D0397144

BLASPHEMY |

European Perspectives

EUROPEAN PERSPECTIVES

A Series in Social Thought and Cultural Criticism

Lawrence D. Kritzman, Editor

European Perspectives presents outstanding books by leading European thinkers. With both classic and contemporary works, the series aims to shape the major intellectual controversies of our day and to facilitate the tasks of historical understanding.

For a complete list of books in the series, see pages 289-90.

BLASPHEMY |

Impious Speech in the West from the Seventeenth to the Nineteenth Century

Alain Cabantous

TRANSLATED BY ERIC RAUTH

COLUMBIA UNIVERSITY PRESS | NEW YORK

♕ *Columbia University Press wishes to express appreciation for*
assistance given by the government of France through the
Ministère de la culture in the preparation of this translation.

COLUMBIA UNIVERSITY PRESS
Publishers Since 1893
New York Chichester, West Sussex

Library of Congress Cataloging-in-Publication Data
Cabantous, Alain.
[Histoire du blasphème en Occident. English]
Blasphemy : impious speech in the West from the seventeenth to
the nineteenth century
Alain Cabantous ; translated by Eric Rauth.
p. cm
Includes bibliographical references and index.
ISBN 0–231–11876–7
1. Blasphemy—History. I. Title.
BV4627.B6 C3313   2001
179'.5'0903—dc21   2001042250

You taught me language, and my profit on't
Is, I know how to curse.

—Caliban (to Prospero), *The Tempest*

CONTENTS

PART SIX | THE AGE OF BLASPHEMY: MEANINGS OF A WORD

A NOTE ON THE TRANSLATION

For the words *le blasphème* ("blasphemy") in French I have sometimes opted for "blasphemous speech" or "impious oath" in English, as context of usage seemed to require. Occasionally, "swearing" is chosen where the original gives *proférer un blasphème* or some other active use; its stronger sense, understood by official sanction as deliberate insolence toward God and divinity, should here be inferred.

Traditionally in French, the verb *jurer*, "to swear," has the stronger sense of blaspheming (as in "Tu ne *jureras* pas le nom de Dieu en vain," "You shall not take the name of the Lord your God in vain"). The noun *jurement* can elicit the less severe reprimand given the venial sin of irreverence. The *juron* generally got by as a merely profane and customary swearword, curseword, or innocuous oath not thought to be maliciously intended to defame the deity and holiness. These demarcations, however, were not absolute; nor were words isolated from their contexts of utterance.

Professor Cabantous generously offered his help with early- and latter-stage clarifications, arcane questions of vocabulary, and fact checks and double checks so that the English edition could maximally fill in the historical context of allusions in the French. Preliminary research for taking on the task proved as rewarding as it was daunting.

I am grateful to Jennifer Crewe of Columbia University Press for saintly patience and a unique opportunity. Sara Cahill's editing—more accurately, collaboration—improved the book's prose with her ear and eye for fluency and readability in English and for the virtues of the subordinate clause and the adverb preceding the verb. For later-stage editing and further adjustments, my debt to Godwin Chu and Anne McCoy cannot be more emphatically acknowledged. I thank also Greg Dawes and Ennio I. Rao for their kind assists with consultations on the Spanish and Italian, as well as the indefatigably gracious staff of the Library of Congress, Duke University, and the University of North Carolina at Chapel Hill, where most of my independent research for the translation was made possible and pleasant.

ERIC RAUTH

| ACKNOWLEDGMENTS

This work could not have been brought to fruition without the indispensable help of a certain number of people who, in one way or another, agreed to support or contribute to this project.

I wish first of all to list, so as to thank, those students at the Universities of Paris I and X who most helpfully participated in the investigation of this topic: Hélène Audard, Véronique Bezault, Stéphanie Debarct, and Nathalie Lourmière. On numerous counts, I owe a great deal to the knowledge, advice, and readings of my friends and colleagues: Michèle and Philippe Bacle, Léandre Boldrini, Félix Bourriot, Philippe Boutry, Gilbert Buti, Olivier Christin, Elisabeth Claverie, Elisabeth Deniaux, Michèle Fogel, Annie Geffroy, Maurice Gresset, Françoise Hildesheimer, and Didier Terrier. May they find here an expression of my total gratitude. My final thanks go to Magali Vautelin of the Institut d'histoire moderne et contemporaine at the Centre national de la recherche scientifique, who kindly saw fit to pick up this manuscript for publication.

BLASPHEMY |

INTRODUCTION: LANGUAGE AND THE SACRED

In this day and age, even a reader keen on things historical might be taken aback by a subject so seemingly trivial, indeed obsolete, as that of this inquiry. The researcher and specialist in the human sciences might also be caught out, aware more than most how semantically tricky blasphemy proves to be, how slippery as anthropological objects go.[1] While not looking to resolve the curious reader's questions or the expert's reservations through overly systematic justification, this introduction does aim to cast light on the meaning and direction of its approach.

A history of blasphemy probably *would* remain an impossible undertaking were it to marshal only a single discipline: in this case, history. What does seem admissible, however, is to propose—for a clearly delimited time and space—a research work about the blasphemer in his and her relation to the official machinery of enunciation and repression, as well as to that machinery's sociocultural setting, through the intermediary of a species of utterance, a *parole*, designated blasphemous. Such an attempt is situated at the convergence of several realities.

It is no secret that the questions historians ask themselves can never be separated from an examination of the world in which they live. One might even surmise that the pertinent and alarming quality of an item in the news of late, which set blasphemy unforgettably at the center of controversy and serious concerns, spurred the writing of this book.[2] But, in this case, the topic's actuality is only a coincidence; the book's original motivation, prior to the late 1980s, came about through observations from my reading.

For a quarter century now, historians' interest in the "mentalities" of the modern period disposed them to adopt, generally speaking, two different attitudes toward the phenomenon of blasphemy. The first consisted, at its worst, in slighting the matter entirely; at its best, in mentioning it only briefly. As a result, major works that took up the subject of criminality or ostensibly turned toward the history of religion (or "popular religion") said not a single word on the subject.[3] The second, and rarer, attitude alluded to the phenomenon, particularly when analyzing administrative rules and rulings. It sometimes underscored how commonplace blasphemous speech was, providing stray examples of charges and sentencings.[4] But it caught hold of the act *as a given*, without reflecting on the meanings it might have carried.

My research on the social world of seafarers, the merchant marine, and the navy had led me to encounter incidents of blaspheming. The disciplinary codes and bylaws of maritime fraternal orders that were in effect and enforced in the merchant and military navies of seventeenth- and eighteenth-century Europe explicitly prohibited blasphemous speech and sought to curb or wipe out its practice. My curiosity aroused, I was quite soon led away from the narrower maritime context. The complexity of the material that turned up through these initial investigations convinced me of the subject's value.

This study partakes of the methodological approach already contained in the research I had devoted to mutinies and, later, to coastal pillaging of sea wreckage in the modern period.[5] In each of these historical cases, it was a matter of orienting commentary around an *event* hitherto considered negligible. These events were, however, also common enough and of sufficient symbolic importance to have favored the emergence of representational mythologies—the reflections of uncontestable social, economic, and cultural realities.

Starting from a given concrete phenomenon—simultaneously a raw fact and a stance arising from it—I had to discover and analyze the multiple implications of the "practice" of blasphemy, the meanings it most likely carried for members of specific everyday communities. This approach to a society and a culture through the exploration of a single gauge of practices was bound to be partial, even as it highlighted the possible influence of such practices in constructing the society and culture. Clearly blasphemy alone did not *determine* the deeper structures of communities. It can now, however, bring to light the collective functionings and individual behaviors of these communities. These workings, in turn, help situate the cultural meanings of communal organizations and the allusions that crop up in connection with blasphemy's practice and prosecution.

Blasphemy was and is about taking the exact measure of the relation between divine and human, about grasping the limit between two worlds that coexisted, yet grew increasingly separate, in the spiritual worldview of modern Europe. Its utterance thus became an intolerably meddlesome interference, or admixture, of the vilest and most profanatory this-worldliness inside the space of the sacred; it became something that cast the shadow of doubt over those traditional reference points that had so starkly traced the bounds of Christian holiness never to be overstepped. But why did these attempts to surmount the bounds of the sacred come about? And who perpetrated them?

The documentation of campaigns to suppress blasphemy's practice affords glimpses of some elements of an answer. And these elements do not always back up the theoretical assertions of the "anthropology" of the blasphemous act—how humanity was time and again implicated in irreligion—that were put forth by clerics on all sides in the Wars of Religion. For the study of "impious speech" quickly uncovers what was essentially at stake: relations between societies and institutional powers. When it came to combating, or professing to combat, blasphemy and its practitioners, the state, the churches, the courts, and even more, the municipalities and pious associations were often in agreement, but they also sometimes contradicted one another, shunned one another's authority, or got in one another's way. Some chose the arduous, often formidable path of their pastoral duties; others, seeking to stake out an ideological position, produced a discourse of norms, wielded primarily by those institutions specially authorized to repress the "crime." It would be erroneous, however, to brand these symptomatic responses as constants, as roles fixed for all time. A detailed chronology brings to light authorities' changing perceptions toward the wrongdoers and their trespasses, remarking the points of contention—even of a total parting of ways—among these authorities. This can be seen, for example, in a consideration of the case of the miraculous events associated with celestial visions reported and scrutinized in France in the first half of the nineteenth century.

Even these few thematic inquiries suggest the extraordinary diversity of the historical field opened up by studying impious speech, with its successive evocation of intersecting and complementary threads of study. Its intricate maze, or skein of imbricate overlappings, to be patiently sorted out and disentangled, commands an absorbing passion and a delicacy of treatment. To take blasphemy as an object of study does not in any way sanction the triumph of things religious over things of the social and political order. Instead, it gathers a whole complex of attitudes around the aberration of a mode of speech that is taboo, thus forbidden, enticing, and *sacred*. Summoning these attitudes redramatizes the blasphemer, as well as his or her judge, the sermoner or pastor, as well as the informer and the district in which the crime was reported.

A multitude of scholarly materials is required to reconstitute blasphemy's many contexts. Works of theology and jurisprudence, priests' handbooks, literary documentation, archives of court cases and tribunals, the reports of individuals in narratives and journals, lists of forbidden terms, dictionaries, treatises calling for punishment of the practice, and much more. All of these materials on which the utterings of profane and blasphemous speech leave their explicit mark have been enlisted in the task. It makes additional sense to ask what distinctions this accusatory denomination concealed behind the unifying taxonomy of blasphemous speech and practices.

Having expounded the method, the problem becomes how to best define the object. This quickly leads to setting forth the most important obstacles facing the historian. Several questions arise at the outset. The extremely broad range of sources and their contextual function assign widely divergent meanings to the concept. If dictionaries and other learned publications, for example, have informational content, theological works, "without closing their eyes to the semantic halo that hovers over *blasphemy* . . . drew argument from these uncertainties in order to interpret selectively, prescribe a meaning, impose a usage."[6] These theological works, in their turn, appear to have influenced, with some semantic consistency, the choices and sentencings by the judicial apparatus of repression. Yet even this does not get to the heart of the matter.

The accusation of blasphemy had a share in all those social organizations in early modern European society that were constructed or justified by references to the sacred. Such references remained essential both to the world's order and its intelligibility. On the same grounds as an act of sacrilege (with which blasphemy, however, is not however to be confused), pronouncing forbidden words was an attack on all things holy, on that "substance radically different from ordinary life . . . which often refers directly to a fundamental and divinized principle."[7] The permanence of this designation over the course of Western civilizations has not led them to grant a comparable meaning to so-called verbal profanation.[8] It is in this sense that Jacques Cheyronnaud and G. Lenclud speak of a separate "blasphem*ic*" category that would be historically conditioned, mobile, and complementary to the "blasphem*ous*" category, unchanging and fundamental.[9] Thus in their estimation "Greek 'blasphemy' is a false cognate of Christian blasphemy."[10] In Hellenic culture, it was considered blasphemous to pronounce any word that may prove to be a bad omen— any word capable of having ill effects on an individual or god, treated (in this case) on the same level.[11] It was, therefore, a crime of irreligion and a political crime, echoed perhaps in references one comes across in Roman history to offensive speech uttered against the Roman people or imperial principate. In the Roman world, however, only the gods punished blasphemy.[12]

While seemingly only a secondary prohibition at Athens or Rome, in the Judeo-Christian world blasphemy possessed an essential status. The teachings of some of the patristic fathers (Jerome, Augustine, John Chrysostom, and Gregory of Nazianzus) laid heavy emphasis on the extreme gravity of impious speech, as based on its treatment in Old Testament texts.[13] This considerable concern stood by the prime importance of the Word and the Name in revealed religion. God could not be called by name as no one knew his Name, as in Tertullian's formulation: "where be His patrimony therein shall be found His attributes." The creator of the world and founder of language "must never thus become an element of His own Creation."[14] Yet the Name was also "the most precious good that God bestowed on men because It delivereth them from false gods."[15] This was why a person could not abuse this gift without running the risk of going astray. So, too, was Jesus called blasphemer and given over to death, condemned not for declaring himself the Messiah or Son of the Blessed but for saying he would be "seated at the right hand of Power, and coming with the clouds of heaven."[16] He thereby had managed to claim for himself a divine nature and breach God's unknowable prerogatives, by the time that an end was being put to a mission that had met with increasing disapproval from the religious authorities. In this one respect blasphemy *founded* Christianity, as it was Jesus' assertion of this role that led him to the cross and, for Christians, to the Resurrection.

The importance of blasphemy in revealed religions is derived also from the place occupied by the Word. Speech opens humanity to the possibility of transcendence and is bestowed with a highly specific intention: that it be placed in the service of glorifying the divine, as emphasized in the second commandment to which the line from the Lord's Prayer "hallowed be Thy Name" answers. Such homage is a pure exercise in accepted grace [*gratuité*], freedom, and identification on the part of mortals. "What meaneth it to say 'hallowed be'?" wrote Saint Augustine. "That He should be deemed holy within you, that He should not be scorned but honored by your innermost person."[17] Blasphemy constitutes, therefore, the perfect inversion of this conception and prayer. It, too, is a veritable exercise of freedom, the expression of a spirited human thought that seeks not so much to harm one's neighbor but, rather, addresses itself to God alone. And just as the authentic and necessary spoken prayer will be "heard" in the sense of hearkened to or answered because listened to by God, so the profanatory word will call forth the often dreadful and immediate punishment of the one who has travestied the essential function of language.

An important fact issues from these few general observations. To arrive at the category of *blasphemy* required a complex and elaborate construction of meanings. It was theological discourse that informed the authoritative categories and called upon the requisite definitions, marking off the prohibited area. This is why "a given utterance is not considered a blasphemy by virtue of the particular *content* but by an act of *judgment*; . . . there is no blasphemy without a jurisdiction," Jeanne Favret-Saada argues persuasively.[18] It is a religious or civil institution that elaborates a corpus of law and other writings in the terms of that corpus's own references, which the institution then interprets and supplements to determine whether a blasphemous act has taken place. To prosecute the act are needed, therefore, an accuser, who may or may not be professionally vested to do so, and some higher authority competent to give the accusation a hearing before implementing sanctions or penalties.

Such a marshaling of institutional machinery entails two kinds of traps for the historian. A good share of the documentary sources professing to reveal blasphemies and blasphemers emanates from "self-appointed" authorities who declared themselves alone qualified to define and flush out the crime. Obviously, to take up such a proceeding just as one found it would simply reproduce the judgment of the said authorities, passively and subjectively reiterating the opinion or finding of the accuser. In addition, the very diversity of voices that fashioned the category makes its exact outlines hard to discern. When we ask, "What *was* a blasphemous statement in modern Europe?" the answers vary according to the actors who passed judgment. Were they clerics or lay persons, theologians or magistrates, jurists or pastors? Much depends, too, on the historical moments. All this makes for the term's semantic multiplicity.

After the twelfth century, the theological approach that had retained such longstanding and exclusive authority in these matters was, indeed, somewhat revised and refined. It ended up agreeing on two definitions of blasphemy, which were not mutually exclusive. The first definition, influenced by Augustine and picked up again by Peter Lombard, stigmatized blasphemy as an assertion of false things about God. The second, emphasized by Aymon of Auxerre, insisted more on its meaning as an insult or offense toward God.[19] In effect, by encompassing so much, these definitions allowed—according to need and the situation's circumstances—for blurring distinctions among blasphemy and imprecation (the invoking of evil by prayer, or a curse), oaths, swearwords or foul language, heresy, sacrilege, and more. This plurality of meanings and their possible amalgamation must be taken into account, inasmuch as they also reflect the stakes and struggles that presided over such distinctions and confusions.[20] Facing blasphemy's polyvalence should not, on the other hand, lead those who research the concept to propose for it *one* absolute definition, pure and simple. Such a definition does not exist insofar as, in David Lawton's words, "blasphemy is essentially rhetorical," a matter for social organization and interpretation of speech [*discours*].[21] The historian's task consists of "learning what he or she is dealing with,"[22] of tracking down the points of exchange between the referential text and the context that bears it up, declaring what is "intrinsically" blasphemous. It consists of reflecting on the meaning that agents of the law or of the church or those charged with the crime seek to give it, of understanding the character of its successive evolutions and the forms of inculpation it assumes or discards, constituting a highly variable interpretive space within an apparently unchanging semantic field.

This methodical series of questions of a rather complex inquiry could only be worked out over a somewhat (though one hopes not inordinately) lengthy duration. Unlike the scholarly undertakings by Lawton or Leonard Williams Levy,[23] I did not think it possible to write a history of blasphemy that embraced the entire course of monotheistic religions, from Moses to Salman Rushdie. This all too often leads to excessively general overviews and episodic analyses, and it does not fit with the method I have laid out above. Clear boundaries of at least the study's framework, if not its object, should be settled on well in advance. The geographic borders of this study comprise, as far as was possible, western Europe, with, however, some favoring of France for a few specific areas and regions.

The study's chronological borders followed slightly more precise historiographical imperatives. The choice to begin with the waning of the sixteenth century simply acknowledged the preexisting claims of scholarly competencies. Blasphemy during the early medieval period has already begun to be explored.[24] The essential sixteenth-century historical work concerning France and Germany remains the province of Olivier Christin, a researcher from whose pertinent analyses I have often drawn inspiration. That my study gets under way with the reigns of Henry III in France or Philip III in Spain meant investigating the reformed church movements' effects on the interpretation of blasphemy and on changes in the behavior of judges and theologians faced with a new confessional deviancy in western Europe.[25] It also meant taking up the historical issue of blasphemy's proliferation, as well as its chronological patterns of occurrence and regulation. Along these lines, the juncture at which the study begins is located within the context of a movement with an already long, tumultuous, and changing history, one whose echoes, at times, can be detected in writings from the seventeenth and eighteenth centuries. Where the study leaves off presents fewer problems, to the extent that heaven itself seems to offer us a signal: it ends with an episode in the year 1846, with the appearance of the Virgin Mary to some shepherds of La Salette, constituting the final, startling, widely reported, and ecclesiastically blessed holy manifestation of the condemnation of blasphemy and of the imminent threats pressing upon French society at that time. This most grave commination, a liturgical recital of divine threats against the sin of blasphemy, came on the heels of other, equally terrible messages that lashed out openly against the French Revolution and its disastrous consequences for Christianity.

This book, then, proposes an analytical framework, a template for reading, an initial assemblage of documentation that might allow other projects, in turn, to enrich with other cases the historical record on blasphemy. Because there is much that still needs to be discovered, filled in and clarified, confirmed or contradicted, above and beyond the question of this taboo's normative function. Especially open to research are the meanings that blasphemy may have held for those who, moving amid a world of perpetual violence, ventured as far as divinity's doorsteps, with words of defiance on their lips.

Blasphemy eludes the historian with its shifting definitions and approaches, with the multifarious perceptions imposed on it by political, legal, and, of course, religious thinking. An evolving object of inquiry, beset by distortions and modulations, it has never failed to generate commentary and investigation, at least up to the end of the nineteenth century. Pride of place has been reserved to theologians and clerical moralists among the many who have gone looking for it and sought a definition so manifold. This is due to the fundamental nature of what they term *blasphemy*, namely, human beings' willful breaking away and falling out in the expression of their relationship to the divine.

 1 | A SIN'S MEANING

Describing Transgression. In the course of the modern era, clerics typically took up the question of blasphemous speech in textual commentary or in sermons on the second commandment that evoked chapter 20 of Exodus, verse 7 ("You shall not take the name of the Lord your God in vain"), quite often including discussion of swearing, uttering curses, and even bearing false witness or committing perjury. Handbooks of priests treated the question similarly.[1] In such writings, produced with a ponderously instructional intent, rarely did the sin of blasphemy benefit from extended examination as a separate subject.[2] It was inscribed in a much wider semantic complex: the perverted misuse of the divinity's name by human speech. Thus framed, blasphemy proper occupied a highly circumscribed space vis-à-vis other sins of speech. Antoine Gambart, for example, believed he had explored the subject in its entirety with four guiding questions, whereas he devotes eight to the category of swearing falsely.[3] He seemed here to be following Azpicuelta, so often

TABLE 1 | References to the Commandments of the Decalogue, by Percent

Commandments	1st	2d	blas-phemy only:	3d	4th	5th	6th	7th	8th	9th	10th
Azpicuelta (1602)	6.5	15.5	.8	3.7	11.9	3.7	13.3	35.1	6.6	(see 6th)	3.7
Bertaut (1610)	12.7	12	3.4	12.4	10.4	8.6	8.6 (with 9th)	19.6 (with 10th)	15.7		
Binsfeld (1640)	17.4	18.7	4.3	2.2	0.9	4.4	0.9	44.2	10.4	0.9 (9th & 10th)	
Eudes (1686)	10	4		4	12	6	36	14	6	6	1
Blanchard (1713)	9.9	3	1	4.2	30.3	12.6	24.4	7.4	8.2	(see 6th)	(see 6th)

SOURCES: Azpicuelta, *Abrégé du manuel et très sage doctrine* (Paris, 1602); B. Bertaut *Le directeur des confesseurs* (Paris, 1638); P. Binsfeld, *La théologie des pasteurs, et autres prestres ayans charge des ames* (Rouen, 1640); J. Eudes, *Le bon confesseur* (Paris, 1686); and A. Blanchard, *Essay d'exhortation pour les estats différens des malades* (Paris, 1713).

consulted, yet who wrote all of one page on blasphemy (5 percent of a chapter concerning violations of the second commandment).[4] By an even wider margin, the study and elaboration devoted to the second commandment are of the most minimal sort in relation to the other commandments.

Without drawing definitive conclusions from these few comparisons, one is led to think that blasphemous practices were relatively undertreated in handbooks on behavior and in basic theology. It's as though discretion in the matter, on the part of most learned ecclesiastics and other confessors, came about from reluctance to write or think anything that departed from their illustrious predecessors, from the church fathers to the Scholastics. In the wake of the forceful and carefully argued patristic condemnations by Augustine (354–430), Origen (ca. 185–254), and John Chrysostom (ca. 347–407), most theologians did not include blasphemy among their lists of sins until the twelfth century.[5] In contrast, during that latter period, Peter Lombard, Alexander of Hales, Saint Bonaventure, Thomas Aquinas, Bernard of Siena, and others were deeply preoccupied with fixing the outlines of this sin, agreeing, for the most

TABLE 2 | References to Sins, by Percent

SINS	Blasphemy	Sloth	Avarice	Lust	Deceit	Theft	Anger	Gluttony	Excessive Curiosity	Pride
Milhard (1611)	4.1	50	4.1	8.4	8.4	25				
Fornari (1674)	6.2	16.7	10.4	18.8			10.4	6.2	18.8	12.5

SOURCES: P. Milhard, *Le vraye guide des curez, vicaires et confesseurs* (Rouen, 1613); and M. Fornari, *Instructions des confesseurs* (Lyon, 1674).

part, that it was to be regarded as the act of "refusing that which belonged or amounted to God Himself or attributing to God that which was not of Him. The insult or verbal articulation in itself doing no more than italicizing an element of affect."[6]

Despite these speculative considerations, the day-to-day function of the church tribunals, whose task it was at that time to judge such matters, highlights the difficulties and uncertainties. In her work on late-fifteenth-century ecclesiastic tribunals, or *officialités*, Véronique Beaulande brings into high relief the fine distinctions that were made by judges in the Champagne region among swearing, repudiations, and blasphemous speech proper.[7]

The clerics of the baroque and Enlightenment eras, relieved of having to pass judgments but still purveying treatises on the topic, produced little that differs on this subject. "To blaspheme," attests Antoine Godeau in 1659, "is to deny the existence of the divine perfections by attributing to God a deficiency He is incapable of having, such as that He is unjust."[8] Not really refining the approach, Pierre Floriot proposed a radical inversion, concluding that blasphemy attributes to the devil what is God's.[9] This intrusion of the wicked one, without lending any great originality, easily leads to likening blasphemy to the language of hell itself.[10] Then again, what sinful behavior does the devil *not* inspire?

When one reads these learned and voluminous handbooks, it is clear from the defiant provocations humanity appears to hurl at God that, for these authors, blasphemy constituted "the most immense, the most shocking, and the most fearful of sins because within it resides a contempt for the Divinity."[11] Richard L'Avocat, Gaspard Loarte, and Valerius Régnault held it the most grievous of all sins. Régnault implored the confessor priest to admonish the penitent as to its dire seriousness, it "being far worse than murder. [For] why, if it be true that he shall have been taken aback by the horror of staining his hands with human blood and his spirit with unfaithfulness, should he not feel shame for having polluted the very tongue given him to praise God?"[12] In such cases, as well as for the global definition of sin itself, assessing the wrong that has been perpetrated takes its inspiration directly from the patristic tradition, from Saint Jerome, Gregory of Nazianzus, or Augustine, all of whom saw blasphemers as criminals more reprehensible than the crucifiers of Jesus Christ. This opprobrium was something Jean Billiot brought to his accusations against blasphemers for "killing God,"[13] and it was revived by Jean Lejeune, who considered blasphemers worse than "the Jew, the Turk, the pagan, and the heretic."[14]

A matter long taken for granted and uncontested, the general reaction to blasphemy (however momentous and consequential the crime's sinfulness) did not, paradoxically, give rise to substantive commentary in the diverse treatises of the modern period. Those few, rather over-elaborate expansions that did arise sought primarily to set forth a certain number of distinctions, not always of striking originality. The first of these revived a distinction made by the great and most angelic medieval doctor of the church, differentiating between blasphemy of the mouth and blasphemy of the heart.[15] This partition opened the way for others to take up the delicate question raised by Jesus' pronouncement on blasphemy against the Spirit, "Therefore I tell you, every sin and blasphemy will be forgiven men, but the blasphemy against the Spirit will not be forgiven."[16] Among the authors of this corpus of commentary, it is Floriot who, after copiously citing Saint Augustine, evokes Jesus' utterance at greatest length. In his *Morale chrétienne*, Floriot writes of blasphemy against the Spirit, "it is to assail the truth, to ascribe to the devil what is God's"; whereas blasphemies against the Son of God, he clarifies, are only harmful and malicious *words*, calumnies against Christ's *human* actions. But blasphemy against the Spirit "slanders his supernatural works and imputes them to the devil."[17] In such terms the theologian continued to inscribe blasphemy within the two customary categories of profanation: unwarranted divestiture of that which is divine and diabolical actions.

As for blasphemy of the heart, a few clerics lost no time denouncing unspoken or gestural blasphemy: "spitting in heaven's direction, gnashing one's teeth," in Ildefonse de Bressanvido's clarification. But the vocal variety was far and away the one most commonly tackled in the priests' handbooks. Some interpreted the second commandment as equating swearing with blaspheming. Jean Laurent Le Semellier, for instance, gave what was presumably a concrete definition: "Blasphemy we understand to be an act of swearing wherein God's name is conjoined with that of death, blood, head, etc."[18] Though all blasphemy is not limited to this verbal genus, clearly all instances of swearing profane oaths of this nature are grouped under it. More exhaustively still, Bertin Bertaut found that cursing to the effect of "saying 'God damn my soul' or 'To the devil with me'; grumbling and fuming with curses against God; and angrily repudiating God, the keeping of Lent, and baptism" are all doubtless allied with blasphemies whose sinfulness is beyond venial.[19]

But most of those authorities consulted do not extend the semantic field of blasphemy this far. Pierre Binsfeld, Bressanvido, Jean Eudes, and Floriot differentiate among blasphemy, insult (sinful speech against loving one's neighbor), oath-swearing (which affirms or execrates; i.e., takes God as one's witness to what one says),[20] and imprecation (which Eudes likens to an ill-intended spiritual oath such as "May I die a miserable death," "The plague take me," and "May I never get to Heaven").[21] In the eighteenth century, Nicolas Girard would, however, encompass under imprecation injurious words against humanity, oneself, or God's unreasoning creatures.[22]

These few notes underscore how precarious it was to delimit categories of peccancy, subordinated first and foremost to the moral orientation of confessors. Yet clergy in no way were prevented from differentiating blasphemies uttered against God and those leveled at saints (even if, following Aquinas, Bertaut concluded that the latter amounted to reaching God indirectly, "for dishonoring the saints conduces to the discredit of their Maker").[23] On the other hand, all were in agreement that impious speech must be deemed a willful and wicked judgment of God and his nature, a provocation that ascribes to the creature that which is the Creator's alone. Along such lines, one was more apt to broaden blasphemous space and use it to derogate all manner of sin in God's presence. For N. Foucault, a priest during Louis XIV's reign, blasphemy became "a sin of rebellion and contempt that shocks the divine power of the Holy Father, a sin of human blindness that attacks the holy wisdom of the Son, a sin of malice and hardened heart that wounds the perfect goodness of the Holy Spirit."[24] An eighteenth-century Parisian sermoner named François Ballet opined that any failure to observe the commitments of the true Christian in daily life, any dissent from the order established by Providence, constituted attitudes that were blasphemous and thus punishable.[25]

A Common Enemy. Existing side by side with these rather convergent interpretations of a Catholic theology largely inspired by the church fathers were a good number of extrapolations differing noticeably in their comprehension of this sin. And if all learned doctors essentially concurred on the meaning of a given error or sin openly scornful of the divine nature, all also agreed on the enormity of "this most grievous of sins." The latter was diagnosed as insolent, detestable, and above all unjust because "the blasphemer has the audacity," as the Jesuit father Loarte contended, "to [scoff at] the holy name of Him from whom he has and continues to receive each day so many blessings for which he should at every instant give expression of thanks and gratitude."[26] This was therefore an unjust crime, and even more a useless and dangerous one, as God could not let it go unpunished. It was, moreover, for this very reason that the theological works one consulted rested firmly on a basis in Scripture and historically attested sacerdotal practice; they readily cited the episode of the Assyrian king Sennacherib having come and failed to attack Jerusalem, and of Hezekiah, king of Judah, who— before the city walls—defies the God of Israel by proclaiming through his official, Rabshakeh, that God "will not be able to deliver his people out of my hand."[27] Responding to the prayers of Hezekiah and Isaiah, that night God sends his angel and slays one hundred and eighty-five thousand Assyrian soldiers.[28] The object lesson of this dreadful incident was to remind listeners and readers that divine punishment was commensurate with the sin's seriousness and that heavenly retribution, horrific and swift, would ever prove ineluctable in the face of human defiance.

"God's terrible vengeance," to cite an expression used by the Orleanist priest Foucault, was something of which worshipers were continuously reminded, even as each commentator lent it singular aspects. For some (in the minority) heavenly retribution fell only upon the individual offender;[29] for most the lone sinner unleashed misfortune on the entire

community. Of the latter group it was L. Loriot who gave the most incisive expression to this collective extension of individual sin. "God pun-
ishes," he wrote in his *Morale*, "not only individuals who are subject to
these vices, but it is in order to exact vengeance that he often sends public calamities."[30] The mid-seventeenth-century Jansenist bishop of Alet,
Nicolas Pavillon, in his *Instructions du rituel*, included blasphemy on the
lengthy list of human offenses that could give rise to the most dreaded of
scourges; "God sends the plague to punish all kinds of sin, principally
those that are made known to all and are scandalous, as: blasphemies, the
swearing of oaths, adulteries, taking of a concubine, sensuality, excessive
celebration, frequenting of taverns, profanation of holidays. The Lord's
ire must be assuaged through a true act of penitence and a sincere confession of sins."[31]

The massive extent of this antiblasphemy purgation, which spared no
one because each is more or less guilty, entailed its own political variant,
which will be anatomized later in this study. At the level of strictly moral
theology, the weighty insistence of the clergy illustrates the defensible
gravity of a punishment for an incomprehensible trespass. Finally, the
occasional rare sermoner, often a missionary, reckoned not only that the
divine arm might unleash itself upon the iniquitous populations but also
that divine forbearance remained ever stronger than the expiation
exacted. "God," wrote Saint Vincent de Paul, "could elect to dash down
blasphemers at any time to the bottom of hell, striking them of a sudden
with death, by dint of the command He could give that very instant for
the earth to open and swallow every living creature."[32] But God did not
choose to do so at least not always. As for Girard, he preferred to address
himself directly to the guilty ones, and laid stress on the reprieve heaven
granted them still, "Oh, wicked and perverse men, where should you be
if the Lord listened to you in His anger?"[33]

Catholic and Protestant theologians as well had thus objectively
reached agreement on a certain number of essential approaches concerning blasphemous speech.[34] For both, it radically compromised the honor
of God's name through its impious and inadmissible attributions. This
was why declaring "I deny God!" was no more abominable than saying
with full deliberateness, "By God's blood" (*par le sang*), "By God's head"
(*la tête Dieu*), or "By his death" (*mort Dieu*). In all these expressions, two
theologically antinomic terms were joined together. "When blasphemy
takes place," observes Christin, "it is knowable not only because the holy

name of God has been spoken but also, and above all, because of the *idea* expressed therein."[35] These verbal errancies, these offenses against or infringements of divine majesty, led priests and pastors to voice forebodings of heaven's inevitable and swift retribution toward the guilty. In light of the tragic divisions that then so shattered the peace in post-Reformation Europe—hardening adversaries and the lines separating professions of the true faith—"the guilty" were, first of all, religionists of the other confession. Here, too, the pope's, or Luther's, or Calvin's Christians made common cause among themselves to confer on the other faithful a label of heretic or potential blasphemer. Scriptural exegesis, celebrations of the mass, consecration of the host, and the cult of saints all constituted so many subjects of conflict, scandal, and schism, all proclaimed in God's name.

During the Colloquy of Poissy, convened to find points of doctrinal convergence that might reestablish the peace in the kingdom, Theodore of Bèze asserted, concerning the Eucharist, that "God's body is as far away from the bread and wine as is heaven from earth." Upon hearing this, the cardinal of Tournon put questions to the king inquiring whether he had "heard this blasphemy."[36] Along the same lines, a Huguenot's adversarial questions to a cleric who was visiting a Bordeaux prison to celebrate the mass, throws light on starkly opposed identities: "Is it your wish that in all places God's name be thus blasphemed? Is it not enough for you that in temples of the faith it already receive such an affront that you now also profane the prisons so that nothing might remain undefiled?"[37] Every gesture, every spoken word of the other confession's adherent became of necessity blasphemous, subject to denunciation, pursuit, and punishment to the point of criminal savagery linked with symbolic violence. Having massacred Protestants in the cantonal seat of Valognes, in a rage against their practices of constant allusion to the Reform Bible, the Vlaognais Catholics stuffed pages torn from the holy book into their mouths, "telling their poor corpses to go preach the truth of their God now."[38] So it was that blasphemy remained similarly for both sides the abominable articulation of a countertruth intended to offend God by obstinately hijacking the meaning of either the Scriptures or the tradition, or even both, depending on the nature of the blame leveled. In short, theirs was the sin of otherness.

Catholics and Protestants were of one mind in condemning one another. They also shared a general reluctance to consider as blasphemous per se the criticism of clerics, be they priests or pastors.[39] On the Catholic side, where clerical organization strengthened considerably from the early seventeenth century on, it would seem that such reluctance was occasionally shed in the century of the Enlightenment, at a time when religious institutions and then the Scriptures themselves came under attack by rational criticism. The appearance in 1764 of the marquis Caesare Bonesana Beccaria's famous work the *Tratto dei delitti e delle pene,* translated from the Italian as *On Crimes and Punishments,* notably led an anonymous author to publish *Notes et observations sur le livre "Des délits et des peines"* (Notes and observations on the book "On Crimes and Punishments"), which accused the Milanese jurist of "pronouncing a blasphemy against religion's ministers by claiming that blood was on their hands." In his response, Beccaria defended himself by setting truth against blasphemy: "Is it not well known that for three centuries the clergy, the abbots and the priests had no scruple about going to war? Can one not say without blaspheming that the hands of those ecclesiastics who were to be found in the midst of battle and taking part in the carnage were bloodstained?"[40]

Separately, and in other domains, the divided brethren strike a note in unison on other terrains and issue convergent indictments aimed at circumscribing blasphemy, historically and socially. Notwithstanding the aforementioned claim of the Oratorian Lejeune, a blind sermoner of the first half of the seventeenth century, that the blasphemer was "worse than the Jew, the Turk, the pagan, and the heretic,"[41] Christians of the modern era held the Turks and the Jews to be genuine blasphemers, practitioners of beliefs that became religious usurpations when set beside the "truth" of Christianity. Such accusations had also been set down in another context: the historical threat of the Turks, from the fourteenth century on, worsened as a Europe divided into East and West proved incapable of joining forces against an encroaching danger that lasted to the end of the seventeenth century. In 1459, Pope Pius II underlined this vision of things and people in an official declaration from Mantua addressed to the princes of western Europe: "We are at war with each other while we leave the Turks free to act out their designs. For the most futile of motives Christians take up arms against Christians and wage bloody war upon each other; and when it comes to fighting the Turks who hurl unholy blasphemies in the face of our God, who destroy our churches, who wish nothing less than to wipe away utterly Christianity's name, no one consents so much as to raise a single hand against them."[42]

Europe's maintenance of the stereotypical figure of the blasphemous Jew owes much, of course, to the tenacious anti-Semitic myths of the Continent. As if to avenge the act of a "God-slaying people" who had condemned Jesus for blasphemy, Christians regarded the presence of nearby Jewish communities as so many ongoing provocations, the incarnate expression of an intolerable blasphemy. Jewish rites, holidays, and collective recitations of prayer were reviled as so many insults to the presence of the "true" God. Did not the humanist and Hebraist Johann Reuchlin (1455–1522), an admirer of the kabbala, nonetheless write, "Every day they offend, defile and blaspheme against God in the person of His Son the true Messiah Jesus Christ. They call him a sorcerer, sinner, traitor"?[43] Enemies "from within" like the heretics, dispersed yet influential and organized, the Jews persisted in professing "a doctrine of blasphemy" which it was deemed proper "to make go away by setting fire to the synagogues," wrote Luther in his rabid pamphlet *Against the Jews and Their Lies*, "and [by forbidding them] on our soil, under penalty of death, from praising God, praying, teaching and singing."[44] In aggravating this anti-Semitic struggle, with blasphemy adding a further reason for accusations, the Catholics hardly lagged behind the Protestants. Using the same presuppositions and observations, they flung themselves headlong against the "impious falsehoods" ascribed to Jewish presence and culture. It was in the name of the fight against blasphemy that the Roman Inquisition ordered a copy of the Talmud publicly burned in 1553. Even more sickening were the virulent proceedings against and imprisonment and executions of the *conversos* during the first half of the sixteenth century. These actions were part of a "unified, theoretically consistent, generalized, and clerically organized anti-Judaism," whose diffusion throughout Europe was promoted by the antiblasphemy proclamations.[45] Soon after the start of the next century, in 1603, five Jews were hanged in Mantua for "having blasphemed." The term was vague enough to encompass the reality of the act's nominal commission and to serve as a simple condonation of the witch-hunt that targeted the faithfully observed Jewish practices and faith.[46]

It seems however, as the remark by Lejeune cited above appears to indicate, that beginning in the seventeenth century, this particular form of denunciation equating Jews, Turks, and blasphemers faded somewhat in the discourse of theologians. Not that the anti-Semitism receded. Instead, the gravity of the offenders' sin, without disappearing, was toned down by such patronizing extenuations as ignorance, originary or ancestral scorn, and blindness—all instigators of so many strayings by these groups abandoned perhaps by God. Thus, in the mid-eighteenth century, the entry under "blasphemy" from the *Dictionnaire de Trévoux*:

> To be a true blasphemer one must speak with intention to blaspheme. That is to say, a blasphemer must know that the things he says are in fact blasphemies; such as would be a Christian who, fallen prey to a violent fit of anger, spews out something offensive toward Jesus Christ. But the same opinion must not be held regarding those who speak on the basis of a false religion. For example the Jews who, through an unfortunate series of errors that they have come to, regard Jesus Christ as an impostor. It is indeed true that these kinds of blasphemers do not cease being guilty before God of so horrible a blasphemy; but it does not follow from this that they should be supposed so in a strict sense, seeing that they believe themselves in no way to be blasphemers.

This relative and belated indulgence did not of course apply to the Christians themselves, Catholics and Protestants. From the mid-sixteenth century on, they began to receive a more or less vigorous religious indoctrination that took it upon itself to illumine for them the reality of dogmas, the meaning of sin, and the depth of respect due to God. It was perhaps from a time when the theologians of the Christian confessions reported "ignorance" among the faithful—understood as a deliberately maintained misbelief inciting to blasphemy—that they continuously denounced (indeed from the sixteenth century on) the proliferation of blasphemous practices in their social world. Errancy that before that time may still have been tolerated in the name of deep ignorance among Christian peoples was no longer pardonable in the wake of intensified efforts to instruct the churches' flock. What before could pass for a wicked abuse of language was turning into the major, apparently worsening sin of heresy. In the Lutheran lands of the waning sixteenth century, pastors and "German" intellectuals professed deep distress at the conspicuous development of this fearsome obliquity. "This heinous [sin]," wrote Jakob Andreä in 1568, "rules in all the conditions of mortal life: among women, children, the old and young, down to the smallest child barely able to form its words; upon the lips of everyone can it be found whose like hath never been seen in the days of our fathers."[47] The same observation and the same lamentations had appeared even prior to the phenomenon's seemingly inexorable emergence at the dawn of the seventeenth century, when a Tübingen teacher named Sigwart took up the refrain:

> Formerly blasphemy was to be heard only among the vilest sol-diery, yet today this vice is become so common that it prevails not in a given guild, house, village, city, or country but has practically invaded the entire world. It is no longer only men who use profane oaths but also women, not only the aged but young persons, [so too] the master and the servant, the mistress and maidservant; the little children who know not yet their prayers swear with such skill that they sometimes exceed their elders in this loathsome art.[48]

Still later, in Hanoverian England, Anglican preachers such as John Shurp or William Howell would lash out in their sermons against the frequency and widening dissemination of blasphemies and oaths, in lockstep with a retreat from familiarity with the most elementary teachings of religion.[49]

Catholic clerics matched the Protestants by similarly bewailing what they found to be, with the advent of the Reformation, less a novel phe-nomenon per se than a preexisting practice that had broadened. Loriot (ca. 1680) and François Ballet (ca. 1740) commented that the speech of "so-called wise men, [of] men about town, as well as the poor and sick" was continuously studded with blasphemies.[50] Bressanvido incriminated not only laborers, carters, journeymen but heads of households who, perhaps unwittingly, inculcated this dreaded vice in their children.[51] Villecourt, in the early 1800s, would also style blasphemous speech as the most readily shared, or infectious, practice in the profane world. It was from now on to be heard "recurring in the public squares, the markets, the workshops, and even places of amusement and leisure." And he was particularly distressed at the youngest children's propensity to adopt such habits: "children who have but recently entered upon the age of reasoning have already received instruction in blaspheming God's holy name."[52]

The perceived omnipresence of blasphemy and profane speech, of their continual and increasingly widespread use, was not just a consequence of the new exactions and impositions of the clergy that accompanied the establishment of Christian education for the masses. Did their propagation not also partly stem, to the minds of sermoners and pastors, from the great rift of the Reformation? Henceforth the division of Christendom registered the shock of a plurality of truths and its concomitant multiple heresies, blasphemous in their very nature. As different confessional spaces were constructed, people everywhere were better able to sniff out both orthodoxy and deviance. In spite of a noticeable decline in some of the more devastating recriminations at the beginning of the eighteenth century, the image of blasphemy triumphant and expansionist did not cease to be a kind of rhetorical figure, cultivated as part of clerics' training in seminaries, bathed in a pessimistic Augustinian gloom. Clergy convinced in advance of this terrible reality ended up flushing it out of their parish's every stronghold. Their moral homilies to the faithful never failed to include it among the most common evils. Alexandre Dubois, curate of Rumegies in the time of Louis XIV, characterized his flock—even as he acknowledged the virtuous and God-fearing of his village, "many of whom one cannot say enough good about"—as "overly fond of things of the earth and [thereby] cruel, given over to blasphemy, and hardheaded."[53] Accounts of pastoral visits in the dioceses of Grenoble or Toul in the seventeenth century, of Bordeaux toward 1730–1770, or of Quebec and Trois-Rivières a century later, all more or less intensely denounced this all too common vice.[54] In records of the parishes in the diocese of Bordeaux, from 1731 to 1734, the only public sinners at whom curates pointed the most accusing finger were blasphemers, residing "within almost all houses" even though the officiating parish minister Lacanau claimed not to know them.[55] It was a finding that had less to do with the pastors of the time observing the intimate lives of the parishioners they frequented than with normal Scholastic theological presuppositions. But, for a while, it helped feed the church's struggle against blasphemous language, aiming at least to contain if not stamp out the practice altogether.

We cannot and do not wish to measure this campaign's efficacy, which, if we rely on accounts by contemporaries in the Enlightenment period, hardly proved decisive. It is far more instructive to focus attention on the motivations and the means put into place by ecclesiastic institutions, particularly the Roman Catholic Church, to root out this terrible evil, which had tilted the human race toward certain damnation.

✤ 2 | BLASPHEMY AND THE COUNTER-REFORMATION

In France proceedings were instituted against blasphemy through ecclesiastic tribunals (until the Villers-Cotterêts ordinance of 1539) and, in Spain and on the Italian peninsula, through the system of the Inquisition. These prosecutions were carried out in accordance with the teachings of the Decalogue and its second commandment. Yet this initial shaping of the issue remains too elliptical. The several interpretations given accused speech, taken with the weight of the political or geographical contexts that disrupted Christendom in the modern era, gave rise to different kinds of contestations and strategies involving the whole of society as much as the individual evildoers.

Reasons for the War Against Blasphemy. The theological handbooks and recorded criticisms by Catholics and Reformers[1] outwardly justified their ferocity in prosecuting blasphemy, likened to a heresy or rather a telltale sign of heresy.[2] This connection, so natural on the surface and so widely used, however, was sure to be ambiguous as the Inquisition had found that certain blasphemous expressions were not tantamount to heresy.[3] Nor was the very notion of heresy necessarily crystal clear. A manifestation of any doctrine that broke with church teaching, heresy effected a rupture and separation whose severity and distance from the "true" dogma must be gauged before making such a determination.[4]

According to a few main currents of philosophical or religious thought, the parameters of the faith set by the magisterium were rather precise. One could, for instance, refer to the condemnation of the five positions put forward by Cornelius Otto Jansen's *Augustinus*. The papal bull *Cum occasione* of May 31, 1653, described two of these positions as blasphemous.[5] By contrast, when it came to the reported situations of everyday life, taking the exact measure of error proved far more difficult. Indeed, it is through official records of the handling of these events that the emerging link between heresy and blasphemy becomes detectable. At the heart of Catholicism in the modern era, legal actions against blasphemers followed the single objective of battling deviances that were most often willful (or perceived as such). A reading of inquisitional documents from investigations and trials of the crime of blasphemy reveals what was indeed at stake: the status of the "true" orthodoxy, and the way in which that orthodoxy was to be properly understood and deemed so with consistency.

When, in August 1599, the sentence was carried out against Matteo Gazzotto, a peasant of the diocese of Modena accused of blasphemy and "vehemently suspected of heresy," Gazzotto was obliged to read out loud a written affirmation presented to him by his judges. It stated,

> I have always believed and believe now all things that are believed, asserted, and preached by the Divine and Holy Mother Church. I swear that I believe in my heart and confess with my mouth that God the Creator of the World is omnipotent, just, holy, infinitely good. That Mary, Mother of God, was always virginal, as much during and after giving birth as before giving birth. That the Holy Roman Church has the power of leadership over all Christians and of commandment under penalty of mortal sin that they not eat meat during certain days among which every Saturday of the year and at the Four Times. Likewise can she compel attendance at the mass every feast day.[6]

Such details incisively limn the breaches and erroneous interpretations of dogma that caused the deviances adjudged blasphemous in the behavior of this Emilian peasant. The delineations of his errancy and theological denials are quite representative of the offending propositions that can be found in other places. Globally speaking, blasphemy was always a matter of interpretive license taken with dogma. A few readings of suspected texts here, some debate or altercation with a monk in stray encounters there: such activities of the accused lent further conviction in the church's eyes to the charge of reprehensible practices. Thanks to the classificatory analysis of historians, records from trials enable these findings of impiety to be sorted into four conceptual, if unevenly represented, configurations.

The first has to do with God himself, with undermining his ontological nature and function as Creator. If some clues of this can be found in Gazzotto's sentence, even more can be found in the trial of Domenico Scandella, the late-sixteenth-century Friulian miller known as Menocchio, whose trial offers the most symptomatic illustration of this first category.[7]

Menocchio's cosmogony squarely declares itself in the course of the cross-examining. "What do you imagine God to be?" the miller asks the villagers. "God is nothing but a little breath, and whatever else man imagines him to be.... Everything that we see is God, and we are gods.... The sky, earth, sea, air, abyss, and hell, all is God."[8] Elsewhere he will identify God not as dispersed among nature's elements but consubstantial with chaos.[9] This at once pantheistic and materialistic declaration would seem to nudge Menocchio's blasphemy toward atheism, as the good fellow refuses to limit his newfound métier as blasphemer to these assertions. In a less original manner, he calls into doubt a certain number of dogmas over which a good many of those fallen into the inquisitors' nets had similarly run roughshod. Like himself, other culprits in Modena, Valencia, Venice, or Toledo were led to subversive wonderings about Jesus' divine nature, the reality of purgatory and hell, the Resurrection, and more often still, Mary's virginity.[10] They took the simple form of doubts expressed by Andrès Feminea, a wool comber of Valencia. Or in the case of Menocchio, a reasonable naturalism ("so you believe Jesus Christ born of the Virgin Mary? It is not possible she shall have brought him into the world and stayed a virgin"). Or, on the Iberian peninsula, the provocative negation tossed off by a drunken man in the company of a prostitute: "Mary has no supernatural power and is about as much a virgin as you are, a public strumpet."[11] This sort of opinion became especially frequent as the Reformation progressed and Mariolatrous worship was radically undermined.

The second manifestation of blasphemous heresy relates particularly to Spain, at the time of forced conversions and religious reconquest. This was the setting for the sixteenth-century Inquisition's efforts to hunt down signs of resurgent Islam or Judaism among the Moorish population and *conversos* by demanding they give palpable proof of their "old Christian" status.

A third species of blasphemy of this order shows up more in literate culture, the culture of writers who contested the foundations of transcendence in order to deny it. Not content to stop at rites and practices or dogmas and their subjective presentation, blasphemous heresy tipped toward frank atheism. Except for a few singular public instances, however, it was mainly still expressed in more clandestine circles of authors and libertines in the sixteenth and seventeenth centuries.[12] This radicalism, whose component social elements will be taken up subsequently, affected the Catholic as well as Protestant confessions. Sites of contestation included Paris and other parts of France, mostly at the beginning of the seventeenth century, and Amsterdam around the 1660s, with the Rokin group and Socinian heresy, whose meetings the consistory of the city described as blasphemous, along with the Koerbagh brothers, relatives of Spinoza who were condemned in 1668 for blasphemous writings "having to do with our Savior Jesus Christ, against his eternal divinity and his Redemption."[13]

A fourth and final definition of this blasphemous heresy concerned the matter of the sacraments and laws of the church. Under this category were grouped doubts about the validity of remission of sin through confession and about transubstantiation during the Eucharist and its efficacy, as well as refusals to attend the performance of either of these sacraments, other forms of divine worship, or mass. But blasphemous heresy might also be judged to include reprehensible daily practices in violation of church observances—as, for example, that followed by Gazzotto, suspected of having expressly taken meat during the fast.

Within this taxonomy of heretical blasphemy, all the different elements might, at times, be hard to keep separate or to isolate from their context. It reveals though, at the very least, the standoff between training that sought to inculcate church teachings in the faithful and other cultural and spiritual inspirations. A majority of those prosecuted by the religious tribunals belonged to the working-class world of the city, and even more to the folk culture of the countryside. The tried offenses sometimes grew simply out of the commonsense observation of daily life or the experience offered by nature. When, toward 1580, Menocchio declared that "all was chaos, that is, earth, air, water, and fire were mixed together; and out of that bulk a mass formed—just as cheese is made out of milk—and worms appeared in it, and these were the angels,"[14] he blasphemed in blending so thoroughly together the sacred and the profane, where the only proper view was that the reality of God and his angels served to explain the homier mystery of cheese and worms. In a similar case Andres de Sepulveda, another miller but from the diocese of Cuenca, was prosecuted in 1659 for having declared that "when a man dies his soul is sent to work a field of thyme or gorse, where he is given to eat and drink his fill; and [that] this afterlife's only torment is to slog away at backbreaking labor with a pickax and that is all." He was also the one to declare "that there was no hell or purgatory and that souls relieved themselves in a corner behind the door."[15]

Scaling down dogmatic arcana into scenarios instantly recognizable by the common person gives a sense of the self-evident ease with which a portion of the populace might take possession—on its own terms—of Christianity's truths in order to better understand, adapt, or reject them. Again, did not the possibility of thinking this way originate with the Reformation's casting into doubt Catholicism's more dogmatic and disciplinary practices, and with its opening toward individual interpretation of the Bible as the sole basis of faith? The development of printing, the spread of works in the vernacular, and the circulation of prospectuses and pamphlets even outside the cities and towns all gave to many the powers and license of literacy, disputation, and protest, of debate and free opinion. De Raemond wrote in 1623 that "the first who heard the truth . . . were goldsmiths and silversmiths, masons, carpenters and other craftsmen working to make ends meet; those even indeed who had never handled anything but a plough and dug the earth became in a trice excellent theologians. . . . Peasants of coarsest manners and the most benighted minds were strong scholars, baccalaureates and doctors all at once."[16] This remark's exaggeration could hardly obscure the undeniable extent of the Bible's reach and the personal enrichment, along with its risks, that some found within its pages. Thanks to Carlo Ginzburg's exemplary inquiry, we know that Menocchio found probably some of his blasphemous assertions in *Il Sogno del Caravia* (1541) and that his cosmogony was drawn from the well of Jacopo Filippo Foresti's thought.[17] Scholarly attention could be broadened to include each of those who, having seen interrogation by the Inquisition, confessed alternate fundamental beliefs, as we try to detect the origin of the those beliefs' cultural influences.

The heretical blasphemer was not content, therefore, to simply misinterpret Christian reality by denying God his veritable meaning, by deciding for himself or herself what he or she must or must not believe. More or less constructing a manner of proceeding along the way, such a blasphemer appropriated the Word at a time when it belonged to the clergy, to those alone capable of knowing and speaking well.[18] Through naïveté, lack of understanding, or malice, blasphemers introduced themselves into a field of knowledge that normally excluded them, and took their turn at speaking—flinging the door open to the worst extremes of thought and language.

Did not, moreover, the malice (and thus consciousness) of evildoing on the part of these challengers of the divine serve to disclose something of blasphemy's sinister origin, and urgently justify its punishment? Numerous theologians, differing in their degree of conviction yet constant in expressing it, held blasphemy to be the very wording of hell itself: "hellish speech," in Vincent de Paul's formulation.[19] As late as the end of the eighteenth century, the Italian Franciscan Bressanvido continued to assert the diabolical nature of "this atrocious sin, hell's language, [just] as praise and hallelujahs are Heaven's."[20] He thereby subscribed to a current of thinking that would follow its own course for a good part of the nineteenth century. This cozy relation between Satan and blasphemy had found its most virulent postulation in the witch-hunts that took place in Europe between 1570 and 1650. There are difficulties in proving conclusively a precise, causal harmonization between the beginning struggles against witchcraft and the early, more systematic repression of impious speech.[21] Still, one can only be struck by the close connection made by demonologists between witches (male and female) and blasphemers. Jean Bodin was one of the chief inspirations of this discourse about witches, adducing that "God sends plagues, wars, and famines via the ministrations of evil spirits, executors of His justice; likewise does He the same with sorcerers, and predominantly when the name of God has been blasphemed."[22] Some decades later, the magistrate Pierre de Lancre of Bordeaux, following others, described the Sabbath as a time when the devil's friends could be seen "dancing indecently, carousing licentiously, coupling diabolically, sodomizing abominably, blaspheming scandalously, taking insidious revenge, racing after all manner of horrid desires."[23] Thus everywhere blasphemy and sorcery were made equivalent, for by striking pacts with the devil to bring about others' ruin and besmirch God's honor, the behavior of sorcerers and magicians systematically became sacrilegious and blasphemous.[24] And yet, every blasphemer was not automatically a sorcerer,[25] even if "intolerable speech" was enough to feed the suspicions of certain investigators.[26]

Generally, to judge by confessions extracted from those accused of sorcery, the very content of the diabolic pact necessarily led to availing oneself of forbidden expressions. In the duchy of Lorraine, or in France under Louis XIII, we know of several examples of people condemned to death for having, like Charles de Manchillon, the baron of Chenevières, "wickedly, maliciously, rashly and recklessly . . . made petition to Beelzebub [sic] containing several blasphemies and impious things against God and His honor."[27] If later in the century the witch-hunts tapered off and repression waned, the two phenomena still remained closely linked. But from the late seventeenth century on, possession by the devil tended to mitigate the circumstances for the individual accused of blaspheming. On May 7, 1698, Susannah Fowles of Hammersmith parish in Middlesex was found guilty before the Old Bailey, the court of justice in London, for "having spoken blasphemies against Jesus Christ and having uttered curses against God." Her husband, one of the foremost witnesses, testified that the devil had appeared to her on several occasions and that she spoke his name while blaspheming as if in spite of herself. Those who examined her treated the affair as an act of fraud bordering on mental imbalance.[28]

An expression of heresy and, for a time, infernal magic, blasphemy beyond these things relativized the transcendent. In the churches' fight against the perversion of speech, this relativizing proved perhaps the most durable cause for action because it was so intimately part of the difficulties met in the course of acculturating the Christian populations of western Europe, led by the respective reform movements.[29]

Instruction of the congregation, particularly within the Roman Catholic Church, aimed to better indoctrinate, to induce more faithful observance of the sacraments, and to encourage performance of the new devotions. It proved equally useful in grappling with what the clerics labeled "superstitions," conveying the need to isolate profane from sacred. Thus set apart, the sacred *space* of church and churchyard, the sacred *time* of Sundays and feast days, the sacred *person* of the priest must henceforth reflect attitudes and individual relations that were imprinted with deference, with reverential silence, with contemplation and rejection of all things vulgar. Beginning with the Counter-Reformation, the sacred was reaffirmed first through a break from daily habits imbued with equivocation, with the nonseparation of heaven and earth. The sacred disclosed the true and only path to the worship owed to God and his saints. From this time on, that which was definitively designated sacred and holy had to be worthy of respect, veneration, and distance, and it represented a distinction that could not be transgressed.

As the social life of individuals and communities experienced the enforcement of this drastic partition between profane and sacred, the clergy of the Catholic Church underwent a thoroughgoing reorganization, which included reform of a liturgy that itself sometimes fell short in respect to the sacred. In 1617 the bishop of Annecy-Genève, François de

Sales, wrote to his clerics telling them they "should see to it that there be sung no carols at Christmas filled with words disgraceful, profane, and contrary to the piety and reverence due to holy places and things, nor that there be superadded into psalms sung to the solemnity of the Nativity of our Lord certain radical words containing blasphemies."[30] Thus it came about that the means of communication, both collective and individual, that people established with God—song, prayer—were now to be expurgated, cleansed of all potentially blasphemous profanation.

Such a context impinged on all those who associated familiarity, vulgarity, or profanity with God when they insisted emphatically on something, made an offhand lively remark, or even heckled someone in the course of ordinary life—without being, for all this, genuine heretics or sorcerers. "And who then are you, O fellow men," the sermoner Ballet reprimanded his listeners, "to be so bold in your furies, your displeasures, or your comments upon public matters as to lay blame on the conduct of the Almighty God, to carry your mortal mouth unto His Glory's throne in order to find fault with Him?"[31] Was not the indispensable distance between Creator and creature suddenly abolished through more or less vulgar disavowals and oaths? When, for example, our Modena peasant Gazzotto, like many others, sprinkled phrases like "*Dio beco*" (That cuckold of a God!), "*Dio poltrone*" (Goddamned lazybones of a God!) or "*Puttana de Dio*" (That damned harlot of a God!) into his familiar conversations, he had probably not yet fully and correctly internalized the holy dimension of Divinity, which—for every reverential mind—must be present in all things.[32] Based on these observations, one would still be mistaken to see in this facet of the larger antiblasphemy battle a charge leveled only at agents of a "popular peasant culture" resistant to the new teachings and strictures of the church. There are at least two reasons for this. First, the offensive to safeguard the sacred was directed at peasants and nobles, dwellers in the countryside and city. Diego de Castro, a Madrilenian functionary, in 1667 expressed shock at the widespread persistence of blasphemy in the Andalusian port of Malaga and the deplorable example Catholics might set, even after so many decades of apparently inconsequential effort by the clergy. "Such a habit is it for the people here that they put no request to the ministers of the holy Tribunal nor the ecclesiastical or civil courts to remedy it. This is why the trespass against Christ, Our Lord, grows greater each day, all the more serious as it is known and seen by all, by those Englishmen, Dutchmen of Hamburg, Moors and peoples of other states who do not embrace the Catholic faith and who live amongst those that do, in this city."[33]

In the second place, the antiblasphemy campaign belonged to the broader context of the moral reform of European society at large that enabled the church powers to mix together the punishable genres of transgression. Did not the courts of the Holy Inquisition in Spain, starting from the year 1574, feel obliged to prosecute for blasphemous speech every person who had declared that sexual relations outside marriage was not a mortal sin?[34] For with this undertaking, the appropriate object of denunciation and prosecution was the person incapable of dominating his or her own instincts or passions. In the same class as fornicators unable to curb sexual urgings, blasphemers could never check their profane language. They refused to discern the sacred meaning of speech because they were unable to master their own impulses of wrath and hatred. This was the stand taken also by Pastor Barbault when he suggested arming against the temptation to blaspheme by reciting to oneself this prayer, "Make us so much the master of the promptings of our heart, the words of our mouth, the actions of our bodily person that nothing may issue from us that be not worthy of the sacred vocation with which you have honored us."[35] No holder of his tongue however, the blasphemer could not break with his other iniquitous proclivities. This was why, as the abbé de Mangin explained in 1757, "blasphemies are almost always accompanied by some other sins, as infidelity, repudiation of faith, etc., which add a new malice to blasphemy."[36]

The Catholic Church, however, was not satisfied with explaining the multiple reasons why blasphemy deserved condemnation; it sought also to implement the means of guiding sinners toward paths of speech more compatible with their aspiration to salvation.

Means of Attack. Manifold and successive advances against the reality of blasphemy and the religious reasons explaining its abhorrence, constantly reiterated by clerics, did not exhaust the churches' relationship to the sin considered "loathsome, [and] which generates no pleasure!" For several centuries of modernity in the West, Christian teaching, along different paths, never wavered in its desire to force a retreat of blasphemy's manifestations. Fighting blasphemy was henceforth written into Catholic efforts to deeply and thoroughly Christianize urban and rural populations. Through ancient but revived practices, the Tridentine program of acculturation was put in place. Catechism, devotions, Catholic brotherhoods, missions, and homilies insistently elaborated the meaning, nature, and several aspects of sin. As part of this larger enterprise of salutary denunciations, singling out blasphemous speech was hardly the least prominent.

Sermons frequently developed the theme—a likely way to rapidly reach the maximum number of people. For example, a collection of homilies from the mid-seventeenth century intended for priests in the mostly rural missionary congregation of the Lazarists, founded in Paris in 1625 by Vincent de Paul, was devoted entirely to the subject. From the outset, it labeled such speech as an "infernal monster and crime highest among all expressions of insolence, blackest of all ingratitudes, most monstrous of all outrageous utterances [*énormités*]."[37] Other model sermons of the seventeenth and eighteenth centuries, just as such sermons had done in the fifteenth century, took blasphemers to task by pointing out to them the perversity of their practices and by bringing the marks of their contradictions to the light of day. Confronting the blasphemer, the sermoner's aggressive questioning was affectedly interrogatory as if unable to understand the sinner's ingratitude. Was not a blasphemer, like everyone, a person on whom God had showered beneficence, "a Christian made by baptism into His adoptive son,"[38] endowed with a heart and a mouth with which to sing creation's praises?[39] What wrong shall God have done the blasphemer that He should deserve such treatment, of what sin were the saints guilty toward the blasphemer?[40] Associating the nature of blasphemies directly with the theology of the Passion, Vincent de Paul then exclaimed,

> Is it because your God became a man for your sake, wished His own head, so worthy of adorations, crowned with thorns that you swear by the head of your God; is it because He died on the cross that you swear by the death of your God? Is it because His paternal breast hath been filled with gall or rather bitterness caused Him by your crimes that you swear by the wounds of your God?[41]

The Lazarists' founder elsewhere encouraged the blasphemer, in the strongest terms, to pose, at each new temptation, the same question: "Unworthy wretch that I am. What harm hath my Lord done me that I should blaspheme?" Writing in the same period, the Jesuit Georges

Fournier asked of the guilty whether it were not God's invisibility that so emboldened them, and whether their verbal audacities would be so shameless in the presence of a great prince.[42]

Contemptuous of evil but also seeking to heal souls, like physicians, these pastors proposed to their Christian audiences different methods for avoiding too frequent lapses into such errors, when such slips were perceived as a dreadful habit. Safeguards proposed were threefold. First, there was prayer. Loarte and Alphonse de Liguori encouraged immediately saying the rosary and ending with a glory-be (*Gloria Patri et Filio et spiritui sancto*) or "some other litany in the name of Jesus or Our Lady."[43] Next was personal resolution to do better: the one made each day, upon waking, to avoid the places, associations, or activities that most promoted this blameworthy deviance. And last, the prescribed punishment favored by many a priest: the blasphemer was to impose his own penitence immediately after sinning "to punish himself for this facility."[44] Normally suggested was a correction of the blasphemer's tongue. Régnault thus proposed striking one's face on the ground at the lips, and kissing the earth after saying a prayer. Loarte advised making the sign of the cross on the earth with the tongue, a suggestion taken up much later by Bressanvido: "Bite your tongue with your teeth and trail it in dust, make use of the most effective means to root out this habit."[45] These proposals—in their personal, voluntary, penitential dimension—did not, however, fit within the typical frameworks of the Catholic clergy. Here, the essential matter rested instead on a heightening of individual consciousness, a realization or recognition of personal guilt, and in this particular case the only recourse was to bridle, without delay, an impulse that polluted communication between God and individual. We do not know, of course, the practical results of these appeals. Still, among the narratives concerning congregational missions devoted to stamping out blasphemy, Louis Châtellier's study evokes certain spiritual exercises imposed by the Jesuit Pedro Catalayud on the populations of Leon, Old Castille, and Andalusia in the middle of the eighteenth century. The recommendations were quite similar to what we have just seen.[46]

Utrera, 1758: the men were told by the mission to circulate through this Andalusian locality. At certain spots they would halt, imitating thereby the stations of the cross, which were often set up along such routes as part of Roman Catholic ritual. At the preacher's order, they would press their mouths against the earth, remaining prostrate during the words of the exhortation; then, following a collective reciting of the act of contrition, they would get up and resume their procession to the cries of "Praise Jesus, death to blasphemies!" This symbolic joining of dirt and impious lips brought together several complementary meanings. First, there was the simple humiliation of having to bow down, abase oneself publicly, touching a ground already trod upon—an impurity and therefore alone most fitting to receive the impurity of blasphemy.[47] But taken in conjunction with contrition and pardon, this prostration and obeisance became a source of purification for "the ground and walls covered with blasphemous refuse and filth through the sin of men." In the end, such abasement recalls the biblical gesture of believers and pilgrims who sought to be regenerated spiritually once they reached the promised land.

Closely connected with sacramental observance, which had been reaffirmed vigorously at the Council of Trent, blasphemy could also be eradicated through frequent confession. But because the sin was so intrinsically serious, it needed to be atoned for through a "grievous penitence," in Jacopo de Benedicti's reminder (based on the decree of the Lateran V council, 1512–1517).[48] Besides this, in the mid-eighteenth century Mangin induced confessors to delay absolution for the penitent who blasphemed too often.[49] He did not, however, any longer suggest actually excluding the offender from the Christian community as, up to the time of the early modern period, penitential canons or papal letters had required. Already cut off by sin from God's communion, the blasphemer was subjected, in turn, to a decree of banishment. For seven successive Sundays, the offender was forced to remain outside the cathedral portal during the service, and, on the Fridays of those seven weeks, was compelled to eat only bread and water, giving of his or her own food to several poor people, before promising to never repeat the offense (under penalty of permanent excommunication). The many decisions by Pius V regarding blasphemers—carrying the force of the law of the land as well as of the church—vividly illustrate the incremental mechanism of such exclusion. If, among the "common people," there were those unable to pay the fine on the first occasion, "they must remain standing for a day before the church portals with their hands tied behind their back; the second time, they were forced along the city streets while being flogged; and the third time they had their tongue pierced and were sent off to the galleys." Should the blasphemer lack the funds to erase his or her sin, the wrongdoer of no means was first publicly expelled from the parish community, then from city or village, and finally from all of society.[50]

The struggle to curb blasphemy, therefore, was not limited to individual control sustained by grace conferred through the sacraments. Society as a whole was implicated; each of its members needed to see to the cohesion of the totality, which, as a rule, came under threat each time blasphemous words were spoken or heard.[51] And were not wrongdoers who had repented of their sin the first ones liable to react to the accursed cursing of others? "They shall take utmost care," Loarte advised, "to give notice in as gentle and suitable a manner possible to those whom they should hear swearing, blaspheming, and making imprecations of what is undeniably for their greater good and for the glory of God."[52] This social perspective on the struggle led the churches to grant a singular role to integrating the individual into society and the ancien régime's structures of political and cultural authority.

At the heart of this strategy lay the family cell, or rather the patriarchal model enshrined by the clergy. Coming out of the Counter-Reformation, the father's role was further defined as "the personification of immortal God; in him [the head of the household] we behold the image of our origin" (catechism of the Council of Trent). The paternal function's rise in religious value—to that of "priest" in the home, lieutenant of God—conferred dignity and duties on the father; high among such duties was the instruction of his children in his home, after the model of the priest in the church.[53] This important responsibility, supposedly overseen by the clergy, granted the individual a considerably wide latitude. According to Charles Borromea, archbishop of Milan (1564–1584), such instruction encompassed giving lessons in prayer and the Ten Commandments, sending children and servants to catechism, and seeing that the fast and Sabbath were properly observed and the mass faithfully attended. It was expressly recommended to fathers that they keep any sin from being committed openly under their roof, notably including swearing or blasphemy. The father consequently made up one fundamental element in the Christian and moral training of Western populations, as envisaged by the church; he acted ideally as one of the foremost foot soldiers fronting the assault on blasphemy. If, gradually, such things as the growing clericalization of the Roman Catholic Church, inequities within the social model, and shortcomings or weaknesses in the family structure markedly diminished these initial ambitions, the paternal function retained certain prerogatives. The father, still held to be an exemplary figure of probity, was expected not to tolerate blasphemous language from the mouths of his children. "Woe unto you, fathers," admonished Liguori, "if you do not correct your children when they blaspheme, and twice woe upon you if you should offer them a bad example."[54] The father remained the one who must guarantee the honor of God and, as occasion demanded, avenge gross insults to it. He was strict with his own children and also with those in his service. "See to the good behavior of your servants," Bressanvido counsels, "reprove them charitably [if they should blaspheme]; if they persist, send them packing."[55]

An echo of this repressive role, which fell to fathers of families, turns up in descriptions of the duties that were assigned to masters with respect to journeymen and ship's mates or apprentices in certain crafts and professional communities.[56] This moral and pedagogical orientation is particularly noticeable in the bylaws and customs of working groups of ship's officers and riverboat crews in France. Through statutes that appear in published rule books and guides, a recurrent injunction can be profiled: blasphemous speech was prohibited aboard ship, under penalty of sanctions, which varied in severity according to time and place. The Brotherhood of Mariners of Marseilles, in its new regulation of 1722, opted to recommend persuasion and to suggest to its members that they avoid "very carefully all kinds of oaths and denials or abjurations [*reniements*] made in the Most Holy Name of God and shall endeavor with all their might to bring about improvement in the behavior of those who observe this abominable custom."[57] Other traditional organized crafts or métiers added various sanctions. The sanctions were simply monetary for the boatmen of Saint-Omer, who were to neither offend merchants and tradesmen by cursing nor "utter a single oath under penalty of being fined forty sols."[58] Sanctions were professional in nature for the canal bargemen of Dunkirk or the codfishers of Le Havre in the seventeenth century. Those who blasphemed might find themselves forbidden from working on boats by the quartermasters. Regulations for the Confraternity of Sailors at the Norman port announced, "Captains will be advised to keep a faithful record of all happenings unfavorable to the honor of God—among the crews—in order to remedy all abuses that shall have been committed during the aforementioned voyages, to prevent repeat offenders, and to draw down God's bestowal of benediction upon sailors and sailing."[59] This insistence on closely monitoring maritime blasphemous speech emerged from both a general inclination to extirpate profanity and blasphemy from all quarters and a more practical situation particular to these spheres of activity. Through sinning, the blasphemer risked drawing down God's wrath and vengeance, creating a permanent threat that weighed heavily on crew and cargo. During an island voyage in the 1720s of the slave ship *Marie-Anne* of Nantes, a second mate named Peyroches questioned a quartermaster who was particularly undisciplined and given to uttering oaths and profanities: "What say, Monsieur Dominic, have you no shame swearing and cursing like that? You shall manage to sink the ship all by yourself with your confounded oaths!"[60]

But if the codfishers' guild of Le Havre showed such professional conviction by busying itself with "rooting out blasphemies, oaths, brawls, drunkenness, and other sinful acts that are habitually committed on the high seas," this was also because it was primarily a religious organization, one of numerous devotional confraternities spawned in the wake of Catholic reform. The Le Havre captains founded the Brotherhood of the Most Holy Sacrament in 1662 with the purpose of "procuring the glory of God and working for the salvation of all who go to sea in ships," through a life of prayer and good example, through the catechesis and moral indoctrination "as much on land as at sea," of sailors under their command. Thus pious associations served as another means for further circumscribing blasphemous behavior and speech within the framework of Christianization and social control.[61]

Many such organizations of this kind, at least in France, were created in the last quarter of the sixteenth century. It was during this period in the diocese of Tarbes (today the department of the Hautes-Pyrénées) that clergy and lay persons alike grouped together to form the so-called *fadernes*, pious associations whose ordinances forbade blasphemous speech among their members.[62] The 1530s had already seen in the parish of Saint-Martin de Morlaix the founding of the Brotherhood of the Holy Name of Jesus to battle swearing, blasphemies, and imprecations.[63] In Paris it was during the continuing anti-Huguenot campaign of the Catholic League, led by the Dukes of Guise, that another brotherhood of the same name was established in 1590. Seated in the Church of Saint-Gervais, the organization exerted influence throughout the capital by copying the municipal administrative subdivisions. Within each unit of ten [*dizaine*], for example, one or two fraternal members "chosen from among the upstanding citizens [*bons bourgeois*]" were specially designated to ward off blasphemous utterances. When such speech was overheard, the monitors were responsible for making offenders' names known to the Parisian administrators. This linguistic surveillance was part of a much more extensive program, the stated objective of which was to disclose any "illicit gathering in which there was conspiracy against God, the pope, the king [Charles X], [or] the Duke of Mayenne." From then on the brotherhood's activities reinforced those of the Sixteen by tightly combining the social, political, and religious surveillance of the city via the struggle against blasphemy and heresy—assaults on the honor of God.[64]

A few cities near the capital adopted similar initiatives. At Orleans, for instance, members of the Brotherhood of the Holy Name of Jesus decreed to "make it their duty that the names of God, the glorious Virgin His mother, and His saints be neither sworn in oaths nor vainly blasphemed, and if so ever someone—which dereliction God wisheth not—come to forget so much as to commit such oath or blasphemy, if he belong to the aforementioned society shall be fraternally and charitably taken aside and admonished according to the stipulation by said general articles and if he be a foreigner shall be brought before the court so that an exemplary punishment may follow."[65] Soon after the Wars of Religion, certain of these brotherhoods disappeared, while others were, perhaps unexpectedly, extended. It seems, for example, that the famous Company of the Holy Sacrament, founded in 1629, took up again a portion of the objectives put forth by the Parisian brotherhood of 1590. From the start, in fact, "they began canvassing against blasphemers" and the company did not fail to make a priority of the 1631 ordinance. Its chronicler René de Voyer d'Argenson points out that indeed it

> enlisted particular individuals to urge the civil lieutenant general [the justice officer of the civil court system] and the provost of the Parisian merchants to make use of their Company in preventing the swearing that went on every day at the Grève and the other ports on the Seine. In all instances where the Company has believed it could avenge insults to God made by impious persons and blasphemers, it has worked hard and fervently, in cases of either episodes in Paris or those to which it has been referred by companies in the provinces.[66]

Concern with such cases is found again in the regulations of the Brotherhood of the Passion, drawn up in the mid-seventeenth century by company members. The professed object was to wage an all-out struggle against duels, blasphemy, and new and suspect doctrines—all considered to be among the many direct causes "of disorder at court and in the army."[67] Enlisted in the aftermath of the Counter-Reformation, these initiatives reverberated in other lands, as well as in a Catholic Europe that had responded to Luther and Calvin with Tridentine episcopal reorganization. In the Spanish Low Countries, the city of Lille saw several brotherhood associations sprout up at the beginning of the seventeenth century, dedicated to the Holy Name of Jesus and intent on battling "blasphemers, most particularly in the parishes of Saint-Sauveur and Saint-Etienne."[68] In the German states, the active propagation of doctrine by Jesuits generated confraternal organizations of the same sort at Dillingen or Kaufbeuren, while those of Saint-Isidora and of the Immaculate Conception in Munich also hitched their wagon to the cause.[69]

The slim data we possess on these pious associations of such aggressive Catholicism show relative homogeneity. Founded mainly during the transition to the seventeenth century, these organizations present similar organizational structures and missions. Often pioneered by religious orders (by Jesuits or Dominicans), they then largely left to lay persons the initiative and responsibility for monitoring the utterances of heresy, of dishonor cast heavenward, and of social infringements on the difficult confessional borderline. Finally, the heavy insistence they laid on the Holy Name of Jesus reflected a devotional current of thought much expounded on in that era. More particularly, for many sermoners the very name of Jesus—which Saint Paul had called "a name above all names"—"contains all the names that we could attribute to God."[70] Jesus was thus "a source of adoration and sublime veneration," worthy of the devotion of all creatures. Yet not only was this name "scorned by the Jews who considered its bearer as the son of a workman," but even more so his name "is today dishonored by all the Christian nations."[71] Yet it was also by this name, open to scorn and blasphemous profanation, and by the favor it represented in the sight of God in heaven, that the sin of dishonor could be erased. Along with the Catholic missions, catechism, theater, or baroque urban stage direction, indeed with the new emphasis on individual initiative itself, the religious brotherhoods participated in the enterprise of social and moral direction that so forcefully accompanied the Christian education of early modern societies in Europe.[72] Nonetheless, this totality of pedagogic and pastoral methods—already so reliant on a diversity of agents of repression—did not exclude the even more coercive forms in those countries

where the Roman Catholic Church disposed of the judicial means of prosecuting and sentencing suspects, recidivists, and recalcitrants.

3 | GOD'S HOLY CHURCH AGAINST BLASPHEMY

Only in a limited number of European states did the Roman Catholic
Church have the power to instigate and carry out proceedings against
blasphemers during the modern era. Without yet evoking the case of
France or certain states of the Italian peninsula (whose ecclesiastic tribunals had lost their primary power over such hearings), we shall recall,
by marked contrast, the Inquisition's role in the matter. Separate studies
of this topic, one directed by Ricardo Garcia-Carcel, another by
Bartholomé Bennassar, arrived at quite similar conclusions.[1]

On the Iberian peninsula, at least during the sixteenth century, the
Inquisition had to work hard to retain the right to prosecute offenses of
blasphemy, maintaining that such offenses must be deemed a form of
heresy. Despite the medieval tradition on which such claims relied, to
assert this prerogative the Holy Office had to make very deliberate, step-by-
step justifications, working against the obstacles of lay or ecclesiastic jurisdictions.[2] Yet, in reality, the hunt for blasphemers never really constituted
a major preoccupation of the inquisitorial workload. As Jean-Pierre Dedieu
has shown, quantitative fluctuations in the number of such trials generally
followed the oscillations in judicial activity, but always at a very low level.
Judging from records on the activity of the Toledo tribunal, only two historical periods (the mid-sixteenth and, much less so, mid-seventeenth centuries) show evidence of a noticeably heightened zeal for prosecuting blasphemers as heretics. The period roughly between the years 1530 and 1560
saw an expressed attempt to eliminate the *conversos*, the newly converted
Christians, and the Protestants. Then, from about 1620 to 1640, there were
campaigns to hound Jews and the dubious Portuguese immigrants. In the
meantime, trials of blasphemers were reduced to a few dozen per decade.
This meant, as Dedieu describes it, a selective withdrawal of the Inquisition's jurisdiction on this particular front. In her research based on complete lists of autos-da-fé from a dozen Castilian court records between 1660
and 1739, Michèle Escamilla-Colin similarly confirmed a relatively minute
portion of offenses (1.3 percent) of this nature.[3]

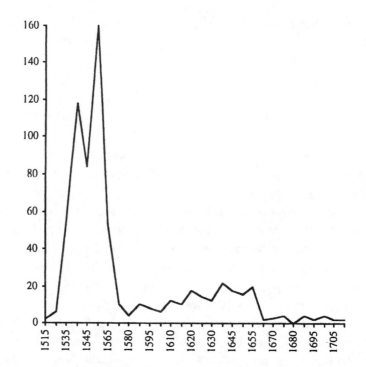

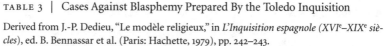

TABLE 3 | Cases Against Blasphemy Prepared By the Toledo Inquisition

Derived from J.-P. Dedieu, "Le modèle religieux," in *L'Inquisition espagnole (XVIᵉ–XIXᵉ siècles)*, ed. B. Bennassar et al. (Paris: Hachette, 1979), pp. 242–243.

Between the horrific theological representations of this sin and the ecclesiastic repression it provoked, the outlines of a veritable divide become evident, especially when seen from the situation in Spain at the end of the sixteenth century. This divide can be further illuminated. For at the same historical moment, calling with fervent piety for the establishment of the Inquisition in France, the members of the Parisian anti-Huguenot League were at once acting (at least from their vantage point) justifiably and making a serious misjudgment. Their intention seemed justifiable to the degree that, seeking to follow the Iberian or transalpine (ultramontane) model, "the [presence of the] Inquisition in this kingdom would facilitate the purgation and extermination of heresy." And it was probably a misjudgment in its belief that this institution could bring about "a prompt, severe, and just judgment in keeping with God's holy commandments, principally regarding those who have offended and continue to offend the divine majesty. [For] several kingdoms and republics are come to such an unbridled depravity and license of all the vices and sins that they are all fallen into ruin and perdition."[4] By reacting in this way, the Parisian rioters were subscribing to the ideological current propounded by the *Dialogue d'entre le maheustre et le manant* (Dialogue between the broadshoulders and the clodhopper), in which the essential workings of society and its proper functions rested on referring all matters to an intransigent Catholicism "springing from the [very] hand of God" himself.[5]

In France, doubtless since the beginning of the sixteenth century, the ecclesiastic tribunals had gradually seen their power to judge these cases taken away. As early as 1510, a decree saw to it that only bishops were referred cases involving clerics who had blasphemed and were to be sentenced "to such grievous punishment that this shall serve as example to all the others." But above all, it was the Villers-Cotterêts decree of 1539 that considerably restricted the right of the ecclesiastic courts to judge such cases, thereby confirming the superiority of secular law over such matters. Against objections from the episcopacy, cases investigated and judged by the Holy Office dwindled, including even those where clergy were suspected of this offense and brought before judges.[6] Thus it was that the Grands Jours, or "Days of Glory," hearings in 1665 and 1666, in the name of the king's justice, forced several priests accused of impious speech to appear in court, sentencing one of them to "a year of banishment and to make atonements for having [uttered in a sermon] impieties and blasphemies attacking heaven and earth."[7]

The Gallican Church of France, its juridical stature somewhat stripped to begin with, of course brought out the need for judgments against a practice that was widespread among clergy and the laity. The church sought to condemn the practice of blasphemy by intervening through various entreaties and at propitious moments such as the calling of the Estates General in 1614. The provincial councils of Bourges (1584) or Narbonne (1609) and the assemblies of the clergy also recommended the strictest vigilance when it came to the liberties with language taken by monks and friars, and recommended the utmost firmness. In an admittedly singular context, the 1579 assembly solemnly declared, "There is no crime that requires a greater diligence on the part of a bishop or his official, and which must be pursued with as much fury, as concubinage and the infamous custom of blasphemies. The number of those who fall into the one or the other crime is so great that one could almost witness the reestablishment of ecclesiastical discipline if the field of the Church were purged of them."[8] Moreover it was in the early seventeenth century, and again through the voice of its assemblies, that the high clergy petitioned the king to instigate coercive measures countering those Christians who were evading the retributions of religious justice.[9] Among the reiterated undertakings, those that issued from the 1645 assembly were accompanied by a circumstantial and interesting explanation: "The Church considers that the calamity of these times is such that all feeling of religion seems extinguished in the greater part of men, and from the defiant contempt for its ministers they pass most injuriously to contempt for God, which brings it about that libertinage, profane swearing of oaths, blasphemies, and impieties are at present considered ordinary crimes that are committed publicly and with impunity."[10]

This text, presented on April 19, 1646, by a delegation of prelates to Anne of Austria and Cardinal Jules Mazarin, was but one among the many times when the church resorted to royal power in an effort to put the scandal of profane language to rest. These interventions sometimes led to reminders of preexisting edicts or to the publication of a new text directed toward repressing blasphemy. Sermoners who took the matter to heart sometimes challenged the responsible powers before groups of listeners they considered influential. Following Séraphin de Paris, the Eudist priest Vincent-Toussaint Beurrier exclaimed (in the mid-eighteenth century), "O honored judges who are guardians and keepers of the sovereign's authority, punish the blasphemers harshly. They are guilty ones so shameful as to not deserve even the full severity of your judgment. But as there shall always be, despite the magistrates' vigilance, impious ones of this sort who evade their deserved prosecution, let us at least endeavor, my dear listeners, to make amends to the Holy Name of Jesus with our praises and our benedictions, for the offenses he receiveth."[11]

But for all this, a real political resolve was still needed for legislative measures to have the efficacy desired by the church. It was no mere coincidence, indeed, that representatives of the clergy would always press the issue harder when the monarch's power seemed the most vulnerable and visibly least effective. The civil wars at the close of the sixteenth century and the regencies of the seventeenth were both periods that did not appear propitious for a thoroughgoing political suppression of blasphemy. As quintessential moments of upheaval, they encouraged much deviance on all fronts. It was a good thing, then, that at such times Providence could be counted upon to continue to watch over and to strike, even more perhaps, with the suddenness a thunderclap, those offenders who had gone unpunished by the king and his minions. This direct intervention by God in the earthly sphere of justice, this immanent manifestation that redressed the failings of human authorities, always appeared in the aspect of an inverted miracle, spectacular and rather theatricalized, only to become a historical event, transmitted orally, as well as by broadsheets, other cheaply printed circulating forms of generally false or sensational news [*canards*], and perhaps by almanacs.[12]

The time of the Wars of Religion, marked by an inevitable dispersion of powers, was a period rich in signs sent by God, all designed to manifest, always with terrible magnificence, his rectifying vengeance. The head-on and violent opposition between the two Christian confessions favored the development of such representative signs. Reflecting on "a great and admirable sign that had appeared in heaven," Artus Désiré, in a vengeful text he composed in 1563, saw in such a sign the foretelling of the Huguenots' immanent extermination. He referred the reader to chapter 12, verses 1 through 4, from John's Book of Revelation, "a woman . . . with the moon under her feet . . . with child . . . a great red dragon . . . His tail swept down a third of the stars of heaven," identifying the Protestants with the ignominious beast that must be slain. "People of God," he went on, "avoid the company of the wretched and cast out children of ire and perdition who composed these thousand blasphemies and defamatory libels against God and our Holy Father whom we are called upon by divine and human right to uphold and defend, for which reason I did make response to the said blasphemy to show the sacrilegious tormenters their infamy." In an earlier epistle, Désiré had appealed to the king to repress the blasphemous Huguenots,

> *In God's name justice give then,*
> *My Lord. By chastisement grand*
> *Be they slain, 'tis God's command.*[13]

When entreaties of this kind remained futile or insignificant and doing nothing seemed unworthy of the dignity of divine majesty despite premonitory cautions clearly signaled by the heavens, God's justice could take no other outlet than to make itself known through punishment of the guilty. What Denis Crouzet dubs "prophetic violence" was thus recognized and designated a true expression of divine ire and will upon the head of offending individuals and communities.[14] In such a context even the butcheries of the St. Bartholomew's Day Massacre and all that went with this—other waves of violence, active participation of children—can be situated in this interpretive line of descent: that of a selective punishment as the instrument of immanent justice restoring order to chaos.

In less tumultuous periods of religious struggle, an equally dramatic divine compensation took over for the lapses in the fight of the political powers against the blasphemer's crime. While communal punishment was held to be exemplary during the periods of most acute concern about the spread of heresies, references to the lessons of individual punishment were favored by orators and pamphleteers during calmer, more ordinary times. Barthélemy de Viette was treasurer of the king's properties in Lyons and a public finance officer. During the regency of Marie de Médicis, he circulated a short account that strove to underscore both "a memorable stroke [that was part] of the infallible effects of Divine Justice in the world" and the notorious weakness of the power to enact justice that God entrusted to kings. On September 14, 1610, during the celebration of the feast of the Exaltation of the Cross, reports Viette, a blasphemer who had been "several times reprimanded for his swearing" was serving his time in prison. Viette writes,

> As the time approached seven o'clock in the evening, he began to play cards in his room, seated at a table with three other prisoners. At the very moment he was uttering and repeating his blasphemies, swearing that he would give himself to the devil, he was observed suddenly to lower his head, become speechless, buckle in the knees, and fall upon the table surrounded by his companions. No sooner had he done this than he did give up the ghost. God shut his mouth and caused him to die of an instant.

By reporting so precisely on the time and place of detention and of the heavenly chastisement, this officer of Lyons (who recurs several times to the ordinances of Saint Louis) issued an indirect challenge to a regency monarchy that had shown such carelessness and laxity in its duty to charge blasphemers, despite the prodigious arsenal of repression at its command:

It is not without mystery that God shall have wished to display the execution of His divine justice in the middle and true heart of this kingdom's capital city, in the very Palace Royal wherein the principal and sovereign justice is served, which giveth splendor and light to all the others, as doth the Sun to all the other celestial Torchlights. He hath wished to show the effects of His divine and supreme justice in this most eminent place and seat of the principal and sovereign justice which communicates its judgments through every means in the kingdom to keep each at his proper station and duty.[15]

The reassertion of one of royal sovereignty's chief attributes poorly disguises the false "mystery" of heavenly intervention. In fact this account, taking the form of an exemplum, reproduces in its executive language of divine mandate the usual model of divine manifestation with regard to impenitent and provocative swearers. After several warnings, more or less readable, the blasphemer who falls yet again into sin has exhausted the grace that a reformed spirit might still have expected from God in His patience. Immediate death is the fate of the fallen, an *unexpected* death: the death feared most by all because no repentance is possible, no sacramental redemption—the death that puts the unredeemed, weighted by the gravity of sin, before the divine Judge and Maker. These quasi-theatrical deaths, which sermoners from Vincent de Paul to Alphonse de Liguori recalled to inspire fright, were always radical, extraordinarily sudden, and instantaneously followed the performance of a terminal transgression. No sooner had the Neapolitan carter let fly his last blasphemy, while crossing the valley of Novi, when he fell into the water and drowned. Likewise it was just after abusing a crucifix that another Campanian peasant was struck by lightning while walking along the road.[16] Need we add that each of these blasphemers was in perfect health? Often, to dispel all doubts, there was a final, postmortem trace of supernatural retribution: a blackened mouth, a twisted tongue clearly visible on the person who had just succumbed, were so many signatures, for the living, of the celerity of heaven's wrath and the material effects of expiated sin.

Other accounts, sometimes later ones written in the seventeenth and early eighteenth centuries, yet retaining the same narrative structure and moral pungency, transform the irreversible chastisement into a (probably only) temporary, if no less meaningful, punishment. When provoked and insulted, God strikes blasphemers mute and simultaneously paralyzes or leaves "crippled all of their limbs." This is the misadventure that befalls some men in a Perigordian inn toward the year 1600, after a mysterious horseman who has arrived on the scene has striven in vain to stop their using such speech.[17] Even more original, in part for its epilogue, is the following story related in correspondence addressed in August 1723 by Monsieur de Rupierre to his father:

> I give myself the honor of writing to you, my dear father, to notify you about a most certain and tragic piece of news relating to what came about at Riom in Auvergne, Wednesday last, on the seventh of July. Several fellows of the town and gentlemen of consideration were amusing themselves in an inn and after having drunk to excess had the impiety to hang a crucifix from a rope, place it upon the table so as to give it drink like themselves, insulting it all the while. The weather being very bad, addressing the crucifix they set to telling it "If you are God, make the storm and hail cease!" (for it was at that moment coming down outside with great vehemence) and other such talk compelled by their impiety. At last by God's just judgment, while three did leave, making contrition for their impiousness and were most penitent, the four others remained seated on their chairs unable to stir, each in the state or posture in which he was, without any movement, one of them holding in hand a glass before the crucifix and without any possibility of making him change position. The crucifix remained on the table. There came to the inn a procession of townspeople from the Church of Saint Amable carrying the reliquary of this same saint, which was brought forth without there taking place any change in all that was there before at this place.[18]

This report, related privately, reiterates the warnings that for decades Catholic apologists and controversialists regularly formulated concerning the Reformers. The Jesuit Jacques Gaultier in the mid-seventeenth century, in his hefty compilation, had even laid out within an ephemeris, or blocked calendar of miracles, the chronology of punitive heavenly interventions against heretics of all ages including blasphemers.[19] Here were so many events capable "doubtless of making a lasting imprint on the minds of persons of the S.R.R. (Supposed 'Reformed' Religion) as long as they wished to pay it some attention, and of convincing them forcefully of the Truth of the Catholic, Apostolic, and Roman Church."[20] Ever since the beginnings of the Covenant—and here one might think of the wife of Lot[21]—all provocation and disobedience toward God was paid for with the stiffest penalty. Even intercession by the saints could do nothing for the petrified blasphemer, frozen in his sin-making stance. Gratuitous, impious defiance remained, therefore, a mortal transgression whose punishment must be exemplary and, thus, public. God's direct intervention, passed along among the faithful in texts and diffused orally by the populace, pointed to a dynamic, dissuasive, and necessarily robust pedagogy. "I well know that some shall take this for a fable," concluded Ollivier de Minière at the end of his edifying narrative. Yet would not God's justice, in place of the faltering justice of men, forever strike down the offending communities or individuals, "sin never making its way forward without an extraordinary vengeance for its commission riding close behind."[22]

The frequency of these expiatory tableaus was not only restricted to the terrifying reality of a divine punishment suddenly delivered. It also reinforced an entire dimension of the theology of *sacrifice*. Telltale traces of blood or mutilations in a number of these edifying tales underscored the extreme cruelty of the offense that blasphemy inflicted—conveniently resembling a reenacted crucifixion, a reappearance of new wounds torn open in the side of Christ. Thus, as Vienna's Archbishop Pierre de Villars reported,

A certain God-fearing person on the way to perform his devotions found in his path a man covered with sores who, when asked how it happened that he should have been so mistreated, answered it was some youths who having feasted and caroused the whole night in a nearby cabaret, had not left off wounding and bruising in such manner that this good personage, moved by compassion, went at once to greatly reproach and reprimand them and induce them to make amends for their error, which deed they did deny hard and fast, claiming not to have offended anyone, having merely jested among themselves, with no other soul having intervened. The good man took them to the place, the battered man disappeared such that they believed it was our Lord Himself appearing as the one rent and wounded by their blasphemies.[23]

Faced with a sin so widespread and so grave, was not the number of guilty speakers designated to be punished by heaven rather disappointing?

And that was without counting on possibilities of repentance, and even more on God's infinite patience, something broken only in extreme cases, as Girard pointed out in the sermon he delivered for mass on the eleventh Sunday after Pentecost.[24] Still, the edifying texts of "popular literature" placed a pronounced emphasis on the possibility of clemency and conditional reprieve.[25] "Believe most assuredly, sinner," one reads in *Les sept trompettes pour réveiller les pêcheurs* (The seven trumpets to awaken sinners),

> that if thy God were not good-natured and pitying as He is, when you sinned the earth would open to swallow you, the water would rise above its embankments and dikes to engulf you, and the air would suffocate you, the fire burn you, the stars unleash their thunder and lightning to blast you to ruin. . . . Do you not imagine, O man and woman of sin, that were it not for God's great goodnesse this wine that you drink would choke you and be converted to poison? It would surely be so, have no doubt. But He reserves this punishment for the next life.[26]

Most theologians, however, preferred to enumerate punishments that fell upon blasphemers here on earth and threatened their tangible surroundings. Just as Nicolas Turlot or Bressanvido would do later, the Oratorian Loriot in the mid-sixteenth century gave a dire warning to the communities he addressed, "You must expect only afflictions, poverty, misery, plagues, famines, hailstorms, sterilities, devastations in your lands so long as blasphemy holds sway and you allow it."[27] Already hauling out the sorry litany of usual calamities, Loriot (along with a good many others) showed no theological originality, simply absorbing the traditional biblical interpretation of evil's origin, catastrophes, and gloom into a heavenly retribution stoked by humanity's innate spiritual incapacity. And yet if the crime of one single sinner could threaten the life and equilibrium of all, did not the struggle against blasphemy from this point enter another category—one in which responsibility no longer fell only to the churches and their pastors?

PART TWO | *The Princes' Time: Powers of State*
Against Blasphemy

The multiplying moral and theological criticism on the practice of blasphemy essentially had a pastoral value: it addressed the care of souls. Warnings, as well as descriptions of the threats of punishment that could fall from heaven upon the guilty, remained separate from the repressive measures of the courts, even as the threats served at times to provisionally attenuate the insufficiency and weaknesses of temporal authorities. This was not, however, for lack of a number of decisions enacted by western European powers in a series of enforceable legislative acts bent on combating "perversities of speech." A congeries of local, provincial, and central institutions, mostly between the late fifteenth and late sixteenth centuries, helped to establish a repetitive and narrow judicial corpus. The offenses covered by this body of law cast a net that, however fine its webwork, still did not always entrap all offenders and was also from time to time diverted from its ostensible primary objective.

 4 | KINGS AGAINST BLASPHEMY

A Flowering of Edicts.   In Europe the first indications of repressive blasphemy laws date back to the drawing up of the Justinian Code (535–540), with its threat to impose "the penalty of death" on those who violated it.[1] In 826, the code's provisions would be enforced with renewed vigor by Charlemagne's son, Louis the Pious, with the offender having to undergo "an adequate punishment" followed by a public atonement and reconciliation.[2] But then apart from a text of doubtful authenticity ascribed to the authority of Philip Augustus dated 1182, the real beginning of royal legislation in this area can be traced to a statute issued in 1263 by Louis IX on his return from the Holy Land.

The king had so deep a love for our Lord and His sweet Mother that
he punished most severely all those who had been convicted of
speaking of them irreverently or of using their names in some
wicked oath. Thus I saw him order a goldsmith of Caesarea to be
bound to a ladder, with pig's gut and other viscera round his neck,
in such a quantity that they reached up to his nose. I have also
heard that, since I came back from overseas, he had the lips and
nose of a citizen of Paris seared for a similar offence.[3]

In accordance with this purism, judges applied prescribed punishments
to the most obstinate offenders, who had their foreheads branded with
hot irons and, for recidivism, their lips and tongues pierced. Pope
Clement IV was struck by the harshness of such unprecedented sentences. Even as he congratulated a king who was later to be canonized for
his zeal, he advised Louis to refrain from inflicting corporal punishments. Here the bishop of Rome was simply following the papacy's pre-
vious decisions on such transgressive behavior. The closest precedent, a
decretal issued by Gregory IX in 1236, had stipulated

> that if anyone be so hardy as to publicly pronounce a blasphemy
> against God or one of His saints, first among them the Holy Virgin,
> the following punishment shall be carried out against him: to wit,
> on seven successive Sundays during the parish mass he shall be
> made to stand publicly outside the church doors; on the last of
> these Sundays he shall wear no coat, shoes, or stockings and have
> fastened around his neck a leather strap; for the seven last days of
> the previous week he shall have eaten nothing save bread and
> water; and for the entire duration he shall offer sustenance accord-
> ing to his own means to one, two, or three paupers the violating of
> which stipulation shall call forth an additional punishment.[4]

Should the offender refuse to undergo this series of humiliations, the
unrepentant would forever be denied entry to the parish church and
deprived of a Christian burial.

The breach separating these two legislative tendencies illustrates quite
well how differently ecclesiastical and temporal authorities approached
these problems, establishing their respective roles. The first evoked the
daunting deterrent of temporary exclusion from the offender's Christian

community. This was a grave but not irremediable sentence, because gradual reintegration, paired with rehabilitative steps for personal conduct and communal involvement, guaranteed the possibility of redemption (except for the obstinately incorrigible). The second approach also involved a form of exclusion, but it was through lasting and unmistakable marks on the body's flesh, singling out in the end, and in the eyes of all, the blasphemer as a marginal figure.

An obedient son of the holy church, Louis IX diluted the severity of the statute's corporal punishments in December 1264. His successors, however, generally renewed the same harsh sentences that ordered mutilation. Philip III (in 1271), Philip VI of Valois (in 1347), Charles VI (in 1397), Charles VII (in 1437 and 1460), Charles VIII (in 1486 and 1487), and finally Louis XII (in 1510) enacted statutes, edicts, and letters patent that, in spirit, were all quite alike: a scale of punishments graduated according to the number of repeat offenses, usually set at four beyond the first conviction. To these were added a call for inculpating and carrying out sentences against summoned witnesses who failed to appear when called to testify against the accused.[5] One might have thought that these legislative means would have been considered sufficient in repressing blasphemy in subsequent periods. However, the period that is customarily called the *ancien régime* in France saw a considerable multiplication of such provisions in the law's assault on blasphemy. This corpus, consisting of twenty-eight texts, merits some attention.

The texts can roughly be sorted into two unequal divisions. First, there are those that have to do with a particular social group and milieu. Six in number, they all address military life. The last monarchical statute passed concerning blasphemy in July 1727 "prohibited soldiers from swearing and blaspheming the holy name of God, the Holy Virgin, and the saints under penalty of piercing of the tongue with a hot iron." The second set brings together texts of a more general import (three of these even were part of the corpus of the most important statutes, the *grandes ordonnances*) whose chronological distribution cannot fail to edify (see the table below).[6]

Its milestone years unevenly balanced toward the Renaissance, the second set essentially concerns the period from 1510 to 1650. In this century and a half, the lion's share of these legal texts was allotted to the sixteenth century and particularly the Wars of Religion (six references) followed by the reign of Francis I. By contrast Henry IV and Louis XIV issued few laws in the name of this cause. Again, the paramount event

TABLE 4 |

16th Century	17th Century	18th Century
1510 ordinance	1606 edict	
1514 ordinance	1617 ordinance	
1523 ordinance	1631 ordinance	
1528 (?)	1647 ordinance	
1534 letters patent	1651 declaration	
1546 edict	1666 declaration	
1549 ordinance	1681 ordinance	
1550 ordinance		
1560 Ordinance of Orléans		
1566 Ordinance of Moulins		
1570 declaration		
1572 declaration		
1579 Ordinance of Blois		
1581 declaration		
1594 ordinance		

was the surge of reformed church movements and the cultural watersheds they occasioned. Impossible to contain in the course of the early sixteenth century, this widespread and far-reaching religious revolution was carried out through an armed confrontation between Christianity's different sensibilities, sustained in the Catholic camp by a reprise of legislation against heretics—always potential blasphemers.[7] It was also in the course of the latter half of the sixteenth century that the hunt for suspected male and female witches further identified impious speech with manifestations of witchcraft, necessitating the prosecution of such deviancies. This parallel between heresy and witchcraft, of course, remains somewhat uncertain or provisional, inasmuch as it considers only the projection of norms onto the situation and not the concrete and detailed application of such norms by the judicial machinery.[8]

This simultaneity cannot, however, be completely brushed aside, even if (or at least apparently) the repression of sorcery was intermittent, while that of blasphemy seemed consistently reconfirmed and pursued (or so suggests the documented intention of the lawgiver). Taking all into consideration, however, was it not the same battle against Satan? The very battle that lawmakers carried forward, albeit in other guises, as long as that same diabolical power, which flourished at yesterday's witches' Sabbaths, continued to express itself through irreverent speech?

On the other hand, the profusion of antiblasphemy texts in the early modern period probably did not reflect an actual increase in blasphemous speech among the population. The exorbitant accumulation of laws targeting this behavior tells us more about the ineffectiveness of pre-existing measures than about the actual frequency of blasphemous offenses. But, even more, this accretion helps us appreciate the expression of a pervasive cultural process in which political and religious upheavals, joined with the emergence of a social "cultivation of manners" [*civilisation des mœurs*] to produce a corpus of law irreducible to simple repetition or reproduction. In fact, the measures taken by the monarchy allow us to identify two textual categories.[9] The laws within the first relate to moderate legislation based on the provisions of the statute of 1510, renewed in full in 1514, 1546, 1651, and 1666. These laws prescribed, through eight stages, a rather extended gradation of penal severity, from the first infraction, punishable by a simple fine named at the judge's discretion, to the last offense, punishable by maiming the tongue. Between these two extremes, some degree of corporal punishment was reserved solely for the last three of the maximum repeat offenses. The laws within the second category, however, imposed far more repressive discipline. Acts promulgated in 1572, 1581, 1594, 1617, 1631, and especially in 1681 exemplify this and are all characterized by a noticeable reduction in the system of graduated penalties and a rather swift application of physical punishment. If the statutes of 1581, 1617, and 1631 mandated bodily punishment for a fourth conviction, and those of 1572 and 1594 for a third, the statute of 1681 (the last of its kind) stipulated that such punishment be administered for a single or the first thoughtlessly uttered invective. In addition the harshest punishments were preceded by a ritual of full apology, or penance, whereby "the offender, bareheaded and barefoot, wearing only his shirt and a rope around his neck, holding a taper, publicly asked God's pardon."[10]

These coercive provisions, which were widely subtended by a collective delirium over the siege of Satan's dominion over the world, could not help but crop up in other European states during similar periods. But they also varied with the specific historical moments and particular situation of each given nation. The fragmentary documentary evidence that we possess mainly illustrates a clear renewal of antiblasphemy laws in Europe during the first half of the sixteenth century. In the kingdom of the Spains, the four edicts of 1492, 1502, 1525, and 1566 called upon and reinforced the repressive legislation by stages, while in the Holy Roman Empire several decrees (especially those of 1530, 1548, 1554, and 1577) inflicted harsh corporal punishments against those found guilty of impious speech. But although the imperial lands bore the full brunt of the growing reform movements and religious atomization, the content of such decrees appeared primarily to view blasphemy as a grave verbal perversion committed in violation of the canons of the nascent civil society of manners rather than as an offense of a purely spiritual nature. Provisions in the text of 1554 condemn "scandalous and quite vulgar words in use among the common people, as for example *bougre* [blackguard, devil or bastard; and, when used with *de*, the adjectival *bloody*; or, by itself, the exclamatory *hell!*], *bersonteu*, *wuyot*, or *cornard* [cuckold], and *mord-Dieu* [goddammit!], detrimental to the honor of one's fellow men [and needing] to be banished in any Republic under proper rule of law and order."[11] At the same moment, in Bavaria, specific provisions in the law held fathers of families, innkeepers, and artisans to the duty of restraining all those living, eating, or working under their roof from blaspheming in their daily practices.[12] In Italy several conspicuous enactments by sovereigns followed in the same course. Besides preexisting papal legislation that had been strengthened between the Fifth Lateran Council and Pius V, it was the city-states of Florence and Venice that proved the most clearly committed to the struggle. In the duchy of Tuscany, Cosimo I in a 1542 proclamation ranked the suppression of blasphemous word crimes as a primary function of state, declaring "It is necessary that every State in addition to its other functions and duties ordain the extinction of these vices in cities and towns." But in confronting the "crime," it was Venice that put in place probably the most exact machinery. The ineffectiveness of extant laws obligated the Venetian Council of Ten to take a more aggressive stance. They established a special judicial institution on December 20, 1537, to deal with blasphemy: the so-called Esecuttori contro la bestemmia (Elders against blasphemy), with three former members of the Council of Ten, which chose the committee. The sentences they issued could not be appealed, and their jurisdiction was gradually extended to other areas. These magistrates "of high morals" were entrusted with stamping out crimes related to gambling, sacrilege, clandestine marriages, prostitution—the gamut, in a word, of infringements of public order.[13]

The kingdom of England seems to have undergone a singular evolution, even as it shared the other monarchies' obsession with blasphemy. Three broad phases in the changing relation between central power and verbal deviance can be discerned through a sparse scattering of printed texts.[14] Under the Tudors and the first Stuarts, the campaign was waged by the High Ecclesiastical Commission and the Star Chamber, with authority to prosecute cases "of a religious nature which could constitute an offense against the soundness of the royal, sovereign, political power."[15] Cases of blasphemy fell under such classification because in a letter of royal commission dated 1559 Elizabeth I granted the high commission authority henceforth to proceed against (among others) heretics, blasphemers, and subjects who behaved wickedly and failed to participate in church services. Despite the lofty titular independence and indeed clerical composition of this level of competent jurisdiction and its extraordinary powers to initiate proceedings (no less than a bishop presided over the high commission), the royal sovereign's hand kept a firm grip on these instruments of judicial power and civil order. This was why they were among the first institutions to be suppressed at the outbreak of the Puritan Revolution in 1641.

One witnessed a prompt filling of the legislative vacuum present at the start of the second historical period running from the English civil war to the death of Queen Anne (1713), as clerics found themselves having to contend with the prodigious efflorescence of political-religious discourses that marked the period. With more and more groups taking their turn at public speaking, with printed tracts circulating in greater numbers, and religious sects multiplying, doctrines and new premises and arguments were put forward which, at times, deviated in pronounced ways from Anglican or Presbyterian Christianity, occasionally negating them entirely. In 1646 a Presbyterian preacher named Thomas Edwards, of Christ Church in London, published *Gangraena*, a collection of "all the errours of doctrine" that were afoot in England. Edwards called in his introduction for a quick restitution of the guidance of the church and of civil officeholders before complete ruin and loss of religion itself ensued. There would, he said, no longer be anyone left to do the governing, as his "*Catalogue, or Black Bill of the Errours, Heresies, Blasphemies and Practices of the Sectaries* of this time, broached and acted within these four last years in England, was increasing more in a single week or month than was the case for an entire year in the past."[16] By the following year fifty-two of London's pastors were signing a petition, *A Testimony to the Truth of Jesus Christ*, in which they urged magistrates to punish all those guilty of "atheism, pernicious doctrine, blasphemy, defilement of the days of the Lord and other sins."[17]

It was in the context of this prolonged disorder and the recapture of the country by the Roundhead army, of which Oliver Cromwell had become spokesman,[18] that the Long Parliament on May 2, 1648, passed a statute aimed at punishing blasphemers and heretics.[19] This lengthy text provides a scrupulous inventory of all the doctrinal deviations that were subject to legal censure: from denying the Trinity, or even God, to rejecting Christ's resurrection and his dual nature. Singled out as well were worshipers of holy relics, images, and saints, those who considered worthless the baptism of children, and those who identified the Church of England with the Antichrist. This document, which prescribed penalties as harsh as banishment and death for blasphemers, put itself forward as veritable creed for the established church. The document's spirit and letter gave shape to the conviction that a strong affirmation of doctrine was necessary in the face of the more or less real threats posed by Quakers, Ranters, the so-called Fifth Monarchists (who were readily accused of atheism), the beliefs of Baptists or Catholics, and the proliferating currents of new ways of thinking and reasoning.[20] Two years later, in August 1650, another act of Parliament targeted "execrable, blasphemous and atheistical opinions contrary to the glory of God." But this time the sin of blasphemy was more directly associated with meanings more explicitly moral than doctrinal. "Notwithstanding this their care," the text of the act stated, members of the Parliament

> find to their grief and astonishment, that there are divers men and women who have lately discovered themselves to be most monstrous in their opinions . . . not onely to the notorious corrupting and disordering, but even to the dissolution of all Human Society[,] . . . who . . . presume avowedly in words to profess that . . . acts of Denying and Blaspheming God, or the Holiness or Righteousness of God, or . . . of cursing God, or Swearing prophanely or falsely by the Name of God, or acts of Lying, Stealing, Cousening and Defrauding others, or the acts of Murther, Adultery, Incest, Fornication, Uncleanness, Sodomy, Drunkenness . . . are not things in themselves shameful, wicked, sinful . . . but are in their own nature as Holy and Righteous as the Duties of Prayer.[21]

It seems that adoption of this text (which limited penalties to imprison-ment or banishment) was primarily aimed at the Ranters and the danger of social destabilization that the ruling classes believed they detected in the sect's designs, mystical pantheism, and moral debaucheries.[22]

This heavy arsenal of repression, which certain historians consider a severe restriction of liberty of conscience (even for the day), was partly derigidified, during the Restoration, when new legislation rescinded the statute of *Haeretico comburendo* (1401) and abolished the death penalty for all religious crimes—even if the text reaffirmed that "atheism, blas-phemy, heresy, schism and other damnable doctrines and opinions must continue to be prosecuted and punished with excommunication."[23] Besides this a new Blasphemy Act was adopted in 1698, now affecting those who—through their writings and words—proclaimed the falsity of the Christian religion and questioned the divine inspiration of the Bible.[24] By identifying blasphemy more closely with a blatant act of unbelief, this measure eloquently distilled the growing fearfulness of public authorities confronting the upswing of agnostic and atheistic thought in England and the publication of several works radically impugning Christianity. From Robert Boyle's *The Sceptical Chymist* (1661) to John Toland's *Christianity Not Mysterious* (1696) worrisome skeptical critiques first took hold on British soil before having a lasting influence on Enlightenment Europe.

Only gradually, during the reign of the first Hanovers, did a third phase take shape as the legislative vise loosened its grip on guilty tongues. But even as late as 1721, at the urging of William Wake, arch-bishop of Canterbury, a royal proclamation condemned "blasphemous societies." By 1745 the Profane Oaths Act decreed that an act of swearing was "only" liable to the imposition of a fine, the amount of which would be determined according to the offender's social rank. Was blasphemous speech proper, however, really any longer the issue? Probably not, if one consults the analyses of the great jurist William Blackstone, who in the mid-seventeenth century clearly distinguished between swearwords and cursing, which were regarded as profane vices, and blasphemy itself, which amounted to "denying the existence or providence of God or insulting Jesus Christ the Savior or holding the Holy Scripture up to ridicule."[25] In any case the violation, still defined at that time as a calumny against the Christian religion, could continue to be prosecuted in accordance with common law. Was not the London bookseller

Thomas Williams charged on this very count for having sold Thomas Paine's *The Age of Reason*?[26]

These chronological layers, broadly sketched and incomplete, are of interest to the historian mainly as part of an explanatory and comparative exposition of blasphemy. As we try to understand the arrangements for authorizing and dispensing political power, which followed lines both alike and divergent in England and on the Continent, what shared preoccupations and ideological orientations does blasphemy illustrate? By juxtaposing the data, however fragmentary, we can draw three broad lessons about the conditions under which the sovereign ruler perceived and exploited the war against impious speech in modern Europe.

The Law's Lessons. The first major development that comes to light throughout Europe, when we turn again to the continent, is the progressive abandonment of turf by ecclesiastic juridical power. In certain regions marked by the reform church movements, the consistories—the lowest courts made up of ministers, elders, and deacons—put up a fight to defend their prerogatives and to sidestep the encroaching jurisprudence of temporal powers. It remained difficult, however, to establish and maintain general rules. In the principality of Neuchâtel, for instance, blasphemy was simultaneously prosecuted by the ecclesiastic and criminal courts. When the occasion presented itself, the secular court could even place the case of the accused in the charge of the seignioral consistory.[27] On the Catholic side, the *officialités*, those ecclesiastic tribunals with the power to try cases in such matters, were gradually dispossessed of that power. In places where the Inquisition was active, before it had become an instrument in the hands of the sovereign political power and to the disadvantage of diocesan courts, it monopolized blasphemy cases. As we have seen in the case of Venice, however, the Inquisition's presence there was no impediment to the Council of Ten's creation, in 1537, of the special prosecutorial functions of the *esecuttori*. In France the situation followed the same general movement, the course of which cannot be confined to an isolated or narrow conception of blasphemy.[28]

The decline of the *officialités* can be explained in two ways. First, there was the undermining of the procedure for bringing charges against offenders, which was open to corruption and without guarantees for the safety of those under the court's jurisdiction.[29] Second, and simultaneously, there was the monarchical power's determination to monopolize the jurisdiction of select tribunals over criminal cases, leaving to such tribunals cognizance over civil cases (concerning debts, nonpayment of the *dîme* [tithes], execution of wills, cases involving marriage, etc.). As early as 1510, in his statute on blasphemy, article IV, Louis XII had already stipulated that any clerics charged with this crime and arrested by the king's men were to be turned over to the *officialités*, whose judges "shall, at the instigation of our counsels and officers, be given such legal and significant punishment as may serve exemplary to all others." It was above all the 1539 Villers-Cotterêts statute that considerably restricted the legal jurisdiction of the church by securing for the monarch a say in those criminal cases, such as blasphemy, that also related to crimes against the faith, the church, and the sacraments. But the lines of demarcation between jurisdictions were not always as clear as the documents made them out to be, and there was real resistance from judges of the ecclesiastic courts. The statute of November 1549 put forward a juridical definition of blasphemy, conspicuously distinguishing between two forms of the crime, with each to be tried by a different legal body. Judges within the church would henceforth have cognizance over cases involving "errors or simple heresy, stemming more from ignorance, delusion or misreckoning [*erreur*], human weakness and fallibility, thoughtlessness and lewdness of language on the part of the accused," and not over those stemming "from true malice or desire to separate oneself from holy union with the Church."[30] Yet should these heresies or public gestures and expressions be accompanied by "public scandal, popular uproar, sedition or other crimes, entailing offenses against the common peace," they were to be tried jointly by the royal and the ecclesiastic tribunals.[31]

This initial grand distinction, in which the royal power affirmed itself as law, was but one of many first steps in what was to be a long process of affirmation, encouraged by circumstances. The eruption of reform movements, and their attendant turmoil, blurred the mutual bonds among society, religious authority, and secular power. From this point on, in facing the threats of shattered spiritual authority stirred up by "heretical" speech and behavior, it fell to the temporal power to guarantee order and to deal, harshly, with all sowers of discord. Divesting the church of its power to prosecute blasphemous speech, as is progressively discerned from the historical record, was always motivated by the need to safeguard public order. At the same time, these shifts in power reconfirmed the finer justifying distinction between blasphemous swearing that was simply improper or out of place and that which was truly heretical (as outlined in the statute of 1666).

In the official history he devoted to this question, Pierre-Toussaint Durand de Maillane stated precisely that in France "secular judges claim jurisdiction over this crime as much because of the infraction it entails against the statutes of our kings as because of its assault on religion in a manner both scandalous and contrary to civic peace." He went on,

> The crime of blasphemy is not seen by us as a case for prosecution by the king's counsel per se even though the examining police magistrate may, at his discretion, undertake in principle to claim competency in all such cases [*quoique le juge de police n'en puisse tout connaître*] (following the decree of January 4, 1710). But if the given instance of blasphemy should constitute a formal intention to decry religion, it is from this moment a crime of heresy with attendant scandal and public disturbance whose punishment is reserved to the king's justice [*au juge royal*].[32]

Between the seminal 1549 statute and this observation about juridical practice, the different nature of blasphemous practices came to no longer refer to distinct spheres of justice but clearly only to degrees of an exclusively royal jurisdiction. This movement over time, which progressively diminished the legal authority of the previously independent administration of justice in repressing blasphemy, underscores the specific relation that blasphemous speech and behavior could maintain vis-à-vis the royal power, justifying the intrusion of the political in a domain that one might have believed belonged to the church. This effort was particularly noticeable in France during the seventeenth century. In strongly consecrating the divine right of kingship, this period was unique in bolstering the prince's claim as sole ultimate authority to punish this crime.[33]

Against the political philosophy of Scholasticism, for which secular sovereigns remained subordinate to the pope (the sole official to hold power directly from God), the theses of Gallicanism developed the idea of the prince's autonomy in relation to all other authority, considering him to be God's lieutenant within the kingdom. The unconditional reference to God thus consecrated the divine origin of the public power, the *plenitudo potestas*. By granting the state a divine foundation, Charles Loyseau's *Traité des seigneuries* (Treatise on seigniories) and later Jacques

Bénigne Bossuet's *La politique tirée des propres paroles de l'écriture sainte* (Political sovereignty derived from the words of holy scripture) remade the "royal throne not a man's but God's Himself."[34] For our purposes, two consequences flow from this theological-political position. Any insult directed toward the divine majesty, first of all, also disparaged the royal majesty. Hurling insults at heaven, therefore, could easily be allied with an offense against royal authority itself. The close connection between these two types of insult is illustrated in the late-sixteenth- and seventeenth-century classification of treason against God and human beings under the same heading.[35] This criminal taxonomy also relied on the divine injunction of chapter 22, verse 28, of Exodus, "You shall not revile God, nor curse a ruler of your people." It would appear to have been in the name of such sanction of the bond between these twin powers that Pierre Ruault, a pork butcher who had come to the Bourg-la-Reine marketplace to purchase meats, was arrested "for insults and blasphemies uttered against God and Monsieur Colbert, the Minister of State."[36]

At the same time, the confidence vested in the royal sovereign was reason to repress blasphemy unflaggingly. One can see here a kind of obligatory reciprocity that theoreticians of law or compilers of jurisprudence have never ceased to point out. Nicolas Delamare, for one, reminded readers of Louis XIII's decisions on the matter of blasphemers,

> The Statutes of our late king will forever be lasting and precious monuments of his piety and the fervor of his zealous devotion to God's glory and the public peace, yet the confusion in which heresy placed the State under his rule did not allow for taking greatest advantage of these good and just intentions of its prince. Thus did it come about that on assuming the throne Louis XIV faced these three colossal forces to combat in his estates: blasphemies, dueling, heresy.[37]

It was the king's duty alone to issue the law in the name of the divine power that had anointed him. "The law of the kings of France," as the future bishop of La Rochelle, Villecourt, pointed out much later at the beginning of the July Monarchy, "by forcing peoples to recognize God's supreme authority made worthy of respect the authority that avenged attacks on His glory."[38] Such was already the meaning of the preamble to the royal proclamation of July 30, 1666, concerning swearers and blasphemers:

In the name of Louis, respective of the truth that there be nothing more capable of drawing heavenly benediction upon our own person and upon the State than keeping inviolably and seeing to the keeping of the holy commandment, and punishing with all severity those who should be so contemptuous as to declaim, by blaspheming, swearing and reviling, against His Holy Name. We did, on the occasion of our entering upon our majority and in deference to those kings our predecessors, make known and explain again a proclamation of 7 September 1651 prohibiting under harsh penalties the blaspheming, swearing profane oaths in the name of, or reviling of the Divine Majesty, and the uttering of any words contrary to the honor of the Most Holy Virgin, His Mother, and the saints: but having learned with displeasure to the prejudice of our prohibitions, to the great disgust and reprobation of the Church and to the ruination of the holy salvation of certain of our subjects, that this crime prevaileth in almost all places in the provinces of our Kingdom, the which doth issue in particular from the impunity of those who commit it. We should consider ourselves unworthy of the title we hold of Most Christian King were we not to bring to bear all possible care in order that a crime so abominable and which so offends and attacks directly first and foremost the Divine Majesty be stifled and stamped out.

Avenging a dishonored God, indeed—but not only that. This delegation of power also made the king a supreme judge here on earth and guarantor both of the natural order desired by the Creator and of the public peace. For blasphemy—the very expression of evil's growing presence since the original sin—cast doubt over both orders.[39] To blaspheme was to contest the hierarchy of fundamental, thus sacred, values, to dislodge the meaning of a subject's obligations of deference, to negate the virtue of obeisance and, at its limit, to question the very essence of the power that established them all. It was, finally, to throw society out of balance. If it spread, the bad example could, in effect, have an impact on the practice of religion in God's name, affecting as a consequence the probity of those customs and manners and moral life whose mainstay was religion. Verbal deviance threatened to chip away at social relations and pull apart public order and religion. It was in the name of this close association regulating the working of the divine-right state that the bishops exhorted their curates to lend their support, even perhaps more than usual, to decisions taken by the crown. Following close upon the issuance of the royal statute of 1666, the bishop of Paris, Hardouin de Péréfixe, informed

all curates of this city, its faubourgs, and the diocese that it [is] entirely just for us to do everything possible to second the pious wishes of His Most Christian Royal Majesty. We send word to you asking that said proclamation be repeated in sermons delivered at your parish masses, that the horrible crime committed by those who blaspheme God's holy Name be represented in strongest terms to your parishioners, and that they be made to understand that nothing so draws down His ire upon the heads of men than this frightful crime which attacks God Himself and the honor of His Holy Name.[40]

It was again in the name of all the troubles and dissensions blasphemy could stir up for public authorities that Guyot, in his *Répertoire universel et raisonné de jurisprudence* (Universal and analytical repertory of jurisprudence), published at the end of the eighteenth century, justified the exclusive right of secular and royal judges to prosecute blasphemy.[41]

If conserving the social organization and balance desired by God required exemplary punishment for all perpetrators of disorder, the blasphemer's chastisement served an added imperative. Indeed even the payment for their sins that God himself sometimes exacted from offenders who escaped the king's justice rarely concerned a lone individual. Often its reach threatened to punish the entire collectivity, and even innocents. As protector of every subject and guarantor of the peace of the realm, the king owed it to himself to spare his people from disturbances and misfortunes by displaying infallible sternness. "Knowing there is nothing that strays farther from God and runs so counter to His honor with as much heedless temerity as blasphemy, which, by its signs of breaking faith, doth often excite and provoke the rigor of His Justice in which He visits the kingdoms, we have felt no better moment might be chosen to ward off the threats of this terrible vengeance and win His more abundant benedictions and graces" (preamble of the 1651 edict).

Legislative acts such as this 1651 edict, then, could be put into effect as preventive measures to ward off the potential retribution of a vengeful

God.[42] Next to these acts, most of the measures aimed at strengthening the arsenal of repression generally were adopted after a natural or political catastrophe, put forth by the king or the local authorities to assuage the vengeance of a scorned divinity. (Such measures also accorded with strong theological speculations about the meaning of suffering and punishment.) At Tarbes, in 1518, sentenced to having his tongue cut out, being hanged, and then burned, Armand Carrière was "punished for repudiating and uttering execrable blasphemies against God and His glorious mother, the blessed Virgin Mary, in one of which [abominations] there was an earthquake."[43] Still, the calamities that followed upon the sin of blasphemy were seldom restricted to a single area. As a good number of theologians emphasized, they ran roughshod throughout whole principalities and kingdoms, overwhelming them with plagues, famines, and other collective misfortunes unleashed by nature. Still worse, if there had been at all such a possibility, the voluntary or involuntary incapacity of the authorities to halt the propagation of such practices was thought to signal dysfunction, sometimes at the heart of the realm. Did not Francis I, in 1528, attribute "to the pullulation of blasphemies [the occurrence of] wars, plagues, and sterilities" besieging the kingdom at that time? And was not the king also thinking of his military setbacks and the recent treaty of Madrid (January 1526), with its terms so disastrous for the French sovereign, even though he ignored them as nonbinding? More marked still was the coinciding of the Republic of Venice's adoption of antiblasphemy measures with its misfortunes overseas. In August 1500, the occupation of Modena by the Turks prompted a law stiffening punishments for blasphemy and sodomy. In August 1537 the siege of Corfu, and then a bit later the danger of losing Monemvasia on the Peloponnesian coast, were accompanied, in December of that same year, by the creation of the specialized magistracy of the *esecuttori*. Finally, in February 1695, an earthquake brought with it the promulgation of a new edict against blasphemy by the Council of Ten.[44] Sovereign authorities wherever they reigned (witness Cosimo I) were persuaded that blasphemy was "a sin that offends God more than all other sins and brings on tribulations."[45] They endeavored therefore to attend to heavenly signs so as to forestall or hinder, through law, future setbacks whose brunt all would have to bear. With this in mind, it is no sterile exercise, at least for the sixteenth and seventeenth centuries, to study antiblasphemy laws along with the chronology of political misfortunes, epidemics, and natural catastrophes.

The example of France confirms this close correlation that (excepting the period of the Wars of Religion) appears to set antiblasphemy laws squarely in the context of the monarchy's consolidation of its sovereignty. It was but a few weeks after his entry into Paris as a Catholic that Henry IV's statute of April 1594 against blasphemers concretized his conversion. The wording of similar texts in November 1617 and April 1631 was also set down in the wake of Louis XIII's victorious struggle over the dangerous political ambitions of those close to him: the marshal of D'Ancre Concino Concini, in 1617, and then Louis's own relatives, between March and July 1631. In the latter event, his conspiratorial brother Gaston d'Orléans and then his mother, Marie de Médicis, were forced to flee France while Cardinal Richelieu prevailed; that August Louis affixed his signature to the statute against blasphemy. Last, and more symbolically significant, the proclamation of September 7, 1651, coincided precisely with the day on which Louis XIV's majority was proclaimed—at a moment when Cardinal Mazarin, declared an exile from the kingdom, was forced to flee Paris. Thus throughout the history of the house of Valois and the first Bourbon kings, royal decrees promulgated against sins of speech were part of a beleaguered authority's search to confirm itself. They foregrounded antiblasphemy's lofty role in reestablishing, totally and spectacularly, the holy office of royalty. In the case of Spain, resolutions and provisions with a similar purpose served more to defend and solidify Catholic exclusivity vis-à-vis the *conversos* (the 1492 edict), the *mudejares* (edicts of 1502 and 1525), and the rebellious Calvinists in the northern Low Countries (the 1566 edict). Yet when all is said and done, by helping unify the faith, these laws also tended to buttress the monarch's position as guarantor of confessional unity.

In this way, through the theory of the divine right of kings and the necessity for social order and peace in the realms, the political vindications for repressing blasphemy took shape. The close relation between church and state (especially in France), and the latter's slowly developing ascendancy over the former, placed blasphemy at the center of a disciplinary action against behavior that was as much a civic as a religious concern.[46] The prince—God's representative on earth, the emanation of the law, a sword of justice executed in the name of all—became the central actor in the drama, the one best positioned to assuage divine anger over the verbal dissipations of subjects in his care. Such a monopoly, of course not confined to this matter alone, had slowly been put in place in countries where the crown had successfully grown stronger. Fighting blasphemy made up one component of a theological-political complex that peaked in the course of the seventeenth century. Compared to this evolution bound up with the structures of the state, the English method of repressing blasphemy offers a contrasting picture: the portrait of a power anxious primarily to address outbreaks of defiance it considered, somewhat reactively, to be only temporary and caught up in the conflicts of the moment.

The Singular Example of the British Monarchy. English public laws covering this vice were one of many responses to the influence of a set of local events and were only later enlisted in a universalizing theory of sovereign power. A reverse image of French statutes on the subject, which were more juridical than religious, Parliament's acts of 1648 and 1650 displayed exceptional theological precision. The rigorously detailed definitions of blasphemous deviance seemed necessary given the situation evoked above, the frenzied profusion of political-religious discourses in the era of the civil war. One of the most prominent figures of the religious movement of Ranters, Abiezer Coppe, went so far as to declare that the "two decrees of 10 May and 9 August 1650 were issued because of [him]."[47] In fact, he reasoned, "from the moment an act is *of* God it is as sacred *as* God," and among these "acts" were to be included "blasphemous speech, drunkenness, adultery, theft, etc."[48] To which argument precisely the Blasphemy Act, of August 1650, responded that it was in effect a blasphemy *not* to hold "adultery, drunkenness, blasphemy or theft to be odious, vile and illicit in themselves." This counterargument did not, however, deter the group's other leader, Lawrence Clarkson, from writing with further clarification on the matter that "none can be free from sin till in purity he commit it as no sin, for I will judge that pure to me, which to a dark understanding was impure. . . . It matters little what sayeth Scriptures, saints or Churches, if what is within thee condemn thee not, thou shall not be condemned."[49] Was he thinking when he put it that way of a sentence of Martin Luther's (by way of drawing Luther's conclusion to its extreme): "The observance you perform out of freedom and love is holy but the one you follow because you are obliged to is sacrilegious"? No one can say. What matters most here is the place given to blasphemy—at the juncture between profane and sacred, at the borderlines of pure and impure.

Certain Ranters went much farther in their dogmatic protest—dissolving Christian belief into a kind of rationalistic pantheism in imitation of Robert Norwood, Jacob Bauthumley, or indeed Clarkson himself. And down to George Fox's declaration "that there was no God the Creator, the origin of all things being found in nature."[50] Christopher Hill's pointed highlighting of these conflicts tracks how adopting such a stance within the revolutionary context of the 1640s inevitably led dissenters to openly question the grounds of ideas, institutions, and society in ways sometimes considered dangerously radical. Richard Bolton, in comparing for example the "worldling" (person of society) with the saint, chose not to favorably contrast the enjoyment of the present with heavenly recompense. He instead denounced the worldling as "a wrongful usurper of the riches, honour and preferments of this life; [whereas] the saint, whilst he continues in this world, is a rightful owner and possessor of the earth."[51] And a Londoner who observed the events from 1641 to 1645, Robert Baillie, in December 1643, wrote in his journal of the Brownists, "to the meanest servant they give power to admonish, reprove, rebuke and to separate from the whole church."[52]

In the name of the tight connection among religion, politics, and society, just as significant in England as in the other countries of Europe, these diverse propositions and new assertions, which were held to be blasphemous, oriented the struggle against blasphemy toward the social field. During the Cromwellian commonwealth, the guiding points of reference in this field became shifting and uncertain. Around 1650 the acts that were voted into effect by the Rump Parliament possessed a strong political function, serving to affirm a new power and to eradicate outbreaks of opposition in the army. The multiplicity and uncontrollability of the dissension constituted a growing threat to the very legitimacy and authority of a still fragile state.

With the Restoration and return of the Stuarts, these measures continued to be applied more or less regularly until the time of the first Hanovers. The chief prosecutors, as well as the grounds for making the charge of blasphemy, meanwhile began to show conspicuous signs of a reasserted link between royal power and confession of faith, clearly emphasizing the function that had devolved to prosecution of the crime. In 1676 at the completion of the trial of the yeoman from Surrey, John Taylor, who at the time was perhaps a member of the sect of Sweet Singers of Israel, the stated grounds for Lord Chief Justice Hale's fairly typical ruling stressed this mutual reinforcement of roles:

> Such kind of wicked blasphemous words were not only an offence
> to God and religion, but a crime against laws, State and Govern-
> ment, and therefore punishable . . . for to say, religion is a cheat, is
> to dissolve all those obligations whereby the civil societies are pre-
> served, and . . . Christianity is parcel of the laws of England; and
> therefore to reproach the Christian religion is to speak in subver-
> sion of the law.[53]

But during the final period of the Stuart dynasty's reign, this relationship
among law, blasphemy, and Christianity assumed a far more singular
direction. With the strengthening of the 1698 law, the repressive arsenal
was now used first to persecute avowed anti-Trinitarians. Had not a
young Scottish student, Thomas Aikenhead, been hanged in 1695 for having announced to his friends that the doctrine of the Trinity was non-
sense?[54] Was not William Whiston, Sir Isaac Newton's successor at Cambridge, removed from his chair in mathematics in 1710 for having pronounced out loud serious words of doubt concerning Trinitarian
dogma?[55] Questioning the most basic tenets of dogma, of course, was not
new; earlier it had been given clear expression by partisan and sectarian
agitators during the Puritan Revolution.[56]

At the turn of the seventeenth century, this unitarian movement took
on a political content that could not be contained by the stiffened orthodoxy of the established church and the alarmed bishops, who, in 1711,
presented to Queen Anne their grievances and exhortations to stamp out
the Socinian heresy.[57] Skeptical doubts, indeed overt negations on the
subject of Jesus' double nature, or the simple relegation of Christ to the
pantheon of wise teachers and philosophers (with Socrates and Confu-
cius), amounted to assaulting the monarchical system itself.[58] Despite the
political and philosophical upheavals brought on by the Revolution of
1640, England continued to belong to that Western cultural sphere in
which the relation between king and Christ remained particularly close.
To be sure, many things, many symbols and values, had changed in the
period from 1640 to 1660. But whereas the extremist episode of 1648–1649
desanctified the royal person, Charles's decapitation in February 1649
gave rise at the same time to "an outpouring of devotion to the crown."
The sovereign's martyrdom on the block recalled the fate of the historical Jesus as human being (*Ecce Homo*), and his beheading was likened to
the Crucifixion. "Among all the martyrs who followed Christ in heaven

by bearing his cross, there was no one who so approached Our Savior by his sufferings [as Charles I]," reported a Restoration theologian.[59] Charles's sentence of execution and death enabled the royalist cause to identify even more interchangeably the figures of royalty and sacrificed divinity. This preferential and blessed association between Christ himself and Charles Stuart—and, beyond the latter's individual person, the sacrosanct Sovereign—could not tolerate a doctrinal contestation of the Incarnation and a denial of the Trinitarian mystery. Refusing to consider Jesus as the Son of God was tantamount to breaking this singular bond, to casting the principle of monarchy to the winds, and therewith the entire social organization that followed from it. One can understand, therefore, how the stakes must have appeared to the judges and clerics facing this ideological current and why they carried out their persecutions of the anti-Trinitarians. Notwithstanding Samuel Clark's efforts to elaborate a reasonable Christianity, precisely around the question of the Trinity,[60] the Socinians gave the distinct impression of being antiauthority intellectual protesters undermining the social and political order. In this context of skepticism and reason, not specific to England alone, the established power's struggle against blasphemy took on an original dimension, even as it laid such stress on the force of reciprocal bonds between the monarch and God.

5 | SOUNDING THE CALL: MUNICIPALITIES, THE BOURGEOIS, AND THE SEIGNIORIES

The battle royal against blasphemy was limited neither to circumstantial measures nor to the effort of royal agents. Other institutional bodies or groups, exercising local jurisdiction and whether they were representative or not, functioned as inferior courts acting locally in lieu of the sovereign power to carry out this daily, diffuse campaign.

The Vigilance of Decentralized Authorities and Provincial Communities. If the specific grievances listed by the Third Estate in 1789 make virtually no mention of blasphemy, those that were drawn up as a prelude to the assembly of 1614 (or at least what fragments subsist of their documentary record) appear to echo an insistent preoccupation with the issue. The recorded grievances of the bailiwick of Troyes, which have been studied and edited by Yves Durand, evoke in several places the quite real existence of blasphemy in contexts, however, that are rather discrepant.[1] Many parishioners of the castellanies of L'Isle, Saint-Florentin, or Neuvy-Sautour asked simply that "the statutes heretofore issued against blasphemers be strictly observed."[2] Other communities denounced the proliferation of sinful speech generally associated with the too regular frequenting of the taverns "in consideration of the considerable abuses that are committed there." Still other communities put the blame on the authorities themselves, supposed guarantors of public morality but incapable of acting with exemplary firmness. In one locale, at Pont-sur-Seine, it was the court judges on whom suspicions focused for being too soft, "not punishing crimes as they deserved to be, especially blasphemies that are regularly committed against the honor of God." In another, the clergy were singled out because of the "vile abuses" they committed and "which should be forbidden them: keeping company with women of doubtful character, tavern-going, engaging in dissolute gambling, uttering blasphemies, taking to hunting and fishing and other worldly pleasures that might bring disrepute upon their vocations and conduce to the lessening of the honor and dignity of the Church and to scandal among the people."[3] As if in indirect response, the local clergy asked that its judicial prerogative be restored for all cases of first-offense blasphemous speech.

This scattered miscellany of means for bringing blasphemers to justice, along with occasional public proclamations against them, might obscure the common threads behind evaluations of and preoccupations with these offenders. Except for the provincial clergy's expanding the notion of blasphemy "to those who pronounce words of impiety against the Catholic Church and offend the superiors of said holy body," blasphemy was defined in 1614 by the *cahiers du Tiers*, or records of the Third Estate (relating to those sessions when the Estates General were convened after Louis XIII had attained his majority and called for the continued regency of his mother, Marie de Médicis). The *cahiers* circumscribed it more narrowly as an offense uttered against the honor of God and the saints. They were unanimous in making it into a serious crime similar to "public fights, murders, thefts, and larcenies committed at night."[4] These open declarations of the sin's wickedness, which emerged in so many guises, and these calls for its eradication corresponded, in reality, to a double preoccupation that was rather widespread at the beginning of the seventeenth century. First was the matter of contributing to setting in place the reform of the clergy, whose moral improvement was expected and needed to instruct the flock and to better save Christian souls. Beyond that, the concerns presiding over the crime's reprobation were proof, in God's eyes, of the population's earnest intent to suppress this scourge and to keep away a wrathful divinity bound to take vengeance. After so many periods of civil or European warfare, disorder, famine, and death in this province of Champagne, with God's help, the path to a restored and preserved peace lay in converting souls and renouncing those sins most hurtful to heaven.

These converging grievances, drawn up in the name of the Third Estate of parishes and castellanies and put in terms of a spiritual neces- sity, were probably more reflective of the preoccupations of certain groups, or perhaps certain personalities, within the rural or urban soci- ety of the times who were sensitized to blasphemy's redoubtable reality.[5] Judges in the lower provincial courts, petty lords of estates, and the bour- geois inhabitants of towns and cities all very probably influenced the composition of the *cahiers* in this direction: that of denouncing and put- ting down a rebellious crime in the name of a moral purification that would shelter the community from the divine anger that was at the very source of the misfortune of their times.

This disposition of a significant part of the social body, at once dis- turbed and vindictive, was translated into rules and police statutes enacted in numerous French municipalities between 1570 and the mid- seventeenth century. Recent studies of Coventry and Norwich, in England during the Great Rebellion, show the town councilors' sustained attention to prosecuting blasphemers.[6] In Spanish Flanders, the magistrate of Lille had ordered a series of sentencings "for heresies and blasphemies," between 1585 and 1614, to be publicly proclaimed by heralds (summarized in the table below).[7]

Partaking in the all-important frontal assault on Protestantism (over two-thirds of the cases), the prosecuting magistrates did, however, distin- guish Reformation heresy from use of terms that were abusive and blas- phemous (a fourth of the cases), even when for some individuals slippage from one category to the other cannot be ruled out. Nevertheless, judicial cases against the crime seem to have become conspicuously rarer after 1615, with the local magistrate's rules and enforcement simply taking over the duty of regulation and disapproval. In June 1636 the magistrate singled

TABLE 5 |

		Percent
Uncatholic Behavior	94	40.71
Protestant Leanings	76	32.90
Having Said the Word "Bougre"	27	11.68
Oaths and Blasphemies	32	13.85
Other	2	0.86
TOTAL	231	100

out "carters along with their wives and children [in the habit of] swearing, blaspheming, denying the Good Lord, and uttering vilifying and offensive words at the least provocation, indeed most often in the absence of any subject."[8] After 1650 and until 1667, the city representatives reiterated their reprobation of blasphemous practices in a series of statutes generally condemning those who uttered "serious and full-blown oaths, blasphemies against God our Creator, the blessed Virgin Mary, and all the Heavenly Host, which cause quarreling, arguments and murders."[9] Despite the grand language, these declarations were not necessarily accompanied by massive or dramatic judicial prosecution.

In the case of France, an examination of archival inventories of thirty-five municipalities between the end of the sixteenth and beginning of the eighteenth century would seem to show that only a bit less than half[10] were locally preoccupied with denouncing blasphemous acts or in some manner repressing them. In fact all, or almost all, depended on the responsiveness of the municipal magistracy to the cause and perhaps, above all, on the legal means at the elite's disposal to successfully carry on the struggle. It appears that those towns and cities that possessed seigniorial powers to pass judgments against blasphemers (the so-called right of high justice) were able to establigh their authority in such cases both within the more immediate urban radius and in outlying areas of the surrounding countryside. However, with some exceptions, documentary records indicate what is essentially a *normative* reality, either by the attention they draw to extant royal statutes[11] or through some municipal code forbidding "oaths, blasphemies and dissolute language in public places," following the models of Château-Thierry (1616), Mende (1623), or Sarlat (1712).[12] More rarely, one finds references to sentences handed down by municipal judges, generally limited to highly varying fines.[13] Even the smallest provincial towns did not fail to impose some sort of fine on blaspheming as reparation for the sin. In his study of the diocese of Tarbes during the seventeenth century, Jean-François Favre-Soulet has pointed to the pecuniary penalties adopted by communities such as Ponzac, Trébons, Mignac, Hiis, or Ordizan, aimed at those who "dared vilify and blaspheme the name of God or the Most Holy Virgin or of a single holy saint, man, or woman, in Heaven." They were to pay five sous to the community in 1616, and fifteen in 1651.[14] Frequently the police statutes prescribed subjection to public humiliation beyond payment of fines. That of Vannes, published in 1672, stipulated that "blasphemers of God's holy name shall be placed and positioned in the square of Main Lievie [?] in a pillory with iron collar and harness at the behest of the mayoral syndic and there be so fastened during such time as justice shall be mandated [and] during which time there shall be publicly registered the terms of the sentence carried out."[15] The frequency of this particular method did not rule out other modes of public humiliation such as the hanging cage, in which, at least in the sixteenth century in the fine city of Puy, offenders were locked up.[16]

Such instances of public display as part of the penalty were also to be found in Italy, and the preoccupations they illustrate were not limited to the municipal functions of the *édiles* (town councilors).[17] Certain landed nobles who were invested with the power to maintain and secure the king's justice on their domains made and enforced public codes in the antiblasphemy cause by closely following the laws of the crown. One illustration is a lord in Languedoc, Hautpol, who proclaimed to the inhabitants of Cassignoles a

> prohibition and injunction upon any person of whatever estate and condition that they shall neither swear nor blaspheme in however a manner using neither the Holy Name of God nor of the Holy Virgin Mary nor saints of Heaven on penalty of paying out a fine of sixty sous one denier for the first offense committed, and for the second shall they be made to have their tongue pierced with a hot iron and other punishments at the law's digression.[18]

In cities and towns where it still exerted some influence, the legal sector controlled by landed nobility—the *justice seigneuriale*—continued during the seventeenth century to be engaged in the collective battle waged by the institutions against blasphemy. In Paris the seigniories able to avail themselves of the right of high justice entrusted an official acting for the public treasury to bring charges against blasphemers and a bailiff's or marshal's tribunal to receive complaints, preside over the hearing of cases, and pass judgments. The functioning of these particular legal bodies was increasingly undercut by royal agents and the intervention of the Châtelet of Paris (the most prestigious of the lower courts) and also of the Paris office of the lieutenant general of police. The authority of the seigniories was compromised by this latter office, whose responsibilities, established in 1667, had the effect first of removing from these courts of justice part of their cognizance over such cases. This reorganization paved the way for those provisions in the 1674 edict that made the seignioral courts part of the Châtelet. Several of these courts, however, still managed to partly escape the monarchical authority's seizure of power. The seigniories of Saint-Germain-des-Prés, Temple, and Saint-Martin-des-Champs continued, up until 1790, to prosecute—more or less pugnaciously—sinful sowers of dissension against the divine order.

In 1718, for example, the abbot of Saint-Germain-des-Prés addressed a letter to the monastics and the bailiff in which

> to establish the union, tranquility and peace in those places that are dependent on us and to acquire a worthy reputation for the dwellers within the walls of this abbey, . . . we decree that proceedings shall be undertaken and carried out against all persons who shall swear, blaspheme, say, sing, write or commit things injurious, abusive and contrary to the respect we have shown the Holy Name of God, of the Holy Virgin his Mother, of all the Saints, of ecclesiastic servants of the secular and monastic orders, against our holy mysteries and further against persons officially recognized in high offices and against all other persons in order that such offenders be punished as required by the case, the atrociousness of the insult, the station of the person insulted, [and] the place and time of the insult, in accordance with the rigor of the decrees and regulations.[19]

This competition from Parisian judicial authorities underscores, all the same, coercive and regulatory proceedings within the framework of urban or seignioral powers that, simultaneous with monarchical power, kept up the pressure against blasphemous practices. Most certainly the legal justice system (whose resources and duties were often more limited) took up and ratified in general those provisions found in the statutes of the sovereign power. Yet this convergent movement of the different royal, municipal, and seignioral civil institutions reflects rather well (at least during 1650–1680) an apparently deep-set preoccupation with, as well as legalistic and cultural sensitivity to, a crime that commanded the careful attention of judges.

Opinions of the Judges. The sensitivity of men of law to blasphemous speech and acts, already rather pronounced in the sixteenth century, was heightened by a number of contributing factors. In her study of the Rouergue, Nicole Lemaître notes that this change in attitude regarding blasphemy and the more aggressive prosecution for the crime during the sixteenth century had begun as early as the mid-fifteenth century.[20] It was to coincide with a need for the "purification of bodies and spirits" associated with the social influence of the aforementioned *civilisation des mœurs* (cultivation of manners), which took hold in jurisprudence and the courts of justice after first having captured the nobility. The robust and highly structured directing of culture and social mores, supported by the ideological orientation of the Counter-Reformation, favored, at the beginning of the seventeenth century, a more vigorously pursued prosecution of transgressive sexual and familial behaviors, of excesses in gestures and speech. Both types of offenses were frequently cut from the same cloth, often feeding one another. On August 23, 1543, had not the aldermen of Arras passed sentence on a shoemaker for having both "denied God and beaten his father"?[21] This express, watchful pursuit of language as crime arose in the midst of the circumstance of religious struggles, in which speech designated as "other" and understood to be harmful necessitated, in turn, a series of interlocking responses. Superadded to the arms of dialectic of limited use to Catholic authorities faced with worsening religious controversy were the more reliable institutional parries and thrusts of the law courts. Recourse to the courts seemed all the more inevitable, given that literary production, cultural interactions, and the growing strength of the European vernaculars during the sixteenth century made the task of controlling discourse and words simultaneously more difficult and more necessary. For such words, of course, were the potential bearers of public deviance.

The organization of the legal proceedings themselves can, on occasion, shed light on the preoccupations of the legal officers and agents involved. We are afforded some revealing glimpses here and there—through the questions organized around the accused's "malicious intent," repeat offenses, and consciousness about such acts—when we read the written statements and accounts of the examining magistrates' interrogations and the responses of those examined. One even encounters formulaic outlines and prepared guides for conducting such examinations.

When these guidelines seem to have been followed, whatever the circumstances of a given offense, the relative uniformity of written orders for conducting the official inquiry and querying the accused limited the scope of this part of the proceedings by focusing on the confirmation of the complainant's initial version of events or of the plaintiff's charges. This mechanism, or protocol, also allowed the crime to be better defined—the charge to be formalized, its limits circumscribed—so as to minimize the extent of its significance and the reach of its influence, authorizing the judges' belief that they had its nature well under control.[22]

The magistrates' vigilance should thus be situated in a much broader movement of the criminalization of the individual, otherwise identifiable as that current of thinking, largely generated by the monarchical power, through which social control was organized to bring society as closely as possible in line with the divinely decreed hierarchical order. But the construction of this social organization, which princes and churches hoped they were gestating through their wise and inspired government, was threatened by Europe's social turmoil, radical skepticisms, and criticisms both structural and dogmatic. So many battles, on so many fronts, unleashed forces that the constituted agents and corpuses of the law were ill-equipped to truly contain, refracted as they were into the multiple gradations of justice and number of respective courts to which causes could be submitted—each autonomous in its own domain, if not indeed in rivalry with the others. This was why the royal sovereign power, ultimate source of all justice, would progressively establish mastery over the territory of the courts, imposing on judges an elaborate taxonomy of criminal behavior. The nomenclature of this taxonomy reflected less the actual frequency of the specified types of offense than the necessary gravity imputed to such offenses by the imperatives of divine law.

Assigning the fine divisions of criminality was the work of jurists in service to the king.[23] Jean Papon in his *Recueil d'arrêts notables* (Compendium of sentencings) in 1562, Claude Le Brun de La Rochette in 1609, the Toulousian Bernard de La Roche-Flavin in 1617, and the Artesian Pierre Desmasures in 1638 all gave distinctive shape to the crimes of high treason against God and humanity (that is, the person of the prince, his estate, and his council) that were considered among the most serious threats to civic peace.[24] More momentous even than theft or homicide, high treason against the divinity—at least in the sixteenth and seventeenth centuries, and according to Le Brun de La Rochette's proposed schema—was the preeminent evil, even as it was in turn broken down into several components. Coming before apostasy, heresy, simony, or sorcery, blasphemy stood out as the most abhorrent crime because, by attributing to God what He could not in his very essence *be*, according to the usual terminology (powerless, unjust, malicious, cruel), blasphemers muddied the divine reality and "left it incomprehensible to us."[25] Such willful interpretive error was tantamount to an act of rebellion—a sign of disobedience that attacked the prince by sullying God.

By giving this deviance such prominence, whether or not it factually corresponded to a measurable increase in this kind of crime, did these early modern tribunal judges truly delimit the concept of blasphemy, and clearly define it, the better to punish it? Certain habits of practice recalled above would tend to bear this out. But the judges' use of these delineations was in no way systematic, and we realize quite quickly that different judges produced rather different responses, wavering with the breeze of circumstances and individual authorities. *For there probably existed no expressions that were intrinsically and "naturally" blasphemous.* Only when such speech became the matter of legal proceedings that repressed the abuse in the name of a right of their own creation, could the abuse be called by its proper name. It was at this system's core that judges said exactly what blasphemy was. The introduction and positive identification of blasphemy as one element within the new sociotheological order of criminalization during the sixteenth and seventeenth centuries were borne on the wave of a sweeping change in which the magistrates were mere instruments. Reflecting in the mid-sixteenth century on charging sinful speakers with the crime, Papon "ranked profanation of holy images and relics without hesitation among other blasphemies."[26] He proposed putting "blasphemy through heresy"—which was not to be confused with mere errancy of speech—first among multiple acts likely to provoke considerable social disruption. Slightly a half century later, Le Brun de La Rochette distinguished heresy from blasphemy, both within

the class of treasonous acts against divine majesty. Yet he too labeled blasphemers "those who put or pull down holy images that have been set up
in the churches or the sacred sign of the cross of whatsoever substance it
shall have been represented, [and either] tear, break, or tread on, trample
and crush them underfoot."[27] These distinctions, entailing progressively
harsher punishments and yet varied, were also applied in the way the
crime was divided among different jurisdictional reviews. The charge of
ordinary blasphemy (and who really took much notice of its banality?)
came under the review of a judge presiding in the crime's local venue.[28]
The serving judges were for a long time ecclesiastical and were gradually
replaced by secular, appointed public officials.[29] Heretical blasphemy,
bringing public scandal and the emotions of the populace in its train,
"was within the province of judges of the crown serving in the presidials
[courts of appeals in the ordinary bailiwicks] and the sovereign law
courts."[30]

Thus the ruling of judges, in part dependent on the frames of reference of their cultural setting, on their experience and religious commitment, increasingly issued from the monarchical judicial system. A
greater visible presence of the royal court was called for to confront the
possible blows that threatened it. Faced with an uncertain religious unity
and the many forms of deviance that were born from such doubt, blasphemy—now infamously revalued as one of the highest crimes—took
part in a new ordering of the social body. Authorized in the lofty names
of God and the king's greater glory, the church and the judges found
themselves serving a function that was more often executive with a
diminishing independence. In the course of the seventeenth century in
France, the subordinate position of the lower courts of justice meant
their increasing divestiture from rulings on blasphemy. The applied
model was primarily of the monarch's devising; the church could only
amplify the meaning of content that he imposed. So that a year after the
royal statute in 1666, Archbishop Hardouin de Péréfixe published his
bishop's letter, imploring "all curates of this city, its faubourgs, and dioceses" to support the monarch's action (see excerpt in chapter 4).[31]

From this point on, blasphemy's religious signification also took on
meaning in manifestations of the monarchy's power, from the issuance of
royal acts to their judicial application. The appearance, in 1686, of the
printed compilation *Des déclarations du roy et arrêts de la Cour de Parlement* (On the king's proclamations and judgments of the king's court

of justice) sought to bring attention to the singular eagerness and indus-
triousness with which the magistrates had increased the sentences in
cases appealed by parties having committed the crime, particularly in the
immediate aftermath of the royal proclamations and statutes of 1651,
1666, and 1681. The circulation of this brief and instructive publication,
relating fifteen noteworthily severe findings of the court, drove home the
judges' disciplined zeal and their compliant role in the crown's exercise of
power. They had sought "to halt the course of the excess of impiety and
root out for good an evil so pernicious, to renew the severity of penalties
applied by the royal court's statutes and decisions."[32]

Sentences that ordered mutilation and hanging of blasphemers aimed
to serve as examples. Yet were they, for all that, as systematic as this circumstantial document would have one believe?

On the simple and legitimate question of blasphemers' social identity, answers quarried from the documentary records for the seventeenth and eighteenth centuries vary rather dramatically, both with respect to sources and observers examined. Hence, our attempt to stake out two complementary approaches here. One approach favors normative texts. The other draws its factual evidence from repression's wellsprings, namely, the seignioral and royal law courts and tribunals. With this evidence, we attempt not so much a point-by-point collation as an outline comparing the different initiatives—initiatives that encompass the complexities of blasphemy as a social phenomenon.

 6 | EMBLEMATIC SWEARERS

Reading the pessimistic and expiatory writings of Villecourt, composed at the dawn of the nineteenth century, leaves the impression that, like René Descartes's "common sense," blasphemy was common as dirt—a universal social habit. For it reared its head "in villages, towns, fields and hamlets, on thoroughfares and highroads and city squares, in public and private. It is enough to cause one to conclude that Christians are your worst enemies."[1]

These hasty summations bolstered, of course, the argument of a rhetorician single-mindedly bent on emphasizing the profusion of such wickedness. Yet well before Villecourt, Henri Estienne, in his *Apologie pour Hérodote* (Defense of Herodotus), entitled a chapter "Blasphemies in Our Times," citing a peasant proverb that singled out a noble, a priest, and a carter as typical blasphemers.[2] In short, with one member drawn from each of the three estates French society was symbolically reconstituted, framed within, and tarred with the sin's everyday practice. The opinions of those leaders and officials of the time working within the reform movements seconded Estienne's social generalizing on this rampant behavior. We recall Jakob Andreä's lament in 1568 that "this heinous [sin] rules in all the conditions: among women, the old and young, down to the smallest child barely able to form its words; upon the lips of everyone can it be found whose like hath never been seen in the days of our fathers." A generation later the situation seemed even worse. To repeat the telling of a seventeenth-century professor at the University of Tübingen, J. G. Sigwart,

> Formerly blasphemy was to be heard only among the vilest soldiery, yet today this vice is become so common that it prevails not in a given guild, house, village, city, or country but has practically invaded the entire world. It is no longer only men who use profane oaths but also women, not only the aged but young persons, [so too] the master and the servant, the mistress and maidservant; the little children who know not yet their prayers swear with such skill that they sometimes exceed their elders in this loathsome art.[3]

The emphasis in such accounts on blasphemy's frequency and ubiquity would become a standard stylistic flourish in the vituperations of clerics distressed at their flock's antisocial behavior. Under Louis XIV, the curate of Rumegies in the diocese of Cambrai typified his colleagues' commonly expressed opinion when he wrote that his "parishioners are too fondly attached to worldly goods, they take an excessive delight in things here below, which is why they are to be found mean-spirited and cruel, headstrongly bent on blaspheming."[4] In their turn, clerics who made pastoral visits also observed how commonplace and habitual the phenomenon had become. Answering some questions treating the most often repeated sins among the faithful, in 1734, priests from a neighboring district of the Bordeaux diocese made mention of "practically no public sinners if not for blasphemers."[5]

And yet going beyond these expected and imprecisely allusive observations, many jurists and clergy members of the modern period portrayed, through legislative documents or moral treatises, a social reality more concrete in its details.

Water and Fire. In his commentary on England's criminal code, Blackstone evoked the 1745 bill on swearing and cursing, noting the frequency of such behavior among sailors and soldiers.[6] By calling attention to the habit of foul and abusive language among these two social categories, above all among the common people, the great English jurist did no more than give a nod to a widely held value judgment about the likely haunts of swearers.

The sharpest-eyed and -eared observers (by virtue of their closeness to the maritime world) included Jesuits, from G. Fournier to Y. Valois, who repeatedly laid stress on this trait.[7] In 1632 Jesuit fathers of the Navalis mission who were doing service with the Flemish navy installed at Ostende wrote that "the greater part of the seafaring multitudes had the habit of making just about every word they spoke an oath and a blasphemy."[8] Bylaws in the charters of numerous fraternal guilds of sailors and especially the important official texts handed down by temporal government authority (more so than the all-too-rare archival fragments) would seem to confirm this widespread practice.[9] The documentary evidence for these vocational communities almost always incriminated sailors, including some officers, as the most occupationally prone to use "abusive speech and blasphemies against God's holy name."[10] In 1662 the codfishing boat captains of Le Havre were still harping on this penchant among sailors of lowest rank, "whose coarse humor not being reined in leads them into many blasphemies, excesses, and much sinfulness which it is difficult to disavow.... Captains, pilots, and quartermasters shall be hard-pressed to put a stop to the profanation of God's Holy Name."[11] When taking it upon themselves to staunch such vile verbal hemorrhaging, the Norman officers conspicuously exempted themselves from this impious brotherhood.

The sources, however, did not censure the sailors alone. They also exposed blasphemous ship captains. Fournier had already noted "that one hears these terms at times among the sailing men but more often still from the mouth of a captain or an angry officer who thinks he can inspire more fear by punctuating his commands or remarks with impious expressions."[12] Though in fact shared by maritime personnel of all ranks,[13] might not the inclination to blaspheme have taken deepest roots among the officer corps, who during the course of the eighteenth century, were won over to irreligious outlooks?[14] Pahin de la Blancherie seemed to have come to just this conclusion when he proposed some edifying examples "that ... may serve as instruction to fathers and mothers of households." He chose to recount, for example, the awful agony of a merchant marine captain who had profaned God's name:

Never had this man given any thought to the consoling ideas of a future life, of an eternity. The priest entered a moment after I did, the entire crew was in the room. Upon our seeing him, his despair became rage; from his mouth there issued only blasphemies. With his hands he rent his own skin; the gnashing of his teeth gave the look that he might attempt to kill the priest. They tied the man to the bedposts, which did but make him all the more furious. The ship's sailing men, despite their insensitivity, could not endure this spectacle; they went out showing their fright by their gestures.[15]

The significant official acts on the organization of the royal French merchant marine and naval fleet that were issued in 1674, 1689, and 1765 specifically provided, each under its chapter covering "the regulation of navy ships," for the harsh suppression of blasphemy uttered aboard ship—particularly toward recidivists, who were condemned to either flogging or mutilation of the tongue, depending on the case. These punishments were applied according to the general and sweeping wording of provisions, but they were invoked with an exemplary pointedness.[16] Even more illuminating is the similarity of such regulations among all the great European navies of the seventeenth and eighteenth centuries. Equally severe were the penalties meted out on board the Spanish armada or the Vatican navy. European states of other reformed or traditional confessions, even if they did not treat the problem at quite such great length, at least gave it prominence and devoted much thought to its eradication. Thus the three first articles of the United Provinces' navy— the statutes of 1692, 1702, and 1705—were devoted to the matter and prescribed a flogging at the ship's mainmast. If the British navy's 1730 statute allotted but a single paragraph to this verbal deviance,[17] the Russian navy's 1720 regulation, by contrast, required seven chapters to describe the gamut of possible cases of this crime, as well as the entire array of repressive measures suited to eliminating this offense against divine grandeur.

This ecumenical consistency throughout the European merchant navies up to the mid-eighteenth century probably did much to reinforce the recurrent popular image of swearing "like a sailor," lending weight to the reputation of members of the occupation as somehow being inherently blasphemous. Yet the deeper reasons for such transnational discipline probably owe less to the chronic utterance of sacrilegious words aboard ship than to the dire consequences the practice might entail. I alluded earlier to the fear of a punishment from God that threatened to fall upon the ship, harming crew and cargo. But the emphatic regulations governing the military navy revealed still other important parameters. Within the closed world of the warship, in which social relations were easily set on edge, the slightest altercation or violent gesture might ignite simmering disgruntlement. As the speech of provocation, blasphemous talk was dreaded for its overlap with dissent and also for the symptomatic protest it might let loose. If such an interpretation (to which we shall return) was not entirely characteristic of the *merchant* naval milieu, for fighting vessels, where victory was thought to be wrested through God's help, by contrast, the battle against blasphemy took on a more concrete purpose. "The Supreme Being offering the source of every good work that bestows victory at the direction of His protective hand which ensures success in warfare, we must pray and put our hopes in Him," wrote the Russian legislators in 1720.[18] Blasphemy, in other words, was tantamount to removing divine blessings, to potentially depriving one's prince of victory, and in the end, to committing a treasonous act of great prejudice.

Was not—and for very similar reasons—the blaspheming soldier inducted as yet another exemplary figure into the rogue's gallery of inveterate sinners of this ilk? Already in the German iconography from the early modern period, military activity seems clearly to have been viewed as "fostering spoken sin."[19] Several other examples are known where, for instance, in the Holy Roman Empire, Low Countries, and France, soldiers were prosecuted for this crime. Witness the horseman who, in 1596, had found his riding gear unfastened and shouted before the camp at Ardres, "God be damned and for Christ's sake! Who in God's name is the bastard who undid my saddle?!"[20] Seeing men of arms brought to justice was also the purpose of specific laws. In France from May 1681 to July 1727, several statutes targeting military infractions "forbade soldiers from swearing or blaspheming the Holy Name of God, the Holy Virgin and the Saints under penalty of searing of the tongue by hot iron."[21] The society of soldiers was maintained—like that of sailors—by strict discipline. It probably first experienced blasphemous speech as a sign of disorder, before seeing in it the vector of ill fortune for outcomes of battle. It was only once an army considered itself invested with a particular, generally God-given mission that its necessary exemplarity and religious morale demanded a jihad against blasphemy. Repressing such shortcomings was more than formality among the Roundhead infantry, or Ironsides, of Cromwell, held to be the instrument of God. In 1643, for example, for having repeatedly blasphemed, a noncommissioned officer was condemned to a tongue-piercing, the breaking of his sword above his head, and dismissal from his command.[22]

And yet, denunciations and the threat of punishment did not actually seem to make much of a dent in the classic trooper's image in the typology of blasphemy, so much "does he take pride in profaning, whenever you meet him, the holiness of God's name. Footsoldiers and swordsmen would think themselves unable to pass muster as brave fighters were they not accomplished blasphemers."[23] This expected aside, however, gives access to still other social categories of blasphemers.

Sword and Quill. Part of military life's very substance, impious speech went hand in hand with many forms of combat. François Billacois's masterful investigation of dueling highlighted numerous direct links, also remarked upon by theologians and individual observers, between this face-to-face confrontation and blaspheming.[24] "Blasphemy and oaths being the very sinews of valor," wrote Arnaud Sorbin in 1578, "these hardy warriors who otherwise surpass even good Christians often expire abjuring God."[25] The need for courage in the heat of battle prodded its antagonists to draw from the wellsprings of linguistic prohibition so as to brave dueling's inherent perils. There was no crossing swords without vindictive taunts, verbal bravado, sacrilegious apostrophe. To go a step further: in their observers' eyes, blaspheming and dueling were genuinely analogous. Both, in a sense, defied God, articulated a provocation that might rush as headlong toward a chosen death as toward a refusal of personal salvation. The violence of a bloody end either from under the sword's blows or heavenly justice striking you down foreclosed all preparation for a *righteous* death. Furthermore, from numerous eyewitnessings, we know that the duelist's last moments were often attended by anathematized expressions—a freedom's final cries or sputterings. "Such a one was seen and heard," Sorbin further reported, "having received a mortal wound who for all his *in manus tua*'s (as they say) during life, now cried out, his end of days so imminent, 'God be damned and bloody blast it, I am dead.' "[26]

The stiff-necked sacrifice of one's lifeblood and the perverse devotional utterance of such last words make these moribund gestures into parodic ritualistic acts in reverse.[27] But by refusing to rein in their passions, the duelist and blasphemer consented to become the devil's instruments, to give themselves to him against God. This satanic influence was not confined to these two desperate acts. It did not fail to corrupt the entire nature of those who gave in to such reprehensible activities, such as that knight of Andrieu, executed in 1638, who was not only a duelist but an incendiary, necrophiliac, rapist, and blasphemer.[28] Far more endemically, Pierre de L'Estoile portrayed King Henry IV's entourage as an assemblage of immoral agents, practicing (all at once) "duels, whoring, and whoremongering; gaming and blaspheming are held by them in high esteem; sodomy taketh there such free rein that one hastens to cover one's breeches."[29]

How, moreover, could those violent and querulous nobles of the sixteenth and seventeenth centuries not have counted themselves among impenitent blasphemers? In this regard the kingdom of Spain could boast a good many lofty and colorfully profiled figures, obviously unfit to serve as role models. During the reigns of Charles V and Philip II, they made up a not negligible portion of individuals accused of this crime.[30] And during the period of civil war in England, were not the Cavaliers, allies of Charles I, nicknamed the "Damned" by their enemies?[31] On the other side of the Channel, Estienne had similarly exposed

> those noblemen in the king's [Henry III's] court who now make use of oaths and blasphemies they once held in abhorrence; such that rather than say "he swears like a carter," it now be more suiting to say "he swears like a lord." In truth they affect a graceful vanity as much in swearing oaths as in other things, such that glory is reserved for whoever shall swear the most elegantly, and that elegance must if possible possess novelty.[32]

Did not the practice reach as far as the king Henry IV himself, obliged as he was to substitute a profane *jarnicoton* (a euphemism; loosely, "I reject Coton") for his *jarnidié* ("I reject God," or "God be damned")? (For more on this, see the conclusion.)

Did certain nobles, buoyed by social standing and worldly finesse, reckon they could express their haughty remove from religious belief by speaking "with the freedom of blasphemers?" Behavior that might be lived with inside limited circles took on a far more delicate dimension when it became public. Paraded before the common citizen, the nobility's oaths made a mockery of the exemplary role that every *sanior pars* throughout the kingdom, that is, those most influential members of society in its towns or villages, should fulfill. Thus it was that in June 1663 Sir Charles Sedley, Lord Charles Buckhurst, the future Count of Middlesex, and Sir Thomas Ogle—all of them sufficiently three sheets to the wind, to be sure—indulged in some curious exhibitionism.[33] Stripped naked and exposing himself, in open day, on the balcony of the Cock Tavern by Covent Garden, Sedley took to miming all manner of unimaginable lubricious and sodomitic postures,

> and abusing of scripture and as it were from thence preaching a mountebank sermon from the pulpit, saying that there he had to sell such a powder as should make all the [women] in town run after him, 1,000 people standing underneath to see and hear him, and that being done he took a glass of wine . . . and then drank it off, and then took another and drank the King's health. It seems my Lord and the rest of the Judges did all of them round give him a most high reproof; my Lord Chief Justice saying, that it was for him, and such wicked wretches as he was, that God's anger and judgments hung over us, calling him sirrah many times. It's said they have bound him to his good behaviour (there being no law against him for it) in £5,000.[34]

This last remark by Samuel Pepys, who reported the incident in his diary, cannot fail to astonish. Sedley did indeed blaspheme by greeting the scriptures with derision and serving his scorn up with doggedly and publicly profanatory conduct. Was it not the social rank enjoyed by Sedley and his troublemaking acolytes that encouraged the court's resorting to a mere reprimand, despite the beginnings of a riot spurred by his provocative demonstration?

The nobility's evident familiarity with speaking blasphemously was sometimes embedded in a wider context of blatant irreligion. It's thus not surprising to find members of the aristocracy forging associations with various libertine poets to the point of becoming their official and effective protectors. The royal court, once again a place of great moral leeway for some, became the site of a war against impiety and debauchery for others. But when it comes to the world of the libertines, the image of the blasphemer turns even more radical and complex.

In the main, this movement emerged at the turn of the sixteenth and seventeenth centuries, under the combined influence of several elements. At first the continuation and extension of humanism's lessons (particularly via the Neoplatonic philosophy of the school of Padua), followed by the disruption of Christian unity relativizing people's relation to dogma, favored the libertine movement's development. Along with witchcraft and mysticism, libertinism was perceived as a genuine menace.[35] In France, however, during its brief period of greatest visibility (from 1610 to 1630), the movement took several forms, anatomized a while back by Antoine Adam into philosophical libertinism, atheistic libertinism, and scholarly libertinism.[36] René Pintard, by contrast, preferred a more sociological classification. He made a distinction between libertines belonging to the nobility—with their ostentatious dismissal of religious gestures and beliefs, following the model of Gaston d'Orléans or, even more so, the great Condé family and their entourages—and the lettered libertines—the gowned lawyers, or *gens de robe*, doctored professors, librarian collectors, and members of the "Putean Academy," gathered around the Dupuy brothers or Pierre Gassendi and Gabriel Naudé.[37]

It is understandable that these close and exclusive intellectual coteries, which were nevertheless in more or less frequent communication with each other, should have found themselves the object of accusation by the devout and the controversialists of the day,[38] or that they should have been made an example of before the public as notorious blasphemers—to the degree that some, witness Lucilio Vanini or Théophile de Viau, lost their lives as a result. The densely discursive Jesuit father François Garasse, author of the *Doctrine curieuse des beaux esprits de ce temps, ou prétendus tels* (Curious doctrine of the great minds of our time, or those said to be) which in 1623 had appeared like a "salvific firebrand to inflame indignation" over *Le Parnasse satyrique* (that collection of libertine works which before that time had circulated individually), accused its authors (Théophile, Frédine, and Colletet) of "pronouncing horrible blasphemies against God, committing abominable brutalities that make Paris into a Gomorrah and lead to the printing of *Le Parnasse satyrique*."[39] A bit further in the text, Garasse expressed suspicion that the authors followed their Christmas confessions by "going on the Day of the Innocents to speak a thousand horrible blasphemies in a cabaret as hath taken place on feast days past."[40] After his arrest, Théophile would moreover be accused of having blasphemed and, in accordance with the laws then in force, witnesses of his crime were expressly called from Amiens and Bourgogne.[41] It was in all likelihood a deposition from R. Leblanc, lieutenant of the provostry in the diocese of Uzès, that lent marked force to the meaning of this accusation.

> He [the lieutenant] encountered Théophile in the house of the Count of Candal [the poet's chief patron], which Théophile had made his place of residence, into which the lieutenant had ingratiated himself and did overhear the accused hold forth with several impious statements against God, the Virgin, and the Saints; did observe him to take up a Bible several times in which he did seek out the most holy words which the aforementioned Théophile turned to mockery and impiety, upon whose beholding the said witness told him and had explained to him several times that he was most grievously wrong to hold forth with such malicious remarks and abominable words of which he should repent.... The accused stated further that he believed in neither God nor Heaven nor Hell and that after death all would be dead to him. In conversation with one Master Joseph, an Italian squire, the said Joseph did implore him to speak ill no longer of the Virgin nor the Saints, to which the said Théophile made answer to the aforementioned Joseph that he was a friend to him and his servant and that he should as soon make lame all the Saints in Paradise than do that which should cause him displeasure.[42]

If the words spoken in this account were accurately reported—something Théophile vigorously denied at his third examining, in May 1624—they would exceed the scenario for merely blasphemous speech and indicate an outright profession of atheism.[43]

In their haste to denounce the danger, contemporaries of the libertines applied the accusation of blasphemy to remarkably disparate sorts of speech. Offhanded commentary and joking that was at times coarse or bawdy and made at the expense of episodes or figures from the Bible, mocking remarks relating to Christ's agony,[44] expressions of derision toward certain Christian dogma,[45] admixtures of lewdness and lechery and Epicureanism: all of this fell into the same category. Answering to the needs of religious revanchism, they helped their adversaries draw bold profiles of blasphemers that strongly emphasized the tiniest trace of a critical attitude toward the culture of religiosity.[46]

Poison Tongues and Throwing Dice. After soldiers and nobles, mariners and libertines, the world of gamblers, though it constituted an autonomous group, embraced the near totality of the blasphemous social types. Duelists, hardened soldiers, and sailors were also chronically addicted to games of chance.

The practice of gambling already carried with it a certain number of suspicions. It should ideally have represented a recreation and pastime to cheer and enliven the soul.[47] But by virtue of the circumstances surrounding it and the consequences it produced, gambling turned, almost overnight, into an extreme public hazard.[48] An activity of leisure that bracketed out the workaday world, it often ended up invading time to the point of devouring the player's life. Nothing came to matter more. Family and managing one's affairs were gradually neglected, then forgotten. For God, too, the gambler no longer found time, putting in doubt his own salvation as much as the fate of those close to him. He might also help bring on a kind of social disorientation if his example produced emulators.[49] How to understand the privileged link between gambler and blasphemer through these dire warnings and moral reservations?

In his *Dictionnaire universel*, published in 1690 in Rotterdam, Antoine Furetière proposed a mechanical association between the two dispositions, with a telling and lapidary definition: "*Blasphemer*. He who blasphemes. Gambling is proscribed by the Turks because of players and blasphemers." For several religious moralists of the seventeenth and eighteenth centuries, on whose sermons we have already drawn, the figure of the gambler (often associated with the soldier)[50] was the archetypal impious character.[51] In fact, the consubstantiality between gambling and blaspheming was based on two inclusive kinds of relations. The first harked back again not to the nature of the distraction itself but its chronic gratifications. High stakes, suspense, and even the repetition stirred the passions. An immoderate taste for this activity "hardened hearts, shut them away from justice and beneficence."[52] But even worse, by the blind frenzy it induced, gamblers were led to lose mastery of their passions, allow impatience and rage to get the better of them, lose control of their language, and even take pleasure in transgressing prohibitions. J. Dussaulx in his work *De la passion du jeu* (The passion of gaming) traced a thumbnail sketch of a Flemish doctor

"who, by this strange destiny, gambled away furiously, whereas he still censured gambling, and at least held blasphemies in abhorrence. 'For my part,'
said he one day in the very grip of his worst disgrace, 'I conceiveth not how
a man, however unhappy he be, shall have forgotten himself to such a
point.' ''Tis that you know not,' another gambler shot back, 'how much it
eases the pain.' "[53] The fellow player's remark, itself an outlet for his tense
anticipation fixated utterly on the rush of pleasure from winning, could
only be drawn from a range of experience that was damned, repressed, and
inhibited, and that welled up under the pressure of a personal and
ungovernable situation.

The second correlation brings out the essential role of luck. Certain
theologians even considered the apportioning of fate "the extraordinary
means by which God makes known His will."[54] It thus constituted a sign
of revelation, obliging God himself and making the gambler an actor
who petitioned heaven to reveal its intentions. Several eighteenth-century authors, however, refuted this interpretation, withholding from
gambling and the gambler this somewhat provocative and implausible
role. "How could Providence," asked Jean La Placette, "so lower itself as to
direct a game of dice between two footmen in the same way it directs the
fate of nations and victory in battles? Nothing in scripture, neither formal
promise nor commandment, instructs us about the presumed fact that
God makes use of fate as a means for making known His will."[55] Jean Barbeyrac added, "Doth it not seem unworthy of this sovereign Being to lend
an immediate assistance to so many things of such meager consequence
as prove to be most of what is decided by fortune among men?"[56]

But the reasoning of those of high morals and reflection, the jurists
and theologians of the Enlightenment period, was not that of the
denizens of the gaming house. Superstitious by nature, gamblers could
not keep from believing that God oversaw their good or bad fortune.
When luck held, the winner would probably forget to praise Providence.[57] The loser, on the contrary (and every gambler is also a potential
loser), would readily take God himself to task and find ways to pay him
back for it. "Not content to tear up the playing cards and toss the dice into
the fire, not content to lament his misfortune or accuse others of cunning
sleight of hand and deceit, he lays blame on God for his misfortune; and
unable to do Him the harm his rage would inflict upon Him as if in
revenge, he defiles His divinity by sacrificing it to his abominable passion."[58] Blasphemous remarks, as a translation of the publicly aired

resentment and spite felt by the man who thought God had betrayed him, constituted therefore a genuine riposte. Far from submitting to a fate he believed to be directed by heaven, the gambler, who was "quite detestable for having resentment against God, seeks to make this obvious and, unable to bring this about through actions, takes the only remaining resort, which is to satisfy himself with vile words. Whence come the horrors he utters on these occasions."[59]

At the heart of the gambler's blasphemy lay the mark of fate played false, of future destiny sealed, the feeling of abandonment by God on which failure had left its signature. And as far as the other figures of impiety were concerned, this sin's nature related directly only to God, ignoring the Virgin and saints who receded from range or remained powerless in the presence of an exclusive Providential will.[60]

Duelist and gambler, soldier and libertine, sailor and noble: here were so many social categories singled out, by speeches and homilies, to edify the more or less responsive throngs and put them on their guard. But upon reconsidering this practical social nomenclature, formed around a shared sin, might there have been some other underlying behavioral consistency beneath the similar appearances and accusations?

A Blaspheming Working World? I do not wish to force the issue by driving out of hiding from beneath this variegated typological underbrush some spurious unity of customs. One can, however, cast further light on a certain number of common characteristics of these groups that, between themselves, already sometimes shared the same members.

A good many of these individuals belonged to a world that partially escaped the institutional or religious framework of modern Europe. The blasphemer faced a Tridentine organizational structure, surrounding the parish and its clergy, as well as a newly assertive state that used its agents to attempt to control the behavior of its subjects. Yet the blasphemer appears to be someone who could elude these structures. Did he, to some degree, not owe this situation to the dynamism of a working world on the move, exemplified most strikingly by sailors and soldiers? And was it sheer coincidence that common lore credited the carter as an exceptionally prolix utterer of blasphemous oaths?

The chief magistrate of Lille was not alone in asserting, on June 10, 1636, that "carters along with their wives and children swear, blaspheme, renounce the good Lord and pronounce all manner of foul and hurtful language on the least occasion, indeed most often without any object."[61] Also belonging to a profession involving travel and transportation, river-boat sailors were at times denounced for being on too familiar terms with these verbal practices. "The occupation of almost all inhabitants in these parts," wrote the curate of Coulanges-sur-Yonne, "is to practice their trade on the water and to work with the floating cargos that must be towed to Paris. It is well enough known that men of this occupation are, as it were, prostituted to blasphemies and oaths. It will be necessary to learn for the other stops along their route of travel in what measure they are given to these kinds of execration."[62] The opinion was formulated in 1682 and can be set beside the attestations of helplessness made by priests in coastal parishes when it came to communities of seafaring personnel.[63] Thus the image of the blasphemer reflected that of Christians unconfined to one locale who, by virtue of occupational practice, more or less avoided the control of religious authorities and, in consequence, *social* control (so interconnected were the two).

This sort of demonstration of independence, of consciously or uncon-sciously rejecting the norm, made for the stock-in-trade common to the social landscape where blasphemies were uttered. Even those characters who took license with language yet were traditionally less emblematic of this profile can be recognized on the horizon of this social landscape. Despite the imposition of the model of the "good priest," standing apart from the faithful by his exemplary life and manners, some ecclesiastics figured in the portrait gallery of rogue blasphemers. Parishioners, having themselves taken the taboos to heart, denounced their own curates. Accustomed to "swearing with ease using the name of God," three Auvergnat priests named Amable Mathieu, Antoine Charbonnel, and Charles Chabrun found themselves prosecuted in 1666 before the Grands Jours, or "Days of Glory," sessions, for having acted out the blasphemous persona to the extremity of caricaturish contradiction.[64]

Socially disordered when compared to the new models of civility, the blasphemer's world, observed from outside, was also the world of risk-taking. When we have related audacious speech to the different social positions considered so far, this audacity emerges as a possible common denominator. To risk one's life making war, writing scandalous words, laboring, or wagering one's money or property—all these amounted to risking one's very salvation, staking one's life on the secret impotence of heavenly punishment, placing one's bets on the gratifications of violent imprecation against the inoffensive silence of God. Behind the exemplary figures of the blasphemers persisted a defiance, a picking up of the gauntlet sometimes thrust at them when battling the elements or the enemy, sometimes gratuitous and even useless to all appearances as in dueling, betting, or creating literature. Forming a whole with attitudes of uncouthness, bravura, freedom but also fear, this defiance through the rough edge of one's tongue was scripted by a structure of representations, by the act of asserting individual and collective identity.

In effect, blasphemy participated here in a system of *recognition*; maintained in large part by notoriety from without, it constituted a mark of belonging. The habit of blaspheming publicly became one of the badges of identity for a part of the court nobility in France or Spain, at least up until the first decades of the seventeenth century. It continued to define the milieus of seafarers and of gamblers, who seemingly would have no way of carrying out their professional or ludic functions without irreverent swearing. Theirs was a world of drives, provocations, and threats but also a world of discursive verbal habits that, taken together, made up the vocational "society of blasphemy" that the edifying commentaries and censures by institutions exposed to all the world.

In the end, this confraternity of blasphemy was a society composed entirely of men. Was this because the incriminated occupations were rarely filled by women or because women—whatever their status or profession—did not blaspheme? Some timely research on the matter seems to indicate that there indeed existed sexually distinguishable uses of forbidden language. In his study of southern Germanic populations in the sixteenth century, E. Labouvie has noted that in contrast to blasphemy in itself it is curses [*malédictions*] that were uttered overwhelmingly by women (71 percent).[65] Châtellier, relying on the testimony of the missionary Catalayud, cites for the region of Galicia the case of women uttering maledictions that shocked the Jesuit. One of these women had even insisted to him that "heaven mattered little to her if she did not find there her daughter who had recently died, and that she preferred going to hell if that was where she could find her."[66] To be sure, the borderline between blasphemy and malediction was a tenuous one, fluctuating probably as a function of the hearer's state of mind. Nonetheless a few quantitative data seem to lend support to this sexual dimorphism thesis. Women comprised a mere 8 percent of those charged by the Toledo Inquisition's tribunal in the sixteenth century.[67] Among those found guilty examined by Elisabeth Belmas, who sifted through forty-one arrest orders issued by French parlements in the seventeenth century, only one was a woman.[68] These historical findings zoom in on the problem with meticulous exactitude. They connect blasphemy to the greater verbal violence, to a more swaggering, boastful bravura, to the "masculine" share of the language, and they would therefore tend to second the teachings of the century's literary and theological production. They do, however, derive from sources other than the ones we have been consulting in this chapter, namely judicial archives. These sources in their turn make it possible to lay out some of the precise social contours of groups of offenders charged with the crime of blasphemy and to compare them with those that have been described for us so far.

7 | THE OTHER REALITY

The documentary archive of repressive measures that warrant another social angle on this offense is, of course, finite.[1] Those who swore oaths against God slipped through the tribunals' nets, probably in high numbers, for a variety of reasons, some of them having to do with how the judicial system functioned under the ancien régime.[2] Their identity was not, moreover, always given even in records of cases prosecuted; one comes across some odd and capricious ways of designating their profession. This necessitates, where possible, a careful comparison between this world of verbal delinquency and that of its surrounding rural or urban social setting.[3] Scrutinizing this (often well-buried) archival data is the only effective means of engaging the two factual constructs open to examination: first, the literary, theological, and political interpretations, which are primarily explanatory, and second, the procedural documentation, which is above all descriptive.

Collectivities and Individuals. If one excludes the more amorphous associations of libertines, there was, strictly speaking, no one group whose members were bound together by an organized practice of and taste for blaspheming. In England, however, owing to criteria of judgment fixed by the established powers, certain sects that were founded during the 1654–1660 Interregnum showcased or domesticated blasphemous speech as an element of prestige and the performance of other actions. The Ranters, though never having constituted an organized movement or (like the Levelers) issued programmatic statements, were most surely composed of individuals whose ideologies harmonized: cottagers, artisans from the urban centers of the Midlands, West Riding, or Lancashire, soldiers in Cromwell's New Model Army such as Joseph Salmon, Lawrence Clarkson, or Jacob Bauthumley.[4] Between the philosophical and theological investigations of the one and the licentious practices of the other, there was enough cohesiveness to make these groups look—at least in the eyes of their contemporaries, from 1645 to 1650—like a group that enlisted blasphemous speech as a powerful means of political and religious contestation. Such speech was also allotted a prominent place in their libations.[5]

Most often, however, collective blaspheming was limited to particular circumstances. In one instance, a family or other association would, for highly variable motives, behave aggressively as a group against an individual; in another, a quarrel after drinking would spread into a feast of invectives or brawl; somewhere else rampant swearing might break out at the dictates of chance. Denis Léger, having been locked up in the Conciergerie of Paris in August 1715, found imprisoned there some men against whom he had brought suit a few months earlier. Recognizing him,

> they shouted a great many insults against the petitioner and blasphemed even the holy name of God concerning a lawsuit he had instigated against them. They told him that he would not leave the said prison without a rope 'round his neck, that they wished to take justice into their own hands against him. . . . This evening at seven o'clock, finding themselves in the prison courtyard, the accused set about mistreating the plaintiff and battering him with blows, holding their fists beneath his chin, and pronouncing the same insults and blasphemies.[6]

Generally, it was on the occasion of these group manifestations that women might enter the scene. Having accompanied their spouses, brothers, or lovers with demonstrative gestures and vocal support during a row or a physical assault, they would then find themselves among the accused. In her valuable study of blasphemy in mid-seventeenth-century Paris, Stéphanie Debaret was able to count forty-four cases (out of 230) in which charges were brought against individual women (numbering twelve) and especially women in conjunction with other accused persons (numbering thirty-two).[7] The majority of these women stated they were married or widowed, and in most cases they belonged to an artisan milieu. The small number of female offenders, most as accomplices or accessories, seems to be the case for other working milieus and periods, reinforcing the conviction that blasphemy was men's business.[8] It remains, however, to determine who these men really were.

A series of surveys of the archives of the seignorial courts from the Parisian region between 1650 and 1750 suggests an initial answer to this question (see table).

It is not very easy to draw general conclusions from such precious but partial data. The quantitative basis remains narrow and its geography limited. Nor can simultaneously highlighting the results for the urban and rural settings bestow any absolute priority on comparative (as opposed to other types of) analysis. Analysis can moreover be particularly delicate due to an imprecision in the descriptive vocabulary used.[9] It is more a matter of juxtaposing these indices with the social organization of Paris and its surrounding countryside. Thus the notable presence of transportation workers at Bourg-la-Reine, artisans and launderers at Boulogne, and winegrowers at Fresnes points to the dominant economic activity of each of these areas: in the one case, to serve as a relay or transition point on the way to the south of the kingdom; in the second, linen manufacture and whitening along the Seine; for the third, cultivation of vineyards on the slopes of the capital city's faubourgs. However, bearing in mind blasphemers' recorded occupational activity in the bailiwick of Saint-Denis, it seems that the Lendit fairs that were periodically held there were not a favorable circumstance, unless one considers that the high percentage of artisans charged with the crime corresponded only to individuals who gravitated to this world of commercial exchange.

Allowing for the pitfalls of shifting taxonomy, a few general observations still command attention. Whether in town or country, the blasphemer was to be found among all walks of social life: the armed services and handicrafts, the wage-earning class and the bourgeoisie, reflecting, more or less conspicuously, the social composition of the given spaces. Yet on closer consideration, one notices that every milieu does not always furnish its proportional share of those prosecuted. Among those charged, it was pri-

TABLE 6 | Milieus of Blasphemy in Paris and Its Environs During the Seventeenth and Eighteenth Centuries, According to Records of Complaints Lodged, Archives Nationales (National Archives), Z2

| | CITY OF PARIS | | | PARISIAN COUNTRYSIDE | |
	1656–71 (by %, based on 149 total)	1701–37 (by %, based on 50 total)		4 Villages,[*] 1660–1710 (by number)	Bailiwick of Saint-Denis, 1655–1735 (by number)
Bourgeoisie of the City					
Officers	11.4	8	Merchants	3	3
Merchants		32			
Trade Masters and Shopkeepers	43	14	Winegrowers	4	
			Garden Workers	3	
			Laborers		3
Street Vendors	14.1	18	Day Laborers	1	
Wage Workers	13.4	16	Artisans	10	12
Domestics	11.4	2	Soldiers	4	3
Soldiers	6.1		Others	5	
Vagabonds	0.7		Vagabonds		3
Unknown		10	Unknown		3
TOTAL	100	100	TOTAL	30	27

SOURCES: H. Audard, "Le blasphème au village: Les pratiques blasphématoires dans les campagnes parisiennes (1660–1710)" (master's thesis, University of Paris I, 1995); V. Bezault, "Le blasphème au XVIIᵉ siècle dans le bailliage de Saint-Denis" (master's thesis, University of Paris X, 1996); S. Debaret, "Le blasphème parisien au XVIIᵉ siècle (1610–1671)" (master's thesis, University of Paris I, 1994); and N. Lourmière, "Le blasphème à Paris dans la première moitié du XVIIIᵉ siècle" (master's thesis, University of Paris I, 1994).

[*]Boulogne, Bourg-la-Reine, Châtenay, and Fresnes

marily the wide social world of the bourgeoisie, both the middle and lower, that was pertinently involved. Those working in the crafts and trades, along with owners of workshops, booths, covered stalls, and small businesses, formed the bulwark of blasphemers in Paris and its environs. In contrast, the very extremes of the social ladder seem far less implicated: few nobles and officers, and few journeymen, day laborers, or vagabonds. Only soldiers, mainly during the seventeenth century, held a more significant place than their actual importance seemed to warrant, thus ratifying one social constant of blasphemous speech.

The upper classes' underrepresentation might have come about from several factors. Perhaps it was due to greater vocal self-regulation among the service-minded ranks of administration and law from which the most active members of the antiblasphemy associations were recruited. Or a dearth of complaints lodged against an impious nobility, which perhaps only employed the reprobate expressions by preference within its own circles as its direct verbal contact with commoners might have been limited. The modest representation of the humblest popular segment of society (wage workers, journeymen, and vagabonds) might be explained, at least for the transient population, by the application of more expeditious judicial measures. The large-scale confinement of the poor to the cities during the second half of the seventeenth century made those who lived on the margins disappear for a time from the public scene. If blasphemous beggars are not to be found in the archives of the seignioral or royal tribunals, it is because they already perhaps were finding themselves shut away in communal rooms of internment houses, which were already filled with blasphemers and all those who committed acts of public profanation.[10] And these sources still mask the presence of another group among the blasphemers: children. Denounced by religious moralists, the precocity of this sin was repeatedly pointed to by Parisian authorities, as witnessed by an ordinance of the ecclesiastic seignioral bailiwick of Saint Jean de Latran passed in 1709:

> On the list of charges that have been submitted to us by the fiscal prosecutor of this benefice there have been made several complaints concerning the disorders committed by children within the walls of the benefice, to the effect that they gather together in groups in courtyards and cloisters firing pistol shots, throwing stones with which they have broken church windows, insulting passersby and even abjuring the Holy Name of God. Addressing such misdoings, we have issued verbal warnings several times to the fathers and mothers that they need keep them within the bounds of their duty.[11]

Finally, the parallel chronology for Paris shows no dramatic changes in the general patterns of the perpetrators' social distribution. In the eighteenth century, the middle bourgeoisie always contributed roughly half of those accused; this proportion allows for a certain social flux inherent in the classification, perhaps linked to specific choices involved in naming vocational affiliation. The share taken up by the artisan class, with a slight progressive increase in representation, always involves less than 20 percent of the full complement of blasphemers, whereas a fall in the percentage of domestics (accounting for an increase of unspecified occupations?) is not so easily explained.

Seemingly, blasphemy continued to be one of the behaviors to show up across the entire range of social identities.[12] It was, however, in the Parisian context as in the others, predominantly an offense committed by men, mostly in their twenties and thirties. The indications relating to age concern a little more than one-fifth of the recorded Parisian legal cases in the seventeenth century and show that nine-tenths of blasphemers were younger than forty.[13]

Recurring scenarios seem to reconfirm the statistical frequency of juvenile offenders. They follow the typical example of three young boys of Aubervilliers, "raising a tremendous din with much insolence one evening in February 1670." The clamor was so loud that "the Most Reverend Father Denemond, priest of the Oratorians in the said village of Aubervilliers, hearing the abovementioned hullabaloo and uproar, is said to have entered their house and severely reprimanded them on the matter of their noisy discord and blasphemies with the name of God, and told them they must be punished."[14] Might taking the Lord's name in vain have been one of the sins of youth, a badge of distinction among young men of promising marriageability and others, a badge that was preserved and handed down in their special youth associations known as abbeys or specific communities? Moreover, it is among the youngest offenders charged that one notes the greatest recidivism. As to those cases detailing the events leading up to blasphemous utterances, the social status of these offenders, too, was of a lowlier sort. Among others, the case of Antoine Lefebvre, a twenty-year-old day laborer of the village of Châtenay, is telling. "Accustomed as he is to swearing and blaspheming, to

TABLE 6.5 |

less than twenty years old:	6.1 percent
from twenty to twenty-nine years old:	49.0 percent
from thirty to thirty-nine years old:	34.7 percent
above forty years old:	10.2 percent

giving thrashings and blows in scuffles, and being someone against whom several writs have been taken out for his arrest, [Lefebvre] is said to have lost his temper against J. Husson, counselor in the parlement and landowner in Chastenay, uttering execrable oaths; to have renounced, sworn with, and blasphemed against the Holy Name of God, and to have foulmouthedly abused [Husson] with atrocious insults."[15] In the Paris of the 1660s, one primarily finds this type of character among the most popular categories: the soldier, the picklock or housebreaker, the woodsplitter, the gardener, and some—such as Simon Erard, who was at first a boy pork butcher then a soldier—who passed from one occupation to another.[16]

Blasphemy and Its Settings. Where was blasphemous speech uttered? Answers to this elementary question cannot be determined from copious quantitative references, but the data shown in the table below evince a real uniformity across differing contexts, especially when we read the results for both Paris and its surrounding villages in the seventeenth century.

Blasphemy's status as a public crime is manifested by the spaces of human transactions and traffic that dominate the list of the crime's scenes: road, square, street, cabaret, and workshop. Each of these, of

TABLE 7 | The Sites of Blasphemy

	Paris, 1656–71 (by %, based on 128 total)		Parisian Countryside, 1660–1710 (by %, based on 39 total)
In one's home	14.1	} 24.2	20.5
In an apartment	10.1		
On the street, on the highway	51.6		48.7
At the cabaret	14.8		23.1
Elsewhere (market, store, workplace, the church's exit)	9.4		7.7
TOTAL	100		100

Derived from: Audard, "Le blasphème au village," p. 49; and Debaret, "Le blasphème parisien," p. 63.

course, did not play the exact same role in the life of the community or individual or have the same importance. But their pronounced presence in the city or village clearly identify blasphemous speech at the end of the seventeenth century as a product of circumstances, of happenstance more or less fortuitous or significant. If impious words spoken in anger on a country road resulted from some unsavory chance encounter where tempers boiled, if those spoken in the urban street (the most common location) were due to some quarrel that turned vicious, blasphemy that was vocalized within the very precincts of the seignorial tribunal took on a completely different dimension because it was the system of justice itself that was being openly scorned. An example had taken place at Boulogne with "insolent remarks proffered within hearing of the court, and of our presence, by Barnabé Moreau who spoke an oath using the holy name of God."[17]

The significant role of prosecutions for blasphemy spoken in the home, however, reveals an erosion of the strictly "private" when it came to this kind of case. At the very core of the house, emitting and carrying from the room that served as living quarters, the blasphemer's blare, the violence of the blasphemer's phrasing and often gestures, made short order of the presumed bounds that kept forbidden words outside the domestic sphere of intimacy, however much one might have wished to preserve such bounds. Thin walls, the promiscuity of utterances overheard on the landing or between floors, doors left ajar—all these could not hold back the sounds or protect their speakers. Neighbors drawn to the noise of disturbing words, something that was easily listened to, contributed in their turn to unleashing blasphemy into a communal domain. Even a more materially delimited domestic space made little difference here, as the workshop or small shop extended out into or over the street, while the blasphemous din occasioned by some young men of the village troubling young girls, as it reverberated off the wall of the house, easily carried the forbidden words to other places.

In this inventory of the topography of unlawful behavior, the cabaret held a singular place. It remained a highly specific public space, suited to favoring and maintaining a steady flow of sacrilegious speech, perhaps even more so in village settings where it continued to be the only genuine, permanent sphere of sociability. In the countryside outlying Neuchâtel during the eighteenth century, the tavern seems even to have been the site where blasphemy was the most commonly heard.[18] In conjunction with this venue should, of course, be added the weekly cyclical rhythm of oath-swearing criminality, whereby Sunday, at least in the rural provinces, remained the (profanable) holy day in all senses of the word as it was divided between time for church and time for leisure.[19] The village cabaret, so often central to daily life, significantly helped solidify this separation between worship and libation. A place to drink and eat, to bond and quarrel, to undergo apprenticeships of all kinds, it remained distinct from all other theaters of social life. Socially broader than the space of occupational life, its clientele in closer contact than they were in the street or marketplace, more impersonal than the home, it became (or at least in the French agricultural areas) a place increasingly monopolized by men, with restricted social and geographical heterogeneity, where associations were kept up, made, and unmade, where the space of being among one's own kind was defended ferociously.[20] In the eighteenth century a Parisian appearing in a village cabaret outside the city, or a bourgeois making an entry in a tavern identified as plebeian, was at times at the root of verbal scuffles and brawls.[21]

Indispensable in its many functions, the tavern maintained a microcosm that thrived with more or less independence at the bosom of every community despite the increasingly futile efforts by the local, civil, and religious authorities to ensure control over it.[22] By the eighteenth century, to some degree, there were visible signs everywhere of overt competition between these two obviously antinomic cultural spaces: the cabaret and the church. From this time on, the cabaret saw its role consolidated as an impious place, a role that had fallen to it a good while before. A 1565 statute issued by the duke of Lorraine had already prohibited the frequenting of taverns on the Lord's day of rest "to remove all occasion for blaspheming."[23] Later, and more distantly, in 1676 the Supreme Council of New France [le Conseil supérieur de la Nouvelle France] required that "all tavern keepers post in each of the rooms in which they served food and drink the bill of regulations regarding the customs and punishment for speaking oaths, blasphemies, and causing other disorders." And more concretely, called before the court of justice of Honfleur, on December 20, 1683, were André Mantor and his older son René, Pierre Gambier, François Gosselin, and the tavern keeper Jacques Lengin, known as Bellot, "for having taken drink during Vespers, Sunday last, and uttered several blasphemies. . . . Guillaume Andrieu, counsel before the assembly, states that he beheld on leaving Vespers the aforenamed persons at the doorstep of the said Lengin quarreling and blaspheming, for which act we have sentenced each of them to pay a fine of twenty sols."[24]

To wage this combat the church mobilized the theologians, who from their desks and studies deplored the cabarets and taverns "where one encounters so much blaspheming the name of God," and the parish priests who impotently offered ever more serious denunciations.[25] Among others the curate of Audrix in the diocese of Périgueux, in 1758, vilified the excesses to be seen during the feast day of the patron saint of Saint-Valéry, when there were "several cabarets filled with people into the night: [where] drunkenness, swearing, blasphemies, speeches, obscene singing, arguments, and fights are what follows from this supposed holy celebration and where plotters can gather and the most scandalous demonstrations take place."[26] The urban and rural bourgeoisie did not lag far behind.[27] In several of the bills of grievances drawn up at the convocation of the Estates General of 1614, the drafters called for a reaffirmation of "the statute of Saint Louis so that there may be removed a great many blasphemies and murders that proceed from the frequenting of taverns, which are a great evil for the French people."[28] This sample of the deliberations indicates the tone for a whole group of official pronouncements that, while originating from different horizons, were united in identifying the cabaret as the blasphemous space par excellence (even if the legal documents, as reflections of plaints at law, transcribed it with less taxonomic specificity).

Its durable reputation, fed voraciously by larger-than-life gallants, portrayed cabaret life as disposed to merrily wanton sallies of profanity—words of mockery and contestation. But the reputation's force was also perennially sustained by the location's chief purpose of serving drink, leading to outpourings of all kinds, often to a blaspheming diarrhea of the mouth, sometimes lasting for hours. A tavern keeper in the village of Ménilmontant lodged a complaint on May 1, 1686, against three men who "are said to have passed a good while at his establishment swearing and blaspheming the holy name of God, then to have left the winehouse without paying for anything, though they had spent more than three livres fifteen sols."[29] A few of the plaints directed at "regulars" afford a closer glimpse of the wine-sodden tipplers' talk. Thus the local authorities of Pontarlier, in 1771, described "the aforementioned Marelier, drunk with wine in the heated room in the house of the Rousselot cabaret, where several persons were present, convicted of having said while arguing about the Christian religion that God was not just, that Jesus Christ never rose from the dead, that the guards at his tomb had been made to pass out from drink while his body was carried away and buried elsewhere." Such remarks went perhaps well beyond simple drunken rantings to betray the true irreligious sentiments of the accused (who was harshly punished for them).[30] It was also innkeeper's wine that, in 1678, turned two butchers and a silk shearer from the province of Toledo into sacrilegious blasphemers. Apparently drunk upon leaving the tavern, they got into a private chapel and in celebrating mass after their own fashion turned the Eucharist to ridicule.[31] It is clear that when consumed at the tavern or at home, alcohol generally helped bring to the surface repressed opinions and rancor toward imposed modes of thought and belief. On Good Friday in 1717, the judicial authorities of Trois-Rivières in New France arrested "the said Durivage, resident of the seigniory of Nicolet, who had become intoxicated and is said to have sworn and blasphemed the holy name of God in the public square ... pronouncing the words 'sacredieu,' 'mortdieu,' 'je renie Dieu,' 'ventredieu,' saying that he renounced Lent and baptism and would not for the rest of his days go to confession, and uttering the oaths 'sacré chien' and 'sacré bougre.' "[32] This is a fine example of mingling cursing with blaspheming, of the usual imprecations with antisacramental oath-swearing. It suggests, more than it explicitly states, the different rankings and bases for reading and reacting to such words. But because of the circumstantial context of the moment of their utterance, it made a case that verbalization of such disowning of Christian obligations and thankfulness could be construed as blasphemy and arraigned by the law. The connection between inebriation and blasphemous practices, finally, was also often invoked when pastoral visits were made. And those parishes reputed to be populated by drunkards—for example, the Xanthis, Boulonnaise, and Bordelaise districts—were also taken to be the ones harboring swearers and blasphemers.[33]

A place of celebration and amusement, the cabaret inevitably hosted gamblers. Card games and dice notably contribute to the chronicle of blasphemy in France. There are many short, edifying narratives that portray future offenders playing cards, seated at table in a tavern, "following their routine custom and by permission of the host who is worth no more than they."[34] But along with these expected images, archives of courts of justice emphasize this frequent association between gaming and forbidden words. How many accused gamblers were there who were brought before the law for having said, with each toss of the dice, "I renounce God,"[35] or for having accompanied those tosses with even more explicit reflections? Consider the words of an *alguacil*, or constable, in the province of Toledo, Pedro Cervantès, who remarked between two gambling bouts, "I do not believe in God if I win; though he even will it, it's the devil I shall have to thank for it."[36]

Such an amalgamation of word, game, and drink was part and parcel of the social relations proper to the cabaret, where everyone could watch one another, size each other up openly or on the sly, play their role with more or less aplomb. Within this framing of codes of sociability, it was understood that the apparent absence of provocation might disappear in a flash and give way to verbal and physical aggressiveness, sparked by the influence of drunkenness or a bad hand at cards.[37] From that moment the pendulum swung away from civility, and blasphemy took part in the ritual of confrontation. Returning from Meudon, in June 1661, four carpenters, most likely from Paris, entered a Vaugirard tavern, modeled on Notre Dame,

> to partake of just a thimbleful of wine. There they encountered in said cabaret Jacques Brossin, head mason, and two other men unfamiliar to them, one of whom stated that he was brother-in-law to the said Brossin through their wives. These [unfamiliars] first made as if to accost the petitioner and those in his company, proceeded to make several insolent remarks and even to break several drinking glasses, throwing them against the walls; and they did seek to make the petitioner and those in his company pay, upon which when the latter refused to do so the aforementioned Brossin did proceed to swear and abjure the Holy Name of God, insisting that they should pay the costs, and Brossin and the others did forthwith fall upon them administering a good many kicks and blows with fists, from which the petitioner was very much wounded, and did cause all of them to bleed.[38]

In their turn, streets and highways could serve as the cabaret's natural extension, a site where customers, intoxicated with wine, sometimes started rows.[39] Frequently, however, violence did not need to be spurred by such circumstances for it to break out with blasphemous words to follow. The numerous studies devoted to the collective behaviors of the ancien régime all draw attention to the essential place of violence in social relations. In a profoundly and visibly unequal society, the risks of contention were quite real and strong—between neighbor and neighbor, owners and renters, masters and journeymen, shop owners and clients, creditors and debtors, natives and outsiders, men and women, young and old. Clashes were inevitable, too, as part of a fragile and often threatened daily life in which the will for and necessity of holding on to one's station, of preserving one's values so as not to fall or lose one's honor, remained essential. A veritable ritual of dos and don'ts led up, or kept one from resorting all too readily, to violence. As a historical researcher of Aquitanian society in the seventeenth century, Gregory Hanlon was able to bring out the main steps in a progression of behavioral interactions associated with imminent violence. Their proper negotiation was to be disregarded only at one's peril and if one wanted to run the risk that they would turn into a scene.[40] Public confrontation, exchange of words, and the intervention of seconds or witnesses were the three obligatory steps to the rites of aggression. Uttering blasphemies was often written into this unfolding face-off at each of its stages. When in 1675 Jacques Pinson confronted Etienne Lecompte in a Boulogne street by telling him, " 'I should drown you both, you *and* your wife, you good-for-nothing thief! You've never amounted to anything, I should see to it you're hanged, you damned old wizard!' " he followed his remarks with "oaths and blasphemies and other abuses not worth repeating."[41] He continued uttering them during the public confrontation that ensued.[42]

This account appositely calls attention to the complementarity between blasphemy and verbal abuse or insult, bringing to light the degree of spoken violence in social relations and the unbearable weight of dependencies and subjections those relations implied.[43] (This weight was even more onerous among the peasantry than among city dwellers, at least in the eighteenth century.[44]) But the strong bond between verbal abuse and blasphemy was not reducible to society's "stage direction" of scenes of verbal violence. It grew out of the common character of both: an assault on one's personal honor, a nullification of the attributes of social distinction, standing, and recognition.[45] If honor remained "the value possessed by a person in his own eyes and its worth in the eyes of those that make up society,"casting doubt and aspersions on it invariably recurred to the same type of denunciation.[46] When it was of a sexual nature turned against women, it directly compromised the dignity of the father, brother, or husband. When turned against men, verbal insult had to do with moral shortcomings, idleness, boastfulness, doubtful parentage, and—more seriously—dishonesty, perjury, and above all thievery. Presumably sustained by factual truths about their targets, these accusations were not really premeditated; they drew from the accepted lexicons of abuse exactly as did blasphemous expressions on the same occasions. Yet by joining actual blasphemous remarks to abusive ones, the aggressor singularly strengthened the latter's range and gravity. Heaping opprobrium simultaneously onto individual honor and onto God's, swearing profane oaths took up a position of absolute defiance. Was this, however, a clear demonstration that the blasphemer *knew* he or she was violating the interdictions? Nothing is less certain.[47] Here again the old vocal habits and automatisms took over, freshly wedding sacred and profane at the very core of denunciation's customary locutions. Rouvilly, by trade a Parisian lathe turner who was found to have accosted a Monsieur Forestier, "is said to have spent a good hour reiterating the said blasphemies, declaring he would kill him, send him to take his supper with the Almighty, that he was a damn idiot and bloody bugger, a rascal, and that he was giving himself over to the devil body and soul."[48]

Uttering blasphemous remarks colluded integrally with a system of individual or collective violence.[49] Festered by the importance and frequency of verbal exchange, one's habit of speech joined blasphemy's excesses with those of invective, but its nature, as well as the circumstances under which it sprang out, augmented its gravity for those it offended directly, not to mention for those who guarded God's honor.

Thwarting the Blasphemer. Civil action to repress blasphemy followed the procedure of preparing a case or suit for judgment and entering an official complaint, either by the plaintiff or by the fiscal officer pleading the case within the system of seigniorial justice. In Paris, during the second half of the seventeenth century, the public administration or ministerial directive was the originator of less than one-fifth of the complaints. The sociological composition of individual plaintiffs was largely that of the Parisian bourgeoisie, at greater than half (57 percent), including those prosperous in the trades—shop owners—merchants— owners of manufactories and other businesses and properties or of otherwise independent means, and officials of the crown or other levels of government. And categories of the working classes—apprentices and journeymen beyond their apprenticeships, trade guild members, day laborers, servants—represented only about a fourth. Contrasting with the social affiliation of the accused blasphemers, the clear imbalance that emerges between the portions represented by these two principal groups of plaintiffs might well indicate the fragility of social relations, with bourgeois *victims* of blasphemous language and abuse to be found in greater numbers than bourgeois *perpetrators* of the offense.[50] On the other hand, members of the clergy against whom verbal aggressions were documented are far less numerous (2 percent) than they would be in the eighteenth century.[51] Should this discretion be attributed perhaps to a momentarily successful policy of Tridentine Christianizing, which imposed respect and reverence toward men of the First Estate? If so, this paying of obedience was singularly attenuated during the following century, at a time when the pressure to maintain spiritual and moral probity weakened.[52]

A magistrate's proceedings against an accused blasphemer were most often the end result of an individual (or collective) denunciation, one which did not necessarily issue from the victim. The gravity of the blasphemy related to the entire community of believers and demanded the immediate establishment of lines of defense, such as the testimony of those who would come forth to inform on the criminal, in order to ostracize the offender. In the early first centuries of the Christian era, Saint John Chrysostom even urged that Christians personally punish those who offended "the name of Supreme Majesty. Should you encounter in the street or public square any of these insolent blasphemers of the holy name of God, approach them and offer the sternest reproaches, do not be fearful of striking them should it be necessary; yea, chastise them publicly and punish this mouth speaking sacrilege."[53]

Even as it reserved its say over matters of law, the state in France or Venice or the Holy Roman Empire held the giving of incriminating information to be the obligation of witnesses to blasphemy, prescribing punishment for those who had refused to point the finger at offenders. In France, from Charles VI on, legislation even exempted the accuser from the costs of the suit and granted him one-third of the total fine imposed on the guilty party. This incentive was a clause of the law regularly cited, particularly in statutes and regulations that were the rule in the smaller jurisdictions. The provost of Champs-sur-Marne, in 1657, stipulated with great precision that out of the eighty-four-livre fine paid by the blasphemer "one-third shall go to the person who made known his act to the authorities of justice, the other two-thirds shall be put toward the church of the jurisdiction and the seigniory."[54] Such a procedure was not without its objective fallibilities. And an accusation that was too vague conspicuously limited its efficacy. In 1640 the judges of Redon had to halt their proceedings in a case for lack of truthful information after "several bourgeois had, in a hearing before the court of this jurisdiction, informed against a great number of rapscallions of the city, port, and outlying districts who utter execrable blasphemies."[55] Proceedings were not always lacking an ulterior motive: in his research on the parish of Bruyères in the duchy of Lorraine, Olivier Christin has clearly shown that, at the end of the sixteenth century, blasphemers were sometimes denounced in order to settle disputes about ancestry or claims on adjoining properties.[56] Often including accusations of witchcraft, instigating legal actions sometimes allowed the plaintiff to favorably resolve family disputes or other conflicts of interest by using the support of legal authorities.[57]

This kind of deviation from judicial impartiality also figured as the motivation behind a case in 1755–1757 involving a dispute between the rich Correr family of Venice and a father and son of the Gualtieri family, who were its agents in charge of one of the properties of the Corrers called La Marina among various Venetian holdings on dry land. The Gualtieris were informed against by a priest in the pay of the owners, whose motives appear suspect and who stated he had often heard them not only swearing by the " 'blood of the head of God' or by the 'blood of God's bonemeal' [*sangue dell'osso della gramola di Dio*] but also denying the soul's immortality and Mary's virginity, as well as saying that the mass amounted to a jolly little pig fest for monks and that licentious sexual intercourse did not constitute a sin."[58] These accusations led to the arrest of the stewards; though they subsequently were released on the terms of a stern warning and pledge, they nevertheless lost their status and reputation, considering themselves victims of the calumny of the Corrers, who—with their accomplices—were eager to get rid of troublemakers.

In many cases, the complainant's statement and the charges were, along with testimony from witnesses, the only documentary records entered and preserved for a given case. Consulting them, while indispensable, also remains delicate to the extent that they often silence what was really behind an event, as if violence and offending words had suddenly erupted without any established prior cause.[59] Yet these records do manage to build up, as if by successive strokes on the canvas, a portrait of the blasphemer who, little by little, sheds the clothing of perfidy, heresy, and headstrong self-willfulness to put on that of a public nuisance in the eyes of his neighbors. Exemplary in this respect were the words recorded at the sentencing of one Simon Erard, exposed by the fiscal prosecutor of the bailiwick of Saint-Germain-des-Prés:

> The aforementioned party, to the great prejudice of that respect and reverence due to God, commits every day several horrible blasphemies, oaths, and disavowals against the Divine Majesty, in public and in plain sight of all, to the great disgust of everyone passing by or living in the vicinity, who have a serious concern in the matter be it either because God is thereby gravely offended against or because of the wicked example given to their children such that said blasphemies are by them so influentially retained in their thoughts that when given to anger they might commit a like sin, as well as disobey their fathers; and notwithstanding this he doth not desist from committing the offense repeatedly with such effrontery and temerity that some of the aforementioned neighbors and persons of piety, having seen fit to reprove him, he did abuse and sought to kill them with jabs of a knife and even in that manner did wound one of those present; and seeing as such crimes are inadmissible being that they are against divine and human law, it is therefore recommended that you be delivered over.[60]

This document puts on vivid display a complete setting down of grievances aired against the blasphemer by his immediate entourage. And, above all, what it meant for such a habit to have become so familiar. Blasphemy was no longer a matter of impious words spoken under precise or passing concrete circumstances but of a full-blown, permanent, and deliberate perversity, something shared by many others. Thus the Parisian Jean Bonnet, a big-time "oath-swearer and blasphemer of God's Holy Name, makes use publicly of words such as '*mortdieu*,' '*sangdieu*,' '*teste dieu*,' '*je renie Dieu*,' which he utters as often in the morning when he arises as in the evening when he goes to bed, and most of the time at those hours when he takes his rest from work and without provocation of anger."[61] Having become a true vice and capable of tipping its agent into the world of madness,[62] blasphemous speech was more a prelude to, than an accomplice of, a multitude of deviancies considered reprehensible and among which might figure drunkenness, licentiousness, violence, and libertinage. In November 1712, a chambermaid named Marie Langrand who lived near Claude Gaudissard, a scribe at the Palais de Justice, described him before the police council as "a man who blasphemes for any reason, who leads a life of debauchery by having young girls visit him in his offices, [and] whose wicked proceedings are held in abhorrence by all in the locality with whom he quarrels when soaked with wine."[63] The life of the blasphemer was indeed dissolute and shocking to the immediate circle of his community. When Anne Evrard, resident of Jaufroy Lasnyer Street in Paris, was said to "constantly deny the Holy Name of God and profess against His holy name several blasphemies and against the holy sacrifice of the mass to which she says she never goes, and all this within earshot of everyone," she outraged the entire community.[64] This was made all the worse as she remained, like the others, generally deaf to remonstrances, to remarks by those close to her. Jean Bonnet, whom we met earlier, "mocked an ecclesiastic who sought to reprimand him for such blasphemies and in derision picked up a flute asking who wished to play along with him." And when a law student named Jean-Baptiste Dujardin de La Motte, encountering Evrard, told her "that she must think of God, she said she did not give a damn about her soul and pronounced several blasphemies by declaring she knew not God, that he was apparently the god by which witnesses swore but that he was not her own and could go to the devil." Marginalized by their way of life, blasphemers brought on their own exclusion also from the community of believers less perhaps by their insults or invectives against the divine than by their provocation toward the practices of worship. Certain people prided themselves on not attending church (while others gloried in not observing the fast on Good Friday) or on shouting scandalous utterances on Easter, All Saints' Day, or Christmas.[65]

Why then did those living in blasphemers' communities rally against these impious persons? Out of piety, adherence to the law, fear of divine punishment? Without discarding these impetuses, which are hard to demonstrate, one can uncover other motivations thanks to the archives of recorded testimonies. Some were motivated by fear of the outlaw characters' inherent violence, of their unpredictable and dangerous reactions, of responding directly to their insults. More often it seems that neighbors could no longer brook this anticonventional life that obfuscated sacred truths, that presented a deplorable model for children, and ended up stigmatizing, with a wicked notoriety, the entire household, the larger residential dwelling, or that street in the city or village. Jean Bonnet, Simon Erard, Jacques Cottier, and many others "administer a slap in the face to the entire quarter and bring great scandal upon its head."[66] Harboring an impenitent blasphemer gave a distinctively unsavory shape to the social representation of those who sought recognition and esteem. Here again, a certain form of honor was at stake. Finally, the offenders' scandalous life could also cause people to feel less secure, as blasphemers drew to their dwelling "all sorts of persons, vagabonds, swordsmen and soldiers, idlers and lackeys who quarrel and wrangle, so that everyone living there is greatly scandalized, notably by public blasphemies."[67] Jean Richard for one was accused of leading "a most scandalous life to the great prejudice of all living around him, into which dwelling he removes debauched women whom he prostitutes to the first passerby and to other such persons as swindlers, vagabonds, and others wearing swords who commit the swearing of oaths and execrable blasphemies against God's holy name."[68]

Owing to such accounts, blasphemers appear increasingly through the course of the seventeenth century as disturbers of the social order, as individuals who, above all, reject the shared rules, who live differently from the others, and make this clear by reprehensible acts and words. Ungovernable in their words and deeds, they unnerve those who surround them through multifarious rejections and refusals out of which they seem to compose their life. The accused's behaviors, associated with officially recorded denunciations in the seignorial Parisian archives of the early eighteenth century, dispel all doubts about the accusers' perception of blasphemers (see the table below).[69]

If flouting moral and spiritual values was still cited, it remained very much in the minority (one-fifth) compared with other ways of describing

TABLE 7.5 |

violent:	28.9 percent
constantly drunk:	25.0 percent
disturber of the peace causes scandal:	24.3 percent
libertine, debauched:	12.5 percent
faithless and lawless:	3.9 percent
impious:	3.3 percent
unwilling to work:	2.7 percent

the blasphemous speaker. From this time onward, the blasphemer was no longer the person who offended heaven alone but became someone who challenged and impugned all social or religious constraint, who chose to defy (beyond the reference to divinity) the order in which he or she was confined to live his or her life. Yesterday scorning God or proclaiming a heterodox word, now the blasphemer gradually became established as a dangerous nonconformist, a fringe element who refused fellow feeling and authority. This mutation of the type turns up in other evidence stressed in the few studies conducted of the phenomenon up to this time. Indications are that the share of informing or official plaints by petitioners for *only* the crime of blasphemy ended up becoming residual, the remnants of an earlier absolutism. And more and more during the course of the eighteenth century, this deviancy can be considered to have been accompanied by a "duty to be discrete" on the part of witnesses or family members, as long as public order was not found to be disturbed. It was, adds N. Dyonnet, "as if each person reckoned or calculated, at least in public, that nothing authorized him or her to judge the quality of the respect that others manifested toward religion."[70] This was therefore to radically depenalize the sin and decriminalize the person who committed it.

The tendency to progressively identify blasphemy as a wrong of private conscience, a misdemeanor of the heart [*un délit du for privé*], seems also to be reflected in the inventory of documented circumstances that produced the lodging of a complaint by petitioners (see the table below).

TABLE 8 |

	Paris, 1656–71 (by %, based on 280 offenders)	Parisian Villages, 1660–1710 (by %, based on 84 offenders)
solely blasphemy (*b*)	1.7	—
b + insults	35.3	34.5
b + threats and anger	11.4	25.0
b + injurious words and blows, injuries	45.0	35.7
b + destruction of property	3.2	1.2
b + an act of rebellion	3.4	1.2
other	—	2.4
TOTAL	100	100

SOURCES: Debaret, "Le blasphème parisien," p. 47; Audard, "Le blasphème au village," p. 31.

It was now indeed violence in all its forms that became the chief incitement to blaspheme. But the tendency that emerged under the reign of the first Bourbon kings was not wholly new. Already at the end of the Middle Ages, blasphemous language and behavior were generally accompanied or preceded by other aggressive manifestations, at least if one is to accept at face value the reasons given for cases tried by the *officialités* in the north of the kingdom of France in the fifteenth century (see table below).[71]

Without disallowing for some possible regressions linked to the religious turmoil of the sixteenth century, one can surmise that between the end of the fifteenth and the beginning of the eighteenth century, the general tendency was toward the pronounced reduction of prosecutions for *only* this crime. Undoubtedly contributing to the gradual modification of the image or picture of the blasphemer were the abatement of religious conflicts and evolution of the status of heresy and heretics in a good portion of Europe in the course of the seventeenth century,[72] the allocation of proceedings against blasphemy to the civil tribunals, and the gradual transformation of repression for the crime into a more irregular occurrence. In France and even more so in the Low Countries or Italy, blasphemers were thus less often inculpated for the ideas they held than for the lives they led. To be sure, the two things were often connected, and the authorities and blasphemers' contemporaries readily accused those persons who held forth with impious declarations and discourses with simultaneously performing other misdeeds and "never going to mass or observing their devotions."[73] But from the local community's point of view, what became of primary concern lay less in the individual's willful self-exclusion from the Christian community by speaking forbidden words or in religious (mis)conduct and more in the disorder and insecurity these misbehaviors engendered among the neighbors. From this point on, religious defiance or the general spread of "the gravest sin" took

TABLE 9 |

Type of Trial	by number	by percent
blasphemy only	199	18.36
blasphemy and gaming	85	7.84
blasphemy and violence	768	70.85
blasphemy and other	32	2.95

a backseat to the damage the blasphemous life did to the reputation and constitution of the larger social body.[74] This was why the equating of blasphemers with malefactors and miscreants became so commonplace.[75] Blasphemers were "people with little conscience, almost without religion, good-for-nothing . . . deceitful and debauched." But were they still even talking any longer about the blasphemer—or was it rather about the thief, the pimp, the drunkard who had usurped the vocabulary?

It remains to be understood how this slippage in perceptions about the blasphemer did or did not corroborate the perception held by the magistrates, and indeed by the theologians, those professionals so adept at interpreting the law and defining what blasphemy betokened.

| *Cleric Versus Philosophe: Blasphemy and Public Space*

The figure of the blasphemer, having been significantly transformed over the course of the late seventeenth century, underwent further changes during the next century. Legal theory and theological reflection kept pace with society's perceptions of blasphemy but had unequal roles in these shifts. By virtue of its prior importance, blasphemy could fade neither abruptly nor completely from the cultural horizon of clerics. As judicial action against it lessened, intellectual and moral inquiry promoted new approaches. These approaches marked the beginning of a questioning and demotion of the sin's ranking among those ways human beings went astray.

8 | A LOOSENING GRIP

Interpretive Difficulties in the Data.   Discerning any long-term trend in the historical unfolding of judicial decisions on criminal behavior runs up against three kinds of obstacles. The first is a classic challenge facing the historian, having to do with both the formidably diverse nature of the written sources and their extreme dispersion. In some cases, the data derive from the seignioral or lower court system of justice, in others from the activity of a bailiwick or a parlement. Second, the small number of blasphemy cases identified as such leads many researchers to logically include them in the general category of crimes of "high treason against the divinity," without always assessing the share of blasphemy proper, as the categorization combined blasphemy with the sins of suicide, heresy, and other effects of witchcraft or the demonic.[1] Might such a meager harvest indicate waning effort to bring the crime to justice during this period?

To these difficulties, on balance quite common, may be added a third: a certain slant in documentary sources that are sometimes used too hastily. Simply counting up the blasphemy cases using lists printed in law manuals or textbooks or alphabetical tables of those found guilty of the crime and judged on appeal before the parlements does not always reflect the reality of the way these cases were judged. For example, the death sentence that the parlement pronounced on March 23, 1724, against Charles Lherbe, an oxen fattener, stipulated that the guilty man bear two "signs, one in front and one behind, with the words 'Abominable, impious, and execrable blasphemer.' "[2] This leads one to conclude the charge was highly specific and defined, consequently sanctioning the retention of an extreme retributive harshness. Yet an attentive reading of the depositions from this trial reveals two facets to the accused's character. Close witnesses who were neighbors or shop assistants testified to the man's frequent extreme gestures and utterances against religion. Marie-Angélique Boulogne overheard him "saying that God was a 'bloody dog' and that if he could grab hold of Him, he would throw him into the fire; witnessed him cursing the crucifix, calling said crucifix a 'bloody devil of a God' [bougre de Dieu]; saying that he knew not the Virgin Mother and continuously swearing with the holy name of God using these words: 'I renounce God!' [Je renie Dieu], 'goddamn!' [sacré Dieu], ''sdeath!' [mort Dieu] and other blasphemies. . . . It seems that he hath not a taint of religion and that she beheld him taking meat during every fast."[3] When his spouse was called to testify, she first put forward his violent behavior when drunk, the blows and bruises and death threats she had suffered, and added "that he had on several occasions sought to force her to go hear Monsieur the Ambassador of Holland's sermon and renounce the Catholic religion into which she had been born." So to the crime of blasphemy strictly speaking had been admixed spousal abuse, disturbance of the peace, and confirmed suspicion of supporting reformist thinking. Which accusations really counted the most in this sentence of such absolute finality? The mere list of "criminal indictments and judgments"[4] cannot by itself, in any event, allow one to ascertain the actual part taken by blasphemy in itself in the final judicial outcome.

These necessary reservations and caveats do not really change the reasons for believing that there is a basic pattern of decline in legal actions against blasphemous speech and that such speech was frequently associated with other crimes attributed to the same culprit. Learned jurists who liked to feather their arguments with exemplary trial precedents unwittingly supply us with quantitative allusions to a progressive loosening of the royal or seignioral judicial body's intervention to suppress blasphemy. Commenting in 1717 on judgments that had been appealed before the parlements, P.-J. Brillon invoked a total of fifteen cases for the sixteenth century and nine for the seventeenth.[5] François Dareau furnished in the case of Louis XVI's reign five examples of blasphemers condemned in the sixteenth century, nine in the seventeenth, and five in the eighteenth.[6] However questionable this strictly quantitative basis may be, it is confirmed by more specific data also provided by the record-keeping of the parlements. At the time of the Grands Jours of Poitiers, in 1634, prosecutions for abusive and blasphemous speech constituted only 1.3 percent of cases prepared against all offenses.[7] During the Grands Jours of Auvergne, of 1666, blasphemy figured in only three cases out of the 283 inventoried.[8] Timely data furnished for the Parlement of Besançon in the eighteenth century broadly verify the phenomenon.[9] And the dated but quite thorough study by Pierre Dautricourt on the activities of the Parlement of Flanders between 1721 and 1790 counted five cases of blasphemy, all before 1740.[10]

The concentration of the latter-day vicissitude of charges for blaspheming during the first half of the eighteenth century is to be found in Françoise Hildesheimer's research on those appeals ruled on by the Parlement of Paris. More than four-fifths (84 percent) of the ninety-one accused individuals were judged *before* 1750.[11] Further, after isolating accusations for blasphemy alone (twenty-three charges), all but one case took place between 1707 and 1745.[12] Dedieu's erudite work on the Toledo Inquisition also highlights the crime's gradual eclipse among the preoccupations of the Holy See. An ebbing, already perceptible after 1560, was furthered by a quasi-disappearance during the seventeenth century, even though until around 1630 a concern with blasphemous propositions, or the actual scandalous words themselves, in some ways took up the slack. With good reason Dedieu believes, however, that the Toledo inquisitors could continue to battle the propensity to blaspheme by means of a less public system, one ensconced within the organs of a judicial authority that hardly left any traces.

Scrutiny of archives of the lower royal courts and seignioral tribunals, however incomplete, would seem to uncover a similar tendency in France. Conclusions shared by a certain number of studies lead to some genuine convergences on this score.[13] Files from the records of the aldermanry or governorship of Arras contain only fifty cases for the period between 1529 and 1628.[14] Christin's research on the registries of the ducal tax officers of Bruyère, in Lorraine, turned up "hardly more than twenty or so cases between 1579 and the mid-1620s."[15] S. Guilleminot's impressive work on the presidial of Caen in the seventeenth century does not allow us to dispel all uncertainty[16] insofar as it does not prioritize the chronological evolution of the judiciary's activity and again, above all, fails to treat blasphemy as an autonomous category because of its close association with verbal aggression or insult. But the very fact that these behaviors were lumped together, as I suggested earlier, is perhaps the sign of blasphemy's weakening representation. Violent speech (perhaps including blasphemy) between 1604 and 1700 was a factor in 15.5 percent of trials in the bailiwicks of Bayeux, Caen, and Falaise; insults applied in 6.3 percent of cases in the ordinary royal jurisdictions of the viscounties and 4.4 percent of those of the presidial structure of governance. Blasphemies, properly speaking, in the end, made up 2.5 percent of the preparation of criminal cases to be judged by the seigniorial courts of La Motte-Harcourt.[17]

During the following century, the decrease in charges of this nature continued at all levels of the judiciary.[18] The provostry of Courbevoie recorded only two plaints brought for blasphemy out of 144 between the years 1726 and 1790.[19] For the bailiwicks, the reduction seems just as marked. Studies of those of Marmers, between 1695 and 1750,[20] and of Alençon, from 1715 to 1745,[21] count no more than one or two cases out of several hundreds, and the work that has been done on the bailiwick of Quingey in Franche-Comté turns up nary a one.[22] The Mitry-Mory bailiwick's archives from the beginning of the eighteenth century (1700–1718) are hardly eloquent on this subject but seem to reflect well enough the loss of blasphemy's autonomy as a criminal act, as it was, from this time on, grouped with other forms of violence.[23] We can add as a final illustration of the tendency the results of a statistical study covering a wide base, namely sentencings in France to the galleys. Between 1680 and 1715, the percentage of common-law criminals given this form of hard labor in convict gangs for blaspheming represented 8 percent of the total and fell to about one-third of a percent (.38 percent) between 1716 and 1748.[24]

From the seventeenth century on, the noticeably reduced importance of this offense—in legal accusations, lawsuits, and trials—conferred on it a progressively secondary status.[25] More and more, blasphemy figured only as an aggravating circumstance in connection with other crimes.

Hildesheimer's work informs us that, during the eighteenth century, a full three-fourths of blasphemy cases were found to be associated with other classes of offense, with physical violence, sodomy, arson, robbery or murder.[26] This left, however, 25 percent in which parties to the crime or suit were involved in a case focused exclusively on determining and judging blasphemy. Might these, then, have been fairly exceptional or notorious cases taken up by the highest level of justice having jurisdiction over the matter? Were the decisions of the judicial authorities in such cases informed by the vestigial aftereffects of traditional repressive sanctions that aspired to make examples of transgressors? This is a highly difficult claim to make, inasmuch as deciphering the conditions of this slow mutation remain a knotty problem. Sometimes, as in the Republic of Venice, they were favored by institutional changes. From the mid-sixteenth century (1540–1550), the growing jurisdictional cognizance granted to the *esecuttori* over penal cases and other offenses that disturbed the moral order facilitated trying cases for blasphemy, along with those involving charges for gambling, urban violence, or obscenity, under a common class of offense calling for repressive measures.[27] Elsewhere, as we will see, a set of new ways of thinking and of cultural valuations loosened the older definition of the object of repression.

As far as the plaintiffs and victims of blasphemous speech were concerned, they perhaps continued to insist before the judge on the slanderous and impious bent of those whose aggression they had undergone, but in spite of their pleas the magistrate did not credit it with quite the same direness as before. A certain Faucon, when he brought suit before the Palais bailiwick in 1727 against a master shoemaker named Claude Gaudissart, having been sorely mistreated by Gaudissart, added promptly in his statement of complaint that "the word 'goddamn' [*sacré Dieu*] was always to be heard issuing from the said Gaudissart's foul mouth" and that he was an "unseemly blasphemer."[28] The accusation does not seem to have given the prosecuting magistrate pause. Nor likewise did the judge of the Cambrai give much weight to an elaboration by the wife of Jean-Charles Houzeau who, backing up her request for a separation from her spouse in 1678, accused him several times of "abjuring God and not only God but an *accursed* God [*le sacré Dieu*]."[29]

Sentencings as Indicator. Judicial authorities' gradual disengagement from proceeding against blasphemous speech was accompanied by an attenuation of judges' severity toward those convicted of it. Numerous gaps in the documentation and files, which for the most part are incomplete, do not always facilitate demonstration.[30] So, too, do the printed lists of detainees leave open the question of how general and representative the phenomenon was.[31] Mere sampling could never make up a completely reliable statistical base transcribing the historical fluctuations of repression.[32] At the very most, all that an analysis of the judgments handed down by the parlements between 1599 and 1718 (grouped under the series labeled A.D. III in the French national archives) can suggest for the thirty-two listed cases is some measure of redirection toward less intransigence around mid-century and a marked diversification of sentencings by magistrates of the sovereign courts.[33] A few studies that rely on a broader and more coherent corpus enable one to crystallize some less tentative conclusions.

Without putting forth specific percentages, we nonetheless note the importance of acquittals among recorded findings by judicial bodies at all levels. Bailiffs of the seigniories of Saint-Lazare and Saint-Germain-des-Prés in Paris announced this type of decision on average probably more than one out of two times. In 1610 Guerrin Michard, though accused of having "greatly blasphemed on several and diverse occasions the name of God" was nevertheless set free.[34] Jean Champion, despite his public provocations, having been "witnessed with his sword drawn, shouting profanities, and using God's holy name blasphemously against several townsmen, striking them on the head with his sword on (the smaller) Bourbon Street" and a writ for his arrest having been issued on May 2, 1669, was released from his imprisonment the very next day.[35] In a context describable with less impressionism and more ample statistics, the Venetian *esecuttori* who issued findings and decrees in a little over six hundred cases of "blasphemies, obscene words and wrongful offenses" in the middle of the seventeenth century, acquitted parties charged with the crime in 51 percent of the cases (without being able to be more specific).[36] The amounts imposed by fines were highly variable but most often were limited to a few livres.[37] Such a sum, however, was not a negligible financial burden for many of those accused who were of modest means. Sometimes these levies were compounded by other punishments more spectacular than physically painful: a penalization of one's honor whereby the convicted "with their hats removed and on their knees begged forgiveness from God, the king, and the law";[38] or the so-called act of solemn abjuration of the levi[39] to which the Inquisition subjected a por-

tion of the blasphemers found guilty in Spain (as Dedieu has recon-
structed it, see table below).

Other, more onerous punishments could evidently be tacked on to
these forced demonstrations of public penitence in France, Spain, or the
Italian principalities, including banishment, the galleys, whipping—or
execution. But by the seventeenth and eighteenth centuries, the repressive
arsenal's main force fell less heavily on offenders. A recommendation by
the Iberian inquisitors during the 1730s seems to have been the longstanding understanding:

> If the case is a grave one, a sentence of exile is given, or a monetary
> penalty is in order if the guilty party has the means to pay, and in
> cases of utmost gravity and scandal, he shall be made to hear the
> mass as a penitent, shall perform the abjuration of the levi, and on
> occasion shall be publicly exposed, notably when there is an auto-
> da-fé, and such a display is good to set an example if the person be
> of low condition and the blasphemy may be such as to merit flagel-
> lation, even though neither the whip nor hard labor on the galleys
> be any longer imposed. However a *motu proprio* issued by Pius V
> says that these must be imposed, although this no longer applies but
> very rarely to blasphemers unless they be persons of base quality.[40]

A little later in the text, its authors evoke the conditions under which the
blasphemer shall be able to incur no punishment: if he should choose to

TABLE 10 | Sentencings by the Toledo Inquisition for Word Crimes
(Blasphemies, Scandalous Utterances, Assertions)

	Atonement & Reconciliation	*Abjuration of the Vehementi*	*Abjuration of the Levi*	*Various & Minor Forms of Penitence*	*Suspension & Acquittal*
1481–1530	2.8	10.3	6.2	76.1	4.6
1531–1560	0.1	2.4	3.5	87.2	6.8
1561–1620	0.8	2.1	56.1	30.0	11
1621–1700	1.6	0.6	27.8	56.6	13.1
1701–1820	0	9.7	24.7	49.6	16

SOURCE: J.-P. Dedieu, *L'administration de la foi: L'Inquisition de Tolède (XVIᵉ–XVIIIᵉ siè-cles)* (Madrid: Casa de Velázquez, 1989), pp. 77–78.

denounce himself or come to do so "as soon as having been denounced by others," providing the blasphemy in question be not too serious. In such a case, a reprimand suffices: "The case shall be expedited with or without issuing a sentence in conformity with the great indulgence of the present times, for in times past one showed oneself in matters of law to be more stern."[41]

The less systematic severity of the royal judiciary through the modern era can be detected largely in cases it decided on appeal. If it is quite difficult to establish that the crown's jurisdictions showed consistent clemency in the majority of their judgments in the seventeenth century,[42] we do know that, over the following century, the Parlement of Paris reduced the sentence in the case of two-thirds of those found "guilty of blasphemy and other crimes."[43] For those judicial actions having to do solely with charges of blasphemy, the distribution of cases whose sentences were modified on appeal have been tabulated in the table below.

If the tendency shown by these results has the appeals to superior judicial authority tilting toward a newfound indulgence, it still cannot be elevated to an acquired rule definitively maintained. Every single blasphemer brought to trial always risked bearing the fullest and harshest

TABLE 11 | Evolution of Sentences Heard on Appeal By the Parlement of Paris in the Eighteenth Century

Sentence	First Rulings	Appeals
Death	2	1
Galleys: for perpetuity	2	—
9 years	4	3
5 years		1
3 years		1
Banishment: for perpetuity	5	
9 years	2	
5 years		2
3 years	1	3
Prison		1
Remonstrance and a Fine		2
Repenting on one's knees	1	
Requiring investigation	1	2
Without cause, case closed		4

SOURCE: F. Hildesheimer, "La répression du blasphème au XVIIIᵉ siècle," *Injures et Blasphèmes*, special issue, *Mentalités*, no. 2 (1989): 71.

punishment provided for by the law against this violation. The fact was that even though a code did exist for investigative criminal procedure there was no uniform penal code, and methods for qualifying facts were established according to a shifting and unpredictable jurisprudence.

There were, as a result, tragic exceptions to clemency during the entire span of the ancien régime. Among others was the sentence given to Simon Bailly, known as Bataille, on June 20, 1684. He was to make

> atonement for the oaths and blasphemies of the Holy Name of God and other cases mentioned at trial, and sentenced to make amends on the porch before the portal of the church of Notre Dame, dressed only in a shirt, with a rope round his neck, holding in his hands a flaming torch weighing the sum of two pounds, and there to say and declare that he did viciously and scandalously swear and blaspheme God's holy name and to ask for forgiveness for it from God, the King, and Justice, bearing a sign both in front and behind writ with the words "Blasphemer of the Holy Name of God." Whereupon he shall have his tongue cut out in the public square of said location and be taken and led to the galleys of the said King or Lord to serve there at hard labor in perpetuity. All his worldly goods are herewith declared to be confiscated and owed to the King and duly recorded, besides which a fine shall be exacted in the sum of three hundred livres.[44]

Whatever gaps there came to be between the cruelties prescribed by royal decrees and statutes and the looser or more sporadic lived reality of judicial practice commonly applied throughout the seventeenth and eighteenth centuries, the letter of the legislative texts might always be reaffirmed under specific circumstances. Even after 1750, there are traces here and there in the bailiwick's archives of severe sentences carried out against blasphemers.[45] The most dramatic model of these, conveying the always possible danger of judicial arbitrariness, remains of course the case of the chevalier de La Barre. Even if, all things considered, blasphemy does not seem to have figured as the true crux of this trial's controversy.

A Chevalier's Fate Between Abbeville and Paris.   This is not the context in which to rehearse this story in all its particulars.[46] Rather we can attempt to understand where exactly the accusation of blasphemy in the trial leading to La Barre's execution should be located, and perhaps to grasp the meanings the trial held at the time.

Sometime on the night and morning of August 8–9, 1765, a crucifix placed on the parapet of the Pont-Neuf of Abbeville in the diocese of Amiens was struck with blows from a sword or knife. The intense and swift shock that took hold among the townspeople led the king's prosecutor, accredited to the city's presidial, to file a complaint with Duval de Soicourt, assistant judge of the lieutenant justice of the criminal court and mayor of the area. Circulating rumors implicated a small coterie of young men, including La Barre, who had already drawn some attention for a brazen act of impudence committed a few weeks before. They had refused to remove their hats when the Corpus Christi procession had filed by. Among those inculpated, a writ was taken out for the arrest of La Barre and Moisnel; they were apprehended on October 2, examined at a hearing, and sentenced at the end of February 1766. La Barre was condemned to death. The automatic appeal procedure referring the case to the Parlement of Paris granted the young nobleman's appearance before the Grande Chambre only to have the chamber uphold the finding and sentence. The chevalier was beheaded on July 1, 1766.

The judgment handed down in the original venue on February 28, 1766, and accepted by the magistrates of Paris described La Barre as an "execrable and abominable impious and sacrilegious person, and blasphemer." It further stipulated that he must

> declare in words loud and clearly heard that he did wickedly and impiously put forth deliberate statements before the Blessed Sacrament without removing his hat and without kneeling, and did utter the blasphemies referred to in the judge's determination. He did also sing two songs filled with execrable and abominable blasphemies mentioned in the examination, and did render signs of respect and adoration unto abhorrent books and defile the sign of the cross, the mystery of the consecration of the wine, and the holy benedictions in use by the Church, for which he doth repent and ask forgiveness of God, King, and Justice."[47]

Thus La Barre's trial could not be boiled down to a case of blasphemy alone. The counts of indictment were more encompassing and, if one examines the inquiry's documents, alluded more to the issues of sacrilege and defilement or profanation. The bishop of Amiens, having come to Abbeville on September 8, to preside over an expiatory ceremony to atone for the outrages visited upon the mutilated crucifix, had likewise laid more stress on these particular classifications of sin in the tenor of the amends that were made, as well as in the selection of ritual observed.[48] The part of local prosecutor Hecquet in the matter was to uphold that "different impious and blasphemous statements" had been made. Yet he hesitated when it came to the exact determination of the crime, as the deeds that had been attributed to La Barre and all the facts adduced by those who informed against him were not clearly and definitively established.[49] Except for the scene of disrespect shown at the time of the procession, not one of the alleged misbehaviors upheld against La Barre and his friends had been witnessed publicly. It was this missing corroboration that the abbess of Willancourt, La Barre's aunt and hostess in Abbeville, emphasized when, having undertaken to organize his defense, she addressed a statement to Joly de Fleury, the king's attorney general, in December of 1765:

> If the chevalier de La Barre had disturbed the order of society and religion by impious pronouncements, if he had given cause for some public scandal, it would be with ample justification that the magistrates should have dealt with him severely. But facts of this nature cannot be imputed to the chevalier de La Barre. He stands accused of irreligious words, but it is not publicly that he spoke them; it is only in private conversation that he forgot himself in ill-considered talk.[50]

Yet if the judges rejected the distinction between public and private in order to secure and assert the singular gravity of the acts themselves, it was because they sought to situate the counts of indictment within a broader and more cunning sphere of criminal behavior they called the "philosophical temperament" [*esprit philosophique*]. Did not the blasphemous formulations and impious acts that the trial had brought to the fore take part in the libertine customs of youthful nobles whose pranks might be readily excused? According to several magistrates of the Parlement of Paris, including Pasquier and Maupeou, the perpetrators had drawn inspiration directly from their reading of philosophical works meant to topple true religion. In this case, it was clearly a matter of reading the writing on the wall, recognizing a danger far more insidious than sixteenth-century heterodoxy, as this was nothing less than the breeding ground of atheism itself.

Thus, in the construction that judicial procedure and discourse placed on the crime in this trial, blasphemy did not constitute the principal motivating factor of the indictment and charges. It dissembled other indictable habits of thought. Did they not burn the chevalier's body along with a portable copy of Voltaire's *Dictionnaire philosophique* (1764)?[51]

Those for whom political and social advantages were at stake also seized on the charge of blasphemy as a pretext. This is not the place to put forth a formal defense of the private vendetta argument which the lawyer Linguet used in his diatribe.[52] Nor can we go deeply into the possible motive of the ambitious commoner Duval de Soicourt, who was bitterly jealous of this young, arrogant, and nonindigenous fraternity of nobles, or of their protector, the abbess of Willancourt, who had derailed the matrimonial prospects of Duval de Soicourt's son. Less arbitrary perhaps, the share that can be attributed to the political environment of the years 1765 and 1766 allows emphasis to be laid, at the very least, on how fast the affair exceeded the reality of the charges brought by the king's justice, situating La Barre at the center of a play of rivalries and trade-offs more or less asserted or confirmed under oath at the time. In short the trial fell prey to struggles, contests of ideas, and special pleadings that went far beyond the immediate issue.

We can briefly allude to a few of the other fragments of a larger contextual history, which doubtless impinged heavily on the turn of events. La Barre's trial was unfolding at a time when the Parlement of Paris had recently succeeded in expelling the Jesuits, in other words in promoting the cause and victory of political Jansenism. So as to not lay themselves open to criticism by those who, such as the bishop of Amiens, held that the expulsion played into the hands of godlessness and "philosophy," the parlementarians were seeking to shore up their image as defenders of religion by condemning the reprehensible deviancies and pernicious influence of the spirit of the Enlightenment. This was the sense in which the jurist Pierre-François Muyart de Vouglans described the parlement's upholding of La Barre's sentence as "a memorable monument of jurisprudence which does too much honor to the zeal and piety of the magistrates from whom it emanated, for us to not give it report here as the very best model we might propose to sitting justices who have say over the matter."[53] But Louis XV, at that time much shaken by the dauphin's death (which he interpreted as an ordeal ordained by God), did not wish to cede to the magistrates the sole privilege of defending a religion under siege. He made known to them his desire that the law make an example. The message made its way from the keeper of the seals, Maupeou, to Maupeou's own son, president of the Grande Chambre charged with deciding cases on appeal.[54]

The unfortunate La Barre's appeal was timed also a few months after the notorious so-called Flagellation Session of March 3, 1766, in which the king reasserted his hegemony before the parlementarians, putting a provisional halt to the violent contestation between monarchical absolutism and the political aspirations proclaimed by the various sovereign courts in the provinces and then, after 1762–1763, by Paris. This warning shot in March 1766 for a time forced the parlement in the capital to adopt a compliant stance toward royal prerogative.

Under the effect of these concomitant and skillfully contained circumstances, a sort of mutual acquiescence or assent on legal matters had emerged among the judges of the presidial, the parlement, and the monarch. These parties, despite their diverging interests, were in agreement "about the show that they were going to present to the king's subjects ... even as they hid their respective reasons for agreeing to it," as Elisabeth Claverie astutely points out.[55] Thus the privately spoken blasphemies of the young noble served as no more than a pretext, a pretext that was plausible but also formidable since to speak them anywhere was designated a weighty criminal act that could in the judge's interpretation still call for the death penalty. Several jurisconsults at the time, moreover, forcefully drew attention to the reality that punishments for blasphemy and sacrilege were always arbitrary and varied with "the seriousness of the facts, circumstances, and extenuating factors."[56] A quite comparable and thus equally serious case had shaken Issoudun twenty years earlier (in 1744) without unleashing similar proceedings against those implicated—"the city's best" according to the testimony of some artisans' wives. For having defiled about twenty crosses, engaged in dissolute talk in the cemetery of Saint-Cyr, and defaced a statue of the Virgin on a street corner, the four chief perpetrators were sentenced to pay a fine of sixty livres.[57] Local context alone cannot, by any means, explain the difference in treatment.

So notwithstanding the tragic reality of 1766, those credentialed to determine, root out, and see to the punishment of blasphemous speech had been asking themselves for some time about the very meaning their predecessors had imparted to this crime. In his defense of the chevalier de La Barre's memory, Voltaire evoked what was at stake in this ill-advised displacement of unlawfulness: "The wise Vauvenargues said, 'What does not offend against society is not the law's business.' A ditty sung among young friends about a sect's religious beliefs," the patriarch of Ferney commented further, "cannot in consequence be an offense against all, against society."[58] Was not blasphemy turning, therefore, into a wholly different object under the joint effect of new and complex thinking?

 9 | MAGISTRATE, THEOLOGIAN, AND THE WAYS OF JUSTICE

The Philosopher and the Judge. It comes as little surprise to learn that philosophes and writers had often felt audacious enough to want to amend the laws on blasphemy and its definition, well before the magistrates and justices. Their discernment of the matter took two directions between the late-seventeenth and mid-eighteenth century. First it was imperative to throw into relief the cultural fluctuations of the very notion itself. "In our own times," wrote Voltaire, "what is blasphemy at Rome, at our Lady of Loretto, and within the walls of San-Gennaro, is piety in London, Amsterdam, Stockholm, Berlin, Copenhagen, Berne, Basle, and Hamburg." He added, for domestic consumption by French readers, "The Jesuits maintained, for a hundred years, that the Jansenists were blasphemers, and proved it by a thousand lettres-de-cachet; the Jansenists, by upwards of four thousand volumes, demonstrated that it was the Jesuits who blasphemed."[1] These summary remarks portrayed the term's referential instability since the time of the great sixteenth-century upheaval within Western Christianity. They led the way to pleas for greater indulgence toward offenders (who, beyond this, were not even guilty of anything in the Enlightenment view) and to assertions of the tolerant superiority of a conciliatory deism over all revealed religions. "One thing equally remarkable and consoling," wrote Voltaire toward the end of the same entry on blasphemy, "is, that never, in any country of the earth, among the wildest idolaters, has any man been considered as a blasphemer for acknowledging one supreme, eternal, and all-powerful God."

This approach was strongly inspired by the La Barre affair, and it went considerably farther than the rather conventional article written by the abbé Mallet, published in Denis Diderot's *Encyclopédie* (28 volumes, 1751–1772). Voltaire's general reflection on this and his criticism of dogmatism did not in one respect, however, break wholly new ground, even when applied to blasphemy. Well before Voltaire, Pierre Bayle's treatise had initiated this removal of the blasphemy issue to another sphere of concern.

> We fashion for ourselves grandiose words to create abhorrence of certain things that quite regularly pass within range of review by our decisions. So-and-so, we say, speaks intolerable blasphemies and dishonors God's majesty, in the most sacrilegious manner there be. What do we have here, after we have given it our close and dispassionate consideration? We have the fact that on the manners in which God may be honorably spoken of, he has ideas other than our own.[2]

This relativity of perception, which should be the customary way of defusing our reaction to things we cannot understand or tolerate, is instead lost insofar as it is still "we" ("*we* say") who announce that our fellow neighbor has said blasphemous words. Our decision that this is so comforts and commits us in our intent to destroy what is different from us, without however entering into relation with God. In a second and more affirmative passage from this text, Bayle discomfits the would-be perceiver of blasphemy in the name of a theology he makes both immemorial and contextual. Commenting on Jesus' command to his servant, "Go out to the highways and hedges, and compel people to come in, that my house may be filled"[3]—a sentence that constituted for some the biblical justification for forcing Protestants to convert in the aftermath of the revocation, in 1685, of the Edict of Nantes—he asked,

> Does a forcer of converts have eyes so piercing they can read a man's conscience? Does he share with God the incommunicable attribute of the teller of hearts? It would be the most extravagant impertinence to think so. Thus when a man whom one has instructed as well as one can in the faith will tell you his conscience remains firm in its belief that the only good religion is his own, one has no right to claim that one has convinced him deep inside and obviously of the error of his ways.[4]

Without naming it as such, the progressive philosopher has nonetheless inscribed blasphemy at the very heart of his observation. The one who insults heaven is no longer the offending wretch nor even the "hard-headed heretic" but rather one among those who believe they can put themselves in God's place to judge another, who take pride in having turned the tables on the guilty conscience of the traditional penitent whom God has persecuted.[5] So the blasphemer becomes the one who takes credit for what belongs to God alone.

We cannot say with assurance how instrumental Bayle's particular analysis was in forming the new appreciation brought to bear on blasphemy in the course of the eighteenth century. Yet if rulings on charges for this grave offense tapered off, it was also because the magistrates and justices, and not just the philosophes, had begun to modify their own perception of the crime. Some had even published and thus disseminated their thoughts before the judicial practice reflected changed attitudes. This evolution, taking shape in slow stages leading up to mid-century before becoming markedly pronounced after 1750, owed much to the personality and conviction of legal theorists.

In the course of Louis XIV's reign and for a long time thereafter, jurists' opinions on blasphemy covered the same ground (out of prudence?) as that of the most classic theologians who commented on the subject. Witness Le Brun de La Rochette, modeling his definition on Catholic teachings: "[This crime] is committed when the Almighty God is written of by attributing to Him that which is not suited to His omnipotence such as powerlessness or inability, injustice, malice, cruelty. Or by taking from Him the divine attributes that render Him incomprehensible to us and that very properly do not suit Him such as providence in all things, omnipotence, knowledge of things to come, goodness, justice and mercy."[6] He adds, a bit further in the text and just as traditionally, that "impious blasphemies uttered against God's honor deserve punishment by death but so also do those spoken against the name and honor of the glorious Virgin, mother of Our Redeemer, and those against the name and honor of the Saints." This rubber-stamping of the extant religious discourse would, for a long while, remain the norm. For example, in 1717 the magistrate Pierre-Jacques Brillon ended an edition of the *Arrêts concernant les blasphémateurs* (Rulings concerning blasphemers) by putting forth an opinion that would not have given the lie to certain moralists of the time: "How many examples of severity have not done anything to correct men? What infernal furor takes possession of them that they attack God and what is most holy to religion? May these visible demons perish from the earth! May eternal abysses yawn before them and swallow them up so that an earth already teeming with maledictions may no longer know such guilty ones nor heaven have such enemies!"[7]

Delamare's treatise from 1727 on policing immoral and ungodly behavior,[8] as well as the *Codex bavarici criminalis* (which appeared in Munich in 1757),[9] similarly depicted blasphemies in terms of theological categories. Both texts distinguished "immediate" blasphemous speech, which directly addressed God, from its "mediate" variety, that which was spoken against the Virgin or the saints but which "reflected adversely upon God."[10] In the second half of the century, a counselor of the Parlement of Aix, admittedly in a dictionary of canonical law, proposed in another context the same distinction between "heretical and simple blasphemy."[11]

Around the 1740s, however, other assessments from the world of officials within legal administration and the systems of justice simultaneously began to take shape. Theological considerations were no longer the only privileged path for justifying the repression prescribed by the statutes. Jurists examining the judicial meaning of the offense leaned toward an authoritative inflexibility. That they brought out this dimension is illustrated in an interesting way by the remarks of G. du Rousseaud de La Combe. Before putting forth the classic definition of blasphemy, this lawyer made it a point to clarify that it was the same blasphemy "of the theologians and doctors of canon law." He then differentiated in precise but classic fashion between "blasphemy of the name of God and the saints, which is committed through swearing, execration, and detestable profane or false oaths, and blasphemy proper, asserted with deliberate, premeditated comments and whose meaning is soberly intended."[12]

In the name of subtleties that still bore their original theological stamp, Charles Clément François de L'Averdy a short time later distributed blasphemies among three headings: profane oaths, vulgar terms of customary usage, and terms that broke faith with God.[13] And the exceedingly conservative Pierre-François Muyart de Vouglans proceeded to make similar distinctions, not failing to separate "blasphemy according to the theologians [from] that which is spoken about primarily in the laws."[14] This clear separation permitted an autonomy of the law over matters of theological judgment to gradually manifest itself. Before Muyart de Vouglans—and with less caution—Daniel Jousse in 1771 had cleared of the charge "those who employing the Holy Name of God or the life, death, or blood of Christ or the Virgin or the saints do not commit blasphemy proper."[15]

A second series of considerations further refined legal thinking on blasphemous speech by taking into account the circumstances of its utterance. This was not a wholly novel idea. In the sixteenth century, nine out of ten letters from blasphemers asking forgiveness from the king's justice sought to excuse their words as the effect of anger, gambler's blindness, drunkenness, or youth.[16] Advancing such attestations of recovery served to minimize the role of exclusive personal will behind the outburst of impious words. But jurisprudential and wider collective rethinking on this matter soon proved more clearly ready to accept the notion that such behavior followed a willfully private course. Jousse and Muyart de Vouglans were in agreement in wishing to see penalties lightened for the blasphemer who spoke rashly, under the sway of drink, or who gave "proof of a sincere repentance." Jousse, however, showed less indulgence when it came to those who spoke in vain the name of God out of simpleness, vulgarity, or because of the coarse customs of their habitual settings.[17] Sounding as if he knew whereof he spoke, Nicolas des Essarts in turn wrote in 1786, "the poor education of individuals in the common populace and one's conviction that their blasphemies are guilelessly uttered work to remove their hearing from our notice and explain our reticence to punish them though they be born from a criminal habit that ministers of the Church must endeavor to root out."[18]

Another element by degrees took part in this falling off of prosecution: public erring and sinfulness in Venice, from the seventeenth century on, came to be attached to scandal. Toward 1640, L. Priori considered blasphemy "so much more serious and villainous as it [was] spoken in a public manner and wittingly, creating a public outcry."[19] The following century would confirm more clearly and frequently this partition between princely prerogative and theological truth, which led by steps to the distinction between public and private. Rousseaud de La Combe illustrated this divide by retaining as the only true sin blasphemy spoken in public against God, the saints, or the church. For Rousseaud de La Combe blasphemy of the heart and "confidential" blasphemy were not the concern of the judge, who instead must be exclusively occupied with words capable of disturbing the social order.[20] For in the latter case, with the public use of disturbing speech, its speaker introduced not merely a lasting and harmful perturbation into social life. But also, as Dareau accentuated the consequences of the offense, by "impudently lacking respect for the divine majesty, the wicked example can weaken the reverence one shows the divine and, as a result, change the sanctity of worshipers' hearts."[21] This essential observation lends a forceful confirmation to the place and role that, at the end of the eighteenth century, religion was expected to assume in Western civilization. "Religion," wrote Jacques-Pierre Brissot de Warville in 1780, "cannot be considered in relation to civil society, save as one of the means Heaven has given society to help maintain its internal tranquillity; religion has the right only to punish crimes that can alter this tranquillity."[22]

Blasphemy thus took on a nefarious exemplarity likely to weaken a church that had become primarily the guarantor of the social order, an especially useful means to this end. Preserving this institution against such incursions meant, for the system of justice, safeguarding the collectivity's harmonious functioning. The collectivity must in turn preserve its responsible members from confusion and receive reparation. "We have indeed to take as a maxim that it is society alone that must be avenged when outrages are committed against the Supreme Being." Dareau finds himself pressing this further by citing sacrilege, irreverence, the casting of spells, heresy, and blasphemy as harming society. All these "crimes that wound society's order are of interest to that society, and its right to vengeance is reserved to those who serve the public ministry."[23]

The state's system of justice, which was, from this time on, more enlightened on the question, and the magistrates who were more apt to judge when there was "an indiscretion, an ignorance with malice aforethought, . . . know that punishment must never exceed the evil that society can suffer from this indiscretion and ignorance, and that sometimes when lending too eagerly its ear to the cries of a populace too easily outraged, it is dangerous in so doing to lean toward severely punishing errors that should merit a certain indulgence."[24] If Guyot sounded so assured here as to the punishment's tempered nature, it was indeed because the very meaning of its suppression had also changed its nature. No longer did magistrates see themselves as blind instruments of divine justice, they regarded themselves as functionaries of criminal law who carefully measured the offense by the litmus test of its danger to society. This refusal to appear as the executors of God's designs eventually became a conviction that was broadly shared, and perhaps even internalized, thanks to the lessons of the philosophe. In De l'esprit des lois, in 1748, Montesquieu was already writing,

> Evil has come out of this idea that the Divinity must be avenged. But divinity must be honored and never avenged. Indeed, if one conducted one's affairs according to the idea of exacting such vengeance, what end would there be to human torments? If it falls to the laws of men to avenge an infinite being, they shall have to take their cue from his infinity rather than adjust themselves to the failings, blunderings, and caprices of human nature.[25]

The jurists who would concretely extend Montesqieu's fundamental reflection relied on two kinds of considerations. First of all, by their reckoning, religion contained rules useful to the successful working of social organization "such as the existence of God, the immortality of the soul, the afterlife, ceremonies that brought human beings together."[26] Each of these was something that the public power had a duty to protect. The churches were to do no more than correct deviancies that overtook their specific dogmas, deviancies that by an abuse of proper judgment had been labeled crimes of high treason against the divine "in order to defend purely human interests under the pretext of defending God's interests."[27] Second and in the name of rejecting an ancient barbarism and an era of fanaticism, other enlightened minds would recall the impossibility that any one individual, judges and clerics included, could divine the thought of God on the question of blasphemers. "We know," wrote Dareau, "that it is not our place to anticipate the sacred rights God has reserved for Himself. How much spilled blood might have been spared by observing the maxim that it belongs to God alone to avenge Himself."[28]

These remarks authorize several possible readings of the perceptions shared by (at least) a fraction of enlightened opinions on blasphemy voiced in the second half of the eighteenth century. Enlightenment criticism was first of all concerned with exposing the clerics and judges' usurpation in determining, in the name of God, what constituted blasphemous criminal behavior. So, too, had the laws repressively imposed the image of a vengeful and cruel God who punished and delegated harsh penalties for offenses against him. It was this specious presumption, already alluded to in the quotation from Bayle, that was henceforth jettisoned in the name of two perceptions concerning the relation among sanctity, society, and politics. The implications of each perception were, apparently, contradictory.

One perception lashed out against humanity's prideful meddling in the innermost and unfathomable depths of the Divine. Did not this ambition, according to one learned critique, mirror the overfamiliarity of the blasphemer's inveighing against God as if he were a mere individual, insulting him as one would a wicked mortal character? After the Council of Trent, the Catholic Church's insistence on distinguishing the domains of the sacred or holy from that of the profane contributed, at a very early point, to deeming the blasphemer as the most vulgarly familiar of all interlocutors, the creature who claimed to put itself on the Creator's plane. In consequence that which was designated truly sacred became inaccessible, out of human reach. The professed will to establish an immeasurable distance between "man and infinite divine majesty" wound up removing blasphemy's function as provocation. This asserted distance helped gnaw away at part of the woven bonds between heaven and earth, expressing, in its own way, one of the aspects of the crisis of the Incarnation. Distancing a God whose glory nothing could alter lent conviction to claims that the very idea of vengeance could be gotten around, indeed done away with, along with the understanding that human agents could serve as the possible instruments of a necessary atonement for sins committed.

This rejection of the notion of such divine agency and divinity incarnate was also seen in the image of religion fashioned by jurists. Religion must be useful to society, promote the emergence of a "civil religion" (Brissot de Warville's term), guarantee the sanctity of manners, and the order of the world. These were the many claims opening the way to considering blasphemy as a counterauthority more secular than Christian. This fundamental mutation in the perception of blasphemous behavior formalized magistrates' more frequent indulgence toward those accused of it. Furthermore it rested on an ever more marked separation between powers of state and Christian values, and it took part in a broader movement that, in France or the Austrian Low Countries, affected the religious orders and the domains of reading and teaching, loosening thereby the traditionally tight link between "the two powers."[29] The "secularization" of blasphemy could not help but contribute to its decriminalization. The reflections of those specializing in law—in certain respects close to the conception of contemporary theology[30]—thus noticeably diverged from the positions adopted by the church at that time. Still, the clergy was not always content to rigidly uphold the inertia of doctrine on a subject that retained a not insignificant spiritual impact.

Some Daring, Much Caution. Affected immediately as it was by this sin still considered "a crime of enormous proportions," the world of theologians, for a long time, found it difficult to reach consensus on the nature of blasphemy as a whole.[31] The directions its pondered interpretations took, when analyzed in greater depth, grew out of a threefold approach.

The first and probably least interesting consisted of safeguarding the most traditional position. Already much present in the seventeenth century and based on rigorism, it was still maintained throughout the eighteenth century, and even persisted with some robustness at the time of the Restoration. It meant, for its defenders, abandoning nothing of the sin's considerable gravity, not entering into the juridical subtleties separating public and private. Quite to the contrary, under the influence of Thomists, Benedicti, Villars, and a few others vehemently denounced mental blasphemy, "thinking blasphemously with the heart without saying anything blasphemous with the mouth."[32] Held to be particularly serious was the propensity to swear by God's head or body. After Jean Eudes, Antoine Godeau, or M. Chevassu,[33] Antoine Blanchard in 1713 and then Jean Laurent Le Semellier in 1753 continued to assert the true blasphemous nature of such expressions: "[As to] these oath-swearers who claim to be speaking of God when they swear by His death, His blood, His head and the rest, it is plain for all to see and hear that they blaspheme as they attribute to God corporal members he does not have; if one [instead] says that they swear by the members that the divine Word took on at its incarnation, they are blasphemers still, because the impious manner in which they voice their oaths seems to record that the Word rendered itself worthy of scorn by adopting flesh-and-blood members similar to our own."[34] At the beginning of the nineteenth century, Villecourt took it upon himself to write that "Jesus Christ wishes it that one not swear by God's creation such as are heaven, earth, or any other thing that is in the universe, by the Blessed Eucharist that is in our divine tabernacles, by the saints or angels who are in Heaven, by the cross, by his own head or by any other created thing."[35]

One fails to find in the authors any leaning toward the idea that the context for an individual's behavior might limit the weightiness of the error. For the curates of Paris at the beginning eighteenth century, anger—regarded as one of the conditions most favorable to the outburst of (mock) holy curses—was not excusable.[36] Bressanvido would later confirm this point of view, stigmatizing lack of restraint, the very sign of the passions' empire over the human mind and spirit.[37] Nor did customs of linguistic practice serve to mitigate and belittle the sin, "to the contrary, they increase it," wrote the Jansenist François Genêt in 1676. And pastors in the kingdom's capital asserted on this matter "that it is sometimes appropriate to refuse absolution to those who are in the habit of speaking such cursed oaths."[38]

These rigid stances more or less explicitly mirrored the battle that had been opened against the casuists. Godeau, in the treatise he composed to the attention of priests in his diocese of Vence, exposed "a casuist [as someone] who excuses from mortal sin all the blasphemies that take place from frequent practice and when one lacks a perfect knowledge of the evil one does and when that knowledge is so inveterate that it is as if become nature."[39] Le Semellier went further than Godeau, thrashing "the new casuists who say blasphemy is only a venial sin when without perjury, without scandal, or without danger of swearing to it, when one has no formal intention of dishonoring God or is not ill-disposed toward God, when one has not hatred or is untouched by spite against God, or finally when it is the anger that utters these words."[40] In reality, well before the rise of casuistry,[41] classical theology that had been sheltered behind certain Thomist developments had not excused itself from questioning the finer distinctions of the blasphemer's guilt. At the beginning of the sixteenth century, Cajetan, taking up the words of Saint Thomas, conceded that although "sins of blasphemy are not of different kinds among its instances, they are nonetheless so different as to the grievousness of the crime that a given circumstance must be explained, much the same as for an act of thievery the quantity of things stolen must be accounted for."[42]

Based on the authority of the Gospels, several doctors of the church had also proposed a second, more nuanced approach. They sharply differentiated blasphemy from the spirit of blasphemy, with only the former being pardonable. "There is difference between blasphemy and the blasphemous spirit," wrote Benedicti. "Simple blasphemy, though it be greatly sinful . . . can be forgiven as the Gospel text says, but the blasphemous spirit can never be forgiven. And what is such a spirit? It is a depraved intent to blaspheme, which is not at all fragility, ire, fear, or ignorance, as much as pure malice."[43] Others, in the course of the sixteenth century, quite readily demarcated heretical blasphemies from all other forms. And from the 1550s on, the Spanish Inquisition claimed to be interested only in the former.[44]

These nuances and discriminations on the nature of blasphemy led to two sorts of consequences. The first was localized, selective, isolated, and limited to "the Supreme." It consisted in only lightly punishing carelessly made phrasing of "little gravity," of which Juan de Rojas had established a list composed of common verbal expressions that borrowed on religious references: "I renounce Saint Peter," "By God's life," "There is no soul," and even "God hath no mercy" were held to be benign expressions as opposed to "true blasphemy." These distinctions thus opened the way to a more conciliatory theology which swallowed up the casuists but not the casuists alone. By increments the theologians would come to recognize blasphemy only in terms of intention, "fully cognizant and entirely consented to"[45] because, in order for an action to be morally good or wicked, in Louis Abelly's assessment, it must be voluntary and chosen freely.[46] And if the penitent, as Liguori wrote in the mid-eighteenth century, takes "to be a sin what is not one, the confessor must educate him thereon."[47] Consequently many of these clerics reckoned that expressions such as " 'sbelly" (*ventre Dieu*), " 'shead" (*tête Dieu*), and " 'sdeath" (*mort Dieu*) were not even blasphemies but simple oaths or curse words, the expression of a sin of irreverence. Bonacina considered them venial sins, and the Jesuit Etienne Bauny (decried so fiercely by Pascal) made this assertion his own.[48] In his *Dictionnaire des cas de conscience* (Dictionary of cases of conscience), published in 1715, J. Pontas informs us that these assessments would already be found in Cajetan, Bilhard, or Vernier for whom they were "a simple form of irreligion." Pontas himself, a little further in the text, wrote that these expressions were "manners of speech and normally neither bad faith nor venial sin."[49]

The more these theologians took into account possible explanatory circumstances, the more they came to relativize the sin by taking into account possible explanatory circumstances. Anger in particular, adjudged a mitigating practice or weakness, was regarded as capable of distorting one's good sense and causing one to utter words "against God's honor without thought to their meaning and without any malign feeling against God."[50] These priests, who were often confessors, insisted furthermore on lenience for behaviors that stemmed from habit or ignorance. The Spanish inquisitors even considered it a necessary part of inquest protocol for the examiner to assess "the capacity, the occupation of the party under investigation, their rusticity, as well as their intelligence" before passing sentence.[51] For custom and practice did lead to expressing words that might sound impious but were involuntary and without duplicity. With ample experience to consult, and in no way capitulating to laxism, Liguori warned the confessors of the Iberian peninsula, "We must observe here that blasphemous speech against the dead is not a grave sin, as it is not a grave sin to say '*Potta di Dio*' because this expression in the Tuscan language is but a simple interjection indicating impatience."[52]

Thus, far from remaining locked into strict categories (which were still maintained and reiterated by some up to the mid-nineteenth century), blasphemy's theological dimension was the object of interpretations and mutations at the very heart of the Catholic world. It nonetheless would be misguided to explain these two tendencies as the expression of a radical and irreducible opposition between inveterate rigorists and laxists. In the course of a joint labor, following Benedicti's lead, many religious moralists put forth several types of ruminations differing in the treatment of the subject. Indeed, the most essential shift lay in weighing the degree of seriousness, along with the more systematic acknowledgment of context and the blasphemer's personality, as requisites for ruling on the sin's nature. Its normative definition was no longer assumed prior to inquiry but deemed part of that inquiry's outcome. The casuistic method ended up having its effect on the practitioners of the confessional, sparing them from monolithically condemning a behavior. The search for the terms of a true moral discrimination guided a fraction of the theologians to minimize a range of blasphemous behaviors, despite their irreducible rootedness in a gospel which was no easy task to interpret: the refusal to forgive blasphemy. This speculative and pastoral step to reducing "true" blasphemy to only a few deliberate heretical situations was probably not adopted by the entire body of curates of the Enlightenment century. But it was a concurrent fact that the law of the state was no longer really punishing this deviance of language, and was contributing to radically attenuate its gravity in the eyes of the Christians of modern Europe. And so: did it not seem imperative that the Roman Catholic Church should continue to speak the rhetoric of disciplinary firmness, faced with the civil power's disengagement from which a host of possible excesses might still ensue? And was it still not up to Rome to portray blasphemy, especially to these consciences turned toward laxism and toleration, to be the most considerable, widespread, and threatening of all sins?

A third approach to the question, more discrete for being rarer and above all infinitely more radical, came into focus side by side with these long, sinuous, and contradictory rethinkings of blasphemy's place. Indeed in the view of a few maverick theological freelances, the sin of language per se, the verbal expression (however heterodox it may be), loomed less large than certain doctrinal assertions allied to the blasphemous speech. Even as it remained within the strict sphere of theology, in this view the sin applied to propositions largely admitted that did not, however, correspond to the reality of the Christian message. There is no disputing that these few and (by necessity) discrete analysts were troubled by adherents of a "reasonable" Christianity and had a good many difficulties with the conception of a God who was good, yet cruel enough to condemn the vast majority of humanity to eternal damnation. It was first and foremost to reassure mortals, to avoid plunging them into discouragement, as Jean Delumeau observed,[53] that Pierre Cuppé, a simple prior-curate in the diocese of Saintes, published in 1716 his *Heaven Opened to All, or, a Theological Treatise by which, without Disrupting the Observances of Religion, it is Soundly Proven by Holy Scripture and Reason that All Men are Sacred.* The casting of doubt on the premise of damnation of the greatest number—a premise which was commonly taught and followed the teachings of numerous doctors of the church—inspired Cuppé to contend that

> Saying God wisheth not to save all of humanity is to go against a point of faith . . . Nor can one say God cannot save the generality of all mankind, this would be to impugn His omnipotence and to blaspheme or at the least to say that He is ignorant because desirous, as it appears in the words of Saint Paul (Timothy 2), to save all humanity [yet] hath not, or hath not known how to find, the means for doing so. Now here one would indeed blaspheme again; there are no signs at all that anyone whosoever they be should dare even conceive the thought of such a thing.[54]

By insisting throughout his work on divine goodness, Cuppé took at its word theology's prime definition of the sin: one blasphemes if one attributes to God something He is not. All of which earned for Cuppé a condemnation of the first version of his work.

Its readers had perhaps included Nicolas-Sylvestre Bergier, who also advocated a theological interpretation that would serve to render Christianity less open to criticism by the best and brightest minds of the second half of the eighteenth century. Quite the reverse of Cuppé, Bergier was an apologist known as much for his reflection on the progressive unveiling of the signs of revelation through human history as for his controversies with the Enlightenment society's philosophes.[55] And one would have to look hard through his numerous militant productions for a deviant or truly innovative thought on the subject of blasphemy. The brief passages he allots to blasphemy situate it within the familiar behavioral range of irreligious faithlessness toward God. But by similarly apprehending blasphemy as an errant dogmatic position, Bergier sought to use it as part of his rereading of salvific theology, an object of fundamental questioning by secular philosophy. Responding to an observation made in his *Le christianisme dévoilé* (Christianity unveiled) on the contradictoriness of a God who was portrayed "as infinitely good but who created the greatest number of mortals only to damn them eternally," the answer of the priest from Franche-Comté was clear. "An opinion that we hold to be a blasphemy must not be imputed to us. Never has a Catholic Christian believed that God ever created a single man in order to damn him; faith teaches us on the contrary that God wishes sincerely to save all men."[56] The discrete traces of this theology that cropped up here and there[57] proved to be more legible and declarative in the correspondence that Bergier carried on with the abbé Joseph Trouillet, curate of Ornans in the diocese of Besançon.[58] Thanks to those letters we know that Bergier was composing (at the same time as his dictionary) a treatise on the redemption in which he wanted to set out to forcefully demonstrate that, with Jesus having died to save the multitude, God offered salvation forever to all men. Thus observant Roman Catholics, of course, but also their unbaptized deceased children, as well as heretics and pagans, could receive forgiveness for their errors or for "their invincible ignorance, and be saved by mercy."[59]

Arguing in such terms went against the tide of Augustinian doctrine widespread in the Counter-Reformation church, to which Bergier's reader, Trouillet, fearing the liberties Bergier took and employing all the persuasion written words could muster to bring Bergier back to the true reason of the Councils of Florence and Trent, did not fail to direct his attention. Before envisaging the publication of his essay, however, Bergier undertook to introduce several elements of his theology of Redemption in a certain number of articles comprising his dictionary (on baptism, God's justice, redemption, the Savior). At the same time that he had few illusions (knowing how subject he was to the corrections and expurgations of his fastidious censor the abbé de La Hogue) and felt resigned to lending his approval to content he actually considered different from his conception of Christian faith, Bergier ventured, "If I find myself obliged to blaspheme a jot against the Redemption, Jesus Christ will not bear me ill will for it; he sees to the bottom of my soul, he knows with how much loathing I consent to be a party to saying that the devil has been stronger than he and that he has lacked either power or good will to redress the wrong the devil has done, does yet, and shall do until the end of days."[60]

Faithful to his interpretation of blasphemy, in private Bergier applied it to this reductive reading of salvation become church law. Here we need to cite in full a passage from one of his last letters to Trouillet, perfectly summing up the essence of the momentous debate.

It is a far different thing to say that a few Christians, filled with grace and the means of salvation, stubbornly persisted in damning themselves by wrongheadedly resisting grace, or to hold that children who had no chance to resist anything and thus could not abuse anything, infidels who seem to us to be in invincible ignorance, or all those who are abandoned by Providence, etc. are prey to the Devil, and that out of a thousand human creatures there hardly be one saved. All of this, according to you and the Sorbonne, in no way breaks with the Redemption of Jesus Christ, and it is thus a deception that Jesus Christ be called Savior, Redeemer, atoner of the world, a victim of the world's sins, a bringer of propitiation not only for our sins but for those of the entire world, etc. The world becomes a handful of those predestined for grace, and the more grace was necessary in the world by virtue of original sin, the stingier God was in dispensing it despite the Redemption and merits of Jesus Christ. You have here in truth a haughtily sublime theology, yet you call it something summoned from the reserves of faith. I confess to you I cannot gainsay all these absurd blasphemies which deliver up Christianity bound and gagged to the derision and sarcasm of the unbelievers."[61]

To thereby admit that God should refuse salvation to those who do not know him or cannot know him, to those deprived of the sacrament of baptism, to believe, what's more, that there shall be a precious few of the elect among all those called to the Roman Catholic persuasion—surely here was blasphemy thrown in Christ's face.

For Bergier, the consequences of the "no salvation outside the Church" slogan, far more than verbal expressions or questionable gestures, embodied the true insult to Christly grace and divine love. Here, too, was the deep-set doctrinal weakness of the teaching of the holy church as it confronted the new questionings. With this realization—and it was yet another overturning—were not blasphemers also to be found among those who professed and supported such contradictions, those comfortably ensconced in a reductionist interpretation of God's goodness, the fulcrum of a theological system that made terrifying demands? This upsetting of the order of grace, from which blasphemy also emerged in a toppled state, placed Bergier in a highly marginalized position. Would the work he foresaw completing have allowed him to gain the conviction of others? Probably not for a long time, especially when gauged by Trouillet's epistolary reactions, which—in the eyes of his colleague—were representative of the French clergy as a whole.

Putting aside the suggestion of the curate of Ornans that Bergier's manuscript be burned as heretical, it seems worthwhile to examine the argument that the curate sought to set against that of his Parisian correspondent. Essentially he tried to maintain that its conception of universal salvation bore the mark of blasphemy to the degree it contradicted decisions of the Councils of Lyon, Florence, and Trent. In the process, Trouillet also identified blasphemy with a heterodox theological position. But unlike Bergier, he gauged error primarily by the yardstick of the Roman Catholic Church's teaching and authority rather than that of Scripture. See, for example, the references supported by the fifth and seventh sessions of the Council of Trent.[62] If therefore for the one blasphemy corresponded above all to a terribly limited awarding of grace, for the other it could be likened to a falsification of the church's proposals about how and when that grace was expressed. For the time being, it was clearly this rigorist theological approach defended by Trouillet that continued to prevail. Clerics saturated with Augustinianism, rooted in "doctrinal immutability,"[63] would uphold the perception of a harsh God parsimonious with the salvation of souls. Bergier's Christ was too charitable and "his" God too good, to repeat the Besançon vicar general's formulation when the *Traité de la miséricorde divine* (Treatise on divine mercy) was posthumously published in 1821.[64]

Without having actually condemned Bergier, the church was absolving herself of any stain of blasphemy before continuing the struggle.

The tendencies plainly manifested at the end of the seventeenth century by judicial decisions, jurists' writings, and the hesitations of theology all took part in myriad ways in a kind of decriminalization of blasphemy throughout Europe. This inclination was illustrated especially in the justice administered by the princes and the nobles of the seigniories. The crime that was always denounced as the most horrible of those committed by humanity was left to itself and to those who sinfully committed it. A few tragic exceptions aside, few blasphemers lost their lives after 1670 for only dishonoring God's name. The abatement of repressive measures, dramatically at odds with the entire arsenal available to magistrates and clerics, was more and more noticeable during the eighteenth century.

This incremental overturning kept pace with several essential and thoroughgoing movements shaping modern Europe's political and religious culture. At an early point, the consolidation of the sovereign's power was already a reason to no longer actually fear blasphemers, to no longer regard them as dread or formidable disrupters of the monarchical order. As it became clear that religious renewal and then the fading of confessional conflicts were undeniable realities, the threat posed by blasphemy was also relativized. Perhaps there should be added to this a certain wriggling out of the shackles of fear of the divinity, a diminished preoccupation with collective punishment, sending each individual to consult his or her conscience. The state's progressive secularization in the eighteenth century, as well as the contestation of the traditional system of justice, probably did the rest.[65] From then on blasphemous speech, whose control had been at stake for asserting power in the sixteenth and seventeenth centuries, receded by degrees from the public sphere, and the blasphemer was recontextualized in the private domain. There the church could still strive to communicate to the blasphemer its word and its judgment. Was the church really heard and understood, however, since, in its very bosom, blasphemy was the object of such differing and nuanced assessments?

Nonetheless, the amplitude of these shifts within the heart of Western society should not be unduly exaggerated. A concern with the valuation of sin, in official discourse, was far from having completely lost its grip. However displaced it was toward the private, blasphemy as object could still be used to expose a relative's or neighbor's bothersome behavior to public condemnation or to the law. In other respects, it continued to provide a label for any attack on or breach of orthodoxy, even including theology. Recall that Beccaria himself would be so labeled by the anonymous critic who authored *Notes et observations sur le livre "Des délits et des peines"* (Notes and observations on the book "On Crimes and Punishments"), accusing Beccaria of having put forth "horrible blasphemies against the ministers of religion by saying their hands were bloodstained . . . [and] that humankind owed all its gratitude to the philosopher and that this philosopher is Monsieur Rousseau."[66]

However radical and widely aired these positions, they did not represent an absolute consensus or any longer dictate the lines of an uncontested collective behavior. The eighteenth century "desacralized" the sin by taking up in detail blasphemy's extenuating circumstances, by asking itself about its variations of meaning, by limiting the coercive interventions of the state relating to its perpetrations. Jean-Baptiste Robinet's *Dictionnaire universel*, published in 1779, keenly illustrated this growing and public uncertainty, which, according to Enlightenment thinkers, should take hold first in the mind of any magistrate faced with what was still being called a crime. The element of contingency that accompanied any offense against organized religion, the unconscious or negligence that so often presided over a blasphemous statement and its effects, the sometimes tragic role of religion in human passions: did these not help along the genesis within the legislator of "a reticence to rule" on this behavior, and within the judge "a discretion in handing down decisions" affecting it?[67] Were both legislator and judge not led, in sum, to surround themselves henceforth with a prudence close to a public withdrawal?

A guiding intent of our inquiry so far has been to collate the outline of large structures of theology, government, and culture with the movement of doctrinal changes, judicial practices, and social realities implicit behind the play of blasphemy's functional operations. At the close of the ancien régime, France and the rest of western Europe entered into a quite different era when, along with a certain number of institutions swept away by the revolutionary upheavals, there also perished the very notions that had founded or helped define them. During the period from the 1790s to the nineteenth century, the status of blasphemous speech, how it was perceived, accepted, or rejected in relation to the new founding referents of political and religious culture in a changing society, plainly shifted place vis-à-vis the relative continuities of earlier centuries. The traditional approaches were not, however, utterly expunged. This chaotic course, at once an immense distance and a circuit characterized by contradictions, needs to be charted. Its turns also expressed those mutations that affected the sacred values to which blasphemy, of necessity, always alludes.

10 | SACREDNESS ELSEWHERE?

Persistent and Novel Interpretations. On the cusp of the ideological shocks of the Revolution of 1789, the recurrent "figure" of blasphemous speech still shows up here and there in certain texts, discourses, and social practices. Bills of grievances from 1789 supply a telling illustration of its persistence, even if the rare deliberative records that allude to it devote only a few lines to its condemnation.[1] The *cahiers* drawn up by the curates of the Auxerre bailiwick, for example, insisted "that it look into the means of suppressing the frenzy of dueling and wanton license of blasphemers."[2] The *cahiers* presented by the Third Estate, contrary to what had been seen in 1614, no longer fixed on this aspect of religious deviance even if, as in some sporadic instances, a parish (possibly acting under the influence of its pastor) made known its devout wish to see the observance of a few Christian rules of behavior long held to be elementary. The parish of La Chapelle-Vallon, in the Troyes bailiwick, recommended "that Sundays be observed religiously and profane games and amusements be prohibited, along with swearing oaths and blasphemies."[3] Yet, collectively, this question no longer preoccupied communities as a rule, and the order of the clergy knew what an uphill battle undertaking proceedings could be. Having said this, other mentions in 1789 seem nevertheless to understand this transgression in its classic acceptation.

A sampling of writers of the latter part of the eighteenth century who in the course of their engagement with contemporaries, their creative production, and their sources of inspiration were likely to use the word, shows in its turn that such classic meanings were maintained.[4] The word *blasphemy* essentially denoted words or gestures apt to be taken as willfully harming divinity, especially as seen in the writings of the Marquis de Sade.[5] Jean-Jacques Rousseau utilized the term in several places in his letter to Christophe de Beaumont and even more in his *Lettres écrites sur la Montagne* (Letters written on the Mountain).[6] The abbé Augustin de Barruel and Louis-Sébastien Mercier both readily understood it as the articulation of an impiety which could, nonetheless, be redirected toward denoting philosophical or moral propositions that challenged Christianity, even to the point of contesting its universality. Thus, after alluding to the text of the Beatitudes in his *Les Helvétiennes*, Barruel added, "This I know, this language is still too sublime for you; your wise men blaspheme against it."[7] Was he thinking here of Rousseau, whom he accuses of having "found a way to revive the voice of the prophets in order to celebrate a god perishing on the cross, while daring to announce, in the figure of Mary's son meditating on sublime truths, nothing but the wise man lost in his contemplations; [as if] paying homage to Jean-Jacques will allow the making of amends for his blasphemies."[8] In spite of everything, one has passed here, without radical alteration of the general idea, from blasphemy as a verbal act ascribing to God what God is not, to blasphemy as another label for an opinion or indeed a widespread and widely known philosophical *system*, a system Barruel denounces following Beaumont and others.[9] Both likened the airing of criticism against the

Roman Catholic Church and Christianity to the expression of an immense blasphemy which, despite an extreme disproportion between the two kinds of statements, possessed (at least in the view of its despisers) both a unifying and destructive power in its ambitions.[10]

More concretely, albeit outside France but not without a link to French history, prosecutions continued for the crime of blasphemy in the old-time style. The example of the Helvetian principality of Neuchâtel, on which Philippe Henry has focused his fine-grained research, emphasizes the perennial nature of the decree against such speech and of its judicial effects.[11] Although we cannot generalize with any comparable exactitude from such research, the Swiss historian informs us that thirteen of the twenty blasphemy cases handled between 1747 and 1806 unfolded between 1787 and 1806. Close inspection leads to the realization that the social contestation blasphemous speech could carry was never very far in the distance. In many instances, the influence of the French Revolution and the radical subversions it may well have engendered were salient. In 1794 was not a clockmaker of the canton arrested at Rochefort for having made "scandalous remarks against religion and the social order; [and having] wanted to gather up all the Bibles and testaments to make a bonfire out of them and dance the [revolutionaries'] carmagnole all 'round"? Two years later a group of inebriate boys let loose their anger against a crucifix, one of them "urinating thereupon, another showing it his behind, a third apostrophizing the figure of Our Savior, bidding it adieu using the term of address 'Citizen,' the entire episode performed to the songs of the Revolutionaries."[12] At the same time, the cantonal law courts, marked in this locality by the influence of Calvinism, hardly shrank from calling before the bench those who laid blame on the pastors, while also proceeding against those who, in deed and word, openly scorned Christianity. In 1795 for instance, a cabaret owner from Valangin had a brush with the law for having asserted that "the Bible was a book of lying, that he had been most delighted to find someone to whom he could sell it, that had he not had this chance to sell it, he would have placed it on the chamber pot, that people were fools for believing in religion and that as for himself he believed it not."[13]

Nonetheless, with the period that began in 1789 (at least in France), could not the disintegration of the traditional values that founded the Catholic monarchy now direct impious speech toward the monarchy's annihilation? Had not the preceding decades of gradual cultural demolition laid the groundwork for this? The careful distinctions of jurists on the question of the crime of high treason against divinity had limited the range of that dishonor that however, had the potential for compromising God's lieutenant on earth. Prosecuted by the sovereign as a simple infraction of the public order, blasphemy had evidently lost a portion of its freightedness as taboo.

More broadly, this gradual destabilization of previously recognized reference points marked a deeper shift in the perception of the political itself, whereby the king was the first to be affected.[14] If one believes that the French under Louis XIV held the king to be a sacred personage,[15] there is little choice but to register the evidence that this image experienced a certain number of alterations during the second half of the eighteenth century. Events that were more or less spectacular, more or less shared by all, helped modify, by degrees, the perception of the function and nature of royalty. Several dramatic episodes, in varying degrees, played a part in possibly altering the king's sacrosanct image and weakening the force of its impression on his subjects, however difficult it may be to accurately measure the intensity of the image. In 1750 a persistent rumor circulated that the monarch had ordered the kidnappings of children in Paris. A madman, Robert-François Damiens, almost took the life of Louis XV with a knife attack in 1757 and was subsequently put to death. A petitioner's bailiff at the Hôtel de Ville, Moriceau de La Motte, was executed for authoring "words seditious and hostile to the authority of the monarch."[16] And the Parlement of Paris had put up popular opposition to Louis XV's assertion of royal authority to legislate at the time of attempts at reform by his chancellor (and ex-president of the parlement) Maupeou.

With these events one should also associate the more diffuse and longer-term influence of writings of the Republic of Letters and the debates they propagated.[17] From that vantage, political Jansenism, though losing some cohesiveness after the 1770s, probably played a more than tentative role in maintaining and strengthening the process inasmuch as its renewed and far-reaching criticisms of Roman Catholic Church theocracy[18] redounded also onto religious and political despotism, despotism that Roger Chartier describes as "ecclesiastic and administrative or ministerial." Besides this, the prior lengthy reflections of the influential Jansenist theologian Antoine Arnauld (1612–1694) of Port-Royal on the civic autonomy of individual conscience had elaborated the outlines of another ethics, a code of conduct in which other frequent connections between religious belief and political conviction had been forged. When we take up the illuminating conclusions of Shanti Marie Singham, Christian activism and patriotic activism, both communitarian in essence, led at the end of the eighteenth century to a portrayal of the nation, or *patrie*, "on the model of family ties which form the Christian community, in a word: the bonds of fraternity."[19] Styles of thinking henceforth promoted not only debate over traditional values, which were undermined and relativized, but helped usher in new concepts owing to shared cultural references. Notions such as the *patrie* and the *nation* were not without their ambiguities, and susceptible to different interpretations.[20] But, little by little, to royalty's detriment, such notions superimposed themselves on the values of the old order and took part in the "sanctification of the political."[21] It was on the basis of this long maturation that the Revolution sanctioned and intensified a dismantling hastened by secular references. Could blasphemy survive the increasingly violent rejection of the monarchy and church, of the king and the God of Christians? Or were the men of the Revolution not, in fact, authorizing blasphemy to fulfill its denunciatory function by their proposal of other values and another source of the sacred?

A Sacred Observance of the Profane, or the Religion of the Political. Affirming the principles of a new sacrosanctity led to the decapitation of Louis XVI, an act that might appear at the time as the blunt negation of all the preceding attestations and affidavits, the end of all ideological compromises.

The event of January 21, 1793, that claimed nothing less than to "put an end to death"[22] was however less allied to the trauma of murdering the father than to the performance of a veritable sacrificial rite, a sacred gesture that accompanies all foundational acts. But if the king's death legitimated thereby the new sacrosanctity of politics by establishing a new scheme of time, it had at the same time to be forgotten, to remain a repressed memory. The deceptive matter-of-factness of the official death certificate of the executed king, omitting as it did to even mention that he had been put to death, ratcheted down this central event to the egalitarian ground level of common fate. One can indeed read it in the tone of any typical death notice:

> *Death of Louis Capet, 21 January last, at ten o'clock twenty-two minutes in the morning. Profession: last king of the French, aged thirty-nine, a native of Versailles, parish of Notre-Dame; resided in Paris, at the Tower of the Temple, married to Marie-Antoinette of Austria.*[23]

This textual treatment thus endorsed the self-sufficiency of an act that had no urgency to owe anything to history. The new sacrosanctity that put the republican ideal at the center of the nomenclature of essential things, enriched as it was thanks to the vagaries of revolutionary events and the threats from abroad, rejected blasphemy and apparent outrage by ousting royalty and its memory. But above all it was the rejection of Christianity that henceforth seemed to confirm the exclusion of royalty.

In this respect the movement of de-Christianization of Year II (fall of 1793), marked by popular costumed parades or masquerades and rampant iconoclasm, aptly illustrates just how drastically religion was dislocated into the new context of politicized practices.[24]

The emphasis of these practices was on breaking forever with references familiar to all, with a community of thought and sensibility; on demystifying Christianity's presumed divine character, assailing once and for all the prohibitions, and breaking through or, rather, erasing, that limit that had been set and maintained between profane and sacred. Everyone could now be shown how (according to the new adopted code) the profane could be transformed into the sacred. Minutely detailed descriptions of the profanatory acts reported by municipal officials or secretaries of popular associations lent support to political grievances. And they put forth the fulfillment of an act that was total and deliberate: to destroy the most powerful symbols through a publicly demonstrated show of force in order to clear a razed space for laying new foundations. Such was the municipality of Corbeil's undertaking when it ordered "consumed by fire the infected cadaver, the wicked mummies of the so-called 'Saints' Spire, Guérin, Lou, and Norbert, and the remains thrown into the river while the people look on."[25] More striking yet was a scene that unfolded on Brumaire 27, Year II [November 17, 1793], in the village of Laître-sous-Amance in Lorraine. François Bouchon, until that time the village curate, gave a speech "on the superstitions of idolatry." He then betook himself to the church tabernacle,

> pulled from it a ciborium and, taking in hand a wafer, asked to perish on the spot if this wafer housed the divinity. He invited his ene mies, in the event there were any among the assembled, to join their wishes to his own that there fall upon his head before he should leave the temple that same vengeance that was visited upon On, Korah [Jude 11, Acts], Dathan [Numbers 16:1, 12, 24, 25, 27; 26:9; and

Psalms 106:17] and Abiram [also mentioned with Dathan in the same verses of Numbers and Psalms] if he were truly a profaner. No one present witnessed any prodigy or miracle. Several citizens in attendance then consumed the wafers, shared them with the curate in the midst of a great calm and the most complete fraternity.[26]

Defiance in such a form, at once dramatic and typical of conditioning by custom, bore much resemblance in its details to scenes of which Protestants during the Reformation had been the cause.[27] But the absence of a sign from God in the face of the profanation of Bouchon's raid on the host stemmed from an interpretation radically different from the reform context. The Calvinists had read such absence as the sign of heavenly approbation, a silent helping hand lent to their determination to expose the smoke and mirrors of Catholic trickery. For the generation of Year II, silence was proof of the heavens' emptiness or, at the least, of a heaven emptied of the traditional God of Christians. Here perhaps is also one reason for identifying those who acted out these deeds and words more as *profaners* (breakers with a sacredness from past traditions) than as *blasphemers* (those in defiance of a sacredness that continues to live on).

And yet, the clerics often at the center of these actions could in fact show themselves to be blasphemers of the truest stripe, though they did so on the occasion of other deeds and developments connected with Year II's program of de-Christianization. The justifications they offered to explain their abdication of the priesthood are telling. A researcher of this phenomenon, Michel Vovelle, is careful, however, not to confuse voluntary ex-priests with blasphemous clerics. In southeastern France the latter comprised roughly 20 percent of those who accounted for their decision.[28] Here one must be clear about what the terms meant. Many of the expository defenses of these acts of abdication denounced, in larger measure, fanaticism and superstition, the use made by the church of its power to cultivate fallacies and illusions and sustain the people in their ignorance so as to exploit their credulousness.[29] According to the more familiar acceptation, only clerics with open scorn for "a religion that degrades man because it forces us to worship, in place of a bastard, the son of Mary" could be considered blasphemers.[30] The negation of Christ's divinity led certain men of the cloth to reject the existence of God; witness a former canon of Puy, Dauthier de Saint-Sauveur, who "regarded with horror as unworthy and destructive of the existence of a creator any opinion that would make him into a bizarre, unjust, and spiteful being."[31] But when one must contend with declarations of atheism, is it still appropriate to speak of blasphemy? All those who acted out these public renunciations of the traditional references, often active members of popular associations or municipal officials, played their part on their respective scales in the symbolic relocation of the sacrosanct. And did not these ex-members of the priesthood foster the conveyance of religious values in which they had been trained into the novel field of the political?

This field was constructed first from notions—fraternity, the people, the nation—which did not, however, mean the same things before and after 1790.[32] For Vovelle, the meaning of *patrie* underwent a revaluation, even a transcendence, informed first by the context of war from 1792 on, and subsequently by the declaration of a nation endangered from without. The notion of "the people" shifted from a plural freighted with particularism (Mirabeau's France as "this aggregate of disunified peoples") to a dynamic, robust singular that would found the cornerstone of democratic speech at the time of the Revolution's bourgeois phase.[33] The historian further inflects this inventory of revolutionary values to insist on the emergence of (or the conferring of new titles upon) happiness, dignity, security, equality, violence, and punishment within a new order of meanings.[34]

This new glossary of founding terms, whose referential intensity varied according to circumstance, was enriched by notions that further defined the individual's share in the sacred: the State, the Republic, the Citizen. The republican catechisms, in this respect, afforded a quite detailed and concrete reflection of the inviolable, essential values that determined the reality of the Revolution's ideological principles.[35] Their maxims and poems and the texts of their anthems confirmed the importance of the liberty of the world, the love of country and hatred of tyrants and traitors. These repositories of the new faith also made other categories salient: familial ones (paternal love, filial piety) and chiefly ethical ones associating (via variable taxonomies) stoicism with disinterestedness, friendship with frugality, courage with good faith. All these patriotic productions laid claim, sometimes with great clarity, to their role of carrying the old into a radically new context: "In place of going to the mass, we shall go to drill. Our catechism shall be the Constitution; our confessionals, the sentry box, and instead of excoriating our sins we shall be on the lookout there for those of others."[36]

These fundamental cultural mutations were accompanied by placement of a high value on securing *words* for the cause. Searching for and maintaining an ongoing practice of democracy gave broad authority to those who spoke in the name of the sovereign people, whether having a true mandate or not. The circulation of words, as well as rhetorical triumph, made revolutionary speech one of the stakes of power, a major form of political engagement. Once this had come about, how could the edification of a new sacrosanctity, the import and urgency of speech in its multiple forms and venues, wholly exclude blasphemous speech from becoming one of the period's preoccupations?

When faced with the public demonstrations and protests, members of the local committees of surveillance and general security in the French departments repeatedly brought up, in their police reports and proceedings against certain citizens, the problem of "uncivil comments."[37] This wording was most often code for defeatist opinions toward military difficulties and setbacks, signs of discontent in the face of problems supplying troops on a daily basis, and criticism of obligatory conscription, which might have even led some to long openly for the monarchical regime by letting loose with a "Long live the King!" These incidents, scattered and spontaneous, were not generally considered blasphemous per se, inasmuch as they were not integrated into larger declarations or speeches, and as they were uttered by individuals who counted themselves outcasts from the circle of republican values. Such suspects, instead, trusted in the time of kings, hoped for the return of the royalist fugitive *émigrés*, and identified themselves with the Revolution's nonbelievers.[38] Official actions taken against these suspects should be seen within the framework of more traditional suppression, directed toward minimizing the slightest signs of opposition, without any need to invoke charges of verbal profanation.

Far different, however, was the content of certain other forms of accusatory discourse: for conspicuous declarations that perverted the republican line of speech against questioning the essential revolutionary bases, there was little hesitation about recurring to the label of blasphemy. This explains why when records of the term's use between 1792 and 1794 are consulted, the charge does not always uniformly apply to the same kind of inculpation or to the same values blasphemy was accused of flouting. The protean category of blasphemy metamorphoses at the mercy of the tumult of circumstances in this period. Unlike those accused of "uncivil" words, the blasphemers who were called on to answer for their crime, for instance in Maximilien Robespierre's addresses, always directly and direly threatened the regime. They were kings or tyrants, federalists or enraged malcontents, or indeed unscrupulous agents of the one or the other. The concern was to inscribe under the denomination of blasphemy the conspiracy's organized world. In a speech delivered at the end of Ventôse II [March 1794], Robespierre tagged the federalists Ducos, Fonfrède, and the corrupted Delauny and d'Espagnac as an "impure horde being paid to blaspheme."[39] And after William Pitt's manifest was published in November 1793, speaking of the other European kings, Robespierre wrote, "They accuse us of rebellion, slaves in revolt against the sovereignty of peoples; do you not realize that this blasphemy can only be justified by victory?"[40] Impious speech was accused of taking aim not only at the symbols of those current newcomers to power—the Republic, the people, and their sovereignty—when it was in fact a matter of targeting the enemies and the crowned heads allied against France, but also at the political representation of the nation, when the *Enragés* or Girondins were already wrongly contesting the legitimacy of these symbols.[41] Blasphemy seemed still more intolerable when it resonated from the rafters of a holy enclosure: the meeting places of the Convention or the Revolutionary Tribunal. At the handing down of the notorious law of Prairial 22, II [June 10, 1794], which practically did away with all rights to a legal defense, Georges Couthon decried

> all those officious defenders [given over to] the tyrant's accomplices, namely all the conspirators. A thing hard to believe, that when liberty was under threat by perpetual conspiracies the law itself persisted in seeking out helpers for its own enemies. The tribunal that was instituted to punish them echoed with blasphemies against the Revolution and treacherous declarations whose purpose was to put it on trial in the presence of the people.[42]

This apparently novel use of the charge of blasphemy was not however exclusive. Revolutionary conditions in fact favored its strange return onto the scene of what truly became religious ritual in a new setting.

The cult of martyrs to the new notion of Liberty, the republican Decalogue, the civic "baptism" or "Lenten sermons" aimed at the new Citizen, all drew more or less directly on a crypto-Catholic storehouse of cultural meanings. But clearly the cult of the Supreme Being and belief in the immortality of the soul did the most to restore the pristine eminence of the blasphemous act. Did the climate of 1794 lend itself to such a rein-stallment? François-Alphonse Aulard contends that it did, by drawing attention to the Christian inspiration behind a good many printed speeches on revolutionary occasions. He cites specifically from the speech by Michault-Launoy to the residents of Vaugirard at the inaugu-ral ceremony for the Temple of Reason on Nivôse 20, II [January 9, 1794]: "Citizens, for the principles of religion, nature and reason and even of Jesus Christ, [words] are written on our doors and hearts: unity, indivis-ibility of the French Republic, liberty, equality, or death. These are our political and moral Gospel."[43] The tilt toward using such rhetoric seems to have steepened after the Hébertistes were eliminated.

But it was the more or less evident passage from the cult of Reason to that of the Supreme Being that markedly modified the spiritual climate.[44] Whereas the cult of Reason's "Great Architect" remained a more remote figure, the invocation of a "Supreme Being" (often alluded to in the eigh-teenth century in the context of a Christian culture) brought God per-haps slightly closer to human beings. Yet setting up a feast day and voting into law legislation that structured belief made the denomination less tol-erant and the accusation of blasphemy more apt to play an integral part therein. The Jacobin Society's address at the National Convention on Floréal 22, II [May 11, 1794], mentioned a certain number of "sacred prin-ciples" held to found the Republic's collective and civic morality: "The existence of the Divinity, the afterlife, the sanctity of the social contract and the laws." These articles of faith were put forth not as "dogmas of religion but as sentiments of sociability."[45] But they led to the exclusion of "the one who dares state he does not believe them [because he] rises up against the French people, humankind, and nature." It was in the name of these principles that the speech concomitantly stigmatized "the wicked clamors of atheism and ... the blasphemy of Brutus repeated by impure mouths."[46] In this context, Robespierre himself had to intervene to have a proposal by Marc Antoine Jullien removed which called for expulsion pure and simple "from the Republic [of] those who did not believe in the Divinity."

In the opinion of the popular societies, the establishment of the cult of the Supreme Being was also viewed as putting a welcome halt to the development of a militant atheism that at the time was viewed as negatively as had been the claims made by the Roman Catholic clergy in earlier days. As the popular Association of Vernoux, for example, reported at the Convention on Thermidor 1, II [July 19, 1794], "The Supreme Being, whom you have avenged for the blasphemies of the impious one, with his all-powerful hand has parried the blows directed against two representatives: we show our thanks to him for it."[47] Intervening on behalf of the Revolution, God justified and sanctified it, dismissing the twin pair of atheism and Catholic "superstitions" alike.

However, despite—or rather thanks to—the success of the celebration of Prairial 20, II [June 8, 1794], Robespierre does not seem to have wanted to drape this new cult in an excessively worshipful reverence. Valier, one of those who publicly mocked the Supreme Being at the end of Prairial, was not reprimanded for doing so.[48] And Robespierre arranged to have rebuffed a petition from Citizen Magenthier from the section of the Unity in Paris, submitted to the Jacobins on Thermidor 7 [July 25], which advocated returning the harshest punishments for blasphemers against the divinity:

> Fellow legislators, deign to pass an act that, for serving to sanction the man who has acknowledged the existence of the Supreme Being and the Immortality of the Soul, and for guaranteeing the memorable celebration of 20 Prairial last, punishes with death the very first individual in the vast extension of the Republic who shall ever harbor within his heart to express and utter with his mouth the infamous blasphemy which is daily to be heard amid the public and the various associations. This blasphemy, punishable by a people who wish to enforce the rule of law and set great examples, is the phrase *Sacré nom de Dieu* ["In the bloody name of God!" or "Goddammit!"]. I tremble from having to spell out these four words, but hope's law dictates my doing so because I dare not believe that they shall be expunged and proscribed from the hearts of every one of my brothers and sisters.[49]

Such a motion before the assembly implies the unstated obverse of a subversive resistance that might cause trouble for an already codified creed which had been imposed by law and was, for some, too near the religion of the old order. This was a proposal to reintroduce blasphemy in its primitive function. Linked directly with the refusal, more or less veiled or mocking, to recognize the existence of God or the immortality of the soul, and denounced in an especially common and traditional verbal form, impious speech once again could only be eradicated through a blunt ruling intended to inspire an exemplary terror. Resort to the death penalty directly harked back to the most draconian legislative acts of the Capetian monarchy. These different emphases managed to reinscribe "damnèd speech" within the long chronology of human beings offending heaven without, however, restoring blasphemy as a strictly *religious* deviation. By changing the field of sacrosanct values, the Revolution endowed blasphemy with a wide semantic latitude, one that annexed the very foundations of common human nature.

What is so forcefully accented by the historical actors of 1789 or 1794 is blasphemy's permanence and its corollary: the necessity of sacred or sacralized references, whether religious or not, as guarantors of social and civil cohesion. Yet the resurgence of incriminations for scandalous speech, with the founding of the cult of the Supreme Being at the end of the Convention, at that time dominated by the Mountain, had the effect of confusing the issue all over again.[50] The attempts by jurists of the Enlightenment to scale down the offense had given way to the sanctification of the political and then the return to an inevitably transcendent meaning. Was blasphemy once again to be heard and practiced everywhere?

11 | SPEECH AND EXPIATION

Does asking whether blasphemy was once again ubiquitous thanks to the Terror allow the historian to consider the events of the early nineteenth century as a simple replication of what had been experienced much earlier with the conquering European monarchies? The answer is not obvious. For if blasphemy was again to be found at the crossroads of the cultures of power, France's unique context during the years of its last kings bestowed on the offense an original interpretive dimension.

The Time for Atonement. If Restoration Catholic Church discourse resoundingly heralded a return to rigorist morality and reiterated its teachings on contempt of things of this world, it also borrowed heavily from the theme of heavenly vengeance. Without being truly novel this appeal to "God, avenger of all crimes," now intended to erase the preceding century's guilty strayings from religion and monarchy, and to castigate the accursed revolutionary decade.[1] This period of chronic sinfulness and recurrent blasphemy—evil to the point of sacrificially executing a king—now demanded an atonement that must be continuous, tireless, solemn, and communal. Renewed emphasis on missions of Catholic ministry in France after 1815 and the important place it accorded devotion to the cross encouraged the equation of Catholicism with an entire kingdom's penitence and expiation. Accounts of these missions regularly insisted on this expiatory obligation and on those reiterated pleas to God for forgiveness.[2] One example is a text written by the abbé Rauzan, in March 1816, at Angers. "We gave three short but very pointed and bracing exhortations," the priest reported,

> the first to prepare the people for a solemn atonement to be made to the cross for all the wrong it had received in France since the Revolution. The first signal was given and this vast people, in all the same instant, made its solemn amends. The second oration prepared all hearts for the general forgiveness extended for all the offenses for which the residents of this diocese might have to reproach themselves during these past twenty-five years. The second signal was given and the people shouted "Yes, forgiveness for all and let it be absolute! We wish forever to be the children of God and the king!" Finally in a third oration we instilled in the people a consciousness of the need to make final solemn and silent amends to Louis XVI, Louis XVII, the august Marie-Antoinette, the inimitable Elisabeth, the king and his august family, for the long and cruel injuries they have received from so many people who have had the evil misfortune of abjuring the character of Christians and the virtues of their fathers. The third signal was given. At which time what cries were raised toward Heaven! What tears of joy flowed! This ritual of reparation for sins committed was ended with the collective vow to spill one's last drop of blood to preserve the Faith and the legitimate king.[3]

As this passage emphatically shows, the church's task during the Restoration was not restricted to leading individuals along the path of repentance to salvation. It consisted also in assuring the monarchical regime that it had the political support of all the faithful. The slightest whim or volition to be disobedient, a clear index of return to sinful erring, would call down punishment from heaven. In this sense, the terrible cholera epidemic of 1832 represented, for certain sermoners, the divine answer to the violently anticlerical Revolution of 1830. For despite the Catholic clergy's efforts and its appeal to the most diverse forms of repentance, the culture born of 1789 and the republican mindset had shaped the behaviors of a population deaf to appeals, definitively impious, and thereby responsible for the misfortunes God's wrath afflicted on the country.[4] This is the climate in which blasphemy's perception and role need to be situated and analyzed.

We recall that the eighteenth century had begun a line of thought of a juridical, then theological, order about the distinctions that could exist in manifestations of blasphemy and their differing degrees of seriousness. Following the period from 1830–1835, the moral theology of Liguori that gained ground through a great many different routes in France unquestionably favored adopting a relatively liberal position on judging blasphemous speech.[5] The abbé Pierrot in an article he contributed to the *Dictionnaire de théologie morale*,[6] following Cardinal Gousset on the question,[7] naturally took up again Saint Thomas's characterization of blasphemy "as the greatest of man's sins." But this he nuanced from the outset by qualifying that this grave sin "can become venial by [there having been a] lack of proper heedfulness, by an impulse of impatience and a disregard for what the spoken words signified." In the same vein, blasphemy's habitual formulations were dutifully enumerated (denying to God what belonged properly to him, ascribing to him what was not godly). But the moralist specified also what was *not* blasphemy and mortal sin: "Introducing the names of God, the Virgin Mary, the saints into ordinary and profane conversations, though they be pronounced in no religious spirit. . . . The uttering, either with composure or in a transport of anger or impatience, the word 'damned' [*sacré*], which one uses most often with certain vulgar expressions more or less insulting to one's fellow Christians[;] . . . nor speaking the holy Name of God in vain. These words which one shouts out most often in a fit of impatience are not at all against *God* according to the intention of he who takes the liberty of using them but against men, animals, inanimate beings." And the article's author concluded that these were simply oaths or swearwords and that if doubts remained upon hearing the sinner's avowal, the confessor must act as if there were no blasphemy proper.

This moral position set blasphemy's "global" limits. It did not confuse verbal habits with deliberate resolve to commit a sin or offense, and refused to consider every profanity as insolent speech against God. Even as it reached back to adopt several casuistic propositions from earlier periods, however, it remained a minority position in the Catholic clergy of the time. The Restoration's religious spirit tended to ratify the traditional broad conception of blasphemy.

From this viewpoint the work of Jacques Marguet, pseudonym of the abbé Daux, who was a priest of the diocese of Metz, was exemplary. His essay on blasphemy of 1820, *Essai sur le blasphème,* was a great publishing success and had a wide distribution: eight editions between 1820 and 1823, followed by nine more between 1823 and 1829. On soil that would become the state of Belgium, the book saw nine editions between 1821 and 1822; its author himself informs us that a translation existed in Dutch and that "the Catholic Society of Belgium" made available "six copies to each of its members."[8] Marguet's approach did indeed equate profane with blasphemous speech, thus encouraging the return to a broader definition of the latter. "In each instance, when one utters one of these oaths or blasphemies deliberately or even without giving thought to it, by the effect of unretracted habit, one closes one's soul to Heaven and deserves Hell."[9] The idea, dwelt on systematically in several of the book's passages, translates a refusal to circumscribe blasphemy within the limited categories of moral theology.[10] Impious speech, perceived in these encompassing terms, seems to go hand in hand with a spreading of the phenomenon into the social and political fields.

A second illustrious example of this tendency is furnished by the reflections and instructions of Jean-Baptiste-Marie Vianney, curate of Ars. In his sermon on the second commandment, inspired mainly by the *Catéchisme des peuples de la campagne et de la ville* (Catechism of communities of the country and city), he proposed a distinctive approach by, at the same time, making distinctions among profane oaths, curses, perjuries, and blasphemies; and defending his rigorist position in refusing to take into consideration extenuating circumstances.[11] "An unfortunate in a moment of anger might say, 'God is not just to cause me suffering.' With such words he has abjured God in His goodness, and this is not swearing but uttering a horrible blasphemy."[12] He must know that "terrible punishments await him in the next life."[13] "To put you in mind of this sin's enormity," Vianney wrote at the beginning of his sermon, "it would need a way of making you understand the greatness of the injury and wrong this sin does to God, something that never shall be given to mortal man to understand; no, my brothers, there is only the wrath, the power, the fury of a God, all concentrated and brought to bear on those hellish monsters, and all of which can force those monsters to feel the enormity of their heinousness."[14] The pastoral work of Vianney and its influence at this time seemed such that several reports testified to blasphemy's eradication in his parish. While on pilgrimage to Ars in August 1841, Laurent Paul-Marie Brac de la Pierrière witnessed,

> on returning home to the hostess of his lodging, a scene that gave him a high idea of the influence of this pastor of Ars. Three men leading two horses hitched together with a large cut tree trunk shorn of its roots arrived at a stream at the same moment we arrived there. They attempted to make the pair of horses ford the stream. One of the horses reared, lost its footing, and fell causing the team to meet with an accident. The man rushed up and got the animal back on its legs. Until this point the occurrence was completely natural, but what was unnatural was to have expressed not the least disapproval in an impulse of anger, to have addressed not a single reproach, and thus directed neither blows nor curses at the poor beast. We looked on with surprise. Such remarkable restraint on the part of peasants threatened in their immediate interests was unknown to us.[15]

After Marguet and Vianney, other priests upheld in their writings this traditional and expanded position on blasphemy. In 1839 Jacques Valentin reendowed the notion with all of its prior signification by defining it as "a harmful locution expressed in words, writings, or signs, and even conceived in the mind alone, against God, against the saints, against things sacred, or other creatures considered works of God. It is a very grave sin admitting of no mildness or leniency in the matter."[16] About twenty years later, the anonymous author of *Le Blasphème flétri* (Blasphemy branded for what it is) persisted in this direction by neatly subdividing blasphemies into the cases included in the text, which numbered eight, and its mega-varieties, numbering six.[17]

Affirming this theological extension of the sin could not help but bear out its increased social prevalence. Marguet followed upon a good many others when he recalled its sustained frequency and its pervasiveness, as if the church's efforts in this instance had been to no avail: "Among poor as among rich, the common people as well as warriors, dwellers in the country as well as the city, among children who can hardly articulate their few words as among old men with one foot in the grave—almost all open their mouths in protest against heaven, bringing forth blasphemies.[18] This "veritable social scourge," as described in *Le Blasphème flétri*, was all the more common as recent French history had contributed to creating and promoting "a huge army of blasphemers that besieges Heaven"[19] by continuing to speak in the name of profane values. Henceforth the blasphemer was no longer only a believer temporarily gone astray. He was an enemy of the church, nourished by the despised memory of the Revolution, and perhaps less a provocateur toward God than an aggressor toward sincere Catholics loyal to the faith of ages.

In short, with the Restoration came forward a new figure of the blasphemer—one who might be found among the liberals, the republicans, the workers. If conformist authors had always singled out to the attention and conscience of their readers those whom heaven had struck down for their defiance, they now chose, besides the drunkards and gamblers, new sinful figures: the Voltairian bourgeois, partisans of progressive or socialist ideas, freethinkers, workers, and protesters from all quarters.[20] It was an entire population, though always male, presented as an enemy of the church, of God, of the king—and which the distinctly anticlerical Revolution of 1830 encouraged and confirmed in this role. Even more, the widening circle of unbelief at the time of the "Second Enlightenment," the church's allegiance to political power, and the forging of a republican identity (often constructed in opposition to clericalism and even Christianity) largely reinforced and consolidated the perennial nature of this negative impression. Thus one can still read in Victor Blateau's *Le catéchisme catholique*, published in the middle of the Second Empire, this characteristic example of how the blasphemer was perceived socially:

In the township of Capian in the Gironde, there was a man of a certain social standing who, being a supporter of Cabet and Proudhon, was spreading communist doctrines in his harangues; he was moreover a skeptic in religion and inveterate freethinker. On the Sunday of the octave of Corpus Christi, he could be found outside a seal maker's near the church. At that spot, he was expounding in front of a few persons his baneful teachings when suddenly a violent storm struck. Our freethinker, looking upward to the heavens on fire, began shouting words of defiance at the thunder and lightning and hurling his irony skyward as he yelled to them, as he would have to a firing squad, "Come on then, fire, fire!" A bolt of lightning, as if having heard his appeal or rather his challenge, flashed from the sky and fell upon this man.[21]

The fierce reprise of this conception of the sin in its wider compass, and all the supernatural effects it engendered, perhaps constituted a desperate response to the total disengagement on the part of the state and its courts from efforts to repress such behaviors. From September 1791, the Constituent Assembly had equipped the system of justice with a penal code that had dropped a certain number of offenses now deemed "imaginary" [*imaginaires*]. Along with the crimes of heresy, that of high treason—against the divinity and the king—had been done away with.[22] High treason *against the sovereign* had been reintroduced for a time in the new penal code of February 1810 and defined by Count Berlier as a "crime reduced to clearest terms; alone is a person guilty who has taken part in an attempt on the life of or a conspiracy against the person of the Emperor."[23] In this way blasphemy found itself excluded from offenses that could be prosecuted. Strong support from the church for the constitutional monarchy did not modify the situation. Yet, without aiming directly at blasphemous speech, legislative decisions did allow for punishing a certain number of infractions or derelictions regarding religion. Such was the statute of Count Beugnot's of June 7, 1814, on the observance of Sundays and feast days, followed by the law of November of the same year, applying to the enforcement of no labor on Sunday, to public displays of leisure, and the closing of cabarets. This stiff prohibition of public merriment and amusements on the Lord's day illustrated the concern to reestablish Sunday's holy character, so ill treated by professional habits, gaming, and dances. And despite numerous derogations foreseen and accorded, this law continued to have bad press up until its elimination in 1880, inasmuch as it showed the influence and open meddling of the clergy in social life.[24]

The same tendency is illustrated just as clearly by the law on sacrilege debated on January 4, 1825, and promulgated on the following April 20. It consisted not only of extremely stern punishment for committing theft in Catholic Churches, all in the name of public order as Count Breteuil, the keeper of the seals, affirmed,[25] but it also had other objectives. Uppermost was its intent to reintroduce the religious dimension into penal legislation so as to break with the legacy of 1791.[26] Adopting the letter of this law, the Bordeaux court expressed its wishes that "one no longer hear the blasphemous statement that the law is and must be atheistic and that in a State whose monarch deems it an honor to wear the title of most Christian king, the objects of worship of the great majority of Frenchmen and the State religion shall find a special protection in the laws."[27] Was it not incumbent on legislators to reestablish or strengthen the meaning of the sacred in peoples' minds through a negative standard of reference, namely, sacrilege, as a reminder that any direct assault on God was an assault on the king, and that this continuing delegate of God on earth had the duty "to remedy such deplorable neglect and error"?[28] Why then choose sacrilege over blasphemy? Sacrilege, a far less frequent offense, remained easier to quell and above all tagged a form of offense, namely theft, still considered by all of society as especially weighty in comparison with the general depreciation of unlawful speech in social relations. It also recalled all the horrendous acts committed against sites and objects of worship during the Revolution, against whose recurrence one must henceforth be armed. Finally, these legal condemnations offered the church a chance to impose, with the state's help, a kind of forced mass expiation, which in turn served to redouble the expressions and practices of redemption it was organizing. Yet, in the church's view, was this enough?

The aforementioned 1820 essay by Marguet suggests the full extent of the offensive undertaken in Catholic milieus that had made their case to public powers. The work's second part was taken up with appeals that recalled to readers the old royal laws against blasphemy, citing a few exemplary precedents and still harsh rulings—as though to insist that the monarchy's regained continuity would require the law to be upheld. To shore up this advocacy, the author invoked judicial rulings by France's neighboring sovereigns. Had not a decree by the Savoy Senate (dated May 6, 1818) sentenced to irons "for two years with public humiliation, at Annecy, François Darriet-Balmatin, convicted of having blasphemed the name of God in the parish of Gonfli in the presence of two witnesses"? Marguet cited next the example of the Spanish king who, in September 1819, on the occasion of his marriage, pardoned a certain number of criminals, excepting blasphemers. And he recalled finally the case of sentencings recently handed down by English tribunals "against several blasphemers." Marguet pointedly reminded readers of the British Parliament's decision, conveniently well timed for his purposes, to "renew the harsh laws brought to bear in the past against blasphemers."[29] "Grandiloquent and forceful speakers," he continued, "held forth on that occasion on respect toward God being the very basis of societies. It is a people separated from the Church who gave this consoling demonstration to the world; why do the Catholic nations not emulate so eminent an example?"[30] This petition, backed up by the edifying example of a heretical monarchy, was not, however, destined to sway the Bourbons of France. No law on blasphemy was promulgated. Lack of legislative action, and thus the absence of officially attested limits, probably encouraged the Catholic Church to make blasphemy cover such a wide area and, perhaps even more so, to use other means to show the offending populations of language-poisoners that God's justice might sternly, and at any instant, substitute for the deficiencies of human law.[31] Recourse to this tactic, as we have seen, was not unknown. But it was much more systematically deployed in a good number of early-nineteenth-century works that took up the topic and that were filled with wretched drunkards found fallen stone-dead on the spot after having blasphemed, with young provocateurs struck down where they stood after insulting a crucifix, with workers wiped out for having presumed to defy their Creator.[32]

Still, these fables with their blunt lesson were not sufficient.[33] In the face of the sin's pervasiveness and the authorities' witting inertia, heaven itself turned out to be once again called upon as it intervened on several occasions to inculpate human sinfulness, a prelude to fearsome catastrophes. . . .

The Voice of Heaven. God's interference in the face of blasphemy's perpetuation took its place in a broad movement of miraculous phenomena generally connected with supernatural apparitions or messages from heaven. Their content was antirevolutionary and most often apocalyptic. It was at the end of the Restoration and under the July Monarchy that these signs proliferated, at first marked by a sure coherence or consistency. Except for the luminous cross that appeared in the sky at Migné, in the diocese of Poitiers in 1826,[34] it was the appearances of the Holy Virgin, or "Mariaphany," that tended to rule the day. In addition, the near totality of visions and celestial revelations concerned women more than men, young people more than adults, the poor more than the well-off. The novice Catherine Labouré in 1830, Mélanie and Maximin in La Salette in 1846, and goat and turkey keepers in the department of the Drôme in southeastern France in 1848 and 1849 formed the first cohort of Mariaphanous visionaries before the other, later waves of them: at Lourdes in 1858, at Saint-Palais in 1876, following those at Pontmain in 1871.[35] A certain number of commonalities shone through the reported content of these supernatural messages: need for conversion and prayer, threats contained in prophetic premonitions. For our purposes, however, it was the testimony of visions experienced by Carmelites at Tours and of the celestial apparition of La Salette that command the most scholarly interest.

On first consideration, the similarity between the two events is not flagrant. The episodes of the Carmelite convent of Tours share an affinity with comparable manifestations witnessed in other monastic settings.[36] The La Salette vision has genuine singularity. It was, in fact, one of the first avouched apparitions in which the seers and especially their accounts founded an eyewitnessed, condoned "proof" at the source of collective gestures organized by the clergy in order to integrate the faith of simple believers into the life of the church.[37] It was also the last significant, heaven-sent antiblasphemy manifestation of the nineteenth century.[38]

Beyond this, each of these episodes introduced very distinct characters into the drama: Christ at the Carmelite convent, and the Holy Virgin in the Dauphiné region; Sister Marie de Saint-Pierre, who was privy to numerous confidences, and the two young Alpine shepherds who heard the same message. Yet for all their differences, their resemblances were not negligible. The two incidents were contemporary: the events at Tours began on August 26, 1843, the day after the feast day commemorating Saint Louis, and continued beyond the apparition at La Salette on the September 19, 1846. The nun at the Tours convent did not fail, moreover, to announce and interpret the vision of the children of Corps. But from this study's perspective the parallelism is most of all justified by the content of the "delivered" messages and their practical injunction: to eradicate blasphemy and compel observance of the sanctification of Sunday. By virtue of the brevity of her sole statement, the Virgin Mary was satisfied to name "those who pull carts [and who] know not how to swear an oath without placing the name of [her] Son in the middle of it."[39] Jesus' reiterated communication allowed her to be more prolix on the subject. "Our Lord gave me to understand just how irritated he was by the French nation . . . how much this atrocious sin wrung painfully his divine heart more than all the other sins," the nun reported. Through blasphemous speech, the sinner execrated Jesus to his face, openly attacked him, negated the Redemption. "He made me look at blasphemy as a poisoned arrow that wounded his divine heart continuously."[40] And then there followed this other avowal at the end of the year 1844: "Our Lord made me aware of the extent of his annoyance with France and his oath to avenge himself in his anger if amends were not paid in honor to his divine Father for all the blasphemies of which she is guilty."[41]

Once again, in these different heavenly declarations, one encounters several of the traditional meanings associated with blasphemy. In the transcribed account based on the reports of the young shepherds, it was identified with angry oaths, frequent in country life and elsewhere, which were spoken under conditions of daily labors and difficulties—a definition which Gousset, at the same historical moment, was removing as a sin. It was, however, just such a skimpy or narrower reprobation of blasphemy that made some ecclesiastics suspicious of these other words reported at the time of Mary's visitation: "When you found rotten apples on the ground you were swearing, you were placing among such oaths the name of my Son." A dubious canon from Angers, H. Bernier, wondered if this truly constituted a message of a supernatural cast.[42]

The account from Tours located blasphemy in a completely different register. After having deplored a widespread use that extended even to children, this text did not exactly specify its nature but did point in several instances to the "blasphemies of France." Pierre Servais, a popularizer of the supernatural Carmelite communications, readily perceived in the latter the shadow of 1789: "The Revolution made blasphemy the capital sin of France," he commented.[43] By so accusing the revolutionary period of having instigated a vast and long-lasting anti-Christian movement, he encouraged connecting the Revolution with the roots of blasphemy, ascribing a history to the sin, and thus an explanatory origin that gave his accusation a causal exactitude.

This double denunciation by heaven of impious speech could thus be stated in two rather separate modes. On the one hand, there would be a theological and political interpretation of blasphemy in which the period issuing from 1789 came explicitly under indictment: "In no other time of history did these crimes approach so closely the very throne of my Father." On the other hand would be a more quotidian, spontaneous perception of the offense, seemingly hardly at all occupied with the contemporary historical context. Did the incontestably less polished and uncouth aspect of the speech of these mountain villagers not also have something to do with the possible sources of inspiration that might have guided the elaboration of this perception? One thinks obviously of those famous and numerous "letters fallen from Heaven" whose legend for a long time had circulated through Christendom,[44] and whose reportings the revolutionary events had helped multiply. The genre was highly stereotyped, and it always associated the denunciation of sin with threats of an eschatological kind. By way of example there was the content of this letter left by Christ himself on the altar of the Church of Paimpol, in 1771:

Receive my warning that should you continue to live in sin and should I see neither your remorse nor contrition nor a sincere and true confession and satisfaction, I shall make you feel the full weight of my divine arm. Were it not for the prayers of my dear mother, I would already have destroyed the earth for the sins you commit against one other. I gave to you six days for laboring and the seventh for resting, for sanctifying my name, for hearing the holy mass, and for dedicating the day's remainder to the service of God my Father.[45]

It was the Jesuit Bollandist H. Delahaye, who, at the beginning of this century, had emphasized the indisputable likenesses between these "letters from heaven" and the La Salle declaration. The comparison was favored by the missives that book peddlers put in circulation (inventories of peddlers' wares in 1818 and 1844 attest to their presence in the Dauphiné region) and that were read and recopied or memorized.[46] However much the structure of the La Salette message recalled that of the heaven sent letters, it was not a mere replication of the phenomenon. Besides the admonitions addressed to those who thumbed their noses at Catholic rites and obligations, and the threats and promises, an account that was related the day following the apparition by Pierre Selme and Baptiste Pra, employers of the children involved, does show some origi-

nality. It manages to blend a general discourse with factual details familiar to the young shepherds, thus becoming a personal and specific address
(directly to the shepherds) that markedly modified the law of the genre.[47]
And beyond a more positivistic reading, does there not shine through the
account given by the children of the mountain a style of speaking all their
own, a language referring us back perhaps to one of the only ways the little early-nineteenth-century country boys could summon to say who
they were, to demand a hearing?

There are other reasons to make a case for the complementarity of the
two accounts. Certain contemporaries did not fail to establish a relationship between the two incidents, first among them Sister Marie de Saint-
Pierre. She did so owing to the trickery of the Christly "communiqués" at
the beginning of the year 1847: "My mother hath spoken to men of my
anger; she hath shown me her bosom and told me, 'Here is the bosom
that fed you, allow it to bestow blessings upon my other children.' Then
filled with mercy she came down to the earth. Place your trust in her."[48]
It was Léon Dupont, known as the holy man of Tours, who communicated this "fact" in a letter to the abbé Mélin, the curate of Corps (parish
of La Salette), and who remarked how struck he had been with the spiritual continuity across time that such events uncovered. Did they not also
highlight the importance of worshiping both Mary and Christ, an importance that had already been strongly felt in the eighteenth century among
Catholic populations and widely encouraged in the following century?

Finally the Tours and La Salette messages both associated blasphemy
with not observing the holy meaning of Sunday. The evocation of these
two sinful slights to God in tandem—also a feature of the heavenly letters and thus of little originality—deserves, however, some attention.[49]
Texts of several legislative promulgations issued under the ancien régime
had often included stipulations to enforce the law against these two derelictions, typically together in the same statute, as when an ordinance of
March 1647 was adopted against "blasphemers and profaners of holy
Sundays." That they were treated in conjunction suggests several interpretations. One, strictly theological, highlights the course and process of
sanctification. A certain share of one's time and speech, which were
works of God as far as mortal Christians were concerned, must be
reserved exclusively for praise. Sunday served to sanctify the Creator; and
language to sanctify his name. Profaning Sunday amounted to a "kind of
apostasy," just as blasphemy disclaimed the need to recognize sanctity

and divine perfection.[50] And did God, in his wrath, not mortify and torment human beings with the same chastisement for both offenses?[51]

Another approach allows for making blasphemy a pernicious consequence of not respecting the Sunday observance. In a letter from the young Louis XIV to the bishop of Pamiers, the king clearly brought out this cause-to-effect phenomenon: "In lieu of betaking oneself to church on Sundays to devote oneself to all manner of good works, there are those who busy themselves in trade and working at all sorts of servile tasks, and others in gaming and tavern-going, from which also follow great blasphemies."[52] This kind of argument crosses the centuries and is to be found in the nineteenth century when the more conspicuous abandonment of Sunday worship openly encouraged the frequenting of cabarets, "where man immolates everything before the god of intemperance and debauchery."[53]

And, then finally, there was a more strategic interpretation. Under the ancien régime the church had, with the help of the monarchy and municipal powers,[54] always fought against the opening of cabarets, places conducive to the temptation of profanation, which led people to miss mass and to blaspheme. After 1815 the support of the monarchy, following the law of November 1814, applied only to the limiting of merriment, in the name of the holy respect due to Sunday. Was the reminder of the privileged association between the two attitudes not designed to favor a reactivation of the antiblasphemy measures? It was, however, without state assistance that the bishops pursued the struggle and, from 1830 on, repeated their denunciation of labor on Sundays but through a new means of attack. Profaning the week's first day was not only an act against divine sacrosanctity, it became a sign of disdain for human dignity. Bosses and owners who required their workers to labor on Sunday were placing material interests before those of religion as the worker "under penalty of losing the bread that sustains his life gave up sanctifying the Lord's day."[55]

Thus blasphemy's incrimination, conjoined with disrespect for the day of rest, were part of the resistance toward a society becoming secularized in its daily practices and behaviors and on the road to the mental secularization of those who had so far been spared from the Revolution's influence.[56] Appeals to God to bless or punish the one or the other was at once the mark of an indispensable independent self-assertion and the sign of an avowed powerlessness. Recurring to implacable and pervasive divine justice effectively constituted the final argument that the church, facing its sense of failure, could try as it pitted itself against rebellious groups. After others had done so before him, the abbé Gaume, in his *Profanation du dimanche* (Profanation of Sunday), confirmed at length this catastrophist interpretation, which he believed was engraved in the event of the Revolution:

Ever since 1789, France has incessantly repeated, "I have worked on Sunday and what harm has it done me? How has my well-being suffered from it?" Well, here is the response. Since 1789 there have come about naught but terrible trials, humiliations, sufferings, miseries, and calamities that France has had to undergo. The earth has rumbled continuously under her trampling, and it rumbles even now: revolutions unrivaled in history have covered it with ruin, blood, and bones. The heavens over its head have become brass [Deut. 28:23], and scourges of all kinds have fallen upon it. No other nation has so often been racked with evil war; twice has she been visited by plague, twice has famine handed over to the strife of abject poverty those of her children whom it did not hand over to the horrors of starvation; for five years have her great rivers overflowed their banks and ravaged her cities and countryside; finally a flood whose like has not been seen in human memory has brought about the desolation of her richest provinces and crowned the general conspiracy of the elements against the people who profane Sunday."[57]

Rereading the history of contemporary France in such professedly clerical terms was not the church's only way to intervene against impious attitudes. Priests and bishops, despite the task's arduousness, must continue to offer to sinners the path of repentance, if only to palliate the thickened ominousness of apocalyptic warnings. In the wake of the reprobative apparitions were organized networks of fraternal brotherhoods and expiatory associations, which also closely entwined the fights against blasphemy and profaning Sunday. Such initiatives were not new. Servais reminds us that in the sixteenth century Pius IV, then Pius V, had set up antiblasphemy associations. A few years before the La Salette incident, under Gregory XVI's pontificate and with his encouragement, Father Caravita had founded a society of this type in Rome on August 8,

1840.[58] But after the 1843 and 1846 episodes and for the first time, it seems, the establishment of a brotherhood to combat blasphemy proceeded from a "marvelous origin." Indeed, on November 24, 1843, Jesus had asked the Carmelite order to form "a well-approved and well-organized association to honor the name of [my] Father"—ongoing public outrage against blasphemy calling for some kind of public amends to be made. The archbishop of Tours, Morlot, at first reticent,[59] on August 8, 1844, authorized the curate of Notre-Dame-la-Riche to establish an association to atone for the offenses committed against divine majesty by blasphemers. It would have as its protectors Saint Michael-Archangel, Saint Louis, and Saint Martin, and each of its members would daily recite an Our Father, a Hail Mary, a patriotic Gloria, and the Arrow of Gold (*Flèche d'or*), a prayer of heavenly origin.[60] The actual work of the atonement association, only alluded to in *Voix de l'Eglise* (Voice of the church) in March of 1847 (echoing the events at La Salette), was not, however, a very effective instrument, lacking both genuine penetration among the general population and real support from the episcopacy. It would require awaiting the aftermath of the La Salette apparition for a structure with like spiritual objectives to be put in place across the whole of France.

It was a few months after the report by the little shepherds in January 1847 that Pierre Marche, in the context of a mission that he was arranging in the parish of Saint-Martin-de-Lanoue of Saint-Dizier to promote the resanctification of Sunday, had the idea of starting such a pious institution, "closely tied," to use his own words, "to the apparition of the Queen of Heaven."[61] The curate Marche explained this pastoral initiative by emphasizing that making reparation for blasphemies and the violation of the Sunday ban "is in reality but a new form of the ever age-old truth Jesus Christ came to bring us." But it was an atonement all the more necessary and urgent as "the presiding evil of our century consists in having an imperfect idea of God, in being without affection toward him and maintaining toward him an inexplicable quotient of suspicion and defiance" because "human hearts are not disposed to concede the supernatural." By these means Satan found a foothold to incite men to attack God himself, after having encouraged them to fight against Christ and his church. Blasphemy became "the great crime of the approaching end of days; salvation will lie only in making execrable amends for this crime."[62]

In this eschatological context, the brotherhood represented a last resort. This handful of concerned watchmen would herald a new humanity at the end of the trumpeted catastrophe, like the occupants of Noah's Ark. The worshipful communities that had formed in this way would surely gather together the elect by whom God would once again spare earthly life's total destruction. But through this struggle against blasphemy, Marche, like others, stigmatized the lack of religiosity he felt to be on the rise, even from the time he had taken up his modest parish observation post.[63] "You shall see," he wrote, "that blasphemy is in the history books, in literature, in philosophy, in novels, and in conversations."[64] This identification of impious language with the creative forms of the human mind vividly displays how condemnation was leveled less at linguistic imprecation, in which the La Salette accounts invested so much passion, than at agnostic or atheistic reflection, dubious or nihilistic sarcasm at Christianity's expense. Blasphemy became the tangible and thoroughgoing manifestation of total de-Christianization, and along with the profanation of Sunday, represented its most immediately accessible and obvious form.

Despite the hesitations of a segment "of the Christian people and clergy,"[65] it was one of the pastors' duties to make known the preferences of divine will and organize a resistance many perceived as last-ditch. Marche's widely acclaimed argumentation resulted perhaps from this feeling, but more probably from the popularity of La Salette and its nascent fame as a pilgrimage site, as well as the support (which this time was immediate) from the ordinary of the premises, Monsignor Parisis, the bishop of Langres. From June 27, 1847, he had recognized the Association to Atone for Blasphemy and Breaking the Sabbath. On July 30 of the following year, a brief pontifical elevated the association into an *archiconfrérie*, the title conferred on those religious or charitable societies most valued for their pastoral contributions. Pius IX, who himself became a member, told Marche in confidence when receiving him in Rome, "It is an admirable association, most necessary for France, but necessary also for Rome. The Romans also blaspheme the Holy Name of God, and even, something which is unprecedented, those who love Saint Peter so much have come in our times to blaspheme with his name. Yes, your work is indeed necessary. You are at the forefront of divine work set upon saving society."[66] The enterprise's belief in the doctrine of salvation by the Redeemer also made each member an actor working at the very heart of society. If, by nature, members committed to abstain from blaspheming and from violating the Sunday injunction, they must, in addition, "protest against those social crimes, prevent them by all means within [their] power, and praise God." A member's expiatory function was also expressed through the veneration of the Holy Face. In imitation of Veronica, who wiped Jesus' face during the ascent to Calvary, the association's brothers and sisters emulated the holy woman's gesture as their prayers sought to efface the insults of the much condemned impiety.[67] From February 1848 on, one hundred fifty parishes of the Langres diocese, uniting approximately fifteen thousand of the faithful, came together on this good work. By the following year's end, 833 groups, spread out among sixty dioceses, were to be counted.[68] Parisis, who had been transferred from the bishop's seat of Langres to that of Arras, continued to propagate these pious associations. Between 1853 and 1858, they took root in twenty-eight parishes of the diocese, of which seventeen could be found in the district of Saint Pol and the upper Artois.[69] In the same period, the Rouen diocese association totaled more than nine thousand members.[70]

For lack of credible and recent research, little is known about the association's operations, social composition, and geographic expansion beyond France. Such expansion took place even though the Christly messages clearly singled out this country as the most threatened. Pius's aforementioned papal observation, however, pointedly conveys that the evil was perceived to have spread among all communities of nineteenth-century Roman Catholics. Perhaps the founding, in August 1895, of the League to Atone for Blasphemy Against the Most Holy Virgin by a third-order Franciscan Corsican named Ignatius Padovani embodied the last social and pastoral avatar of any substantial scope in this struggle of the church against blasphemy as a public manifestation of social secularization.[71]

But was not the new dimension blasphemy had taken on—this time limited to profanation of Mary, by the final years of a century that had so heartily favored Mariolatry—the sign of a double failure? It might even be that fighting blasphemy against God was being abandoned, retreating to a line of defense drawn to save the coherence of a worship that nevertheless remained popular.

"Blasphemy," wrote Richard L'Avocat, "is but the fruit of violence or pleasure. And thus what is it, messieurs? Pure malice, blindness of spirit, hardening of the heart, brutishness, faithlessness, ingratitude, atheism."[1]

What then indeed *is* it? This study's recurrent question can at this juncture be reformulated to accommodate the possible meanings of blasphemy's changing historical importance. In the course of our reconstructions, successive disclosures by documentary sources have yielded disparate factual material. But this information perhaps best lends itself to comprehending blasphemous speech from the point of view of its utterers themselves. By such a method we can approach the question of their religious commitment and gain a better understanding of their social practices.

12 | THE TELLTALE SPEECH OF SIN?

We know that interpretations of blasphemy on the plane of *judging* it lock it in the box of "misbelief in God [*malcroyance en Dieu*] or, perhaps, failed faith." This is an expression of sufficient vagueness not to be inflected in a plural mode, following the example of that seventeenth-century sermoner L'Avocat, from whom we have just heard above. Between "blindness" and atheism more than a nuance intercedes, but we are left with a single appellation. Nonetheless, beyond the clerical definitions, particular circumstances, and episodic range of behaviors, is blasphemy to be found somewhere *inside* the spectrum of belief? Can it in fact be associated with specifiable spiritual attitudes, durable ones, ones advocated as such? Can it, without distorting them, accurately translate the forms of relation between human beings and Christianity?

Blasphemy, Dogma, and the Clerics. During the entire sixteenth century uttering blasphemy could signify passing an errant judgment (whether voluntary or not) on the teachings of dogma. It thus functioned as an inculpating marker, unmasking dubious converts from Islam in the Iberian peninsula, the Inquisition having arrogated to itself the right to consider impious language an expression of ex-Muslims' deceptive profession of Christianity.[2] At the same historical moment, Catholic authorities could see blasphemies uttered against the Virgin, saints, or Roman sacraments as glaring badges of the demands of an unequivocal Protestantism. Such was the impression made by Nicolas Boivin, summoned before the Troyes *officialité* in 1528, for having declared, among his other pronouncements, that "the Virgin is like a bottle which was filled with once fine wine; afterwards the wine is out, the bottle just like all the rest."[3] Conversely, a certain Jean Cathalan of the Cordelier order, who had gone over to the Calvinists and then returned to the Roman Catholic Church and defended the mass, was branded a blasphemer by John Calvin. "The said mass," Calvin fumed, "is a consignment shop of blasphemies which has nothing in common with the promise of God."[4]

Blasphemy was not simply the hollow of the rock or photographic negative of a strong religious identity. It could also signal an *unintentional* way of understanding dogma, an approach in error, without having to be an actual deviance deliberately embraced. The Dutch historian Johan Huizinga even understood this "degeneracy" of language to be the expression of a naïve familiarity "that could spring only from a deep faith."[5] Still, the explicit use of certain formulations condemned by the clerics would seem to indicate less the speaker's undermining of dogma than his or her insufficient appreciation of its fundamental dimension. Oaths such as *mort-Dieu, ventre-Dieu, tête-Dieu,* and *sang-Dieu,* long scourged as "horrible blasphemies," struck theologians as radical sabotage of the very bases of Christianity. Blurting "*tête-Dieu*" or "*ventre-Dieu*"—was this not to vulgarize the mystery of the Incarnation, to rob it of its holiness by scandalously insisting on a reality more human than divine, scorning the gift of a mysterious fragility? Saying "*mort-Dieu*" juxtaposed two deeply contradictory words claimed by Christianity's vocabulary, closing the door on the Resurrection. And, finally, uttering "*sang-Dieu*" would (from the same vantage point) be a double denegation: of the New Covenant sealed by the Crucifixion and of the eucharistic sacrifice that repeated its terms.

Yet for all this, were those who used or abused such expressions really even thinking about the theology? In the sixteenth and seventeenth centuries, the Spanish Inquisition judges did not appear to believe so.[6] We would need to know—and can we?—whether such expressions issued from a genuine and deliberate choice or whether they were simple squibs of vulgarity among others. For lack of a precise and encompassing answer, their reiteration at least bore some likeness to the marks of an elementary ignorance of or indifference to dogma that muddled the corporal object and transcendence, belittling the Incarnation to a triviality shorn of salvific qualities. Beyond that, their spoken frequency would draw attention to the early modern churches' uphill battle to permanently inculcate Christianity's most essential doctrinal principles.

From the dawn of the modern era, under the same heading as other similar abductions or defacements of holy signs and their meanings as well as the hypostasis of the profane seen on the sites of pilgrimage and the adoration of saints and their relics, blasphemy, too, would still in a sense fully belong to Christianity. At the same time, for the blasphemers themselves, the act manifested only a faint degree of guiltiness, as opposed to others who held it to be a sin of considerable proportion.[7] The setting in place of Protestant and Catholic reforms in western Europe initiated, as it were, a new relation between blasphemy and Christianity. Theologians wished to combat the blasphemous, as they did heresy and witchcraft, by radically excluding from speech any profane language so as to turn thoughts always toward the divine. This meant that the political power was under obligation to prosecute and pass sentence on it. Taking on the traits of heresy and witchcraft, blasphemy became the devil's language, an audible trace of possession by him. The demon's failure to keep the world under his spell drove him henceforth to pursue his works by inspiring each person to pronounce words of disavowal and denial.[8] In this markedly new context, can we not cautiously observe that the repetition of these kinds of formulations in the seventeenth and eighteenth centuries must have carried, at least for certain people, an appreciable awareness of the importance of the Incarnation, the Resurrection, and (for Catholics) transubstantiation? Did such words not in their time translate into an oblique refusal of a theology that had become rigid and intellectualized, putting up a sort of cultural resistance to an enterprise of moralization and dogmatic discipline?[9]

The blasphemer's verbal world of refusal would also possess its own social geography, its crossovers departing dramatically from the contrast scholars have sought to draw between elites and the working populace. Between the mid-sixteenth century and the 1660s, blasphemers could be found in one heterogeneous cross section, stretching from rural aristocrats and peasants to urban artisans and the court nobility. Without again recalling the firsthand account, alluded to earlier, by Estienne at the beginning of the sixteenth century, we can call here upon Ezechiel Spanheim. An observer at Louis XIV's court, Spanheim reported that "the debaucheries, dissolutions, blasphemies, and other scandalous vices were formerly quite ordinary in the palace up until a more recent period."[10] He was probably differentiating these crudely defined classes of behavior from those of the *bourgeoisie de robe*—the world of official appointments and administrative service. This latter class, along with the clergy at least in France and Spain, likely offered a frontline offensive of those devout who were prepared to monitor and track down any impious speech in order to impose their version of a Christianity "purified of superstitions."[11] Was it not against these acculturative claims of a part of society that one Pigeonneau, imitating many others, was determined to blaspheme as he pleased and when he pleased, to demonstrate a kind of independence from a religious sensibility tied to the stringent new norms? In August 1656, near the abbey of Saint-Germain-des-Prés, Pigeonneau

> is said to have entered the cabaret that displays its sign in the form of a White Cross, cursing and blaspheming execrably the holy Name of God; and having been reprimanded as much by . . . the witness Nicolas Duquesnoy, master carter, as by the [assembled] company, for wrongly blaspheming God's Name, notwithstanding said remonstrances, is said to have uttered in reiterating said blasphemies "by God's death, by God's head," and "the first damn bugger among you who so much as goes for me by a hair, you've only to move two steps toward me and so help me I'll knock out [*estoubisse* for the text's *estourpille*] all these bourgeois who act so high and mighty citing dogma [*font ainsy les docteurs*] and want to keep me from swearing." And that was all he said he knew.[12]

The reasonable caution shown by the witness to this incident and by his drinking companions when faced with the fiercely maverick arrogance of the offender does not prejudge the elocutionary comportment of each and every oath-swearer and still less their failings of commitment to church dogma. It mainly highlights, so that justice might be served, a kind of self-discipline of speech through a mutual, or reciprocal, organization of surveillance in a place well known for its verbal excesses. Hardly, however, does it allow us to draw firm conclusions about any presumed victory of the advocates and defenders of the new religious culture. Abundant indications are that blasphemous speech continued to be used widely in the eighteenth century. And in those aristocratic or bourgeois milieus in which it seemed to no longer be current, its very absence might betoken a possible slackening of religious respect. During the 1740s, did Montesquieu not observe within the social milieus with which he was in close association a growing shortage of sallies of intelligence inspired by Christian thinking, adding "that one proof irreligion has won is that our bons mots are no longer lifted from Scripture and the language of religion; an impious remark no longer has bite."[13]

But if the abandonment of blasphemous references marked a retreat of Christian values, might not their continuation by some still be interpreted as a sign bordering on outright atheism?

Blasphemy and Atheism. On first perusal associating blasphemy and atheism is contradictory. From the start of the seventeenth to the mid-nineteenth centuries at the least, theologians never ceased heckling "blasphemous atheists" by striving to underscore the incoherence of their position: why if they did not believe in God did they get angry at Him? "The blasphemer swaggers and talks big pointlessly, behaving as if he were having a good time hurling insults at a stone," wrote the anonymous author of the *Le manuel du marin chrétien* (Christian sailor's manual) in 1851.[14] But if on the one hand clerics clearly dissociated atheism from blasphemy and implicitly acknowledged the latter only as a counterimage or negative of true faith, on the other they continued to identify impious speech as a manifest sign of unbelief. At first allied with humanity's disloyalty, blasphemy could not fail to lead to impiety, the latter an open invitation to genuine atheism.[15] Such also was the viewpoint expressed in the official Remonstrance of the Assembly of French Clergy in 1645 for which, we recall, blasphemy verged on a drastic negation of God's existence.

Does this deductive direction of thought on the subject not find its flagrant illustration in the famous scene from act 3 of Moliere's *Don Juan*, where the debauched nobleman proposes the "immoral" bargain to a beggar of alms in exchange for a blasphemy?

> FRANCISCO. Most days, your Lordship, I haven't a crust of bread to chew on.
>
> DON JUAN. My dear man, I should find another profession, fast. Never mind. I'll give you a gold piece. Right this minute. All you have to do is curse God.
>
> FRANCISCO. I can't do that. It's a mortal sin.
>
> DON JUAN. One curse, one gold piece. It's up to you.
>
> FRANCISCO. Your Lordship!
>
> DON JUAN. No curse, no cash.
>
> SGANARELLE. Go on. Say it quickly, it'll hardly count.
>
> DON JUAN. Here, feel it, all you have to do is curse.
>
> FRANCISCO. I'd rather starve.[16]

Following Dorimon and Villiers, Molière was perhaps basing his character on the life of the chevalier de Roquelaure, the notorious libertine nobleman of the mid-seventeenth century, who when he encountered a pauper speaking blasphemies in a street in Toulouse, encouraged him "to blaspheme some more and he would give him more silver."[17] But for our purposes what matters in the offending scenario is that blasphemy does not amount to a flagrant indicator of Don Juan's atheism. His irreligion has been brought out more definitively in the preceding scene, when he admits to believing only that "two and two make four; and four and four, eight." Molière's detractors, however, were quick to tar these multiple professions of the rationalist's credo with blasphemy, following the example set by the prince de Conti. Conti saw in *Don Juan*'s feast of stone

> a school of atheism . . . in which after having made a quick-witted atheist pronounce the most horrible impieties, the author then confides God's cause to a valet who is made to speak every conceivable impertinence in defending him. And he has the gall to try to justify it all at the end of this play so filled with blasphemies by means of pyrotechnics to which he gives the role of ridiculous executor of divine vengeance.[18]

And yet, in conformity with the theologians' opinion, Don Juan does not blaspheme because he does not believe in God. This does not prevent him in places, though, from certainly behaving like a blasphemer. Does he not prefer "the love of humanity" to the goodness of a God who bestows no gratitude on the prayer of the poor man?[19] Does he not resemble the classic blasphemer by adopting the gambler's stance, the man who will wager on anything, on any subject? Here he places his bets on blasphemy against faith and engages his dialogue with the beggar like a game of chance in which he is indifferent to winning or losing in an ultimate sense. Does he not put on the very face of the tempter himself, that blasphemer par excellence, renewing his proposal three times? In this episode Don Juan exploits blasphemy instrumentally as a means to inflict his test on the penniless Christian who, being a man of prayer and faith, refuses any transgression of language, any betrayal of his God, even at the price of his own hunger.[20]

The exemplarity we see in this singular excerpt from the creative literature is at least twofold. Atheism would continue in the mid seventeenth century to remain the prerogative of worldly wits, more numerous particularly in aristocratic circles and thus preserving a kind of tradition already pointed to by J. Gerson in the fifteenth century: "What now, truly must one say to the lord who addresses the peasant, 'You give your soul to the devil and you deny God and yet are not noble.' "[21] Blasphemy moreover does not reveal humanity's atheism but rather simply confirms it, went the theologian's argument, to the extent that the atheist pronouncing it would not be seeking to offend a hypothetical or nonexistent God but instead to provoke or cast aspersion on a prospective faithful interlocutor, so as to elicit a reaction of opposition, to measure the force of a conviction.

Set beside this engaging if primarily literary example, does the study of individuals who incessantly made remarks such as "I renounce God," "I don't believe in God," or "God be hanged" [*malheur à Dieu*] prove more enlightening in view of a connection between blasphemy and atheism? Again, it would seem rash or risky to assert that the first was the second's vector. Dedieu, who has turned up and scrutinized such numerous locutions in the inquisitorial trial records of Toledo, explains skillfully what seems to have been at stake in both using and prosecuting such words. He concludes that an ontological negation was not the issue. For sixteenth- and seventeenth-century Spaniards—Don Juan excepted?—

God *was*.[22] A personal misfortune or a collective accident such as a bad harvest, epidemic, or drought, however, seemed for a time to release human beings not from their credence but from their perfect obedience to their Lord, as He was no longer protecting them. So such blasphemous expressions would thus have indicated the *momentary* refusal to recognize God's power,[23] the transitory negation of "He who is not good for the poor."[24] They would have brought out the bitterness of those for whom a kind of basic contract with heaven had not been honored. Granted the plausibility of such interpretations, could blasphemy in this context always be interpreted in this way?

We can see how fragile it is to use blasphemy alone as a cornerstone of unapologetic irreligion. It was ideas and opinions, readings and writings, social relations, and cultural nonconformism that, in the long run, identified an atheist—and not, first and foremost, vindictive language dubbed blasphemous by those who wished to equate atheism and blasphemy. Faced with these hypothetical and hesitant determinations of loyalty to faith, could one more confidently regard blasphemous speech as the stamp of an avowed anticlericalism?

Blasphemy and Anticlericalism. On principle itself, there could not exist any direct link between the discrete phenomena of blasphemy and anticlericalism, one addressed to God, the other to his servants; and the treatises of moral theology of the modern era made practically no allusion to this more encompassing interpretation of blasphemy pertaining to criticism of the church as an institution. The reality, however, was rather different. The French bishops of the mid-seventeenth century, for example, when denouncing the extinction of "every last religious sentiment," had directed attention on every possible occasion to the close link between blasphemy and anticlericalism, given that "out of scorn for His ministers, men pass with great harm to scorn for God."[25] The opinion was reiterated by their distant successors at the time of the Restoration. There did not, properly speaking, exist any legal condemnation for blasphemy against priests or pastors.[26] A certain number of signs would tend to demonstrate that its use could sometimes translate deep-set anticlerical feeling, particularly after the implementation of certain decisions issued at the Council of Trent. The priest gradually became a person apart, a holy and necessary, and thus respected, intermediary between God and humanity.

This situation could only favor an overlap and identification between gestural or verbal attacks against clerics and offenses perpetrated against God himself. This was why after the years 1660 to 1680 insulted parties considered it within their right to identify this verbal aggression as a sign of impiety. "It is important to defend God who is offended and myself as well who am treated with indignity," a curate of Beaujolais declared in the mid-eighteenth century, after having endured several verbal abuses from his parishioners.[27] One of his brethren from the same diocese of Lyon, the curate of Blacé, deplored "the appalling insults that do considerable prejudice to the sacerdotal character of the said complainant," while during the same period another curate, of Villefranche-sur-Saône, found the insulting attitude of one of his female parishioners likely to "compromise the honor and duties of his holy ministry."[28] These attacks on the priest seemed all the more offensive when they pointed out shortcomings with respect to ecclesiastic discipline, especially inebriation and concubinage—discipline that the council had brought up and that had been imposed little by little in the dioceses and parishes. In 1669 the court of justice of Saint-Germain-des-Prés in Paris was taken up with a case that pitted Jacques Hardy, the priest with charge over the benefice of the abbey of Nesles, against the husband and wife Duplessis. The couple "said of the abbey priest that he was a nasty, infamous, and squalid person, that he participated in debaucheries, [was] a man who made known the confessions of his penitents, repeating the said insults and accompanied these with their like even in the Saint Sulpice church, in which place the petitioners [heard him] swearing and abjuring in an execrable manner."[29]

Thus when a priest's reputation was publicly undercut—François Neveu would call the curate of the Paris diocese of Chatenay a "whoremonger" in 1667[30]—it was the sacramental holiness and solemnity of his ministry that were affected. Also impugned, by extension, was the honor of the defied God, as the theology of the time emphasized that God himself had founded the organization of his church. The seriousness accorded these kinds of assaults was not necessarily conveyed by a proliferation of expressions, each more impious sounding than the last. Such was the accreted sacral aura of the people and places ordained for Christian worship that a simple offensive remark, a profane oath tossed off toward or directly against a priest (or even worse his holy function) were enough to found an affront against the divine.

What can be said, then, about such phraseology or comments when they were uttered within the sanctum of the church or during the celebration of a rite?[31] In this context, the interpretation of a word that was simply coarse or vulgar was unequivocal. Invectives and clashes between priests and the faithful in the seventeenth and eighteenth centuries could, however, have origins other than religious ones: personal animosity, disparities of economic levels, taxation, etc. This long-tolerated anticlericalism was transformed for the large majority of the clergy into an undeniable practice of blasphemy. It is moreover highly illuminating to note that Protestant Europe in the eighteenth century knew a similar slippage of definitions and equation of the two. Did not the court at Neuchâtel consider as blasphemies "certain public insults toward pastors," notably those spoken inside the temple or during worship?[32]

But what was going on in the mind of the blasphemer who "disturbs a priest in the exercise of his pious offices by swearing oaths, accosts him with abusive words, and even wishes to lay profane and murderous hands on him and thereby cause scandal"?[33] Was this not also one way of showing the blasphemer's rejection of a change the churches had imposed? Was it not an implicit refusal to recognize the new status assigned to sanctified time (Sundays and holidays) and holy space (church and cemetery)? And was it not a reflection of persistent disregard for that increasingly radical separation between profane and divine, bridged personally and instrumentally by the priest?

One might therefore encounter in "anticlerical" blasphemous speech yet another form of that cultural resistance (already met with earlier) opposed to the new spiritual ambitions of the church. Given the current state of fragmentary evidence and various contextual analyses, this would seem to be the most plausible meaning in the case of many blasphemers. Except for known atheists, the more or less chronic and unseemly use of impious words offensive to God, to the saints, and then perhaps to clerics represented an *alternate* "religious sensibility" even as it harked back to an older practice of speech that was part of Christianity. In the end the two blasphemous sensibilities—atheistic and anticlerical—amounted somewhat to the same because both cases had to do with rejecting an acculturation, challenging forced assimilation into that oral civility which suppressed one of the signs of the culture of violence. Blasphemy was the persistent and tenacious avatar of *other* human relations. Together on its verbal palette it mixed expressions whose origin was indeed religious with the terms of the profane, sacrilegious wording with seditious talk.

🐝 13 | WHAT BLASPHEMY SAID ABOUT SOCIETY

Blasphemy's plurality of meanings cannot be reduced to the domain of Christian belief. "The devil's speech" presents its own, quite extensive autonomy. Indeed there exists a purely *social* aspect of such speech that, as it evolves between the early modern period and the Enlightenment in its turn gives rise to a variety of interpretations.

Blasphemy and Ways of Being. In the sixteenth and still in the seventeenth century, blasphemous words often spontaneously figured in spoken language. They punctuated sentences, added flourish at the end of dialogues, lent punch to convictions in a way that reflected medieval Christianity's venerable and customary confusion between profane and sacred. François Rabelais's meditation on this subject in a brief dialogue is revealing:

> "So," said the monk [being feasted by Gargantua], "here's to all those devils, while they last! Power of God! what would that limper [the devil] have done with it? 'Odsbody! ["*Le cor Dieu!*"] He gets more pleasure when someone presents him with a pair of good oxen!"
>
> "How's that?" said Pontocrates, "you're swearing, Frère Jean?"
>
> "That's only," said the monk, "to adorn my speech. Those are colors of Ciceronian rhetoric."[1]

This imbuing of everyday language with impious remarks, of which numerous traces can be found in farces and other theatrical productions of the fifteenth and sixteenth centuries,[2] affected clerics as well as lay people. And Ponocrates's (feigned?) surprise seems to have been inscribed in that mixture of "genres" widely practiced by all, and especially by men. For the expressions that were in principle prohibited were largely part of the asseverations of male speech: during the workdays of carters and sailors (whose cursing reputations were well established); in the heat of battle and invective between soldiers and duelists; during leisure time, when remarks made in the cabaret, under influence of drink or not, might easily accompany some liberal or indecent pleas- antry, affront, or snub, often in prelude to other aggressions; and finally, in the sometimes commotion-filled home environment, as recorded in a wife's complaints over her husband's violent behavior and the blasphe- mous language that attended it. But the very frequency of this usage sometimes served to truncate or dilute blasphemous expressions that as a result, in the context of verbal exchange, lost their shock value, their scandalous import. Putting a challenge to Jean Charrière at Agen, in May of 1669, Jean Brethès exclaimed, "By his death, head, and blood! It is *you,* you insolent bastard who made it your business to speak ill of *me.* 'Sdeath! but you'll learn to speak that way about people who amount to more than you and who'll stand up to you wherever you show your face!"[3] This snippet calls to mind yet again the importance duly accorded the circumstances of utterance, as familiarity with these cir- cumstances helps us grasp the impious remark's meaning. Using for- bidden expressions in this kind of situation was less allied with willful intent to transgress a religious rule than with sheer habit. At best, and in most cases, the habit accompanied an intense physical effort or simply made annoyance more emphatic; at worst, it over strengthened an indi- vidual's demonstration of force and defiance toward one fellow man. The latter is also the sense in which blasphemous speech became encoded as part of the ritual of male violence in the sixteenth and sev- enteenth centuries.

Since the development of a separate field of the history of criminality, the role of animosity in the social relations of modern Europe has received much attention. Highly frequent use of impious words in the externalization of interpersonal conduct took part in a kind of dramatic staging, mutually recognized by its antagonists. Certain codified ges- tures, for example, allowed the person who was attacked not to lose face, not to admit total defeat thanks to the opportune participation of a third party who intervened to separate the enemies by siding with the weaker.[4] Blasphemous words might obviously emerge at any moment in this "rit- ual of aggression." Successive bursts of them were all part of the bluster- ing, the invectives, the affronts to honor, the noisy and publicly witnessed cavalcade of every provocation, clash, settling of accounts.

Most documentations in the archives of court cases in this area clearly emphasized blasphemy's presence early in the preliminaries of public confrontation. The aggressor was indeed the one who threatened to strike or even kill, "swearing and blaspheming God's Holy Name." Blasphemy further punctuated the verbal face-off that followed the first provocations, and it accompanied the coming to blows as often as it did the intervention of witnesses (who, according to their own accounts, were frequently alerted "by the said blasphemies," a sure sign of disorder and flagrant index of violence). In 1671 near the abbey of Saint-Denis, Jean Letellier came to Guillaume Freimein's aid because he "heard all those blasphemous curses and, given the lateness of the hour, is said to have come forward to break up this quarrel and discover who it was that was swearing and blaspheming in such manner the Holy Name of God."[5]

In such an environment, blasphemy exceeded its function as an attribute of customary male speech. Along with other symptoms, it had its part in constructing a code that imposed, such as it was, an ordered sequence on social violence in the sixteenth and seventeenth centuries. In the course of a verbal joust, the blasphemous utterance represented a sort of warning preface, a crystallization of intention addressed to the one attacked to an onlooker(s). It took its place in a progression in which jeers, jests, sarcasms, and bantering or cruel joking, in reference to recognized codes and through an effect of escalation, prepared those involved for what would happen next.[6] For the one who shouted them, blasphemous remarks lent force to the process of social transgression, since, through a vocal habit, forbidden words became agents of public violence.

In this way, civil authorities and intellectuals gradually grasped the meaning of blasphemy's social function. And, acting in the name of the conventions of civility that imposed themselves little by little starting in the Renaissance, they, along with a good fraction of the rest of society, thereby indelibly marked blasphemous speech with its stamp of marginality.

Blasphemy and Its Margins. The spiritual acculturation that succeeded the Reformation era was accompanied and sometimes preceded by another emerging sensibility, another social morality: new manners at table and in conversation. In a word, a strictly coded civility took shape. Civility opened onto mastery of self, domestication of the body, guilty introspection. These were so many attitudes that would reinforce the

movements of Christianization even as they took on their own independent life in society.[7] One can also conclude that the gradual clarification and regularization of syntax, its maturation especially in France and
England, the state's appropriation of a particular vernacular, deployed in
specific registers to affirm the grandeur of monarchical power or the
order of society—all contributed at the end of the sixteenth century to
promoting a purification of vocabulary and taste for refined speech.
These tendencies managed to help fix in place norms that, from the
Republic of Letters or from the royal court (actions in these two cases
being probably not closely associated), defined what was and what was
no longer correct on the basis of literary and aristocratic references.[8]
They also combined to lend language a keen and strong social responsibility, setting ever more markedly apart the acceptable expressions used
by elites from the "bad" words used by the people. Although we can add
that we know that the cleavage between the two was not to have been as
drastic as all that,[9] it is in this context that another possible interpretation of blasphemy needs to be considered.

Increasingly, in the seventeenth century and even more the next, blasphemous cursing would be chalked up to poor education, to rudeness.
During a mission to the parishes of Bavaria in 1725, one of the fathers
attested that "a good number of blasphemous words form part of the
daily parlance, such that people will need to be led to speak in another
manner."[10] Henceforth eradicating impious speech could only come
about through reeducating individuals. This age-old and coarse habit did
not fail to go hand in hand with the religious ignorance of many. "Blasphemies and profane oaths," wrote Nicolas des Essarts, "are routine
among the masses because of the inferior education of these people."[11] A
more thorough assimilation of Christianity's principles (and thus of
God's eminent holiness) and well-attended worship would enable the
church to modify the moral attitudes of each person, erasing indecencies
from mind and conduct.

Apprenticeship in civility consisted in curbing impulsiveness, revers-
ing the triviality of acts and words, giving up any habits of gesture that
might lead to an irreverent or vulgar verbalization. Catechism and elementary instruction, from the collèges down to the petites écoles, took up
this apprenticeship slowly.[12] But daily observations, the threat of judicial prosecution, in short, public remonstrance administered by village
officials or curates lent further emphasis to these cultural intermedi-

aries' efforts to edify. Among other examples was the intervention, in October 1664, of a tax procurator at Boulogne, in the Paris diocese, insisting that a gambler and potential blasphemer "desist from said gaming and attend vespers without any scandal or blasphemy but, to the contrary, with civility."[13] Certain individuals yoked their fortunes and dedication to the task, especially those active in the rural societies, which were judged to be more receptive and also consisted of rank and file with more potential than the urban rabble. In 1746 for example, "after a long period spent [visiting her] landholdings," Catherine Villiers de Billy believed it her duty to publish *Instructions historiques, dogmatiques, et morales en faveur des laboureurs* (Historical, dogmatic, and moral instructions for bettering agricultural laborers), so much had she observed "with great distress the degree to which those who lived in the rural villages are ignorant of their religion and practice it badly."[14] The work's title vividly highlighted its determination to mix edifying genres, and its section devoted to God's second commandment labeled blasphemous speech a sin dishonoring God. Such speech came about through absence of education, misunderstanding connected with a bad habit: "Many blaspheme among the country population while not even thinking they do so."[15]

From this outlook, all those who refused to receive the enlightenment of civility, education, or morality and who kept on submitting to such unseemly gestures and words consigned themselves in a space of social marginality where idlers, paupers, and delinquents rubbed shoulders.[16] Blasphemy was increasingly regarded as a form of expression that automatically attended reprehensible acts. It effectively became a circumstance adding heinousness to the guilty party's crime, insofar as it was spoken by someone already marginalized by offensive behavior. Accusations and testimonies regularly insisted on the inevitable association between aggressive gestures and impious speech, not to acknowledge their ritualistic complicity but to denounce their criminal collusion. Accused by her neighbors for scandal and prostitution, appearing before the superintendent Chauvin in June 1723, Anne Evrard of the Parisian parish of Saint-Germain-l'Auxerrois was inevitably called a blasphemer who spoke "using the most vulgar abusive language against the residents of the house."[17] Damned speech could spring forth only from those who were themselves cursed by living on the margin of social and religious rules.

Blasphemy as the language of evildoers in the eighteenth century belonged also, following Louis-Sébastien Mercier's portrayal of it, to the world of the mentally ill, who in the later years of the ancien régime saw themselves clearly cut off from the human community. The author of *Tableau de Paris* (Panorama of Paris) based his opinion on a rather typical incident. Every Thursday eve before Good Friday in the Sainte-Chapelle, a relic of the True Cross was displayed so that epileptics could be delivered of their "diabolical affliction." Touching the relic was supposed to favor a cure that would manifest itself through an outpouring of public curses and blasphemies, a sign of delivery from demonic possession. So, during Holy Week in 1777, Mercier was indeed an ear- and eye-witness to

the most brazen, the most incredible of blasphemers. Imagine all the adversaries of Jesus Christ and his divine Mother; imagine all the impious unbelievers all brought together and forming but one single voice. Well, they have never approached this man's sacrilegious, abusive, and derisive audacity. For myself and for the onlookers it was a truly novel spectacle to hear such a man publicly and thunderously defying the God of temples, insulting his worship, inciting his wrath, spewing forth the most abominable invectives, while all of these emphatic blasphemies were chalked up to the devil. The terrified rabble crossed themselves, and prostrate with their face to the ground said that it was the demon himself who spoke. After he had been made by force to pass three times before the cross (and eight men barely restraining him), these blasphemies became so outrageous and so appalling that he was put outside the church doors, as though forever abandoned to Satan's Empire and not deserving a cure by the miraculous cross. Imagine a public guard presiding on that night at this inconceivable farce.[18]

This account invites a range of possible readings. A standard observation, to begin with: the credulous populace always associated relics with thaumaturgic power; in this case, the holy cross against possession. Blasphemous words themselves, the devil's speech, were vomited forth when Satan, vanquished by the holiness of the cross, released his hold over bodies and spirits. But this explanation does not seem to convince our memorialist. He instead attributes the episode of blasphemous swearing to one of two possible explanations, when it comes to this somewhat exceptional incident of 1777. One was that of a theatrical hoax, cleverly arranged since "the would-be 'possessed' only cried out their curses precisely at midnight, at the precise moment when the instrument of the Savior's agony was pulled from its container."[19] Besides which, relating the anecdote, Mercier believes that the so excessive imprecator may be a paid actor. The other was that the cursing partook in a frequent and grave expression of pathology that was erroneously attributed to the demon and placed those who showed symptoms of it at the fringes of society. These blasphemy-spouters would have been considered unbalanced and, as such, destined to commitment in an asylum, far removed from ordinary folk so as to not disturb social harmony. Interpreting blasphemy as the language of madness was not truly new to the eighteenth century. What became so was the abandonment, from that time on, of any religious dimension. The mentally ill person who spoke delivered himself or herself from prohibitions, not from the devil. It became suitable to propose not a spiritual but a clinical treatment for the sufferer. In the meantime, the applied social therapy was to lock up the unstable. In the buildings that held them, one could find, mixed in among the condemned by common law, the libertines, the debauched, marginal people to a one.[20]

In aspiring to construct possible approaches to blasphemy in the modern period, this study has put forward a few elements of an answer. These have been separated into a few interpretive categories, somewhat out of convenience, as the reality of the time most often blurred any stark partition. A classic religious valence emerges in its several guises, according to the observers or the actors, ranging from disrespect to impiety. The disrespect might, of course, be toward God but also his ministers, who were often not far from thinking that anticlericalism might indeed take the form of impiety. As to atheism, it was only recognized by the reverse image that molded it or by the resonance of its context of reception; the atheist actually did not only blaspheme for him- or herself at all but as a test of the true believer's mettle. There existed also a social function: blasphemy played a part in the verbal expression of a good many fringe sectors of the male population and of coded acts of violence before belonging mainly to a marginalized realm—of criminals, the mentally ill, and more generally all those who (consciously or not) refused the efforts of moral and religious education undertaken since the sixteenth century.

This helps us understand the artificiality of drawing a line between the categories of social and religious interpretations of impious speech. Finally, must one not also take into account, if it were possible, the *psychological* approach to the individuals in question? Did not each person modify and mold, according to whim of character or circumstance, his or her own meanings in speaking blasphemously? This likelihood made John Wright, an English Unitarian minister, write in 1817 that "blasphemy ... has been applied so variously, that all who make use of it attach their own signification."[21]

And so we are left with these diverse, potentially explanatory openings, with the eminent place of the performative context, and consequently blasphemy's permanent presence in the field of the Christianity and society of modern times. Do these more global contexts, however, authorize the idea of what has recently been called a "civilization of blasphemy"?

A *"Civilization of Blasphemy"*? This "historian's question" deserves at least to be laid out insofar as the use of such a formulation by specialists in the subject leads to a certain number of needed clarifications. It was Jean Delumeau's pioneering focus on blasphemy, *La Peur en Occident* (Fear in the West), which seems to have first used this expression.[22] Delumeau was giving a name to the apparent feeling "of uneasy observers confronting a general cultural phenomenon that concerned all of Europe at a period of its history," but which chronologically was less uncertain than Jeanne Favret-Saada suggests in her pertinent critical analysis on the subject. Delumeau did in fact not limit the "civilization of blasphemy" to the seventeenth and eighteenth centuries, as Favret-Saada reminds us,[23] but very explicitly confined it to the sixteenth, citing for example Calvin, the Venetian retreat before the Turks, and the decisions of Charles V and Philip II. He implicitly included the first half of the seventeenth century by evoking the English statute of 1648.[24] The historian Robert Muchembled, though not mentioned by Favret-Saada, also used the same phrase to link an earlier period with the sixteenth century: the fifteenth century would for him be another period rife with the practice of blasphemy.[25]

Might this apparent discordance of periodization, even as it stressed the cinquecento's importance, encompass an alternate appreciation of the very terms "civilization" and "blasphemy"? To answer the question would require that each historian apply himself or herself to defining the expression. Yet Delumeau used the phrase as a given, and Muchembled followed his predecessor's example, without citing him, by taking up the expression in turn. Neither of these works makes an attempt, or even wants, to offer an analysis of the christened phrase in the few pages that follow their mention of it. These lexical and chronological uncertainties, it seems to me, make it hard to guarantee the reliability of such a coinage. Indeed, the very expression "civilization of blasphemy" "amounts to anointing a particular feature of culture to characterize this civilization in its entirety and contrast it to others that do not supposedly have this feature available to them. From the moment we realize this, it is essential to *define* this particular feature because it is the basis of a distinction," Favret-Saada reasonably observes.[26] And if Muchembled timidly tries his hand at filling in the outlines of the object of blasphemy and removes or curtails its sense of semantic ambiguity, Delumeau takes it as a given, according it simply the status of a "feature of mentality that it would be necessary to study in the light of a history of Christianization."[27] But does that suffice?

The expression's inaptness results just as easily from the availability of other possible phrases that can lend their name to the period. Could one not bestow on the fifteenth and sixteenth centuries the names "civilization of the Renaissance" or "civilization of the Reformation" or identify a distinguishing characteristic (the book, European expansion, merchant capitalism) just as legitimate, but also just as reductive, as blasphemy? That is, short of contending that blasphemy constitutes an invariant powerful and dominant enough to become for several centuries the essential indicator determining all of Western society. And who can believe that? To be sure, customs of forbidden speech remained considerably widespread between at least the fifteenth and eighteenth centuries. It is not, however, the period's predominant singularity, even if fundamental theological or political considerations (of variable intensities) are attached to blasphemy. Blasphemy thus was but one "cultural" component among others (the book, the musket, algebra, etc.), though to its historical credit it has duration, a positive geographic diffusion, and the fact that the powers that be took a keen interest in it.

The term "civilization," furthermore, generally implies "productions" and intellectual behaviors closely associated with objects that will serve to give that civilization a label. But blasphemy gives rise only to works based on opposition to or negation of it, and they are few in number:

spiritual treatises without any great originality, a few poetic works (see Eustache Deschamps already at the end of the fourteenth century!),[28] an iconography (mostly engravings), all of them centered on excoriating its grave and harmful effects. Christin in a recent article tellingly emphasizes the phenomenon in the countries of the Holy Roman Empire during the early modern period. He analyzes Germanic representational production from Albrecht Dürer to Hans Baldung, from M. Gerung to Abraham Bach, their works dramatizing the symbolic figures of blasphemy and the blasphemer and taking an active part in the virulent polemics between Catholics and Protestants from the 1520s to the mid-seventeenth century.[29] Is this a case in which we are obliged to speak of a "civilization"? Christin rightly makes no use of the term, inasmuch as this iconography represents after all only a very minor portion of artistic works and is not the dominant reflection of pictorial culture in the German-speaking countries between 1450 and 1700 (drawing elsewhere for the essential sources of its subjects of inspiration).

It seems, then, that the association between "civilization" and "blasphemy" is pertinent neither at the level of chronology nor in relation to the word's meanings and implications. At the very most, one can conclude that blasphemy's multifarious forms and significations take their place alongside other practices in a history of incivility, that they belong to the record of a "civilization" of violence and proximity. Concurrently, blasphemous speech represented one of the forms of aggression in social relations and of overfamiliarity in religious behaviors. Before being a stigma of marginality or assumed faithlessness, it for a long time translated a cultural heterogeneity that it helped maintain and foster between the divine and the human.

So if there is not exactly a "civilization of blasphemy" there is, nevertheless, an abiding class of speech judged as forbidden—at once through its facility of verbal expression, its disrespect or negligence vis-à-vis the ineffable, and its insistence on a notorious distinction. Prosecuted more and more in the name of correcting customs and rejecting coarseness and incivility, blasphemy nonetheless continued to endure during the entire modern period and beyond. It managed to do this precisely by playing in the alternate ranges or registers of a populist voice that spoke through it. And it is these different registers to which theologians, judges, common people, as well as latter-day historians have all seen fit to harken.

Approaching historically a speech behavior called *blasphemy* by the authorities that denounced and repressed, it gives the researcher the opportunity to bring out the originality of the chosen historical period with respect to its handling of the concept. What becomes clear is the permanence of the frameworks that define blasphemy.

The period labeled "modern" in the wider (or postmedieval) sense seems to have favored not a dramatic "upsurge of blasphemy" but rather a developing consciousness of its social frequency and discovery of its bearing on religious and political levels. In the midst of the religious wars of the sixteenth century, defining "blasphemy" helped identify the Christian who *thought differently*: the blasphemer was the Other. A classification of speech whose inside meaning was the denunciation of errant thinking, forbidden speech (so designated) could not help but call upon the political power in the name of mutual support between churches and states. But by voicing taboo words, the blasphemer also became a provocateur, a sower of social discord. The slow and dramatic abatement of religious antagonisms, the published commentary of clerics and judges on the essential import and meaning of impious speech, its practical depenalization all ended up disuniting the coordinated struggle of prince and priest. The first half of the nineteenth century, in France more than elsewhere in Europe, consummated this parting of ways when the state gave up ascribing to the blasphemer that opprobrious social role that had become distinctively his or hers. Only the Catholic Church, with heaven's aid, from then on waged the battle against an expansionist "society of blasphemers." Clerics voiced their determination to take vengeance against this nation rocked by revolutions and "the progress made by unbelief."

Bearing in mind these difficult and decisive changes highlights how important the church-state conjuncture was to properly apprehending the practice of blasphemy. On the other hand, one cannot neglect the very bases of this class of speech, established well before the period we consider here and maintained well beyond it. Blasphemy in fact was always seen with respect to a point of reference that was sacred, absolute, and, especially in Christianity, none other than the God of the Revelation and the Incarnation. As long as divine transcendence defined the very essence of what was holy, the publicly issued challenge against that transcendence was a radical summons to believers and witnesses. Moved by the sovereign's law and/or assaulted in their spiritual convictions, true believers and accusers demanded the blasphemer's eviction from the shared field of culture and society, because whoever had just abused God's name laid their community open to a formidable chastisement by committing (according to the guardians of orthodoxy) one of the gravest of all sins.

Under these conditions, how has the gravity of this sin, driven home at every possible opportunity from Deuteronomy on and marking such a breach between humanity (who truly took on its consequences?) and God, become a matter no longer discussed in Western society until very recent times? Has a tradition on which the Catholic hierarchy is happy to bolster its authority ended up blotting blasphemy out of its picture of human life? This contradiction, already noticeable in modern Europe through the gap between the sin's radical judgment and how it was treated, is even more strident in the contemporary age. At bottom, to be sure, nothing has changed, at least outwardly. The archconservative *Catéchisme de L'Eglise catholique* (Catechism of the Catholic Church), recently published,[1] adopts the habitual stance in the few passages it accords the subject, calling blasphemy a "seriously illicit" act and "a mortal sin."[2] Yet the leaders of today's Christian churches, it appears, have given up sustaining a vehement and continuous pastoral charge against what remains a sin against the holy name.

This prominent lack of interest shows its own progressive stages and processes whose beginnings we have been able to grasp here. It came about as the state's secular culture took up and made plainer its distance vis-à-vis theological perception during the second half of the eighteenth century, examining the "true" nature of blasphemy and hesitating between unbelief and customary speech practices. A return to virulently denouncing impious utterance in the course of the nineteenth century remained a strictly ecclesiastical matter in which heaven was called upon to punish the oblivious and the perverted. The accusatory movement eventually ran out of steam.[3] But this did not stop a few prelates from interpreting historical catastrophes as so many divine punishments unleashed against the blasphemers. A pastoral letter that Cardinal Jean-Marie-Rodrigue Villeneuve, archbishop of Quebec, addressed to the faithful during Lent in 1943 lashed out at the responsibility of these sinners implicated in the tragedies of the historical moment:

> We express amazement, dear Brethren, that the war prolongs itself and increasingly wreaks its havoc and devastation on humanity. Many there are who have sought to reproach the Almighty for not staying His vengeful hand faster in all this. But when one hears this blasphemous clamor that rises from so many Christian mouths, even in our own country, is there not rather good reason for surprise that the war and other divine scourges shall not have fallen upon us more heavily; and were there not present within the holy cloisters and our families those praying and atoning souls who hold back the full wrath of the Lord, should we not have already seen the war let loose upon us its fires and instruments of death?[4]

The growing silence regarding blasphemous transgression can be understood in several ways that sometimes functioned cumulatively. A civil decriminalization that followed the increasingly rarer application of the law's provisions concerning offenders compounded what is called de-Christianization.[5] Finding expression in western Europe in the gradual loss of markers of religious orientation (and even the oppressive use of those markers), this de-Christianization has put on the clothing of indifference. That indifference, in turn, also has rendered less efficacious an anticlericalism that was otherwise militant and apt to be gleefully blasphemous. Reduced pressure on individual consciences from the churches (at first Protestant, then Roman—both with more reservations about being punitive) and, perhaps above all, the possibility to more freely choose which confession of faith to embrace weakened blasphemy as an index of resistance toward an imposed religious culture, and reinforced the divestiture of religious authority.[6] Nevertheless, blasphemy's gradual erasure from pastoral preoccupations and the increasingly manifest absence of impious expressions in the language do not entitle us to conclude that those expressions have disappeared altogether.

The weight of an interdiction reiterated for centuries and sustained daily by the vehicle of the word has, for example, favored the emergence of euphemism: expressions that "correct and disarm blasphemy."[7] Already and without great success, Father Coton, the Jesuit confessor to a converted Henry IV, had attempted to induce his famous penitent to try euphemism, lending his own family name as a (hardly attractive) substitute for the swearer who defied God. "I reject Coton!" [*jarnicoton*] was supposed to supplant "I reject God!" [*jarnidieu*]. In similar fashion, the same type of verbal word play would later create nonsensical forms such as " 'Sblad!" [*palsanbleu*] instead of "by God's blood!" [*par le sang de Dieu*]. Likewise expressions that dropped or garbled syllables, or substituted more innocuous locutions—"Lordy!" [*pardi*], "Yegads!" [*parbleu*], "For Pete's sake!" or, literally, "By a pipe's name!" [*nom d'une pipe*], and "For cryin' out loud!" or, literally, "By a little chap's name!" [*nom d'un petit bonhomme*]—coined such detoxified modifications. They transformed the sinful word into an innocent interjection, while preserving the phraseological framing device: a quaintly masked a blasphemy to send out into the world. Was the very oblivion into which many of these substitutes fell a by-product of the saltier locutions' too effective makeover?

Here again, to announce blasphemy's total demise would be premature. All lexical neuterings aside, the recent present has, it seems, reignited the antiblasphemy battle. Along with Salman Rushdie's condemnation to death in absentia by a fatwa in 1989,[8] other better or lesser known writers (the Egyptians Alla Ahmed, Farag Foda, Naguib Mahfouz) were prosecuted for blasphemous writings. And even the unexpurgated edition of *The Thousand and One Nights,* published in 1985, was judged to be "pornographic and blasphemous" by al-Azhar University in Cairo.

As for Catholicism, it has revived to much fanfare or notoriety its reprobation of blasphemy. We recall the polemics surrounding Martin Scorsese's *The Last Temptation of Christ.* But is it commonly known for instance that showings of *El Jardin de las Delicias* (The garden of delights) by Spanish filmmaker Carlos Saura were forbidden in 1970 by an agency for the direction of popular culture under the Ministry of Culture because of the film's "irreverent presentation of religious practices, beliefs, and ceremonies, with a malicious intent that borders upon blasphemy"? Is it known that German and Austrian Catholic authorities relied on legislation still in effect to recently bring charges against people or associations who openly accused Christianity and its ministers?[9] More discreet these days in the discourse of contemporary moralists, forbidden speech is undergoing only a provisional relegation, always ready to resurface, less through any particular verbal formulation per se than through the intermediary of other forms of expressive communication: a written work of fiction, visual art and media, or a musical work rapidly and widely circulated.[10] For all that however, the conception of the term is not clearly agreed upon. And religious authorities can easily attach the label of blasphemy to an artistic production just as to a profession of atheism, to the subversion or loose interpretation of a dogma, or indeed to the criticism of a clerical institution.

If these spiritual forces' resurgent combativeness has been in sympathy with the rise of fundamentalism, one cannot however limit oneself to that aspect of things. The 1992 Catholic catechism itself seems to propose a complementary interpretation with the clarification that it "is still blasphemous to recur to God's name to conceal criminal practices, reduce peoples to servitude, torture, or put to death." Was it not in explicit reference to this authorized statement that Cardinal Decourtray, taking stock of the conclusions of the Touvier report at Lyons in 1992, avowed, after the surrender of principle by several clergy members in favor of the militia of Vichy, that he was unable "to hide [his] amazement at what appeared to be a particularly grave, objective blasphemy"?[11]

And yet the obvious collusion between the religious field (Christianity or Islam) and blasphemy can no longer be reduced to only this relation, as impious speech refers less to the religious than to the sacred (whatever the equation for centuries between the latter and Christianity). Other values that yesterday were held to be profane have also acquired the freight of sacredness through a process of "profanization."[12] We have analyzed in the historical case of the French Revolution this transference of sacrosanctity which turned the *Patrie*, the People, and the Republic into references off-limits to the sacrilege of profanatory language. Much more recently in 1979, did we not witness some deeming blasphemous the version of the Marseillaise sung by Serge Gainsbourg?[13] And what of human beings themselves, sacred in their person:[14] are they, too, not the object of blasphemy when assailed in their wholeness, image, dignity—as, in these times, the human rights or the "Rights of Man" are also authorized to found another locus of the sacred?

This probably does not exhaust the list. It shows simply that blasphemy continues to be lost to definitive scrutiny from the moment one rejects a priori accusatory labels. For its persistent and necessary history refers us back, before all else, to the part of ourselves that is the most fragile, the most secret, and the most human.

| NOTES

The French edition followed an abbreviated citation style, supplying only the author's first initial with surname and no mention of the publisher. The bibliography reflects that style. Wherever possible these notes have been expanded to provide fuller publication data—including publisher name (for works appearing after 1900) and full names for authors. At times only the author's surname is given. Numerous frequently cited works belong to the multivolume set abbreviated as *CHO* for J.-P. Migne, ed., Collection of holy orators [*Collection des orateurs sacrés*] or to the National Archives (Archives nationales) abbreviated as *NA*.

For ease of reference, notes that mention a previously cited work give the author's surname and shortened title. When there is considerable space between references to the same citation, the note number of the first citation is provided. French editions cited by Cabantous are accompanied by their English-language translations.

Translator's notes are set off in square brackets. —Trans.

INTRODUCTION

1. I refer to the noteworthy article by Jacques Cheyronnaud and G. Lenclud, "Le blasphème d'un mot," *Paroles d'outrages,* thematic issue, ed. Jacques Cheyronnaud, Elisabeth Claverie, and Jeanne Favret-Saada, *Ethnologie française* 22, no. 3 (1992): 261–270.

2. More will be said about this episode in the conclusion.

3. Among others, one can consult Jacques Ferté, *La vie religieuse dans les campagnes parisiennes (1622–1695)* (Paris: Vrin, 1962); Nicole Castan, *Justice et répression en Languedoc à l'époque des Lumières* (Paris: Flammarion, 1980), and *Les criminels de Languedoc: Les exigences d'ordre et les voies du ressentiment dans une société pré-révolutionnaire (1750–1790)* (Toulouse: Association des publications de l'Université de Toulouse-Le Mirail, 1980); Alain Croix, *La vie, la mort, la foi en Bretagne aux XVIe et XVIIe siècles* (Paris: Maloine, 1981); Robert Sauzet, *Contre-Réforme et Réforme catholique en Bas-Languedoc: Le diocèse de Nîmes au XVIIIe siècle—Etude de sociologie religieuse* (Lille: Université de Lille, 1978); and Bernard

Peyrous, *La Réforme catholique à Bordeaux (1600–1719)* (Bordeaux: Fédération historique du Sud-Ouest and Institut d'Histoire, Université Michel de Montaigne-Bordeaux III), 1995.

4. See, for example, Jean-François Favre-Soulet, *Traditions et réformes religieuses dans les Pyrénées centrales au XVII*ᵉ *siècle: Le diocèse de Tarbes de 1602 à 1716* (Pau: Marrimpouey, 1974); Jean Delumeau, *Le péché et la peur* (Paris: Fayard, 1981) [*Sin and Fear: The Emergence of a Western Guilt Culture, 13th–18th Centuries*, tr. Eric Nicholson (New York: Saint Martin's Press, 1990)]; and Alain Lottin, *Lille, citadelle de la Contre-Réforme? (1598–1668)* (Dunkirk: Westhoek Editions/Editions des Beffrois, 1984). At the same time one must acknowledge the pioneering perspectives of Bartolomé Bennassar and his students Jean-Pierre Dedieu and M.-G. Lefranc on the subject, which use as sources the archives of the Spanish Inquisition.

5. See my *La vergue et les fers: Mutins et déserteurs dans la marine de l'ancienne France* (Paris: Tallandier, 1984), and *Les côtes barbares: Pilleurs d'épaves et sociétés littorales en France (1680–1830)* (Paris: Fayard, 1993).

6. Cf. Cheyronnaud and Lenclud, "Le blasphème d'un mot," pp. 269–270. I closely follow this excellent article for the information in my passage.

7. R. Otto, cited by Robert Tessier, *Le sacré* (Paris: Cerf; Fides, 1991), pp. 28ff. Mercea Eliade, *Le sacré et le profane* (Paris: Gallimard, 1985), pp. 26, 43ff. [*Mystic Stories: The Sacred and the Profane*, tr. Ana Cartianu (Boulder, Colo.: East European Monographs, 1992)].

8. Cheyronnaud and Lenclud, "Le blasphème d'un mot," p. 264.

9. Ibid.

10. Ibid., p. 263.

11. But on the whole there are few (evident, at least) traces of blasphemy. Not a one appears in the Greeks' sacred laws of which recorded texts have survived; and there are only a few allusions in the literature—in Pindar, Euripides, Menander, and above all Plato (*Laws, Republic*, and *Alcibiades I and II*). I owe all of these clarifications to Professor Félix Bourriot, whom I thank warmly for his most helpful research into the question.

12. For this information I am very grateful to Jean-Pierre Martin and Elizabeth Deniaux. Cf. also Daniella Piattelli, "L'offensa alla divinità negli ordinamenti guiridici del mondo antico," *Memoirie de la Società dei Lincei* 8, no. 21 (1977): 410–448.

13. Fernand Cabrol, ed., *Dictionnaire d'archéologie chrétienne et de liturgie*, vol. 2, bk. 1, (Paris: Letouzey et Ané, 1925), s.v. "blasphemy."

14. Nancy Houston, *Dire et interdire: Eléments de jurologie* (Paris: Payot, 1980), p. 27.

15. I refer to the excellent elaboration by Bernard Lauret, "Tu ne prononceras pas à tort le nom de Dieu," in *Blasphèmes et libertés, Colloque de Bruxelles, 10 février 1990, organisé par la Ligue pour l'abolition des lois réprimant le blasphème et*

le droit de s'exprimer librement, ed. Patrice Dartevelle, Phillippe Denis, and Johannes Robyn (Paris: Editions du Cerf, 1993), pp. 33–47.

16. Mark 14:62. Clouds in the Old Testament manifest the presence of God (Exod. 34:5; Num. 11:25). [These and subsequent references to biblical passages follow *The New Oxford Annotated Bible with the Apocrypha*, Revised Standard Version, ed. Herbert G. May and Bruce M. Metzger (New York: Oxford University Press, 1977).—Trans.]

17. Augustine, *De Diverso*, 48, quoted by Pierre Floriot, *Morale chrétienne rapportée aux instructions que Jésus-Christ nous a données dans l'oraison dominicale* (Rouen, 1672), bk. 3, p. 297.

18. Jeanne Favret-Saada, "Rushdie et compagnie, préalable à une anthropologie du blasphème," *Paroles d'outrages*, thematic issue, ed. Jacques Cheyronnaud, Elisabeth Claverie, and Jeanne Favret-Saada, *Ethnologie française* 22, no. 3 (1992): 257.

19. Carla Casagrande and Silvana Vecchio, *Les péchés de la langue: Discipline et ethique de la parole dans la culture médiévale*, translated from the Italian by Philippe Baillet (Paris: Editions du Cerf, 1991), pp. 174–175.

20. Olivier Christin, "Sur la condamnation du blasphème (XVIᵉ–XVIIᵉ siècles)," *Revue d'histoire de l'Eglise de France* 80, no. 204 (janvier–juin 1994): 43–64.

21. David Lawton, *Blasphemy* (Philadelphia: University of Pennsylvania Press; London: Harvester Wheatsheaf, 1993), pp. 2–3.

22. Favret-Saada, "Rushdie," p. 257.

23. Leonard Williams Levy, *Treason Against God: A History of the Offense of Blasphemy* (New York: Schocken, 1981); and Lawton, *Blasphemy*.

24. Students of Claude Gauvard (at the University of Paris I) and Albert Rigaudière (at Paris II) are currently investigating the question through their theses, respectively, in history and legal history.

25. On this score, it seems that the accusation of blasphemy made against Christians professing "the other religion" after 1530 was more frequent in France than it was under the Holy Roman Empire (except in the case of the Anabaptists). See Olivier Christin, "Matériaux pour servir à l'histoire du blasphème," *Bulletin de la Mission historique française en Allemagne*, no. 3 (1996): 68.

1. A SIN'S MEANING

1. I am relying on a corpus of readers and instructional handbooks for priests, church homilies and exhortations, and casuistic treatises for "cases of conscience" [*casus conscientiae*] drawn up by a good fifty or so French or foreign authors, published between the beginning of the seventeenth century and 1809. The exact list of them can be found in the bibliography.

2. See, for example, E. Bauny, *Somme des péchez qui se commettent en tous estats* (Paris, 1633); or, a century after that, Antoine Blanchard, *Examen général sur tous les commandements* (Paris, 1713).

3. Blanchard, ibid.; A. Gambart, *Instructions sur les commandements de Dieu* (1666), vol. 89 of *Collection intégrale et universelle des Orateurs sacrés du premier at du second ordre . . . et collection intégrale, ou choisie, de la plupart des orateurs du troisième ordre* [hereafter abbreviated as *CHO*], ed. J.-P. Migne (Petit Montrouge, 1844), columns 804–811.

4. Azpicuelta, *Abrégé du manuel et très sage doctrine*, Fr. tr. (Paris, 1602).

5. Perhaps this is because of the semantic imprecision of the term *blasphemy*. Such, at least, is the viewpoint of Casagrande and Vecchio in *Les péchés*, pp. 173–180 (see intro., n. 19).

6. Ibid., p. 176.

7. In her thesis for the postgraduate D.E.A. [*diplôme d'études approfondies*, a certificate for study and research prior to the doctoral thesis], Véronique Beaulande turned up two declared cases related to the sacrament of the Eucharist, emphasizing, as far as this issue is concerned, that "blasphemy consists here not in a list of swearwords (*jurons*) but rather in another offense that is not elaborated." See her "Le blasphème et les blasphémateurs à la fin du Moyen Age dans la France du Nord," (D.E.A. thesis, University of Rheims, 1994), pp. 84–88.

8. Antoine Godeau, *La morale chrétienne* (Paris, 1709), vol. 2, pp. 145ff. See also Azpicuelta, "It is blasphemy . . . to attribute to God what is not suited to Him or to take away from Him what is suited to Him, or to give to God's creatures what belongs to God" (*Abrégé*, p. 93). The idea is also in the works of Bauny, Jacopo de Benedicti, Bertin Bertaut, and many others.

9. Floriot, *Morale chrétienne*, bk. 4, sec. 4, art. 4, p. 427 (see intro., n. 17).

10. Gambart, *Instructions*, col. 808. See also Nicolas Girard, curate of Saint Loup, *Petits prônes* (11e dimanche après la Pentecôte) (1776), vol. 92 of *CHO*, col. 1099; Jean Lejeune, *Sermon XLVII*, vol. 3 of *CHO*, col. 526; Vincent de Paul, *Sermons pour les missions des campagnes*, ed. Jeanmaire (Paris, 1859), 25th sermon, vol. 1, pp. 448–465; Ildefonse de Bressanvido, *Instructions morales sur la doctrine chrétienne* (1809), Fr. tr. from the Latin by l'abbé Pétigny (Lyon, 1859), p. 198.

11. François Ballet, *Sermon XVI*, vol. 49 of *CHO*, col. 260.

12. Valerius Régnault, *De la prudence des confesseurs* (Paris, 1616), pp. 520ff.

13. Jean Billot (1709–1767), *Prônes réduits en pratiques, pour les dimanches et fêtes principales de l'année*, vol. 40 of *CHO*, col. 820.

14. Lejeune, *Sermon XLVII*, col. 584.

15. Casagrande and Vecchio, quoting Thomas Aquinas (*Les péchés*, p. 176).

16. Matt. 12:31. See also Mark 2:7. [The French original gives Mark 2:23, but in *The New Oxford Annotated Bible*, Jesus' specific mention of blasphemy occurs in 2:7.— Trans.]

17. Floriot, *Morale chrétienne*, p. 428. Benedicti, Godeau, and Villecourt devote significant, if shorter, passages to the question.

18. Jean Laurent Le Semellier, *Conférences ecclésiastiques sur le Décalogue* (Brussels, 1759). The author distinguishes among other, less grievous acts of swearing (such as imprecation or perjury). Gambart, *Instructions,* also likens blasphemy to a type of oath-swearing ritual or ceremony (*jurements*). In the later medieval period (ca. 1460 in Nantes), a popular preacher, Olivier Maillard, delivered a sermon in which he grouped together, under the name of blasphemy, lies and curses uttered against God and shameful speech. See Maillard, *Sermons et poésies,* ed. Arthur de La Borderie (Nantes, 1877), p. 99.

19. Bertin Bertaut, *Le directeur des confesseurs* (Paris, 1638), pp. 140–143.

20. Pierre Binsfeld, *La théologie des pasteurs, et autres prestres ayans charge des ames,* Fr. tr. from the Latin (Rouen, 1640), pp. 331–332.

21. Jean Eudes, *Le bon confesseur* (Paris, 1686), p. 260.

22. Girard, *Petits prônes,* col. 1100 (earlier this chap., n. 10). An anonymous pastor, a convent superior of Saint-Mark's of Vendôme, distinguished among blasphemy, swearing, and execration ("blasphemy without thought of God"). See *Essai d'exhortation pour les états différents des malades* (Paris, 1713), vol. 2, p. 186.

23. Bertaut, *Le directeur.* Other theologians will call this "mediate" (versus immediate) blasphemy.

24. N. Foucault, *Prônes des dimanches,* vol. 88 of *CHO,* col. 758.

25. "To blame the course of Providence in relation to the unequal distribution of the goods of the earth" (Ballet, *Sermon XVI,* col. 270 [earlier this chap., n. 11]).

26. Gaspare Loarte, *Instructions pour les confesseurs,* Fr. tr. from the Italian (Lyon, 1674), p. 175. [An English-language translation is available as *Instructions and Advertisement* (1613), facsimile reprint (Menston: Scholar Press, 1970). The work is bound with an English-language translation of Etienne Binet, *The Admirable Life of Saint Aldegond* (1632).—Trans.]

27. 2 Kings 18:29. See Exod. 20:7; and Lev. 24:15–16: "Whoever curses his God shall bear his sin. He who blasphemes the name of the Lord shall be put to death; all the congregation shall stone him; the sojourner as well as the native, when he blasphemes the Name, shall be put to death." See also the passage of the Gospel reprised in the Synoptics.

28. 2 Kings 19:35; Isa. 37:36; 2 Chron. 32:18–31. See also the least frequently invoked example of Benadab, another blasphemous Assyrian king, whose 127,000 soldiers are slain by God.

29. For example Girard, *Petits prônes,* or Nicolas Turlot, *Thrésor de la Doctrine chrétienne* (Lyon, 1651).

30. L. Loriot (1633–1715), *Morale,* sermon LXI on blasphemy, vol. 31 of *CHO,* col. 881.

31. Quoted by Françoise Hildesheimer, *La terreur et la pitié* (Paris: Publisud, 1990), p. 57.

32. Vincent de Paul, *Sermons pour les missions*, vol. 1, p. 453 (earlier this chap., n. 10).

33. Girard, *Petits prônes*, col. 1101 (earlier this chap., n. 10).

34. Jean Delumeau, *La peur en Occident (XIVᵉ–XVIIIᵉ siècles); une cité assiégée* (Paris: Fayard, 1978), p. 221.

35. Olivier Christin, "Le statut ambigu du blasphème au XVIᵉ siècle," *Paroles d'outrages*, thematic issue, ed. Jacques Cheyronnaud, Elisabeth Claverie, and Jeanne Favret-Saada, *Ethnologie française* 22, no. 3 (1992): 339.

36. Donald Nugent, *Ecumenism in the Age of Reformation: The Colloque of Poissy* (Cambridge, Mass.: Harvard University Press, 1974), cited by Christin, "Sur la condamnation," p. 46 (see intro., n. 20).

37. Quoted by Nathalie Zemon Davis, *Les cultures du peuple: Rituels, savoirs et résistances au XVIᵉ siècle*, tr. from the English by Marie-Noëlle Bourget (Paris: Aubier-Montaigne, 1979), pp. 160–161. [Published as *Society and Culture in Early Modern France* (Stanford, Calif.: Stanford University Press, 1975)].

38. Denis Crouzet, *Les guerriers de Dieu: La violence au temps des troubles de religion* (Seyssel: Champvallon, 1990), vol. 1, p. 286.

39. An attentive reading of the recorded acts of the Consistory of Saint Mary-of-the-Mines in the seventeenth century (1635–1685) leads to the surmise that instances of blasphemy (of a very small number—2 to 3 percent of cases considered) were distinguished from affronts to pastors and elders. This leads me to modify what I have written about in my study "Du blasphème au blasphémateur: Jalons pour une histoire (XVIᵉ–XIXᵉ siècle)," in *Blasphèmes et libertés, Colloque de Bruxelles, 10 février 1990, organisé par la Ligue pour l'abolition des lois réprimant le blasphème et le droit de s'exprimer librement*, ed. Patrice Dartevelle, Phillippe Denis, and Johannes Robyn, pp. 11–32 (Paris: Editions du Cerf, 1993). For example, when David Antoine was called before the city consistory in February 1672, he was accused on two clearly distinct counts: blaspheming against God and verbally attacking the deacons. (I wish to thank M. Magdelaine for information on this subject.) Did things "evolve" over the centuries in a retrograde direction in regions under the reformed church? Philippe Henry's *Crime, justice et société dans la principauté de Neuchâtel au XVIIIᵉ siècle (1707–1806)* (Neuchâtel: La Baconnière, 1984) would appear to demonstrate this; between 1804 and 1806, legal authorities of this canton prosecuted several people accused of blasphemy for verbal attacks against church pastors, made openly at the church or during services (p. 647).

40. Cesare Bonesana Beccaria, *Des délits et des peines*, 6th ed. (Paris, 1773), p. 288. The eighteenth-century accusations by Beccaria's adversary also pointed to the mark of blasphemy because, according to this detractor, by writing that

humankind owed its gratitude to Jean-Jacques Rousseau, Beccaria had committed "the most impious blasphemy." [There are several English translations of the Milanese marquis's influential work *Tratto dei delitti e delle pene* (1764): *An Essay on Crimes and Punishments* was published, with a commentary, and attributed to Voltaire, in London in 1767. Another was produced in London in 1775; one in Glasgow in 1770; and another in Philadelphia in 1793. Alessandro Manzoni's *The Column of Infamy* opens with Beccaria's *Of Crimes and Punishments*, tr. Kenelm Foster and Jane Grigson (London: Oxford University Press, 1964). A standard scholarly edition is *On Crimes and Punishments*, tr. Henry Paolucci (Indianapolis: Bobbs-Merrill, 1963).—Trans.]

41. Lejeune, *Sermon XLVII*, col. 534 (earlier this chap., n. 10).

42. Ludwig von Pastor, *Histoire des Papes*, Fr. tr., vol. 3, p. 73, quoted by Delumeau, *La peur*, p. 265. [Von Pastor's original work was titled *Geschichte der Päpste seit dem Ausgang des Mittelalters* (Freiburg im Beusgau: Herder and Co., 1925–1933). It exists in English translation as *The History of the Popes from the Close of the Middle Ages: Drawn from the Secret Archives of the Vatican and Other Original Sources* (St. Louis: Herder; London: Routledge K. Paul, 1938–1961).—Trans.]

43. Quoted by Delumeau, *La peur*, p. 284.

44. Ibid., p. 286.

45. Ibid., p. 304.

46. Claudine Fabre-Vassas, *La bête singulière: Les Juifs, les chrétiens et le cochon* (Paris: Gallimard, 1994), p. 145. [Translated by Carol Volk as *The Singular Beast: Jews, Christians, and the Pig* (New York: Columbia University Press, 1997).]

47. Quoted by Delumeau, *La peur*, p. 402.

48. Ibid., p. 403.

49. Françoise Deconninck-Brossard, *Vie politique, sociale et religieuse en Grande-Bretagne d'après les sermons préchés ou publiés dans le nord de l'Angleterre (1738–1760)* (Lille: Atelier national de reproduction des thèses, 1984), pp. 114, 379.

50. Ballet, *Sermon XVI*, col. 270 (earlier this chap., n. 11); Loriot, *Morale*, col. 882 (earlier this chap., n. 30).

51. Bressanvido, *Instructions morales*, p. 202 (earlier this chap., n. 10).

52. Villecourt, *Explication sur des commandements de Dieu*, vol. 82 of *CHO*, col. 398.

53. Alexandre Dubois, *Journal d'un curé de campagne*, ed. Henry Platelle (Paris: Editions du Cerf, 1966), p. 76.

54. Etienne Le Camus, *Le cardinal des montagnes, Etienne Le Camus (1671–1797)*, ed. Jean Godel (Grenoble: Presses Universitaires de Grenoble, 1974). In many of his pastoral visits (to Villard d'Arène, Pierre-Châtel), Le Camus vilifies blasphemy. Cf. Michel Pernot, *Etude sur la vie religieuse de la campagne lorraine à la fin du XVIIe siècle: Le visage du Xaintois d'après la visite canonique de*

1687 (Nancy: Faculté des Lettres et Sciences Humaines de l'Université de Nancy, 1971), p. 105. For the dioceses of Quebec, see René Hardy, "A l'origine du juron religieux au Québec," *Injures et blasphèmes,* thematic issue, *Mentalités,* no. 2 (1989): 104.

55. Departmental Archives of the Gironde, G 651, heading labeled "Etat des paroisses, visites pastorales 1731/1734."

2. BLASPHEMY AND THE COUNTER-REFORMATION

1. Cf., for example, Ephraim Pagitt, *Heresiography or, A description of the Hereticks and Sectaries of These Latter Times* (London, 1647). "Today," writes Pagitt in his dedication to the lord-mayor of London, who had denounced fifty-three heresies," I do purpose, to the Honour of God and great Benefit of the Church, to give a Description of these impure sects, who blaspheme God's name and are spread wide in the midst of us like unto the Locusts of Apocalypse."

2. "Heresy's consequences?" asked F. Pena in his additions to the 1578 edition of N. Eymerich's *Manual of Inquisitors.* "Blasphemies, sacrileges, blows to the very foundations of the Church."

3. The inquisitors' handbooks, through the use of separate listings, sometimes distinguished oaths or blasphemies that were heretical from those that were not.

4. See the comments of Jean-Pierre Dedieu, *L'administration de la foi: L'Inquisition de Tolède (XVIᵉ–XVIIIᵉ siècles)* (Madrid: Bibliothèque de la Casa Velázquez, 1989), p. 243.

5. On the first proposition, which stated " 'some of God's commandments are impossible to observe for the Just despite their will and efforts, given the powers they presently possess and as well because the Grace is not theirs which would allow them': this is a reckless, impious, blasphemous proposition, worthy to be declared anathema and heretical." The fifth fared no better: " 'It is semi-Pelagian to say that Jesus Christ died and shed his blood for all men without exception.' A false, reckless, scandalous proposition, understood in the sense that Jesus Christ shall have died only for the salvation of the predestined. This proposition is declared impious, blasphemous, slanderous, injurious to God's goodness and heretical." Cited by Françoise Hildesheimer, *Le jansénisme en France aux XVIIᵉ et XVIIIᵉ siècles* (Paris: Publisud, 1991), p. 59.

6. M.-J. Piozza-Donati, "Le procès contre Matteo Gazzotto, modénais soupçonné d'hérésie à la fin du XVIᵉ siècle," *Mélanges de l'Ecole française de Rome* 89, no. 2 (1977): 978.

7. Carlo Ginzburg, *Le fromage et les vers: L'univers d'un meunier du XVIᵉ siècle,* tr. Monique Aymard (Paris: Flammarion, 1980.) [In English as *The Cheese and the Worms: The Cosmos of a Sixteenth-Century Miller,* tr. John and Anne Tedeschi

(Baltimore: Johns Hopkins University Press, 1980); and originally published as *Il formaggio e i vermi: Il cosmo di un mugnaio del '500* (Rome: Giulio Einaudi, 1976).—Trans.]

8. Ginzburg, *Cheese,* p. 4.

9. Ginzburg, ibid., pp. 5–6. Yet, elsewhere, the miller Menocchio had proposed other images of God to the inquisitors: that of army captain, noble lord, father, property owner (*Fromage,* pp. 94–95; 105).

10. A. Coll, a sacristan of the convent of Augustinian sisters of Valencia in Spain, was condemned in 1643 for having said that "Christ was just a wooden timber and that if one struck him and broke him with an axe he would not bleed" (in M.-G. Lefranc, "Blasphèmes et blasphémateurs dans le royaume de Valence [XVIe–XVIIe siècles]," [master's thesis, University of Toulouse-le-Mirail, 1976]. One could also cite the case of a peasant in a market town in the region of Murcie who, in front of a crucifix, had said to his wife during a quarrel that "all this is only lies" (Michèle Escamilla-Colin, *Crimes et châtiments dans l'Espagne inquisitoriale, 1659–1734* [Paris: Berg International, 1992], vol. 2, p. 228). Cf. also Maureen Flynn, "Blasphemy and the Play of Anger in Sixteenth Century Spain," *Past and Present* 149 (November 1995): 29–56.

11. Lefranc, "Blasphèmes et blasphémateurs," trial of 1584; Ginzburg, *Fromage,* p. 37; Christin, "Le statut ambigu," p. 338 (see chap. 1, n. 35). Many other examples can be found in the archives of the Parisian *justices seigneuriales.*

12. In 1582 a schoolmaster named Noël Jumet was burned alive at Metz for having repudiated the entirety of Christian dogma. Ten years later at Nîmes, a philosophy professor was "merely" exiled from the city for having declared Christianity "twaddle and stupid rubbish" (*fadaises et niaiseries*). Cited by François Lebrun, ed., *Histoire des catholiques en France* (Toulouse: Privat, 1980), p. 122.

13. In February 1668, Adriaen had put out "a florid garden composed of all matter of lovable things, planted by Peaceful Speaksincere, searcher after truth." Arrested, he died in prison. The following year one reads in the records of Amsterdam's consistory, "the Assembly learns with deep sadness that the blasphemous heresy [of the Socinians] is audaciously rearing its head, and we judge it eminently necessary to remain attentive within the full extent of its means." For a complete account of this episode, see Koenraad Oege Meinsma, *Spinoza et son cercle* (orig. 1896, in Dutch), Fr. tr. S. Roosenburg (Paris: J. Vrin, 1983), pp. 355–385.

14. Ginzburg, *Cheese,* pp. 5–6.

15. Escamilla-Collin, *Crimes,* p. 224.

16. Quoted in Bernard Dompnier, *Le venin de l'hérésie: Image du protestantisme et combat catholique au XVIIe siècle* (Paris: Le Centurion, 1985), p. 101.

17. Ginzburg, *Fromage,* pp. 62, 91.

18. See also the pertinent remarks of Christin in "Sur la condamnation," pp. 6off. (see intro., n. 20).

19. Vincent de Paul, *Sermons pour les missions*, vol. 1, p. 456 (see chap. 1, n. 10). For the seventeenth and eighteenth centuries, one can consult Loriot, Turlot, Girard, Lejeune, Loarte, and Le Semellier.

20. Bressanvido, *Instructions morales*, pp. 198–199 (see chap. 1, n. 10).

21. In Spain, where there were few witch-hunts, the struggle against blasphemy ran out of steam before 1560. In Venice—where attacks against witchcraft were rare—the campaign against blasphemy went on for a century and a half; after 1570, there was a concurrent antiblasphemy campaign in the duchy of Modena (Piozza-Donati, "Procès," p. 945 [earlier this chap., n. 6]). In France there seems to have been an upswing in condemnations of blasphemy (at least as attested by written accounts and books on it) toward 1580 at a time that saw the initiation of vociferous witch-hunts. A more precise chronology, however, would be needed to demonstrate unequivocally the correspondence. According to Alfred Soman, *Sorcellerie et justice criminelle, le Parlement de Paris, XVIe–XVIIIe siècles* (Brookfield, Vt.: Variorum, 1992), it was after 1630—thus when repression against blasphemy was ebbing—that stories of witches' sabbaths, along with gossip about devils, were no longer associated with the accusation of blasphemy (p. 197).

22. Jean Bodin, *De la démonomanie des sorciers* (Paris, 1580), p. 122.

23. Pierre de Lancre, foreword to his *Tableau de l'inconstance des mauvais anges et démons: où il est amplement traité des sorciers et de la sorcellerie* (1613), n.p. [A recent edition of Lancre's *Tableau* has been edited by Nicole Jacques-Chaquin (Paris: Aubier, 1982).—Trans.]

24. R. Mandrou, *Magistrats et sorciers en France au XVIIe siècle: Une analyse de psychologie historique* (Paris: Plon, 1968), p. 359.

25. Exceptions to this are known; consider the example of Antoine Millet, whose profane speech placed him under suspicion for sorcery, having pronounced "that he no longer wanted to pray to God and that he truly knew not if the devil should not lend him help rather than God" (Archives Nationales, X2A-959, 30 August 1597, cited by Soman, *Sorcellerie*, p. 400).

26. Christin, "Sur la condamnation," p. 51 (see intro., n. 20).

27. Mandrou, *Magistrats*, p. 185. Mandrou also gives the example of the woodworker Michel de Moulins, who was condemned in 1623; Christin cites the 1622 sentencing of Barbe Martin of Vézelise for having treated with the devil "and by the works and ministry of the aforementioned did cause several persons to fall sick with illness and made an animal to die and by execrable blasphemies did impiously and scandalously declare she was innocent" ("Sur la condamnation," p. 51). One might also consult the examples cited in J.-C. Deidler, *Démons et sorcières en Lorraine: Le bien et le mal dans les communautés rurales (1550–1660)* (Paris: Messene, 1996).

28. Lawton, *Blasphemy*, pp. 17–19 (see intro., n. 21).

29. In the case of France, Mandrou observes that the ordinance of July 30, 1666, against blasphemers "nowhere mentioned conjuring the devil or committing devilish sacrilege" (*Magistrats*, p. 439, n. 31).

30. Synodal statues of the diocese of Annecy, vol. 23, bk. 2, pp. 397–398.

31. Ballet asked this in a sermon (*Sermon XVI*, col. 261 [see chap. 1, n. 11]).

32. Piozza-Donati, "Procès," p. 963 (earlier this chap., n. 6).

33. Quoted by Escamilla-Colin, *Crimes*, p. 229 (earlier this chap., n. 10).

34. Dedieu, *L'administration*, p. 247 (earlier this chap., n. 4).

35. T. Barbault, *Prières pour ceux qui voyagent sur la mer* (Amsterdam, 1688), p. 25.

36. Abbé de Mangin, *La science des confesseurs* (Paris, 1757), vol. 2, pp. 125–126.

37. Quoted in Jean Delumeau, *Un chemin d'histoire: Chrétienté et christianisation* (Paris: Fayard, 1981), p. 172.

38. Bressanvido, *Instructions morales*, p. 196 (see chap. 1, n. 10).

39. Vincent de Paul, *Sermons pour les missions*, vol. 1, p. 453 (see chap. 1, n. 10). The same idea can be found in G. Fournier's *Hydrographie universelle contenant la théorie et la pratique de toutes les parties de la navigation* (Paris: 1643; Grenoble: 1975): "Doth not the blasphemer make use in attacking God of one of the most signal gifts he hath received from His most generous Hand?" (p. 692).

40. Alphonse de Liguori, *Instructions et sermons sur les preceptes du Décalogue et sur les sacrements* (1768), Fr. tr. from the Latin (Paris, 1827), p. 64. [Later editions of this work from 1832, 1834, and 1844 are all catalogued in the Bibliothèque Nationale bearing the slightly variant title *Instructions familières au peuple sur les préceptes du décalogue . . . et sur les sacrements*, tr. Jean-Baptiste-Avit Verdier.— Trans.]

41. Vincent de Paul, *Sermons pour les missions*, vol. 1, p. 455. [The original has "*ventre*" (side). I have chosen *wounds* as the English equivalent, since Christ's side was pierced by the lance of the centurion. Blasphemous French oaths that used the word include the euphemistic "*ventrebleu!*" (equivalent to the Elizabethan "zounds!") and "*ventre de Dieu.*"—Trans.]

42. Fournier, *Hydrographie*, p. 692.

43. Liguori, *Instructions*, p. 65; Loarte, *Instructions* (see chap. 1, n. 26); also discussed by Régnault, *De la prudence*, pp. 519–520 (see chap. 1, n. 12).

44. Antoine Blanchard [often catalogued as Joseph-Antoine-Esprit Blanchard], *Essay d'exhortation pour les estats différens des malades* (Paris, 1713), vol. 2, p. 187.

45. Bressanvido, *Instructions morales*, p. 202.

46. I closely follow the account that L. Châtellier draws on in his *La religion des pauvres: Les missions rurales en Europe et la formation du catholicisme moderne, XVIe–XIXe siècles* (Paris: Aubier, 1993), pp. 135–136.

47. "To reestablish it [i.e., the impurity of blasphemy] in the low condition it should never have left" (ibid., p. 136).

48. Jacopo de Benedicti [also known as Jacopone da Todi], *La somme des péchez et des remèdes d'iceux*, Fr. tr. from the Italian (Paris, 1601), p. 70.

49. Mangin, *La science*, p. 128 (earlier this chap., n. 36).

50. Nicole Lemaître, *Saint Pie V* (Paris: Fayard, 1994), p. 230.

51. The reformed churches, attempting to suppress sinful behavior by bringing it to the attention of the consistory, also oversaw the religious and moral cohesion of communities. For the years between 1635 and 1671, the archives of the Lutheran consistory of Sainte-Marie-aux-Mines contain some thirty recorded cases of blasphemy (less than 5 percent of the total contained in the archives); the perpetrators of which are sometimes "censured," more rarely "sent away by the Elders."

52. Loarte, *Instructions*, p. 179.

53. Jean Delumeau and Daniel Roche, eds. *Histoire des pères et de la paternité* (Paris: Larousse, 1990). See in particular the essential contributions by M. Carbonnier-Burkard and O. Robert.

54. Liguori, *Instructions*, p. 68 (earlier this chap., n. 40); Girard, *Petits prônes*, col. 1101 (see chap. 1, n. 10); Gambart, *Instructions,* col. 89 (see chap. 1, n. 3).

55. Bressanvido, *Instructions morales*, p. 201 (see chap. 1, n. 10).

56. The statutes of the Tailors and Dressmakers of Carpentras of 1592 specifically encourage members to take diligent measures against blasphemy. Cf. R. Sauzet in Lebrun, ed., *Histoire*, p. 121 (earlier this chap., n. 12).

57. D. Alezais, "La confrérie des gens de mer de Marseille: Le nouveau règlement de 1722," *Mémoires de l'Académie de Marseille* (1935): 142–147.

58. Quoted by C. Memheld, "Le fait associatif chez les gens de mer français du XIe au XVIIIe siècle" (graduate thesis, University of Paris IV, 1979). Among the orders given by one J. Pellet, a mid-seventeenth-century merchant from Bordeaux, to the captain of the vessel *La Pallas*, one may read "that said captain keep a firm hold on his crew, that he keep the peace and punish with utmost rigor blasphemers who use the Holy Name of God" (Jean Cavaignac, *Jean Pellet, commerçant de gros* [Paris: SEVPEN, 1967], p. 59).

59. Quoted by J.-B. Le Comte, *Messire de Clieu, les églises et le clergé de la ville du Havre (1561–1861)* (Le Havre, 1851), pp. 267–276.

60. Departmental Archives of the Seine-Maritime, 216 BP 305 bis (1717).

61. This material is drawn from Le Comte, p. 225.

62. Favre-Soulet, *Traditions*, p. 47 (see intro., n. 4).

63. Georges Minois, "Le réseau des confréries pieuses est-il un indice valable du sentiment religieux?" in *L'Espace et le sacré, Annales de Bretagne et des Pays de l'Ouest* 90 (1983): 341.

64. Marcel Poète, *Une vie de cité: Paris de sa naissance à nos jours* (Paris: Auguste Picard, 1931), vol. 3, pp. 241–244. [For an overview of the context of the

religious wars in France during the latter part of the sixteenth century when these brotherhoods were formed, see Georges Livet, "France: Failure or Spiritual Heritage?" part 3 of *The Reformation*, ed. Pierre Chaunu (Gloucester: Allan Sutton, 1989), pp. 168–183.—Trans.]

65. Articles granted and sworn to by the brothers of the Brotherhood of the Holy Name of Jesus, Orleans, 1590 (printed texts, Bibliothèque Nationale, Paris).

66. R. de Voyer d'Argenson, *Annales de la compagnie du Saint-Sacrement*, ed. Don Beauchet-Filleau (Paris-Poitiers, 1900), p. 18, quoted by Alain Tallon, *La compagnie du Saint-Sacrement, 1629–1667: Spiritualité et société* (Paris: Editions du Cerf, 1990), p. 20; and by Raoul Allier, *La cabale des dévôts: 1627–1666* (Paris: A. Colin, 1902; reprint, Geneva: Slatkine, 1972), p. 215.

67. Quoted by François Billacois, *Le duel dans la société française aux XVIe et XVIIe siècles: Essai de psychologie historique* (Paris: Editions de l'Ecole des hautes études en sciences sociales, 1986), p. 286.

68. Lottin, *Lille*, p. 263 (see intro., n. 4).

69. Châtellier, *La religion des pauvres*, p. 133 (earlier this chap., n. 46).

70. Jean-Louis de Fromentières, *Sermon pour le jour de la circoncision*, vol. 8 of *CHO*, col. 18. [This sermon appears to be in Fromentières's *œuvres complètes: Collection intégrale et universelle des orateurs sacrés du premier et du second ordre*, vol. 8 (Petit Montrouge: Imprimerie Catholique, 1844).—Trans.]

71. Séraphin de Paris, *Sermon XXXII* and *Panégyrique du Saint Nom de Jésus*, vol. 33 of *CHO*, cols. 659/668 (respectively).

72. At Fribourg-am-Brisgau the Jesuits staged a theatrical production to denounce blasphemy; at Trent they adorned the street with pictures of Christ with lit candles set before them (first third of the seventeenth century) (Châtellier, *La religion des pauvres*, p. 133 [earlier this chap., n. 46]). As for the emphasis on directing individual initiative and faith, Christin points to the founding of a special mass of the Holy Spirit by Marie Rollier de Vaudelainville in 1680 "for the conversion of jurors, blasphemers, and speakers of curses" (Christin, "Sur la condamnation," p. 53 [see intro., n. 20]).

3. GOD'S HOLY CHURCH AGAINST BLASPHEMY

1. Ricardo Garcia-Carcel, *Origenes de la Inquisición española: El tribunal de Valencia* (Barcelona: Ediciones Península, 1976); Bartholomé Bennassar et al., eds., *L'Inquisition espagnole (XVIe–XIXe siècles)* (Paris: Hachette, 1979); Dedieu, *L'administration* (see chap. 2, n. 4). One can also consult the Actes du Colloque de Trieste (May 1988) on the Italian Inquisition; see A. Del Col and G. Paolin, eds., *L'inquizizione romana in Italia nell' età moderna: Archivi, problemi di methodo y nuove ricerche* (Roma, 1991).

2. The Toledo Inquisition received 53.3 percent of the first declared cases of blasphemy; 16.7 percent were referred to ecclesiastical courts, and 30 percent to the lay or secular justice system (Dedieu, *L'administration*, p. 138).

3. Escamilla-Colin, *Crimes*, vol. 1, p. 231; vol. 2, p. 216 (see chap. 2, n. 10).

4. *Advis et exhortation en toute humilité et obéissance à Mgrs du Conseil d'Etat général de la Sainte Union de l'Eglise C. A. et R. contre les blasphémateurs du Saint Nom de Dieu et ceux qui seront trouvés en adultère et paillardise* (Paris, 1589) (printed texts, Bibliothèque Nationale).

5. [A *Dialogue d'entre le maheustre et le manant*, published in Paris in 1593 or 1594, has been variously attributed to a *procureur* (comparable to *attorney* or *solicitor*) named Crucé and one Lazare Morin called Cromé. One scholar (Brunet) has argued that in successive publications this dialogue shifted its original pro–Catholic League sympathies toward favoring Henry IV. Both Yale University and the Newberry Library in Chicago are listed as having editions of the work. *Maheustre* was apparently a term of insult applied to Huguenots and members of the *parti politique* (Frédéric Geodefroy, *Dictionnaire de l'ancienne langue française et de tous ses dialectes du IXᵉ au XVᵉ siècle* [Paris, 1888; reprint, New York: Scientific Periodicals Establishment and Krauss Reprint Corporation, 1961], s.v. "*maheustre*"). In France, the *maheustre* was a pad, or wadding, placed in the upper part of the sleeve of a garment to increase the apparent breadth of the shoulders and to upraise them, following the fashion of the fifteenth and sixteenth centuries. The Old French word (also seen in the forms *mahustre*, *mahostre*, and *maheutre*) became the English *mahoitre*, describing the same padding for the fashionable upper sleeves (*Oxford English Dictionary*). Precisely how, when, and why the term came to be associated with Huguenots is harder to trace.—Trans.]

6. For more on this whole question, see Anne Lefebvre-Teillard, *Les officialités à la veille du Concile de Trente* (Paris: Librairie générale de droit et de jurisprudence, 1973).

7. Arlette Lebigre, *Les Grands Jours d'Auvergne: Désordre et répression au XVIIᵉ siècle* (Paris: Hachette, 1976); Esprit Fléchier, *Les Grands Jours d'Auvergne: Oraisons funèbres*, ed. Philippe Bernard (Paris: Union générale d'éditions, 1964), pp. 115–116. [Fléchier, *The Clermont Assizes of 1665: A Merry Account of a Grim Court, Being a Translation of Abbé Fléchier's "Mémoires sur les grand jours d'Auvergne*," tr. William Wistar Comfort (Philadelphia: University of Pennsylvania Press, 1937).]

8. Quoted by Jacques Marguet (pseudonym of the abbé Daux), *Essai sur le blasphème*, 8th ed. (Besançon, 1823), p. 77.

9. *Table raisonné des matières contenues dans les procès-verbaux des Assemblées générales et particulières du clergé de France* (Paris, 1780). The texts of synodal statutes from the seventeenth and eighteenth centuries add nothing concrete on

this subject, except the express prohibition that priests not swear or blaspheme (as laid out in the 1647 statues of the diocese of Rheims) (Bibliothèque Municipale, B 5 595).

10. The remonstrance accuses "blasphemers and libertines whose habits are everywhere to be seen" (quoted by René Taveneaux, *Le catholicisme dans la France classique: 1610–1715* [Paris: Société d'édition d'enseignement supérieure, 1980], vol. 1, p. 249).

11. Vincent-Toussaint Beurrier (1715–1782), *Sermon VII* ("Day of Circumcision"), vol. 56 of *CHO*, col. 1148. [The Eudists were named for Saint Jean Eudes (1601–1680), who founded at Caen, in 1643, this congregation of priests devoted to teaching in seminaries and preaching.—Trans.]

12. The widespread and notorious circulation of false news, or canards, in the seventeenth century echoed these "marvelous and frightening stories" of blasphemers being punished with a cruelty commensurate with their defiance. See Jean-Pierre Seguin, *L'information en France avant le périodique: 517 canards imprimés entre 1529 et 1631* (Paris: Maisonneuve et Larose, 1964), pp. 111–114.

13. Artus Désiré, *Le grand et admirable signe de Dieu apparu au ciel, contraire à la blasphème* (Paris, 1563).

14. Crouzet, *Les guerriers de Dieu*, vol. 2, p. 93 (see chap. 1, n. 38).

15. Barthélemy de Viette, *Punition divine et exemplaire d'un blasphémateur* (Lyon, 1612) (Historical Library of the City of Paris).

16. Liguori, *Instructions*, p. 64 (see chap. 2, n. 40). In an interesting variation on the motif, the Jesuit Fournier cited the case of a blasphemer carried off by the devil into the depths of Etna, " 'and so that I might be believed,' said the diabolical voice, 'here is what [the offender] held in his hands when he was borne off,' and at that same instant the thing that this unfortunate wretch had been holding fell into the middle of the audience" (*Hydrographie*, p. 692 [see chap. 2, n. 39]). Cf. also *Récit véritable, merveilleux et espouvantable relatif à la punition d'un blasphémateur d'Ancône* (Paris, 1627) (Bibliothèque Nationale, K 16024).

17. Ollivier de Minière, *Discours véritable de ce qui est advenu à trois blasphémateurs ordinaires* (Angoulême, 1600).

18. Departmental Archives of Puy-de-Dôme, 1 J 284, August 1723.

19. Jacques Gaultier, *Table chronologique de l'estat du christianisme comprenant . . . le rapport des vieilles hérésies aux modernes et douze principales vérités catholiques établies contre la R. P. R. par l'Ecriture Sainte et preuvées de siècle en siècle par les Saints Pères de ce temps-là*, 7th ed. (Lyon, 1673). The author cited the cases of two blasphemers who were punished immediately by God: an Arian bishop of Carthage in 502, and an English soldier in the twelfth century (pp. 517, 687). ["R. P. R." stood sardonically for "Religion Prétendue Réformée," "Religion Supposedly 'Reformed.'"—Trans.]

20. Puy-de-Dôme archives (earier this chap., n. 18).

21. Gen. 19:24–26. ["Then the Lord rained on Sodom and Gomorrah brimstone and fire from the Lord out of heaven; and he overthrew those cities, and all the valley, and the inhabitants of the cities, and what grew on the ground. But Lot's wife behind him looked back, and she became a pillar of salt.—Trans.]

22. Anonymous, *Histoire merveilleuse et épouvantable de la punition d'un parjure blasphémateur* (Lyon, 1608).

23. Pierre de Villars, *Traité sommaire et invectif contre les vains sermens, fréquens juremens et exécrables blasphèmes dont ce siècle est tout infect* (Lyon, 1596), p. 145.

24. Girard, *Petits prônes,* col. 1101 (see chap. 1, n. 10).

25. Lebrun has clearly pointed out how a work such as *Les sept trompettes,* which was used in primary schools as well as in the collected tales of the *Bibliothèque bleue,* served as a vehicle for "a message emanating from the elite—in this case the clergy of reformed Catholicism—and intended for the instruction of the popular classes." See his "Les échanges entre culture populaire et culture des élites," in *Les échanges culturels à l'époque moderne* (Association des historiens modernistes des universités), no. 10 (1985). [Robert Darnton describes the *Bibliothèque bleue,* in a rather more populist vein, as "the primitive paperbacks that were read aloud at *veillées* in villages where someone was capable of reading. These little blue books featured Sleeping Beauty and Little Red Riding Hood as well as Gargantua, Fortunatus, Robert le Diable, Jean de Calais, les Quatre Fils Aymon, Maugis l'Enchanteur, and many other characters from the oral tradition that [Charles] Perrault never picked up" ("Peasants Tell Tales: The Meaning of Mother Goose," *The Great Cat Massacre and Other Episodes in French Cultural History* [New York: Vintage, 1985], p. 63).—Trans.]

26. *Les sept trompettes pour réveiller les pécheurs,* translated from the Latin by C. Jouye (Rouen, 1645), p. 130.

27. Loriot, *Morale,* col. 881 (see chap. 1, n. 30).

4. KINGS AGAINST BLASPHEMY

1. Novelle 77, quoted by Nicolas Delamare, *Traité de la police* (Paris, 1727), vol. 1, p. 544.

2. Jean-Pierre Pichette, *Le guide raisonné des jurons* (Montréal: Quinz, 1980), part 2, chap. 1.

3. Jean de Joinville, *The Life of Saint Louis,* in Joinville and Geoffroy de Villehardouin, *Chronicles of the Crusades,* tr. M. R. B. Shaw (Harmondsworth: Penguin, 1963), p. 336. [Cabantous's note cites *Histoire de Saint Louis* (Paris, 1958), p. 246. The nearest complete citation for an edition of about this time is *L'Histoire édifiante et merveilleuse de la vie du Saint roi Louis, de ses croisades en Terre Sainte,*

de ses vertus et de sa sagesse, ed. Jacques Desforges (Paris: Le Livre Club du libraire, 1957). A recent edition is *Histoire de St. Louis écrite par son compagnon d'armes le sire de Joinville*, ed. Nathalis de Wailly (Paris: J. de Bonnot, 1994).—Trans.]

4. For a complete account of the legislative measures, see Delamare, *Traité*, title 6, chap. 4. One can also consult N. Meury, *Code de la religion et des mœurs* (Paris, 1779), vol. 1, pp. 66–92.

5. According to Elisabeth Belmas, "La police des cultes et des mœurs en France sous l'Ancien Régime" (graduate thesis, University of Paris I, 1980); this is subject matter that Guyot rounds out in his *Répertoire universel et raisonné de jurisprudence civile, criminelle, canonique et bénéficiale* (Paris, 1776), vol. 6, s.v. "blasphème," pp. 208–212. [Belmas's thesis is apparently available as a subsequent publication in two volumes (Paris: Editions de l'Ecole des hautes études en sciences sociales, 1985).—Trans.]

6. Cabantous, "Du blasphème," pp. 11–31 (see chap. 1, n. 39); Christin, "Le statut ambigu," pp. 337–343 (see chap. 1, n. 35).

7. This is also Delumeau's finding concerning the Inquisition's activity at Modena (*La peur*, p. 402 [see chap. 1, n. 34]).

8. Here I follow closely Elisabeth Belmas's elaboration in "La montée du blasphème à l'âge moderne du Moyen Age au XVIIe siècle," *Injures et blasphèmes*, thematic issue, *Mentalités*, no. 2 (1989): 14–16, even if I have qualms with the choice of title, which relies on the gearing down [*démultiplication*] of legislative documents to prove the resurgence of blasphemy during the sixteenth and seventeenth centuries.

9. Over the course of the first four convictions, the fine was doubled, with the amount for each instance determined arbitrarily. Prison terms for blasphemers unable to pay fines were at the magistrates' discretion. Five-time offenders were sentenced to wear the ignominious iron collar on a feast day or the Sabbath. Judgments for the three last repeat offenses prescribed cutting off the upper lip, then the lower, and finally the tongue, with a stint in the pillory each time.

10. Belmas, "La montée," p. 15.

11. Quoted in Robert Muchembled, *Le temps des supplices: De l'obéissance sous les rois absolus (XVe–XVIIIe siècles)* (Paris: A. Colin, 1992), p. 151.

12. Siegfried Leutenbauer, *Das Delikt der Gotteslästerung in des bayerischen Gesetzgebung* (Cologne-Vienna: Böhlau, 1984), pp. 107–108.

13. R. Derosas, "Moralità e giustizia a Venezia nel '500–600: Gli esecutori contro la bestemmia," in *Stato, società e giustizia nella Repubblica veneta (sec. XV–XVIII)*, ed. Gaetano Cozzi (Rome: Jouvence, 1981), pp. 433–528.

14. It has not been possible to consult Courtney Stanhope Kenny's "The Evolution of the Law of Blasphemy," *Cambridge Law Journal* 1 (1922): 127–142, which may well take detailed bearings of the question. It is noteworthy that Parliament in the Scottish kingdom drew up, on at least two occasions, a list of proscribed

expressions considered to be blasphemous. Cf. Geoffrey Hughes, *Swearing: A Social History of Foul Language, Oaths and Profanity in English* (Cambridge, Mass., and Oxford, U.K.: Blackwell, 1991), p. 120.

15. "Blasphemy," *New Catholic Encyclopedia* (New York: McGraw-Hill, 1967); Maurice Braure and Léon Cahen, *L'evolution politique de l'Angleterre moderne (1485–1660)* (Paris: A. Michel, 1960), pp. 57–230, 308.

16. Quoted by Elizabeth Tuttle, *Religion et idéologie dans la Révolution anglaise (1647–1649)* (Paris: L'Harmattan, 1989), p. 35. [Thomas Edwards's *Gangraena or a Catalogue and Discovery of Many Errours, Heresies, Blasphemies and Pernicious Practices of the Sectaries* (1646) is available in a facsimile edition, introduced by M. M. Goldsmith and Ivan Roots (Ilkley: *The Rota* and the University of Exeter, 1977). I was unable to locate, in the original English edition of *Gangraena*, any passage corresponding to a section cited by Cabantous of Elizabeth Tuttle's French translation—in either Edwards's "Epistle Dedicatory to the Lords and Commons Assembled in Parliament" or his preface (*Gangraena*, part 1), his dedication entitled "To the Christian Reader" or the second preface (part 2), or his preface to part 3. (There is no English original of Tuttle's book.)—Trans.]

17. Tuttle, ibid., p. 98.

18. It was in the spring of 1648 that Cromwell and the Roundhead army subjugated Kent, Wales, and the northern part of the kingdom (Bernard Cottret, *Cromwell* [Paris: Fayard, 1992]).

19. In *Acts and Ordinances of the Interregnum (1642–1660)*, ed. Charles Harding Firth and Robert Sangster Raits (London: Her Majesty's Stationery Office, 1911), vol. 1, pp. 1133–1136.

20. Christopher Hill finds that there existed among the people a long tradition of materialist skepticism and anti-clericalism that was not necessarily well organized, even if he cites, for example, the Familists. See *The World Turned Upside Down: Radical Ideas During the English Revolution* (London: Temple Smith, 1972); translated into French by Rachel Ertel as *Le monde à l'envers: Les idées radicales au cours de la Révolution anglaise* (Paris: Payot, 1977), pp. 31–32. [References to pages are to the French edition.—Trans.] This assertion, for which Hill does not adduce a good deal of serious support, is open to some doubt.

21. In Firth and Raits, *Acts and Ordinances*, vol. 2, pp. 409–410.

22. J. C. Davis, "Fear, Myth, and Furor: Reappraising the Ranters," *Past and Present*, no. 129 (1990); B. Coward, "The Experience of Gentry (1640–1660)," in *Town and Countryside in the English Revolution*, ed. R. C. Richardson (New York: Manchester University Press, 1992), p. 210.

23. Roland Marx, *Religion et société en Angleterre de la Réforme à nos jours* (Paris: Presses universitaires de France, 1978), p. 77. G. E. Aymler cites the case of a certain Taylor who was tried and sentenced to prison and public penitence by the King's Bench for having blasphemed and professed atheism. See his "Unbelief

in Seventeenth-Century England," in *Puritans and Revolutionaries: Essays in Seventeenth-Century History*, ed. Donald Pennington and Keith Thomas (Oxford: Clarendon Press, 1978), p. 44.

24. R. Webb, "From Toleration to Religious Liberty," in *Liberty Secured? Britain Before and After 1688*, ed. J. R. Jones (Stanford: Stanford University Press, 1992), p. 162. Three months' imprisonment was given only in the case of repeat offenses.

25. William Blackstone, *Commentaries on the Laws of England*, 3d ed. (Oxford, 1768); Fr. tr. (Paris, 1776), p. 54.

26. Cited in Patrice Dartevelle, Phillippe Denis, and Johannes Robyn, eds., *Blasphèmes et libertés, Colloque de Bruxelles, 10 février 1990, organisé par la Ligue pour l'abolition des lois réprimant le blasphème et le droit de s'exprimer librement* (Paris: Editions du Cerf, 1993), p. 100.

27. In December 1710 Blaise Borel, standing accused of "blasphemy and superstitious acts," saw his case transferred from the court of the state council to that of the Consistory of Lordships of the Val du Travers (cf. Henry, *Crime*, p. 157 [see chap. 1, n. 39]).

28. Here one can refer to V. Demars-Sion's article for information about the particular arrangements which Charles V (in 1521) and then Phillip II (in 1559 and 1587) explained to the *officialités* of the Low Countries, which were more autonomous institutions than those of the French kingdom ("Les monarchies européennes aux prises avec la justice ecclésiastique: L'exemple des anciens Pays-Bas espagnols," *Revue du Nord* 77 [July–September 1995]: 535–565).

29. Lefebvre-Teillard, *Les officialités*, pp. 73ff. (see chap. 3, n. 6).

30. Cf. the quotation provided by Christin, "Le statut ambigu," p. 339 (see chap. 1, n. 35).

31. A quite similar division of juridical responsibilities could be found in England, at least up until the middle of the eighteenth century.

32. Pierre-Toussaint Durand de Maillane, *Dictionnaire de droit canonique et de pratique bénéficiale*, 2d ed., vol. 1 (Lyon, 1770).

33. In 1625 the bishop of Chartres considered any declaration that went against the following theory to be blasphemy in itself: "It should be noted that aside from the universal consent of peoples and nations the prophets announce, the apostles confirm and the martyrs confess that kings are ordained by God and, not only this, are themselves Gods. . . . No one can refute it without blasphemy nor question it without sacrilege (declaration of the bishop of Chartres to the 1625 Assembly of the Clergy)." A telling illustration of a closed system.

34. Jacques Bénigne Bossuet, *La politique tirée des propres paroles de l'écriture sainte*, bk. 3, art. 2, proposition 1.

35. See among other texts Claude Le Brun de La Rochette, *Le procès civil et criminel* (Rouen, 1609), bk. 1, "Les Crimes."

36. French National Archives, Z-2-482 (July 22, 1670), quoted by H. Audard,

"Le blasphème au village: Les pratiques blasphématoires dans les campagnes parisiennes (1660–1710)" (master's thesis, University of Paris I, 1995), p. 28.

37. Delamare, *Traité*, bk. 3, title 6, chap. 3 (earlier this chap., n. 1).

38. Villecourt, *Explication*, col. 395 (see chap. 1, n. 52).

39. Monarchical intervention in this area enlarged the category of "royal cases" to include a certain number of other crimes (crimes committed on the crown highways, the setting of fires, heresies, dueling, perjury, and unlawful carrying of arms). See Philippe Sueur, *Histoire du droit public français (XVe–XVIIIe siècles)* (Paris: Presses Universitaires de France, 1989), vol. 1, "La constitution monarchique," p. 177.

40. Quoted by Delamare, *Traité*, bk. 3, title 6, chap. 3.

41. "As blasphemy offends against public order by offending against religion, lay justice can try crimes of this nature under its jurisdiction" (Guyot, *Répertoire universel*, vol. 6, p. 211 [earlier this chap., n. 5]).

42. Louis XII's 1510 statute concerning blasphemers was enacted after the outcome of his Italian conquests, the king "considering the great victories bestowed by God, not wanting to remain ungrateful but to present and have presented homage and immortal graces [to Him in return]."

43. Departmental Archives of Haute-Garonne, B17, bundle 91/92, quoted by Nicole Lemaître, *Le Rouergue flamboyant: Le clergé et les fidèles du diocèse de Rodez (1417–1563)* (Paris: Les Editions du Cerf, 1990), p. 208.

44. Delumeau, *La peur*, p. 402 (see chap. 1, n. 34).

45. Proclamation of Cosimo I in Florence, 1542.

46. Under both categories fell acts of impiety, indecency, iconoclasm, sacrilege, etc. (N. Dyonnet, "Impiétés provinciales au XVIIIe siècle," *Histoire, Economie, Société*, no. 3 [1990]: 391).

47. Cited by Hill, *Le monde à l'envers*, p. 168 (earlier this chap., n. 20).

48. Ibid., p. 165.

49. Quoted by Arthur Leslie Morton, *The World of the Ranters: Religious Radicalism in the English Revolution* (London: Lawrence and Wishart, 1970), p. 133.

50. George Fox, *The Arrangement and Tryall with a Declaration of the Ranters* (1650), quoted by Hill, *Le monde à l'envers*, p. 163.

51. Hill, ibid., p. 149.

52. Ibid.. This interpretation is radically contested by J. C. Davis in his *Fear, Myth and History: The Ranters and the Historians* (Cambridge: Cambridge University Press, 1986). In Davis's view the statute of 1650 was not aimed first and foremost against the Ranters. After a close reading of the text, Davis argues that the charge of blasphemy against Abiezer Coppe and his *Remonstrance* (1651) does not appear to be self-evident (pp. 19, 54–55).

53. Following Lawton, *Blasphemy*, p. 26 (see intro., n. 21). See also Aymles, "Unbelief," p. 44 (earlier this chap., n. 23).

54. Lawton, ibid., p. 126.

55. B. Cottret, *Le Christ des Lumières: Jésus de Newton à Voltaire, 1680–1760* (Paris: Editions du Cerf, 1990), pp. 72ff.

56. Hill, *Le monde à l'envers*, pp. 149–150 (earlier this chap., n. 20).

57. Cottret, *Le Christ des Lumières*, p. 78.

58. B. Cottret, "Ecce Homo: La crise de l'incarnation royale en Angleterre (1649–1688–1701)" in *Le Christ entre orthodoxie et lumières: Actes du colloque tenu à Genève en août 1993*, ed. Maria Cristina Pitassi (Geneva: Droz, 1994), pp. 77–100. Here I closely follow Cottret's fine development of the question.

59. Ibid., p. 86.

60. Samuel Clarke, *The Scripture Doctrine of the Trinity* (London, 1712).

5. SOUNDING THE CALL: MUNICIPALITIES, THE BOURGEOIS, AND THE SEIGNIORIES

1. Yves Durand, ed., *Les cahiers de doléances des paroisses du bailliage de Troyes pour les Etats généraux de 1614* (Paris: Presses Universitaires de France, 1966).

2. Ibid., pp. 140ff., 237ff., 245ff.

3. Ibid., parish of L'Isle, p. 140.

4. Ibid., *cahiers* of Saint-Florent and Crancey, p. 314. [For an account of the extraordinary convening of the Estates General in October 1614, and the tensions between the ultimately pro-monarchical clergy and commons and the nobility, see Victor-L. Tapié, *France in the Age of Louis XIII and Richelieu* (Cambridge: Cambridge University Press, 1974), tr. O. McN. Lockie, pp. 72–75.—Trans.]

5. Lemaître, *Le Rouergue*, p. 208 (see chap. 4, n. 43).

6. E. Bourcier, "Pouvoir, religion et société à Coventry (1655–1656)," pp. 474–475, and C. Lacassagne, "Les avatars du pouvoir épiscopal: Norwich (1642–1656)," p. 467, both in *Pouvoir, ville, et société en Europe, 1650–1750: Actes du colloque international du C.N.R.S. (Oct. 1981)*, ed. Georges Livet and Bernard Vogler (Paris: Editions Ophrys, 1983).

7. Lottin, *Lille*, p. 427 (see intro., n. 4).

8. Municipal Archives of Lille, catalogue heading "statutes" (*ordonnances*), no. 388, folio 286, quoted by Lottin, *Lille*, p. 427.

9. Cited by Hildesheimer, *La terreur*, p. 57 (see chap. 1, n. 31).

10. Those inventories in the archives that were consulted included only those in the following cities where regulatory or prosecutorial actions were undertaken: Aix-en-Provence, Amiens, Angoulême, Avallon, Béthune, Château-Thierry, Chauny, Grenoble, Hagueneau, Honfleur, Laon, Le Puy, Mende, Nantes, Nevers, Nîmes, Pontarlier, Sarlat, Troyes, and Vannes.

11. Cf. Nîmes in 1636, and Laon in 1714. At Brest in 1599, commissioners were

charged with seeing that the Edict of Nantes was carried out, with its reminders of "punishments to be applied by the king's edicts and statutes." Cf. Elisabeth Rabut, *Le roi, l'Eglise, et le Temple: L'exécution de l'édit de Nantes en Dauphiné* (Grenoble, 1987), p. 81.

12. Belmas, "La police," p. 207 (see chap. 4, n. 5).

13. Thirty livres for a blasphemer convicted at Laon in 1714 (Communal Archives, Plumitif, FF 52); seven livres and ten sous for a François Martin found guilty in Pontarlier in 1650 (Communal Archives, CC 33 reports). More drastically, in August 1618 the city magistrates of Toulouse ordered the arrest of G. C. Vanini, "terrible blasphemer," before turning him over to the parlement of the city. See D. Foucault, "G. C. Vanini, un libertin martyr à l'époque baroque: Mise au point bio-bibliographique," *Bulletin de la Société d'histoire moderne et contemporaine* 1–2 (1996): 81–90.

14. Favre-Soulet, *Traditions*, p. 289 (see intro., n. 4).

15. Statute of April 1, 1672, quoted in the *Bulletin de la Société archéologique du Morbihan* 3 (1859): 15.

16. Cf. also the Communal Archives of Béthune (BB6, 1530). At Puy-en-Velay in 1581 the *édiles*, or town councilors, had ordered that a cage be installed in one of the city's public squares to exhibit blasphemers (Augustin Chassaing, ed., *Mémoires de Jean Burel: Journal d'un bourgeois du Puy à l'époque des guerres de religion* [Saint-Vidal: Centre d'étude de la Vallée de la Borne, 1983]).

17. Hardly unique, the 1571 municipal ordinances of Casteldelpiano in Tuscany prescribed fines as punishment for blasphemies (cf. Ildefonse Imberciadori, "Spedale, scuola, e chiesa in popolezioni rurali dei secoli XVI–XVII," *Economia e storia* 6:442).

18. Communal Archives of Cassagnioles, FF 1, quoted in the *Bulletin de la Commission archéologique et littéraire de Narbonne* 4 (1986): 248, n. 1.

19. Pierre Lemercier, *Les justices seigneuriales de la région parisienne de 1580 à 1789* (Paris: Domat-Montchrestien, 1933); and S. Debaret, "Le blasphème parisien au XVIIᵉ siècle (1610–1671)" (master's thesis, University of Paris I, 1994), pp. 11–13.

20. Lemaître, *Le Rouergue*, pp. 207–208 (see chap. 4, n. 43).

21. Muchembled, *Le temps des supplices*, p. 147 (see chap. 4, n. 11).

22. Cf. the case of Jean Leblanc at Bourg-la-Reine, investigated in 1672 (French National Archives, Z-2-482, cited by Audard, "Le blasphème," pp. 9–10 [see chap. 4, n. 36]).

23. Cf. Muchembled, *Le temps des supplices*, p. 147, who also cites the Fleming Josse de Damhouder, *Praxis rerum criminalum* (Antwerp, 1554), pp. 134–136.

24. Jean Papon, *Recueil d'arrêts notables des cours souveraine en France*, 4th ed. (Lyon, 1562); Le Brun de La Rochette, *Le procès* (see chap. 4, n. 35); Bernard de la Roche-Flavin, *Recueil des Arrêts notables du Parlement* (Toulouse, 1617); and P. Desmasures, *Des observations concernant la matière criminelle* (1638) (a copy of

the 1743 edition can be found at Lille's municipal library [cf. Muchembled, *Le temps des supplices*, p. 135]).

25. Le Brun de la Rochette, *Le procès*, p. 134.

26. Olivier Christin, "L'iconoclaste et le blasphémateur," *Injures et blasphèmes*, special issue, *Mentalités*, no. 2 (1989): 35–68.

27. Le Brun de La Rochette, *Le procès*, p. 136.

28. The November 1549 statute specified that cases "of errant behavior or simple heresy originated more from ignorance, error, human weakness and fragility, carelessness and lewdness of the accused's tongue than from truly malicious intent."

29. Lefebvre-Teillard, *Les officialités*, p. 128 (see chap. 3, n. 6).

30. Edict of Châteaubriant, June 1551.

31. Delamare, *Traité*, bk. 3, title 6, chap. 3 (see chap. 4, n. 1).

32. Bernard de la Roche-Flavin, *Recueil des déclarations du roy et arrêts de la Cour de Parlement* (Paris, ca. 1686), p. 16.

6. EMBLEMATIC SWEARERS

1. Villecourt, *Explication*, column 400 (see chap. 1, n. 52).

2. Henri Estienne, *Apologie pour Hérodote* (Paris, 1566), vol. 1, chap. 14, p. 164: "He swears like a nobleman, he swears like an abbot, he swears like a carter."

3. Andreä quoted in Johannes Jansen, *La civilisation en Allemagne depuis la fin du moyen âge jusqu'au commencement de la guerre de Trente Ans*, vol. 6, tr. from German by E. Paris (Paris: Plon, Nourrit, 1902), pp. 453–454; Andreä and Siwart are both cited in Delumeau, *La peur*, pp. 402–403 (see chap. 1, n. 34).

4. Dubois, curate of Rumegies, *Journal*, year 1691, p. 76 (see chap. 1, note 53).

5. Departmental Archives of the Gironde, G.651.

6. Blackstone, *Commentaries*, p. 54 (see chap. 4, n. 25).

7. Fournier, *Hydrographie*, p. 691 (see chap. 2, n. 39); François Valois, *Entretiens et exercices théoriques sur les vérités de la religion* (La Rochelle, 1747).

8. "Brevis Narratio eorum quae gesta sunt a Patribus Nostri (ab anno 1623 ad 1629) in Missio Navalis," reprinted in E. Hambye, ed., *L'aumônerie de la flotte de Flandre au XVII siècle, 1623–1662* (Louvain: Nauwelaerts, 1967), p. 171.

9. On the few examples that can be found in the files of the French Admiralties Archives, see Cabantous, "Le blasphème en milieu maritime à l'époque moderne," *Injures et blasphèmes*, thematic issue, *Mentalités*, no. 2 (1989): 83–89.

10. Departmental Archives of the Seine-Maritime, 216 BP 233 (1735), *La Concorde* (from Dieppe) case.

11. See the statutes of the Fraternal Order of the Blessed Sacrament (Confrérie du Saint-Sacrement) of the Cod-Fishermen of Le Havre (1662)(Cabantous, "Le blasphème en milieu maritime," p. 87).

12. Fournier, *Hydrographie,* p. 652.

13. In 1637 the crew of the *Tenth Whelp,* of London, refused to go on board a ship whose captain was known as an inveterate blasphemer. Cf. Keith Thomas, *Religion and the Decline of Magic* (New York: Charles Scribner's Son, 1971), p. 92.

14. Alain Cabantous, *Le ciel dans la mer: Christianisme et civilisation maritime (XVIᵉ–XIXᵉ siècle)* (Paris: Fayard, 1990), pp. 269ff.

15. Pahin de la Blancherie, *Extraits du Journal de mes voyages* (Paris, 1775), vol. 2, p. 26.

16. "All those caught blaspheming shall be put to irons and punished on their first offense by forfeiture of one month's pay, and when found to have repeated the offense shall be made to appear before the War Counsel for sentencing to the piercing of their tongue, in conformity with ordinances." The 1786 text (despite a regulation on disciplining the crew), however, says nothing on the subject.

17. Ordinance of 1730, part 2, title 2, art. 2: "If any man should be heard using the name of God to swear an oath, utter a curse or blaspheme, the captain is absolutely enjoined to punish those guilty of such statements by seeing that they are made to wear for as long a time as he shall judge fit a wooden-harness collar or some other likewise visible mark of his baseness."

18. Regulation of 1720, bk. 5, chap. 1.

19. Olivier Christin, "Du Solt nit schweren bey Sein Namen: Matériaux pour servir à l'histoire du blasphème (1450–1550)," *Bulletin d'information de la Mission historique française en Allemagne,* no. 29 (December 1994): 66.

20. Quoted in Robert Muchembled, *La violence au village: Sociabilité et comportements populaires en Artois du XVᵉ au XVIIᵉ siècle* (Paris: Brepols, 1989), p. 374. ["Je renie Dieu, teste Dieu, qui est ce bougre qui a deslié mon cheval?"—Trans.]

21. Ordinance of May 20, 1681; cf. also article 36 of the ordinance of July 1, 1727.

22. Cited by Ashley Montagu, *The Anatomy of Swearing* (New York: Macmillan, 1967), p. 167.

23. Richard L'Avocat, *Sermon XLVI,* vol. 18 of *CHO,* col. 528.

24. Billacois, *Le duel* (see chap. 2, n. 66). R. Bénichi's "Le duel et le blasphème à Paris au temps de Louis XIII" (thesis for the D.E.S. [*diplôme d'études supérieures,* roughly equivalent to the master's degree], University of Paris, 1956).

25. A. Sorbin, *Exhortation à la noblesse pour la dissuader et détourner des duels* (Paris, 1578).

26. Sorbin, ibid., p. 24. Other examples can be found in Billacois, *Le duel,* p. 340. ["Je renie Dieu par la mort et par le sang, je suis mort"—Trans.]

27. Billacois, ibid., pp. 145–146.

28. Ibid., p. 189.

29. Pierre de L'Estoile, *Journal,* ed. L. R. Lefebvre (Paris, 1886), vol. 9, p. 187 (December 1608); in the same vein see also vol. 8, p. 278 (February 1607).

30. Jean-Pierre Dedieu, "Le modèle religieux," in *L'Inquisition espagnole (XVIᵉ–XIXᵉ siècles)*, ed. Bartholomé Bennassar et al. (Paris: Hachette, 1979), p. 249.

31. Hill, *Le monde à l'envers*, p. 161 (see chap. 4, n. 20).

32. Henri Estienne, *Deux dialogues du nouveau langage français* (Paris, 1591 ed.), vol. 2, p. 163. One can also consult his *Apologie* (earlier this chap., n. 2), which sketches either a portrait of Albert of Gondi or Pierre Strozzi, notorious blasphemers at court (pp. 165, 174). See also the observations of Tallement des Réaux concerning the chevalier de Roquelaure, in *Historiettes*, ed. Antoine Adam (Paris, 1961), vol. 2, pp. 385–387.

33. As related by Anthony à Wood, *Athenae Oxonienses: An exact history of all the Writers and Bishops who have had their education in the University of Oxford* (Oxford, 1820), p. 732.

34. Samuel Pepys, *The Diary of Samuel Pepys* (1825), ed. Henry B. Wheatley (New York: Random House, 1946), July 1–2, 1633, entry, p. 670.

35. The admirable thesis of S. Van Damme on this subject can be consulted, "Théophile de Viau et les Jésuites: Procès et polémique littéraires au XVIIᵉ siècle" (D.E.A. thesis, Ecole des Hautes Etudes en Sciences Sociales, 1994).

36. Antoine Adam, *Théophile de Viau et la libre-pensée française en 1620* (Geneva: Slatkine, 1966), and his *Les libertins au XVIIᵉ siècle* (Paris: Buchet/Chastel, 1964).

37. René Pintard, *Le libertinage érudit dans la première moitié du XVIIᵉ siècle* (Paris: Boivin, 1943).

38. See Van Damme, "Théophile de Viau," part 1, chap. 1, which skilfully highlights the Parisian Jesuits' role in organizing this controversy by the mediation of the *maison professe*, or convent house for taking of vows, on the Rue Saint-Antoine and of the Collège de Clermont.

39. François Garasse, *Doctrine curieuse des beaux esprits de ce temps, ou prétendus tels* (Paris, 1623), p. 38.

40. Ibid., pp. 73–74.

41. Van Damme, "Théophile de Viau," p. 107.

42. Deposition of October 1623, reprinted in Frédéric Lachèvre, ed., *Le procès du poète Théophile de Viau* (Paris: Honoré Champion, 1909), vol. 1, p. 215.

43. Adam casts serious doubt on the testimony of Leblanc and suspects him of merely repeating what the *Mercure François* had printed about Vanini so as to show the affinity between the two men and, thereby, condemn the disciple to the same punishment as the master (*Théophile de Viau*, p. 137, n. 4).

44. Adam cites as examples in this vein numerous minor pieces of irreverent poetry (ibid., pp. 129–137).

45. Here for example is what the Baron of Blot, kin to Gaston d'Orléans, wrote regarding the Annunciation,

That a dove in wingèd flight
Hath enshadowed a damsel bright
Of this I believe not a jot.
In Phrygia they say as much
And fair Leda's swan as such
Is worth Mary's pigeon's plot.

[Qu'une colombe à tire d'aile
ait obombré une pucelle
je ne crois rien de tout cela.
On en dit autant en Phrygie
et le beau cygne de Léda
vaut bien le pigeon de Marie.]

(from R. Sauzet, quoted in Lebrun, ed., *Histoire*, p. 124 [see chap. 2, n. 12].)

46. The nebulosity of the libertine "movement" and its decline in France after 1660 do not allow one to discern what perhaps amounted to a veritably blasphemous fellowship of feeling, akin to that which may have been manifested in Hanoverian England; see also chap. 7, n. 5 (below).

47. J.-B. Thiers, *Traité des jeux et des divertissements qui peuvent être permis ou qui doivent être défendus aux chrétiens selon les règles de l'Eglise et le sentiment des Pères* (Paris, 1686).

48. I direct attention here to the useful development by Elisabeth Belmas, "Le jeu dans la société au XVIII* siècle," in the thematic issue entitled *Traditions et innovations dans la société française au XVIII* siècle* of the *Bulletin de l'Association des historiens modernistes des universités*, no. 18 (1995): 182–200.

49. J. Frain du Tremblay, *Conversations morales sur les jeux et les divertissements* (Paris, 1685), p. 100. See also the account by Jacques Fontaine, *Mémoires d'une famille huguenote*, ed. B. Cottret (Montpellier: M. Chaleil, 1992), pp. 101–102 (1684). [Two translations of the latter work, under different titles, are available in English. See *Memoirs of a Huguenot Family: Translated and Compiled from the Original Autobiography of the Rev. James Fontaine and Other Family Manuscripts; Comprising an Original Journal of Travels in Virginia, New-York, etc., in 1715 and 1716*, tr. Ann Maury (New York, 1853; facsimile reprint, Baltimore: Genealogical Publishing Co., 1967); and *Memoirs of the Reverend Jacques Fontaine, 1658–1728*, tr. Dianne W. Ressinger (London. Huguenot Society of Great Britain and Ireland, 1992).—Trans.]

50. A good many *exempla* begin their narrative by describing soldiers playing at dice on Sunday. Did this association refer back to the episode in the Passion in which, at the time of the Crucifixion, Roman soldiers gambled with dice for Christ's tunic?

51. Cf. L'Avocat, *Sermon XLVI*, col. 528 (earlier this chap., n. 23); Loarte, *Instructions*, p. 176 (see chap. 1, n. 26); Turlot, *Thrésor*, part 3, lesson 10 (see chap. 1, n. 29).

52. J. Dussaulx, *De la passion du jeu* (Paris, 1779), p. 134.

53. Ibid., p. 216.

54. P. de Joncour, *Lettres sur les jeux de hasard* (La Haye, 1713).

55. Jean La Placette, *Traité des jeux-de-hazard défendu contre les objections de M. de Joncourt, et de quelques autres* (La Haye, 1714), pp. 11, 37.

56. Jean Barbeyrac, *Traité du jeu*, 3d ed. (Amsterdam, 1737), p. 28.

57. Ibid., p. 362.

58. Richard L'Avocat, *Dictionnaire moral ou la science universelle de la chaire*, vol. 19 of *CHO*, col. 416. See also Rivals, who around this time declared in his *Essai sur la fureur du jeu* (Essay on the gambler's frenzy), "gamblers [are] scoundrels who end up believing nothing, they deny the existence of a Supreme Being Himself, flatter themselves that after their death all is put to an end with them and that punishments for the wicked and rewards for the good are but illusions" (p. 29).

59. La Placette, *Traité*, p. 65.

60. Some rare variations were sometimes to be found. If Dussaulx is to be believed, an abbot who was an avid gambler took it out "on the Church whose minister he was, holding Her responsible for his misfortunes. 'If I lose again,' he would say, 'I shall reveal Her secret.' This madman did lose, and he claimed to offer assurance that there was no Purgatory" (*De la passion du jeu*, p. 216).

61. *Registre aux ordonnances* (Register of statutes) of the chief magistrate of Lille, Lille Communal Archives, no. 388, folio 286, quoted by Lottin, *Lille*, p. 263 (see intro., n. 4).

62. Quoted by Gabriel Le Bras, "Le contrôle canonique de la vie chrétienne dans le diocèse d'Auxerre sous Louis XIV," *Etudes de sociologie religieuse* (Paris: Presses Universitaires de France, 1955), vol. 1, p. 44. Police ordinances of April 1738 and March 1782 forbade riverboat crews that transported merchandise and passengers upriver to Paris "from blaspheming and swearing" (National Archives [hereafter abbreviated as NA], A.D. IX, 458, files or bundles 230; and H1.1954, file or bundle 389).

63. A. Cabantous, *Le ciel dans la mer* (earlier this chap., n. 14), pp. 277ff.

64. NA, X2B 1267 and 1268. Cf. also Lebigre, *Les Grands Jours* (see chap. 3, n. 7). Along the same lines, see the examples Muchembled examines in *La violence*, p. 373 (earlier this chap., n. 20); G. Mandon's *Le société périgourdine au siècle des Lumières: Le clergé paroissial* (Périgeux: Médiapress, 1982), p. 32. See also R. Bompard, who in combing through the archives of the *officialité* of Lyons between 1660 and 1789 uncovered ten charges of blasphemy among the ninety-three priests sentenced ("Les ecclésiastiques indignes jugés devant les officialités de Lyon," *Histoire et criminalité de l'Antiquité au XXe siècle: Nouvelles approches; Actes*

du colloque de Dijon-Chenove, 3–5 oct. 1991 [Dijon: Editions universitaires de Dijon, 1992]).

65. E. Labouvie, "Verwünschen und Verfluchen: Formen der Verbalen Konfliktrezelungen in der ländlichen Gesellschaften der Fruhen Neuzeit," in *Die Flucht und der Eid,* ed. P. Blicke (Berlin, 1993), pp. 121–145. See also Christin, "Du Solt," p. 57 (earlier this chap., n. 19).

66. Châtellier, *La religion des pauvres,* pp. 134–135 (see chap. 2, n. 46).

67. Bartolomé Bennassar, *L'homme espagnol: Attitudes et mentalités du XVIᵉ au XIXᵉ siècle* (Paris, 1975), p. 75.

68. Belmas, "La police," p. 203 (see chap. 4, n. 5).

7. THE OTHER REALITY

1. It amounts, for France, to judicial documents in the *B* series of the Departmental Archives and the *Z2* series (records of courts of seignioral justice) of the National Archives.

2. Muchembled, *Le temps des supplices* (see chap. 4, n. 11).

3. Beaulande's study, which consults the archives of the *officialités* of Troyes and Châlons from the end of the Middle Ages, makes it possible to only roughly differentiate offenders from within the laity (82.3 percent, of whom 81.8 percent were male) from ecclesiastics (clerics, monastics, and priests comprising the other 17.7 percent) ("Le blasphème," pp. 98–100 [see chap. 1, n. 7]). Even for modern periods the exact breakdown of sociological-vocational affilations is far from systematic. Audard ("Le blasphème" [see chap. 4, n. 36]) has turned up twenty-eight different professions for forty-two cases of blasphemy prosecuted in a few of the villages just outside Paris. Debaret ("Le blasphème," [see chap. 5, n. 19]) was able to come up with 149 such documentary detailings out of 230 recorded blasphemy cases.

4. Morton, *Ranters,* p. 11 (see chap. 4, n. 49).

5. While dining with others on a prodigious meal, a guest grabbed a piece of beef and said, "Here is the flesh of Christ, take of it and eat." Another hurled a tankard of brew against the fireplace and said, "Here is the blood of Christ" (in Hill, *Le monde à l'envers,* pp. 159, 161–165 [see chap. 4, n. 20]). In eighteenth-century England a club would enshrine the sociability of blasphemous speech as one of its reasons for being: The Robin Hood Society that was created in 1747 had a reputation for welcoming among its forty-six members "libertines, blasphemers and atheists" (Joseph Robert Allen, *The Clubs of Augustan England* [Cambridge, Mass.: Harvard University Press, 1933]).

6. NA, bailiwick of the palace, Z2-2984, quoted by N. Lourmière, "Le blasphème à Paris dans la première moitié du XVIIIᵉ siècle" (master's thesis, University of Paris I, 1994), p. 88.

7. Debaret, "Le blasphème," p. 58. Fifty-seven percent of this latter category (i.e., codefendants) were explicitly accused of blasphemy.

8. But was this only, as Muchembled believes, because the women "trusted in the males to translate into action the hatreds and rancors of the mothers, wives, and daughters" (*La violence*, p. 195 [see chap. 6, n. 20])? Called before the Toledo Inquisition tribunal in the sixteenth century, forty-seven women were charged with blasphemy, versus 598 men (Bennassar, *L'homme espagnol* [see chap. 6, n. 67], p. 77). In examining Spanish inquisitorial prosecution during the seventeenth century, Escamilla-Colin finds that less than 10 percent of those charged were women (*Crimes*, vol. 2, p. 216 [see chap. 2, n. 10]).

9. Among the difficulties that are already so well known to scholars of the modern period must be added lexical fluctuations in the terms that were used to describe occupations of the accused. Such discrepancies were often due less to the court clerks than to defendants and witnesses themselves.

10. Michel Foucault, *Histoire de la folie à l'âge classique* (Paris: Gallimard, 1972), p. 107.

11. NA 22-3671, Saint Jean de Latran (ecclesiastic seigniory within Paris).

12. Before further advancing or refuting this hypothesis, the need exists to pluralize research on separate regions. For a comparative study, one can refer to R. Ferrand's *Blasphémateurs et sacrilèges en Lyonnais et Beaujolais (1679–1789)* (master's thesis, Lumière University [Lyon II], 1989), which confirms the social diversity of people charged with blaspheming:

TABLE 12 |

rural elites:	14
craftsmen:	18
agricultural workers:	13
carriers or carters:	2
merchants:	5
MISCELLANEOUS:	2

13. Debaret, "Le blasphème," p. 61; and Audard, "Le blasphème," p. 36. Escamilla-Colin notes that one-half of those charged by the Inquisition were between the ages of twenty-five and thirty-four, and one-third between thirty and thirty-four (*Crimes*, p. 216).

14. NA Z2-4 032, quoted by C. Hofmann, "Justice et société dans le bailliage seigneurial de Saint-Denis en France dans la seconde moitié du XVIIe siècle" (thesis, Ecole Nationale des Chartes, 1992), p. 277.

15. NA Z2-452, Z2-483, Z2-781, quoted by Audard, "Le blasphème," pp. 39–40.

16. Debaret, "Le blasphème," pp. 61–62.

17. NA Z2-452 (December 1669).

18. Out of the twenty-seven cases of blasphemy recorded for the principality of Neuchâtel in the eighteenth century, with a place and date for the occurrence of the offense appearing only eighteen times, the cabaret was mentioned twelve times (Henry, *Crime* [see chap. 1, n. 39]).

19. In the principality of Neuchâtel, twelve out of eighteen incidents occurred on a Sunday; in the Parisian region, eleven out of nineteen (Henry, *Crime*; and Audard, "Le blasphème"). In eighteenth-century Paris, the prevalence of incidents on Sundays does not seem as well established (Lourmière, "Le blasphème," pp. 77–79 [earlier this chap., n. 6]).

20. According to P. Clark's study, English taverns would seem to have evolved in the opposite direction. From the Restoration on, social intermixing became commonplace. Well-off bourgeois and officers of the crown were frequent customers, and women visited in increasing numbers. And although some taverns still had bad reputations, debts for drinks owed to the establishment were not (or, perhaps, were no longer) the cause of social unrest. See P. Clark, *The English Alehouse: A Social History (1200–1830)* (London, 1983), pp. 195–245.

21. On this question and others pertaining to the system of justice in the provincial countryside, I refer the reader to the noteworthy essays that F. Billacois and H. Neveux have assembled for the 1990 thematic issue of *Droit et Culture* (no. 19) entitled *Porter plainte, stratégie villageoise et justice en Ile-de-France (XVIIe–XVIIIe siècles)* and, most especially, pp. 90–91 of J.-P. Burriat's article for the journal, "Villageois et parisiens."

22. Aside from Clark, *The English Alehouse*, one can read the remarks of Robert Muchembled in *Cultures et société en France du début du XVIe au milieu du XVIIe siècle* (Paris: SEDES, 1995), p. 354; and, above all, Daniel Roche, "Le cabaret parisien et les manières de vivre du peuple," in *Habiter la ville (XVe–XXe siècles: Actes de la Table ronde organisée avec l'aide de la D.G.R.S.T. et de la Mission de la recherche urbaine*, ed. M. Garden and Y. Lequin (Lyon: Presses universitaires de Lyon, 1985), pp. 233–251.

23. Information that was kindly relayed to me by J.-C. Deidler.

24. The Supreme Council's requirement is cited in Jean-Pierre Pichette, *Le Guide raisonné des jurons* (Montréal: Quinze, 1980), p. 145. The Honfleur court's sentencing of the blasphemers appears in Charles Bréard, *Honfleur, la police des ports et des marchés* (Brionne, 1980).

25. Benedicti, *La somme des péchez*, bk. 1, chap. 9, p. 66 (see chap. 2, n. 48). Similarly, see the denunciation made by the bishop of Pamiers in 1649 against "those who drink in cabarets and often pronounce blasphemies there" (Departmental Archives of Ariège, G.145, no. 4).

26. Mandon, *La société périgourdine*, p. 240 (see chap. 6, n. 64).

27. "In cabarets are spoken great and atrocious oaths and blasphemies against God our Creator, the Blessed Virgin Mary, and the heavenly host," wrote the magistrate of Lille in 1667 (cf. Lottin, *Lille*, p. 154 [see intro., n. 4]).

28. *Cahiers*, or bound legislative memoranda, of grievances of the Third Estate of the castellany of Grève, see Durand, *Les cahiers*, p. 213 (see chap. 5, n. 1). In the same vein, see also the *cahiers* of Saint-Florentin and Pont-sur-Seine.

29. NA Z2-1 327.

30. The punishment was nine years of banishment from the province, with a fine that must be paid first (cf. Roger Martine, "Etude sur la criminalité dans le bailliage de Pontarlier au XVIII siècle" [master's thesis, University of Franche-Comté, 1975], p. 80).

31. Escamilla-Colin, *Crimes*, vol. 2, p. 223 (see chap. 2, n. 10). Escamilla-Colin also cites other instances of blasphemies spoken by drunkards.

32. Quoted by Pichette, *Le guide*, p. 119 (see chap. 4, n. 2).

33. Pernot, *Etude*, p. 105 (see chap. 1, n. 54); A. Playons-Chaussis, *Le diocèse de Boulogne au XVIII° siècle* (Arras, 1976); Departmental Archives of the Gironde, G 558.

34. Minière, *Discours* (see chap. 3, n. 17).

35. Numerous examples can be found in Dedieu, *L'administration*, pp. 138–140 (see chap. 2, n. 4); Escamilla-Colin, *Crimes*, p. 222; Lefranc,"Blasphèmes et blasphémateurs," chap. 1 (see chap. 2, n. 10); Nathalie Zemon Davis, *Pour sauver sa vie: Les récits de pardon au XVI° siècle*, tr. Christian Cler (Paris: Seuil, 1988), pp. 254ff. [The original text from which this is translated is *Fiction in the Archives: Pardon Tales and Their Tellers in Sixteenth-Century France* (Stanford: Stanford University Press, 1987).—Trans.]

36. Dedieu, *L'administration*, September 1544, p. 138.

37. Muchembled, *Cultures et société*, p. 355 (earlier this chap., n. 22).

38. NA Z2-3 545, seignioral minutes of Saint-Germain-des Prés (1661), in Debaret, "Le blasphème," p. 128 (see chap. 5, n. 19).

39. NA Z2-452 (August 1675); or the examples given by Ferrand, "Blasphémateurs," p. 138 (earlier this chap., n. 12).

40. Gregory Hanlon, "Les rituels de l'agression en Aquitaine au XVII° siècle," *Annales E.S.C.*, no. 2 (March–April 1985): 255–256.

41. NA Z2-453, provostry of Boulogne (July 22, 1675), quoted by Audard, "Le blasphème," (see chap. 4, n. 36).

42. Cf. Debaret, "Le blasphème," p. 67.

43. Castan, *Les criminels de Languedoc*, p. 241 (see intro., n. 3).

44. H. Lecharny, "L'injure à Paris au XVIII° siècle: Un aspect de la violence au quotidien," *Revue d'Histoire moderne et contemporaine* 36 (October–December 1989): 559–585.

45. C. Ditte, "La mise en scène dans la plainte: Sa stratégie sociale. L'exemple de l'honneur populaire," *Porter plainte, stratégie villageoise et justice en Ile-de-France (XVII°–XVIII° siècles)*, thematic issue, *Droit et culture*, no. 19, (1990).

46. Julian Alfred Pitt-Rivers, *Anthropologie de l'honneur: La mésaventure de*

Sichem, tr. Jacqueline Mer (Paris: Le Sycomore, 1983), pp. 18–27. [Originally *The Fate of Shechem or the Politics of Sex: Essays in the Anthropology of the Mediterranean* (Cambridge: Cambridge University Press, 1977).]

47. On this issue, the unsupported assertion of Hanlon's on p. 255 of "Les rituels" seems to me debatable.

48. NA Z2-3 522 (1656), seignioral minutes of Saint-Germain-des-Prés, quoted by Debaret, "Le blasphème," p. 67.

49. It would also be worth bearing in mind the place of blasphemy in the collective violence of popular revolts. Cf. Alain Croix, *L'âge d'or de la Bretagne (1532–1675)* (Paris: Editions Ouest-France, 1993), p. 524; and Yves-Marie Bercé, *Histoire des croquants* (Geneva: Droz, 1974), pp. 13, 626.

50. Debaret, "Le blasphème," p. 62.

51. Ferrand, "Blasphémateurs," pp. 113–114 (earlier this chap., n. 12).

52. In Ferrand's study, ibid., p. 114, the corpus of recorded crimes of blasphemy is too small (twenty cases) for the response to be certain.

53. John Chrysostom, "Homélies sur les Statues (I)," in *Les Pères grecs*, ed. Jacques-Paul Migne, vol. 49, pp. 32–33. [Efforts to locate and give a fuller citation for this work were unsuccessful. An English translation, "Homelies on the Statutes," however, can be found in John Chrysostom, *A Select Library of the Nicene and Post-Nicene Fathers of the Christian Church*, vol. 1 (Grand Rapids: Eerdmans, 1979–1986).]

54. Departmental Archives of Seine-et-Marne, B 10 (1657).

55. Quoted by Christiane Plessix-Buisset, *Le criminel devant ses juges en Bretagne aux XVIᵉ et XVIIᵉ siècles* (Paris: Maloine, 1988), p. 124.

56. Christin, "Sur la condamnation," p. 54 (see intro., n. 20).

57. After blasphemy's decriminalization at the end of the eighteenth century, informing and taking legal action against certain injurious instances of speech served to favor the settling of accounts and vendettas in much the same way as earlier charges along similar legal lines, in several regions in Europe. For more, see the studies David Warren Sabean has devoted to the context for this question in Germany: *Power in the Blood: Popular Culture and Village Discourse in Early Modern Germany* (Cambridge: Cambridge University Press, 1984), and *Property, Production, and Family in Neckarhausen (1700–1870)* (Cambridge: Cambridge University Press, 1990). I again thank Olivier Christin for alerting me to both these works.

58. G. Cozzi, "Note su tribunali e procedure penali a Venezia nel '700," *Revista Storica Italiana*, no. 4 (1965): 931–952. One can also point to the case of Valerio Camerino, who in 1588 was accused by some young persons of having gravely blasphemed on several occasions. It came out that all of the informers were tenants of Camerino's whose relations with him had soured because they had not met the terms of their lease for several months (Piozza-Donati, "Procès," p. 954 [chap. 2, n. 6]).

59. NA Z2-3 523 (1656), cf. Debaret, "Le blasphème," p. 124.

60. NA Z2-3 547 (1661), cf. Debaret, ibid., p. 70.

61. Among other accepted definitions of a *madman* was "a man who spends his nights and days uttering blasphemies" (Foucault, *Histoire de la folie*, p. 151 [earlier this chap., n. 10]).

62. NA Z2-2 983, minutes of the palace bailiwick, quoted in Lourmière, "Le blasphème," p. 59 (earlier this chap., n. 6). Along the same lines, one could cite a request made in 1725 by Charles Giraudot, a Parisian domestic, asking the lieutenant general of police to curb the escapades of his wife, a "prostitute for two years [who] swears and blasphemes endlessly" (Archives of the Bastille, Bibliothèque de l'Arsenal, MS 10 884).

63. NA, Conseil de Police, Paris Châtelet, Y-9 523-A (November 1723). In his important article on Venetian blasphemy, Derosas gives numerous examples concerning the immorality of blasphemers, see "Moralità," pp. 456–464 [see chap. 4, n. 13]).

64. Several examples are in Debaret, "Le blasphème," pp. 72–76; Lourmière, "Le blasphème," p. 95; and also NA Y6 9 523-A.

65. Debaret, ibid., p. 73.

66. NA Z2-3 588, seignioral minutes of Saint-Germain-des-Prés (1671).

67. NA Z2-3 522, minutes of Saint-Germain-des-Prés (1651); cf. Debaret, "Le blasphème," p. 74.

68. On the decisive role of neighbors living nearby or in the same building in the determination that the crime should or should not be declared to and be denounced by the authorities, see A. Soman, "Le témoignage maquillé: Encore un aspect de l'infrajustice à l'époque moderne," in *Les archives du délit, empreinte d'une société: Actes du Colloque Archives judiciaires et histoire sociale, 24–25 mars 1988*, ed. Yves-Marie Bercé and Yves Castan (Toulouse: Editions universitaires du Sud, 1990), pp. 99–110.

69. Lourmière, "Le blasphème," p. 58.

70. Dyonnet, "Impiétés provinciales," p. 394 (see chap. 4, n. 46).

71. Beaulande, "Le blasphème," p. 93 (see chap. 1, n. 7).

72. Elisabeth Labrousse, *La révocation de l'édit de Nantes* (Paris: Payot, 1985), pp. 81–87.

73. Cf. the case of Zuanne Bertilli in Venice (1692), in Derosas, "Moralità," p. 457 (see chap. 4, n. 13).

74. The way sodomy was perceived seems to reflect the same evolution. Cf. M. Rey, "Police et sodomie à Paris au XVIIIᵉ siècle," *Revue d'histoire moderne et contemporaine* 29 (1982): 123–124.

75. "For the aid that it pleased the king to give to Canada in the year 1664," quoted by Louise Duchêne, *Habitants et marchands de Montréal au XVIIᵉ siècle* (Paris: Plon, 1974), p. 95. [*Habitants and Merchants in Seventeenth-Century Mon-*

tréal, tr. Liana Vardi (Montréal: McGill-Queen's University Press, 1992).]
[Cabantous uses the word "*malfaiteurs*," or wrong-doers. Like blasphemous
behavior in this chapter, the etymology of the English word *miscreant* similarly
evolved from a heretical to a secular-ethical meaning. From the Old French
mescreant, present participle of *mescroire* (to disbelieve), the word archaically
named the infidel, the heretic, the unbeliever. These connotations receded as the
word came to signify "an unscrupulous villain or rascal destitute of conscience"—a meaning for which the question of religious faith seems of decidedly
secondary importance.—Trans.]

8. A LOOSENING GRIP

1. Between the beginning of the sixteenth century and the middle of the seventeenth (1500–1659), the provostry of Maubeuge brought charges in thirty cases
of "treason against the divinity." Among a total of 343 cases, thirteen concerned
witchcraft, and four concerned blasphemy (following Pascale Raux's findings, as
cited by Muchembled, *Le temps des supplices*, pp. 161–162 [see chap. 4, n. 11]).

2. NA, Y 10 031.

3. Quoted by Françoise Hildesheimer, "La répression du blasphème au XVIIIe
siècle," *Injures et blasphèmes*, thematic issue, *Mentalités*, no. 2 (1989): 75.

4. NA, A.D. III-2 (1592–1664), and A.D. III-3 (1665–1718).

5. P.-J. Brillon, *Dictionnaire des arrêts ou jurisprudence universelle*, vol. 1 (Paris,
1717).

6. François Dareau, *Traité des injures dans l'ordre judiciaire* (Paris, 1775).

7. NA, X2A-251.

8. Lebigre, *Les Grands Jours*, pp. 137–138 (see chap. 3, n. 7).

9. The statistical study carried out by Maurice Gresset, a postgraduate student
doing research for the *diplôme d'études approfondies* (D.E.A.), turned up one case
between 1680 and 1684, and five cases between 1779 and 1782; communicated in
personal correspondence with Gresset.

10. Pierre Dautricourt, "La criminalité et la répression au Parlement de Flandre au XVIIIe siècle (1721–1790)" (doctoral thesis, University of Lille, 1912).

11. In J. Lecuir's article, which focuses on Montyon's statistics concerning the
activity of the Parlement of Paris at the end of the eighteenth century, one finds
no allusion to blasphemy ("Criminalité et moralité: Montyon, statisticien du Parlement de Paris," *Revue d'histoire moderne et contemporaine* 21 [July–September
1974]: 445–474).

12. Hildesheimer, "La répression," pp. 69–73.

13. Cf. the chart reprinted by Dedieu, "Le modèle," pp. 242–243 (see chap. 6, n.
30). The offense of blasphemy represented 1.3 percent of the criminal caseload of

the Inquisition between 1660 and 1737, according to the work of Escamilla-Colin, *Crimes* (see chap. 2, n. 10). For the principality of Neuchâtel, between 1707 and 1806, Henry found that 3.8 percent of the total crimes were against religion and social morality. One percent of the latter were blasphemy cases (*Crime*, p. 641 [see chap. 1, n. 39]).

14. Muchembled, *Le temps des supplices*, p. 151 (see chap. 4, n. 11).

15. Christin, "Sur la condamnation," p. 52 (see intro., n. 20).

16. S. Guilleminot, "Litiges et criminalité dans le Présidial de Caen au XVIIe siècle" (graduate thesis, University of Caen). See also Guilleminot's article on which my discussion draws, "La justice d'Ancien Régime au XVIIe siècle: Onze mille cas dans le présidial de Caen," *Histoire, Economie, Société*, no. 2 (1988): 187–208.

17. Guilleminot, "La justice," pp. 193, 194, 197, and 198.

18. Also worth looking at are the negative indications drawn by Yves-Marie Bercé from the presidial archives of Angoulême and Lectoure, from the years 1643 and 1644, in his "Aspects de la criminalité au XVIIe siècle," *Revue historique* 239 (January–March 1968): 38–39.

19. Y. Allain, "La criminalité dans la prévôté de Courbevoie au XVIIIe siècle" (master's thesis, University of Paris X, 1995), p. 36.

20. A. Margot, "La criminalité dans le bailliage de Mamers (1695–1750)," *Annales de Normandie*, no. 3 (October 1972): 185–224. This study bears on 704 cases.

21. M.-M Champion, "La criminalité dans le bailliage de Bayeux (1715–1745)," *Annales de Normandie*, no. 2 (March 1972): 47–84.

22. H. Brugger, "La criminalité dans le bailliage de Quingey au XVIIIe siècle" (master's thesis, University of Franche-Comté, 1992). Also pertinent is Dyonnet's fine article, "Impiétés provinciales," pp. 391–422 (see chap. 4, n. 46).

23. M.-C. Fouquet and M. Ollivier, "La criminalité rurale dans le bailliage de Mitry-Mory (1700–1718)" (master's thesis, University of Paris X, 1978), p. 54.

24. André Zysberg, *La galériens: Vie et destin de soixante mille forçats sur les galères de France (1680–1748)* (Paris: Seuil, 1987), p. 66.

25. In the second half of the seventeenth century, blasphemous speech in the environs of Paris is almost always accompanied by other violent behaviors— insults, threats, fisticuffs. Cf. Audard, "Le blasphème," p. 31 (see chap. 4, n. 36).

26. Hildesheimer, "La répression," pp. 72–73 (earlier this chap., n. 3).

27. Derosas, "Moralità" (see chap. 4, n. 13). Starting in 1541, the *esecuttori* saw the fight against sacrilege (1541) and the censuring of printed texts (1543) turned over to their care. They were subsequently made into a tribunal of appeal for prostitution cases (1553 and 1615), instituted proceedings against clandestine marriages (1577), and were given responsibility for the surveillance of foreigners (1583) ("Moralità," pp. 446–447).

28. NA Z2-2 990 (August 27, 1927), quoted by Lourmière, "Le blasphème," p. 101 (see chap. 7, n. 6).

29. Departmental Archives of the North, 5 G 379.

30. Many incomplete trial records do not include the sentence that was handed down. Sometimes we simply have the sentence without information supplied about the real tenor of the accusation (except for the very vague and insufficiently qualified term *blasphemer*).

31. Papon; La Roche-Flavin; and Brillon. In the A.D. III 2 and 3 collections of the National Archives can be found records on the overturning by the Parlement of Paris of thirty-two sentences between 1599 and 1718.

32. This is, however, what is forcefully suggested by the work of Belmas who, using the printed documentation drawn from guides or textbooks for jurists, establishes statistical tables based on less than fifty cases over two centuries ("La police," pp. 624ff., and tables 31, 34, and 39 [see chap. 4, n. 5]).

33. Following the National Archives (NA, A.D. III, 2/3):

TABLE 13 |

	Pillory	Banishment	Galleys	Tongue Split	Death	Total
1599–1655					13	13
1656–1718	1	4	4	2	8	19

34. Jail-book entries of Saint-Lazare, NA Z2-3 695, quoted by Debaret, "Le blasphème," p. 52 (see chap. 5, n. 19).

35. Jail-book entries of Saint-Germain-des-Prés, NA Z2-3 401, quoted by Debaret, ibid., p. 53.

36. Derosas, "Moralità," p. 470; 602 sentences pronounced between 1642 and 1657.

37. See the examples supplied by Debaret, "Le blasphème," pp. 53–54 (see chap. 5, n. 19) and Audard, "Le blasphème," pp. 45–46. See also the inventory of the *B* series of the Departmental Archives of Eure-et-Loir (bailiwicks of Chartres, Gallardon, Courtalain, 1573–1754). Among several other examples, there is that of J.-F. de La Tour de Gouvernet, lord of Mitry, who gives the reminder in a statute of 1712 "that every person, no matter of what quality and condition, is forbidden to swear or blaspheme the Name of God under penalty of a fine of ten livres and imprisonment" (quoted in Fouquet and Ollivier, "Criminalité," p. 56 [earlier this chap., n. 23]).

38. NA, Z2-482 (July 1670), seigniory of Bourg-la-Reine.

39. The *levi* abjuration "was practiced in the context of offenses that the inquisitors deemed possible indicators of heresy in order that they might have the legal justification to rule on them without truly believing that the accused were guilty of heresy." This clarification was kindly communicated to me by Jean-Pierre Dedieu.

40. Quoted by Escamilla-Colin, *Crimes*, p. 218 (chap. 2, n. 10). In accounts of autos-da-fé, the author reveals that this punishment was given to every one out of five people found guilty.

41. Escamilla-Colin, ibid., p. 218.

42. In an article already cited, Belmas asserts this implicitly without supplying proof for it. See "La montée," p. 25 (see chap. 4, n. 8).

43. Hildesheimer, "La répression," p. 70.

44. Bibliothèque Nationale, Joly de Fleury collection, 2-498, "Crimes of treason against the divinity," folio 52.

45. In March of 1774 the Dijon parlement's *tournelle* sentenced a young wig-maker, P. Dubois, to the galleys for five years for uttering (only?) blasphemies (D. Ulrich, "La répression en Bourgogne au XVIIIe siècle," *Revue historique du droit français et étranger*, no. 3 [1972]: 427). [One finds in the case of the French provincial parlements that legislative-judicial authority could be shared between a *tournelle* and a *Grande Chambre*, as in Toulouse, where Vanini had appeared before both convened bodies.—Trans.] See also the proceedings instigated against Jacques Chassevant "for having sworn and blasphemed" (bailiwick of Loupe, Departmental Archives of Eure-et-Loir, B. 640[1754]).

46. There is a lack of satisfying research on the subject. Elisabeth Claverie's noteworthy work bears primarily on the system of construction and deconstruction of an "affair" that became a tried legal case—one that created a critical space in the midst of absolute monarchy. See her "Sainte indignation contre indignation éclairée, l'affaire du chevalier de La Barre," *Paroles d'outrages*, thematic issue, ed. Jacques Cheyronnaud, Elisabeth Claverie, and Jeanne Favret-Saada, *Ethnologie française* 22, no. 3 (1992): 271–290.

47. Decree quoted in the not very nuanced treatment by M. Gallo, *Que passe la justice du roi: Vie, procès et supplice du chevalier de La Barre* (Paris: R. Laffont, 1987).

48. Marc Chassaigne, *Le procès du chevalier de La Barre* (Paris: Lecoffe, 1920), p. 9.

49. D. Holleaux, "Le procès du chevalier de La Barre," in *Quelques grands procès criminels aux XVIIe et XVIIIe siècles, présentées par un groupe d'étudiants sous la direction de Jean Imbert*, ed. J. Imbert (Paris: Presses Universitaires de France, 1964), pp. 165–179.

50. Quoted by Claverie, "Sainte indignation," p. 278.

51. Voltaire wrote at the beginning of his fight, upon the death of La Barre, "I fear that they shall say those people are [partisans of] the Encyclopedists" (Voltaire, *Correspondance* [1765], ed. Theodore Besterman [Paris: Gallimard, 1953–65].

52. Linguet, having previously spent time in Abbeville, became a resource for Douville de Maillefeu, the city's ex-mayor, whose son had fled the authorities, having been incriminated in the desecration of the crucifix.

53. Pierre François Muyart de Vouglans, *Les lois criminelles de France dans leur ordre naturel* (Paris, 1780), bk. 3, art. 1, p. 96.

54. In a development disadvantaging the chevalier, the Maupeou family was on bad terms with the Ormesson family—the principal defenders of the chevalier's interests there.

55. Claverie, "Sainte indignation," p. 273.

56. D. Jousse, *Traité de justice criminelle en France* (Paris, 1771), vol. 3, p. 265, n. 12. This position can already be found expressed by G. du Rousseaud de La Combe, *Traité des matières criminelles* (Paris, 1741), part 1, chap. 2, sec. 4, p. 65.

57. Dyonnet, "Impiétés," pp. 394–396 (see chap. 4, n. 46). Jean Nagle thinks that this discrepancy in treatment was perhaps not unrelated to the development of devotion to the Sacred Heart during the second half of the eighteenth century. I am keenly grateful to him for this detail and acknowledge his *La civilisation du cœur: Histoire du sentiment politique en France (XIIᵉ–XIXᵉ siècles)* (Paris: Fayard, 1998).

58. Quoted by Claverie, "Sainte indignation," p. 285.

9. MAGISTRATE, THEOLOGIAN, AND THE WAYS OF JUSTICE

1. Voltaire, *Dictionnaire philosophique* (1764). [See, *A Philosophical Dictionary*, translated from the French (London: E. Truelove, 1850), s.v. "blasphemy," vol. 1, pp. 213–214.]

2. Pierre Bayle, *De la tolérance: Commentaire philosophique sur ces paroles de Jésus-Christ "Contrains-les d'entrer,"* ed. Jean-Michel Gros (Paris: Presses Pocket, 1992). The first dramatic effects of the revocation of the Edict of Nantes of 1685 directly impacted on Bayle's life with the death of his brother Jacob.

3. The "compel people to come in" scriptural exhortation was taken from the twenty-third verse of the fourteenth book of the Gospel of Luke.

4. Bayle, *De la tolérance*, p. 185.

5. Cf. the remarkable introduction to the 1992 edition of Bayle's essay by J.-M. Gros, ibid., pp. 27–28.

6. Le Brun de la Rochette, *Le procès*, p. 134 (see chap. 4, n. 35).

7. Brillon, *Dictionnaire* (see chap. 8, n. 5); cf. also J.-B. Denissart, *Collection de décisions nouvelles et de notions relatives à la jurisprudence* (Paris, 1754), vol. 1, p. 235.

8. Delamare, *Traité*, vol. 1 (see chap. 4, n. 1).

9. Cited by Christin, "Du Solt," note 17 (see chap. 6, n. 19).

10. *Dictionnaire de théologie catholique*, article on "blasphemy"; or *Catholicisme hier, ajourd'hui, demain: Ecyclopédie en sept volumes*, ed. Abbé Gabriel Jacquement (Paris: Letouzey et Ané, 1949), vol. 2.

11. Durand de Maillane, *Dictionnaire* (see chap. 4, n. 32): "Heretical blasphemy

is the type that is accompanied by heresy; simple blasphemous speech, without being contrary to the articles of faith, does not cease to be very serious."

12. Rousseaud de La Combe, *Traité* (see chap. 8, n. 56).

13. Charles Clément François de L'Averdy, *Code pénal ou recueil des principales ordonnances*, 4th ed. (Paris, 1777).

14. "Following the theologians, it is committed through refusing to Divinity the attributes proper to it, through attributing what is not proper to it; when one ascribes to God what is only fitted to the creature, while ascribing to the creature what is only fitting to God. . . . But blasphemy taken in its most common signification, and of which it is principally spoken in the laws, is the blasphemy that consists of verbal imprecations spoken not only against God's honor but further against the honor of the Blessed Virgin and all the saints, men and women, in Heaven" (Muyart de Vouglans, *Les lois criminelles*, bk. 3, vol. 1, chap. 1 [see chap. 8, n. 53]).

15. Jousse, *Traité*, vol. 3, pp. 267ff. (see chap. 8, n. 56).

16. Claude Gauvard, *De grace especial: Crime, Etat, et société en France à la fin du Moyen Age* (Paris: Publications de la Sorbonne, 1991), pp. 2:809ff.; and Davis, *Pour sauver sa vie* (see chap. 7, n. 35)

17. Muyart de Vouglans grouped together "blasphemies committed under the effects of drunkenness, rusticity, the custom of the place of utterance" even as he separated all these from those issuing "from malice aforethought and irreligious thinking" (*Les lois criminelles*, p. 96).

18. Nicolas des Essarts, *Dictionnaire universel de police* (Paris, 1786), vol. 1 (s.v. "blasphemy").

19. Lorenzo Priori, *Pratica criminale secondo il ritto delle leggi della Serenissima Repubblica di Venezia* (Venice, 1644).

20. Durand de Maillane stated clearly that "secular judges are familiar with this crime . . . because it assaults religion in a manner scandalous and contrary to civil order" (*Dictionnaire*). Along the same lines: Rousseaud de La Combe, *Traité*; and Essarts, *Dictionnaire*.

21. Dareau, *Traité des injures*, p. 97 (see chap. 8, n. 6).

22. Jacques-Pierre Brissot de Warville, *Les moyens d'adoucir la rigueur des lois pénales en France* (Châlons-sur-Marne, 1781), p. 81.

23. Dareau, *Traité des injures*; and Lecharny, "L'injure," pp. 559–580 (see chap. 7, n. 44).

24. Guyot, *Répertoire universel*, vol. 6, pp. 208–212 (see chap. 4, n. 5).

25. Baron de la Brède et de Montesquieu [Charles-Louis de Secondat], *De l'esprit des lois* (1748), part 1, bk. 12, chap. 4, in Montesquieu, *œuvres complètes*, ed. Daniel Oster (Paris: Seuil, 1964), p. 599.

26. Brissot de Warville, *Les moyens*, p. 80.

27. Ibid., p. 81.

28. Dareau, *Traité des injures*, p. 98.

29. Here one should recall the establishment of the Commission of Regulars in 1766, the loss of control over teaching after the Jesuit order was suppressed (1763–1764), and the lessened influence over censure and bookselling (cf. Daniel Roche, *La France des Lumières* [Paris: Fayard, 1993], chaps. 11 and 18).

30. In a superb study, the theologian Bernard Lauret has shown decisively that, in the Bible, the gravity of blasphemy was not founded by injurious words spoken against God ("because God cannot be assailed") but by "the abuse leveled at man's liberation instituted by the law of God" ("Tu ne prononceras" [see intro., n. 15]).

31. Cf. Benedicti or Ballet.

32. Benedicti quoted by Christin, "Le statut ambigu," p. 338 (see chap. 1, n. 35).

33. Jean Eudes, *Le bon confesseur*, p. 261 (chap. 1, n. 21); Blanchard, *Essay*, vol. 2, p. 186 (see chap. 2, n. 44); Godeau, *La morale chrétienne*, p. 262 (see chap. 1, n. 8); M. Chevassu, *Conférences sur les commandements*, vol. 94 of *CHO*, col. 676.

34. Le Semellier, *Conférences ecclésiastiques*, vol. 2, pp. 24ff. (see chap. 1, n. 18).

35. Villecourt, *Explication*, col. 395 (see chap. 1, n. 52).

36. Decisions of the curates of Paris (1707, 1714, 1718), reprinted in Le Semellier, *Conférences ecclésiastiques*, p. 158.

37. Bressanvido, *Instructions morales*, p. 203 (see chap. 1, n. 10).

38. The Parisian pastors' words are cited by Jeanne Ferté, *La vie religieuse dans les campagnes parisiennes (1622–1638)* (Paris: Plon, 1962). Genêt's conviction that ingrained habits of speech did not excuse the sin was advanced in François Genêt, *Théologie morale* (Paris, 1676), p. 167.

39. Godeau, *La morale chrétienne*, p. 149.

40. Le Semellier, *Conférences ecclésiastiques*, p. 147.

41. Albert R. Jonsen and Stephen Toulmin, *The Abuse of Casuistry. A History of Moral Reasoning* (Berkeley: University of California Press, 1988); and Pierre Cariou, *Les idéalités casuistiques: Un directeur de conscience au XVIIᵉ siècle: Jacques de Sainte-Beuve, 1613–1677* (Lille: Atelier Reproductions des thèses; Paris: Champion, 1979) [originally a doctoral thesis for the University of Paris I, 1974].

42. Tomasso de Vio, known as Cajetan, quoted by Domingo Banes (often cited as Bannes), ed., *Scholastica commentaria in universam primam partem angelici doctoris* (Venice, 1602). For Saint Thomas blasphemy could only be a venial sin if one uttered it without believing it to be a blasphemy. But did not the good Dominican doctor also add that the true blasphemer, because of the perversity of his intention, was more guilty of sin than a murderer?

43. Benedicti, *La somme des péchos*, p. 556 (see chap. 2, n. 48).

44. Dedieu, *L'administration*, p. 247 (see chap. 2, n. 4).

45. *Dictionnaire de Trévoux*, s.v. "blasphemy."

46. Louis Abelly, *Les principes de la morale chrétienne* (Paris, 1670).

47. Alphonse de Liguori, "Avertissements aux nouveaux confesseurs" in

Liguori, *œuvres complètes du bienheureux*, ed. abbés Vidal, Delalle, and Bousquet (Paris: Parent-Desbarres, 1935), vol. 27, p. 44.

48. Bauny, *Somme des péchez*, p. 51 (see chap. 1, n. 2).

49. J. Pontas, *Dictionnaire des cas de conscience* (Paris, 1715); see also P. Milhard, *L'inventaire des cas de conscience* (Toulouse, 1611), p. 60.

50. Mangin, *La science*, p. 125 (see chap. 2, n. 36). Cf. also Bauny, *Somme des péchez*; or, delving into the question further, Azpicuelta, *Abrégé*, p. 93 (see chap. 1, n. 4).

51. *Advertimientos para consultas (fornicacion, blasfemio)*, quoted by Escamilla-Colin, *Crimes*, p. 221 (see chap. 2, n. 10).

52. Quoted by Jean Delumeau, *L'aveu et le pardon, les difficultés de la confession, XIIIe–XVIIIe siècles* (Paris: Librairie Générale Française, 1991), p. 162. [*Potta di Dio* is a milder sounding equivalent to "goddammit!" in Italian. —Trans.]

53. Jean Delumeau, *Rassurer et protéger: Le sentiment de sécurité dans l'Occident d'autrefois* (Paris: Fayard, 1989), p. 511.

54. Pierre Cuppé, *Le ciel ouvert à tous les hommes ou Traité théologique par lequel, sans rien déranger des pratiques de la religion, on prouve solidement par l'Ecriture sainte et par la raison que tous les hommes sont sauvés* (1716; reprint, London, 1783), pp. 25–26.

55. F. Laplanche, *La Bible en France entre mythe et critique (XVIe–XIXe siècles)* (Paris: A. Michel, 1994), pp. 100–106; and M. Cottret, "Le catholicisme face au déisme: Autour de *L'Emile* (1762–1770)," *Revue d'histoire de l'Eglise de France* (July–December 1993), pp. 301–319.

56. Nicolas-Sylvestre Bergier, *Apologie de la religion chrétienne* in *Œuvres complètes* (Paris, 1770), vol. 1, p. 229.

57. Cf. Cottret, "Le catholicisme," p. 309.

58. *Un théologien au siècle des Lumières: N. Bergier, Correspondance (1770–1790)*, ed. Ambroise Jobert (Lyon: Centre André-Latreille, 1987); see, for example, letter no. 90 (May 18, 1781), p. 220.

59. Ibid., letter no. 112 (October 13, 1783), p. 337.

60. Ibid., letter no. 118 (July 21, 1785), p. 358.

61. Ibid., letter no. 120 (December 11, 1785), p. 361.

62. Ibid., letter from Trouillet no. 101 (July 29, 1782), p. 309; and letter no. 119 (November 30, 1785), p. 359.

63. The meaning of this static dogmatism can be found in the writings of certain eighteenth-century lay authors. Thus Malesherbes, "staking out the borderlines of the domain of legitimate censureship" (in Roger Chartier's formulation), concluded that "the science of religion acquired all its perfection from the moment it was handed down to us, and a taste for discoveries has never been aught but prejudicial to it" (Chrétien-Guillaume Lamoignon de Malesherbes, *Mémoires sur la librairie et sur la liberté de la presse* [Paris: Agasse, 1809], pp. 129–130).

64. Quoted by A. Jobert in his preface to Bergier, *Correspondance*, p. 36.

65. In the period of 1750 to 1760, Venetian jurists put up a resistance against the operations of the tribunal of the *esecuttori*, their secret methods, and their use of witnesses to denounce people to the tribunal (Cozzi, "Note su tribunali," p. 933 [see chap. 7, n. 58]).

66. Beccaria, *Des délits*, supplement to the 7th ed. (Paris, 1773), p. 288. [See chap. 1, n. 40, for English-language translations.—Trans.]

67. Jean-Baptiste Robinet, *Dictionnaire universel ou bibliothèque de l'homme d'Etat et du citoyen* (London, 1779), s.v. "blasphemy."

10. SACREDNESS ELSEWHERE?

1. A good forty or so (forty-three to be exact) of the *cahiers* drawn up in the different parishes of the bailiwicks were examined.

2. *Cahier des curés du bailliage d'Auxerre*, ed. C. Porée (Auxerre, 1927), p. 360.

3. *Cahier du bailliage de Troyes*, ed. J.-J. Vernier (Troyes, 1909), vol. 1, p. 564.

4. I have made the selection of these authors (Jean-Jacques Rousseau, the abbé Augustin de Barruel, Louis-Sébastien Mercier, and the Marquis de Sade) insofar as during the thirty-year period leading up to the end of the ancien régime, they were the ones in whose works the word *blasphemy* appears most often. This generalization was made possible through a consultation of the Frantext database, which statistically calculated the word's frequency in print. Thanks are due to Annie Geoffroy for accommodating this research request and for providing indispensable help with it.

5. Marquis de Sade, *Justine: Les infortunes de la vertu* (1791), ed. Jean-Michel Goulemont (Paris: Garnier-Flammarion, 1969). In two instances (pp. 99 and 232) Sade's use of the term can also be read as a simple semantic swerve, or careless variation, as in the remark, "Will I go to make sacrifices to blasphemies, to sophistries that disgust me?"

6. Jean-Jacques Rousseau, *Lettre à Christophe de Beaumont* (1763), p. 141, and *Lettres écrites sur la Montagne* (1764). [A contemporary edition of the latter was published in 1962 by Ides et Colindes, Neuchâtel.—Trans.]

7. Abbé Augustin de Barruel, *Les Helvétiennes* (1781), letter no. 76, p. 383.

8. Ibid., letter no. 35, p. 74.

9. Ibid., p. 97. Rousseau writes, "But you who dare to reproach me with [speaking] blasphemies, what else are you doing when you take the apostles for accomplices of offensive ideas which it pleases you to maintain on my account?" (*Lettre*, p. 141). Cf. also his *Lettres écrites*, letter no. 1: "My books, they say, are impious, scandalous, rash, full of blasphemies and calumnies against religion" (p. 103); and letter no. 2, p. 78.

10. To perceive blasphemy in this way did not however exclude a return to the original Greek etymology of speaking ill about someone and attacking their reputation. In his dedicatory epistle to his work *On the Theater*, Louis-Sébastien Mercier alluded to those "people who . . . will cite for your benefit what they have read a thousand times; they will speak to you about what one knows already, they cry foul with the accusation of 'blasphemer!' the moment they are mocked" (*Du Théâtre* [1773], p. xi).

11. Henry, *Crime* (see chap. 1, n. 39).

12. As quoted in Henry, ibid., pp. 646–647.

13. Ibid., p. 646.

14. See Roger Chartier, *Les origines culturelles de la Révolution française* (Paris: Seuil, 1990), particularly chap. 6, "Le roi désacralisé," pp. 138–166. [Available in English as *The Cultural Origins of the French Revolution*, tr. Lydia G. Cochrane (Durham: Duke University Press, 1991).] From this purview J. W. Merrick's analysis in *The Desacralization of the French Monarchy in the Eighteenth Century* (Baton Rouge: Louisiana State University Press, 1990) is less incisive and its passage on blasphemy (pp. 38–40) especially underdeveloped.

15. Alain Boureau, *Le simple corps du roi: L'impossible sacralité des souverains français (XVᵉ–XVIIIᵉ siècles)* (Paris: Editions de Paris, 1988). And see especially Alain Boureau and Claudio Sergio Ingerflom, eds., *La royauté sacrée dans le monde chrétien. Actes du colloque de Royaumont, 1989* (Paris, 1992). In his contribution to this collection, "Un obstacle à la sacralité royale en Occident: Le principe hiérarchique," Boureau concludes that the Western monarch in the Middle Ages was never able to cultivate an intrinsic, autonomous sense of the sacred because "of his immersion in a powerful hierarchical system that subsumed him functionally" (p. 29). Boreau believes, concerning this question, that the church's overbearing role in determining and consecrating what was holy or sacrosanct significantly reduced "the sacred virtualities of the monarchy." The theory is further nuanced, with an uneven intensity, by Jacques Le Goff and A. Guéry in the recorded discussions at this same conference.

16. Chartier, *Origines culturelles*, pp. 143–144; and, above all, Arlette Farge, *Dire et mal dire: L'opinion publique en France au XVIIIᵉ siècle* (Paris: Seuil, 1992), pp. 190–196, 278–282. The Joly de Fleury archival collection at the Bibliothèque Nationale (2074–2077), "Mauvais discours à Paris et en province, 1756–1775," can also be profitably consulted.

17. Chartier (ibid.) discusses this point of view in his chapter 4.

18. In addition to the *Nouvelles Ecclésiastiques*, see the part taken by Duguet, Maltrot, and Mey favoring circulation of the analyses of Montesquieu's *Spirit of the Laws* prejudicial to despotism (cited by Hildesheimer, *Le jansénisme*, p. 93 [see chap. 2, n. 5]).

19. Shanti Marie Singham, "Vox populi, vox dei: Les jansénistes pendant la

Révolution Maupeou," in *Jansénisme et révolution: Actes du Colloque de Versailles tenu au Palais des Congrès les 13 et 14 octobre 1984, Chroniques de Port-Royal*, 39 (Paris: Bibliothèque Mazarine, 1990), p. 189.

20. François Furet, in his *Penser la Révolution Française* (Paris: Gallimard, 1983), pp. 75ff., shows that the terms "constitution" and "nation" contained in the *cahiers* of grievances "were inscribed within old power structures."

21. On Jansenism's role in "the sanctification of the political" during the last third of the ancien régime, see Singham, "Vox populi," pp. 190–191.

22. Quoted by Jacques André, *La Révolution fratricide: Essai de psychanalyse du lien social* (Paris: Presses Universitaires de France, 1993), p. 105.

23. Quoted by Boureau, *Le simple corps du roi*, pp. 5–6.

24. The Revolution's brand of iconoclasm was quite unprecedented in that iconoclasm during the Reformation was aimed at destroying the error and strayings symbolized by statues and stained glass so that the Truth could triumph. This destructive movement was located at the very heart of the Christian religion, whereas the Revolution's iconoclasm completely erased this religious objective.

25. Quoted by Serge Bianchi, "Recherches sur la déchristianisation dans le district de Corbeil (1793–1797)" (graduate thesis, University of Paris I, 1976), p. 80.

26. Quoted in Albert Muthiez, ed., *Annales historiques de la Révolution française* (Rheims, 1926), pp. 79–80. [The four Old Testament rebels mentioned in Bouchon's anti-sermon were all coconspirators against Moses and Aaron in the wilderness; the conspirators perished together and are alluded to in Numbers, Deuteronomy (11:16), and Psalms. See Robert Young, *Analytical Concordance to the Bible* (Grand Rapids: Eerdmans, 1976), s.v. "Abiram," p. 5.—Trans.]

27. Olivier Christin, *Une révolution symbolique, l'iconoclasme huguenot* (Paris: Editions de Minuit, 1991).

28. Michel Vovelle, *La Révolution contre l'Eglise: De la Raison à l'Etre Suprême* (Brussels: Editions Complexe, 1988), pp. 121–124.

29. Robert Quillet, curate of Athis-Mons, in Brumaire of Year II [calendar of the Revolution; October 23–November 1793] "wished not to sully himself fulfilling a ministry of trickery and deception" (cf. Bianchi, "Recherches sur la déchristianisation," p. 148).

30. Quoted by Serge Bianchi, *La Révolution culturelle de l'an II, élites et peuple (1789–1799)* (Paris: Aubier, 1982), p. 165.

31. Vovelle, *La Révolution*, p. 123.

32. Only perhaps the *patrie* (nation) alone, after 1789, preserved its virtues of power, eternity, and protective emanation conferred on it earlier by the abbé Coyer in 1754. See G. F. Coyer, *Dissertations pour être lues: La première sur le vieux mot de patrie, la seconde sur la nature du peuple* (Paris, 1775), quoted by Mona Ozouf, *La fête révolutionnaire, 1789–1799* (Paris: Gallimard, 1976), p. 338.

33. Michel Vovelle, *Idéologies et mentalités, 1789–1799* (Paris: Gallimard, 1992), p. 316.

34. Ibid., pp. 318–320.

35. Volnay, *Le catéchisme du citoyen* (Paris, 1793); La Chabeaussière, *Catéchisme républicain, philosophique et moral* (Paris, Year II [according to the revolutionary calendar, ca. September 1793–September 1794]); Serane, *Catéchisme du citoyen* (Paris, n. d.); C. Gouriet (the son), *Office Républicain* (Paris, Year II). Cf. also M. Kennedy, "The French Revolutionary Catechism," *Studies on Voltaire and the Eighteenth Century* (1981): 353–362.

36. Quoted by J.-R. Surateau, Albert Soboul, and François Gendron, eds., *Dictionnaire historique de la Révolution française* (Paris: Presses Universitaires de France, 1984), p. 194.

37. F. Hildesheimer, "Parler dangereusement en 1793," in *1793, La patrie en danger: Actes du 2ème colloque international organisé par les Archives départementales de l'Oise, samedi 23 et dimanche 24 octobre 1993* (Beauvais: Conseil général de l'Oise, 1996), pp. 157–171.

38. " 'You are not a republican!' shouted Jacques Delacroix to a fellow citizen of Beauvais at the end of a debate 'on the current law.' 'No,' the citizen answered, 'I am not a republican and will never be one.' With that, Delacroix told him he was a knave and a scoundrel, [to which the citizen shot back,] 'and they can put me on the block and I still won't change my mind' " (quoted by Hildesheimer, ibid., p. 166).

39. Maximilien Robespierre, *Œuvres*, vol. 10, ed. Marc Bouloiseau (Paris: Presses Universitaires de France, 1958–1967), p. 403.

40. Robespierre, ibid., speech of Frimaire 15, II [December 5, 1793], p. 229.

41. Ibid., speech delivered against the factions and *Enragés*, end of Ventôse, Year II [ca. March 1794], p. 400.

42. Report by Couthon on the Revolutionary Tribunal, Prairial 22, II [June 10, 1794].

43. François-Alphonse Aulard, *Le culte de la Raison et le culte de l'Etre Suprême (1793–1794)* (Paris, 1892), p. 235.

44. Vovelle, *La Révolution*, pp. 189–192.

45. This and subsequent quotations in this paragraph are from François-Alphonse Aulard, *La société des Jacobins* (Paris, 1897), vol. 6, pp. 135–137.

46. The reference is to Lucius Brutus, Roman first consul who banished royalty and did not hesitate to condemn his own son to death for his complicity in a conspiracy with partisans of the exiled monarchy. It was the value judgment made by the Revolution's adversaries that was alluded to here. Brutus and certain others (Cato, Scaevola) were among the Roman figures most invoked in political rhetoric—so commonly were the French and Roman republican situations paralleled. Was not Brutus presented as one of the founders of Roman liberty after

the tyrant's murder? Cf. J. Bonineau, *Les toges du pouvoir ou la révolution du droit antique (1789–1799)* (Toulouse: Association des publications de l'Université de Toulouse-le-Mirail, Eché, 1986), pp. 116, 145.

47. Vovelle, *La Révolution*, p. 179.

48. This was the famous affair of Catherine Théot, the "Mother of God."

49. Quoted by Aulard, *Le culte de la Raison*, p. 361.

50. For interpretations of the celebration of the Supreme Being, see the fine elaborations by Ozouf, *La fête révolutionnaire*, pp. 126–132 (earlier this chap., n. 32). [The revolutionary calendar's date for instituting worship of the Supreme Being (Prairial 20, II) correlates with June 8, 1794. Napoleon abandoned Fabre d'Eglantine's time-keeping innovation in 1805. —Trans.]

11. SPEECH AND EXPIATION

1. See Gérard Cholvy and Yves-Marie Hilaire, *Histoire religieuse de la France contemporaine*, vol. 1 (1800–1880) (Toulouse: Privat, 1985), which attempts, in many places, to minimize the image of this harsher church (pp. 58–66).

2. Ernest Sevrin, *Les missions religieuses en France sous la Restauration (1815–1830)*, 2 vols. (Paris: Vrin, 1948–1959).

3. Ibid., vol. 2 (*Les missions* [1815–1820]), pp. 36–37.

4. As if to reflect this climate, George Sand writes in *Lélia* (Paris: H. Dupuy, 1833): " 'Do not blaspheme, young man,' said the priest with a fearsomely grave air. 'God would strike you with his curse, would make you crazy; I fear you may be this way already, as you speak like a being deprived of reason' " (p. 80).

5. Jean Guerber, *Le ralliement du clergé français à la morale liguorienne: L'abbé Gousset et ses précurseurs (1785–1832)* (Rome: Università gregoriana editrice, 1973); and especially the clarification by C. Langlois, "La difficile conjoncture liguorienne de 1832," *Penser la foi: Mélanges offerts à J. Moingt*, ed. Joseph Doré and Christoph Theobald (Paris: Editions du Cerf, 1993), pp. 645–661.

6. L'abbé Jacques-Paul Migne, ed., *Encyclopédie théologique ou série de dictionnaires sur toutes les parties de la science religieuse, offrant en français, et par ordre alphabétique, la plus claire, la plus facile, la plus commode, la plus variée et la plus complète des théologies*, vol. 1 of *Dictionnaire de théologie morale* (Paris, 1849), vol. 31 of *CHO*.

7. Cardinal Thomas-Marie-Joseph Gousset, bishop of Rheims, *Théologie morale à l'usage des curés et des confesseurs* (Paris, 1844).

8. Marguet, *Essai sur le blasphème*, pp. ix–x (see chap. 3, n. 8).

9. Ibid., p. 21.

10. Ibid., pp. 28, 32, 101–104.

11. Jacqueline Genêt, *L'énigme des sermons du curé d'Ars: Etudes sur la prédica-*

tion de Saint Jean-Marie Vianney suivie de l'analyse critique et du texte de six ser-mons (Paris: Editions de l'Oronte, 1961), pp. 377–403. Avid thanks to Philippe Boutry for having put me on to this very erudite study. *The Catechism* dates from 1800; Jean-Baptiste-Marie Vianney, in any case, acquired an 1844 edition of this work. See P. Peyronnet, "La bibliothèque de saint J.-M. Vianney," *Revue française d'histoire du livre*, no. 72–73 (1991): 287–308.

12. Genêt, ibid., p. 379.

13. Ibid.

14. Ibid., p. 373.

15. Laurent Paul-Marie Brac de la Perrière, *Souvenirs de deux pèlerinages à Ars* (Lyon, 1868), pp. 8–9, a text about which P. Boutry has kindly informed me. Another example can be found in P. Boutry and M. Cinquin, *Deux pèlerinages au XIXᵉ siècle: Ars et Paray-le-Monial* (Paris: Beauchesne, 1980), p. 27. Did a parish have to be favored with an exemplary curate in order to be spared from blasphemy? The inquiry made by Monsignior Rendu in 1849 into 122 different parishes of his Annecy diocese, and in the absence of an apparently exceptional curate, made reference to no parish given over to this practice—with the sole exception of that of Serraval, "where the people were not trash; one hears there however vulgar and blasphemous words, though rarely." *Mœurs et coutumes de la Savoie du Nord au XIXᵉ siècle: L'enquête de Mgr Rendu*, ed. Roger Devous and Charles Joisten [Annecy: Académie Salésienne, 1978]).

16. Jacques Valentin, *Examen raisonné ou décisions théologiques sur les commandements de Dieu et de l'Eglise* (Paris, 1839), vol. 1, pp. 100–108.

17. Anon., *Le blasphème flétri* (Paris-Toulouse, 1861). Among the six kinds were: blasphemy out of ignorance, blasphemy in the course of one's occupation, blasphemy while in a group with others, blasphemy out of loss of self-control, blasphemy out of sorrow and melancholy, and blasphemy with impiety.

18. Marguet, *Essai sur le blasphème*, p. 16.

19. G. Clément, *Souvenirs de La Salette, les deux plaies de la France* (Grenoble, 1872), p. 11.

20. *Le blasphème flétri*, pp. 11–12; the canon J.-M. A., *Le blasphème* (Paris, 1882) gives examples of punishments that were administered between 1820 and 1882, pp. 25ff.

21. The abbé Victor Bluteau, *Le catéchisme catholique, d'après saint Thomas d'Aquin, disposé suivant le plan du catéchisme du concile de Trente, à l'usage des catéchistes, des institutions religieuses et des fidèles avec un choix de nombreux traits historiques* (Paris, 1860), vol. 3, p. 711.

22. J.-P. Royer, *Histoire de la justice en France: De la monarchie absolue à la République* (Paris: Presses Universitaires de France, 1995), pp. 280ff.

23. Count Berlier, speech before the legislative body (February 5, 1810) in the *Code pénal* (Brussels, 1810), p. 23.

24. Robert Beck, *Jour du Seigneur, jour de fête, jour de repos: Les mutations du dimanche en France (1700–1900)* (Paris: Editions de l'Atelier, 1997). [The page citation is from the doctoral thesis of the same (University of Paris VII, 1995), pp. 215ff.]

25. At the end of the eighteenth century, the archives of the convict-prison of Toulon noted the harsh sentences against profaners of church property: three years given to P. Lenormand (1760), ten to J. Guibert (1761), fifteen years to J. Marguet, and life to L. Filiachy (1765) (from the S. H. Marine sources, Toulon, 10 126–127). I thank G. Buti for having passed along to me this information. A provision in the 1825 law on sacrilege required the death penalty for persons guilty of profaning holy receptacles in the churches if "the holy containers were filled with consecrated wafers when the crime was committed, [and] if the profanation was committed publicly." In the event of only one of these conditions, the law allowed for forced labor for life.

26. The 1791 penal code had made no provision for sacrilege as a crime but did require fines against any person who committed a hostile act against objects of worship and veneration, who struck ministers, or who instigated threatening actions or disrupted services of worship (articles 260–264).

27. Quoted by E. Lamour, "Le débat sur le sacrilège (loi du 4 janvier 1825)" (master's thesis, University of Paris I, 1987–1988), whose very fine elaboration I follow here. See also Jacques-Henri Lespagnon, *La loi du sacrilège* (Paris: F. Loviton, 1935).

28. Parlement archives, vol. 42, January 29, 1825 (document of the Toulouse court), p. 724. Lamour brings up one particular trial that was heard on appeal in Bouches-du-Rhône in which, in June 1829, a man was condemned to prison for life for an act of theft in the Saint-Theodorus Church of Marseilles (ibid., p. 45).

29. It is hard to know exactly what kinds of case Marguet is referring to because the proceedings undertaken against blasphemers in England seem to have had to do with Thomas Williams, bookseller prosecuted in 1797 for having sold Thomas Paine's *The Age of Reason*, and then, in 1840, with a similar case in which another bookseller, Henry Hetherington, was accused of having sold copies of *Haslam's Letters* (Lawton, *Blasphemy*, p. 132 [see intro., n. 21]; and P. Dartevelle, P. Denis, and J. Robyn, eds., *Blasphèmes et libertés*, p. 94 (documents on blasphemy lesgislation in Europe) [see intro., n. 15]). [Joss Marsh relates that the radical printer Richard Carlile would make Paine's book the national symbol of the struggle for "blasphemous" free publication in 1819. Marsh picks up the thread of the whole question of the offense in England during the romantic period (1817–1830) on through to key historical trials in the 1840s and in 1883, as well as the controversies surrounding the works of Thomas Hardy. See Marsh, *Word Crimes: Blasphemy, Culture, and Literature in Nineteenth-Century England* (Chicago: University of Chicago Press, 1998).—Trans.]

30. Marguet, *Essai sur le blasphème*, pp. 99–101 (see chap. 3, n. 8).

31. A work from 1666 by the abbé Thomassin, reedited in an expanded but anonymous volume in 1847, was titled *Le blasphème foudroyé par les carreaux du ciel et de la terre*.

32. The canon J.-M. A., *Le blasphème* (earlier this chap., n. 20); and the anonymous author of *Le blasphème flétri* (earlier this chap., n. 17).

33. On the level of individuals, the fight against blasphemy could take on unexpected, but revealing, aspects. Monsieur Dupont, "the holy man of Tours," sought to punish Voltaire, "the greatest blasphemer of them all," in a strange manner. He buried Voltaire's works in his garden, raised a plot of potatoes in the soil above them and fed the vegetables to pigs. See O. Métais, "Monsieur Dupont, le saint homme de Tours" (thesis, François Rabelais University, Tours, 1990).

34. C. Langlois, "La conjoncture miraculaire à la fin de la Restauration," *Revue d'histoire de la spiritualité* (1973): 227–241; and also by Langlois, "La conjoncture mariale des années 1840" (paper presented at the "Colloque sur La Salette," Institut Catholique de Paris, 1996; published acts forthcoming).

35. René Rémond, "Une vitalité religieuse toujours forte," *Histoire de la France religieuse*, ed. J. Le Goff (Paris: Seuil, 1991), vol. 3, pp. 494–505.

36. According to the account given by Pierre Servais, author of *La sœur Marie de Saint-Pierre de la Sainte-Famille* (Saint-Dizier, n. d. [ca. 1880]), "The Lord had communicated his wishes beforehand to Mother Superior Adélaïde of the Carmelite order of Poitiers" (p. 11). One might also allude to the apocalyptic visions of a Trappist contemplative nun of Gardes in Les Mauges, the southern part of Anjou, in 1820.

37. Here I follow closely P. Boutry's notable treatment in his paper "Le fait de La Salette" (paper presented at the "Colloque sur La Salette," Institut Catholique de Paris, 1996; published acts forthcoming).

38. Condemnation of blasphemy could still be found in the message delivered by the apparition of Saint-Martin-en-Vercors in 1910.

39. Jean Stern, ed. *La Salette: Documents authentiques, 1847–1849* (Paris: Editions du Cerf, 1984), vol. 1, document 1 (the report by Pra).

40. August 26, 1843, quoted by Guy-Marie Oury, *Sœur Marie de Saint-Pierre: Carmélite de Tours: 1816–1848* (Chambray-les-Tours: C.L.D., 1983), pp. 87–88.

41. R. P. Huguet, *Notre-Dame de La Salette mieux connue* (Paris, 1857), p. 119.

42. H. Bernier, *Le doute légitime sur l'apparition miraculeuse de la Très Sainte Vierge Marie* (Angers, 1859), p. 15.

43. Servais, *La sœur Marie de Saint-Pierre*, p. 8.

44. Claude Guillet reminds us that they had been reported since the sixth century. See his *La rumeur de Dieu: Apparitions, prophéties et miracles sous la Restauration* (Paris: Editions Imago, 1994), pp. 36–37.

45. Voltaire, *Dictionnaire philosophique*, pp. 622–623. [See chap. 9, n. 1, for the

citation of the English-language edition. Here the original specifies neither the article of Voltaire's from which the quote is drawn nor the particular edition used.—Trans.] Stern, *La Salette*, also describes this "letter" by Jesus.

46. H. Delahaye, "Note sur la légende de la lettre du Christ tombée du ciel," *Bulletin de l'Académie royale de Belgique* (1899): 171ff.; "Un exemplaire de la lettre tombée du ciel," *Recherches de sciences religieuses* 18 (1928): 164–169, reprinted in Hippolyte Delehaye, ed., *Mélanges d'hagiographie grecque et latine* (Brussels: Société des Bollandistes, 1966), pp. 150–178.

47. Cf. Boutry, "Le fait de La Salette."

48. Stern, *La Salette*, vol. 2, p. 193. After having taken cognizance of the La Salette apparition, Sister Marie of Saint-Pierre would write, "I thank you, O divine Mary, for having given me these two little shepherd boys to be the sonorous trumpets upon the mountain by which the resounding echo of what was communicated to me in the solitude of the Carmelite convent shall reach all the ears of France" (Oury, *Sœur Marie de Saint-Pierre*, p. 124).

49. On the other hand, in a "heavenly letter" particularly renowned for having served as model to many others ("The Commandment of Our God and Savior Jesus Christ sent by the angel Gabriel"), and which turned up in the village of Maton near Loudun in 1586, only the profanation of Sunday was lambasted.

50. D. Moulinet, "Episodes de la lutte pour la sanctification du dimanche au XIXe siècle," the La Bussière Group, *Le Temps*, 1995, p. 76.

51. In 1856 Father Debreyne foresaw, as a consequence of this dual deviance, "revolutions, revolts, conspiracies, riots, civil wars, disturbances," bringing the political dangers to the fore (cf. Beck, *Jour*, p. 354 [earlier this chap., n. 24]).

52. Departmental Archives of the Ariège, G. 142, no. 2, letter of the king to M. de Pamiers.

53. Cardinal de Bonald, bishop's letter for Lent (1842), vol. 81 of *CHO*, col. 656.

54. D. Biquard, "La lutte de l'Eglise contre les fêtes païennes, les jeux et les divertissements aux XVIe et XVIIe siècles" (thesis, Ecole des Hautes Etudes en Sciences Sociales, 1986).

55. For a development of this question, see D. Moulinet, "La sanctification du dimanche," p. 75. Moulinet underscores the influence of D. Ozanam, one of the first (1839) to associate the respect of Sunday observance with human dignity.

56. One trace of this much warned-against secularization can be found in the La Salette message, "People fail to observe fasting on Lent, they go to the butcher's shop like dogs."

57. J. Gaume, *La profanation du dimanche* (Paris, 1850), p. 133. And, yet, were not certain clerics already observing that "now unbelievers could care not less about such threats, and to the simply unmindful they are imperceptible"? See Marguet, *Essai sur le blasphème*, p. 49 (see chap. 3, n. 8).

58. Servais, *La sœur Marie de Saint-Pierre*, pp. 13ff. (earlier this chap., n. 36); under the heading "The Association of the Name of God."

59. Guillet, *La rumeur de Dieu*, p. 154 (earlier this chap., n. 44); and especially Stern, *La Salette*, pp. 2, 22–33 (earlier this chap., n. 29).

60. "Praised, blessed, loved, glorified forever be the most holy, most sacred, most adored, most unknown, most inexpressible name of Jesus in heaven, on earth and in Hell, by all creatures come from the hands of God and by the Sacred Heart of Jesus Christ at the Most Holy Sacrament of the Altar" (quoted by Servais, *La sœur Marie de Saint-Pierre*, p. 14).

61. Pierre Marche, *Nouveau manuel d'Archiconfrérie réparatrice* (Paris, 1858), p. 37. But the bishop, Monsignior Parisis, would persistently refuse to link this foundation to the revelations of the Carmelite convent of Tours (cf. Stern, *La Salette*, p. 127).

62. Marche, ibid., p. 21.

63. Marche described his parish as "a parish of sailors and infrequent practice of religion" (ibid.).

64. Ibid., p. 23. The idea would be taken up again and developed by G. Clément, *Souvenir de La Salette: Les deux plaies de la France ou le dimanche non gardé et le blasphème* (Grenoble, 1872), p. 13.

65. Marche, ibid., p. 20.

66. Ibid., p. 344.

67. The abbé Parisot, *La réparation des blasphèmes et de la profanation du dimanche* (Nancy, 1883), p. 16.

68. Charles Guillemaut, *Pierre-Louis Parisis* (Marconne-les-Hesdin, Pas-de-Calais: Brunet, 1916–1924), vol. 1, p. 355. [The citation in the original gives Arras and 1916–1917 as place and dates of publication.—Trans.]

69. Yves-Marie Hilaire, in his great work on the diocese of Arras, says very little else on the pastoral dynamism and social composition of this association in his *Une chrétienté au XIXe siècle? La vie religieuse des populations du diocèse d'Arras (1840–1914)* (Villeneuve-d'Ascq: Université de Lille, 1977), vol. 2, pp. 150–152.

70. Beck, *Jour*, p. 360 (earlier this chap., n. 24), N.-J. Chaline, "Repos du dimanche et loisir sacré: Autour de l'exemple normand," in *Oisiveté et loisirs dans les sociétés occidentales au XIXe siècle: Colloque pluridisciplinaire organisé par le Centre de Recherche d'histoire sociale de l'Université de Picardi, Amiens, 19–20 nov. 1982*, ed. Adeline Daumard (Abbeville: F. Paillart, 1983), p. 151.

71. M. Bertoni, *La ligue réparatrice des blasphèmes contre la Très Sainte Vierge Marie: Une démarche de la pensée religieuse, mariale, et franciscaine de la Corse et plus particulièrement de l'Ile Rousse au début du XXe siècle* (Sisco: Editions Santa Calina, 1982). The author points out the development of this pious work in Venice between 1905 and 1910 (pp. 90ff.).

12. THE TELLTALE SPEECH OF SIN?

1. L'Avocat, *Sermon XLVI*, col. 525 (see chap. 6, n. 23).

2. Bennassar, *L'inquisition espagnole*, pp. 159ff. (see chap. 3, n. 1); and Lefranc, "Blasphèmes et blasphémateurs," part 2, p. 87 (see chap. 2, n. 10).

3. Quoted by Christin, "Le statut ambigu," p. 338 (see chap. 1, n. 35).

4. Jean Calvin, *Réformation pour imposer silence à certain bélitre nommé Anthoine Cathelan*, in his *œuvres françaises* (Paris, 1842), pp. 330ff.

5. Johan Huizinga, *Le déclin du Moyen Age*, tr. Jean Bastin (Paris: Payot, 1932), p. 168.

6. Bennassar, *L'inquisition espagnole*, p. 249.

7. Delumeau, *Un chemin d'histoire*, p. 172 (see chap. 2, n. 37).

8. Robert Muchembled, *L'invention de l'homme moderne* (Paris, 1988), p. 77.

9. In the same vein, see the remarks of Châtellier, *La religion des pauvres*, p. 132 (see chap. 2, n. 46).

10. Ezechiel Spanheim, *Relation de la Cour de France en 1690* (Paris: Mercure de France, 1973), pp. 287–288.

11. On the ambiguous and very unsystematic relation between elites and their perception of blasphemy, see the remarks of Christin, "Sur la condamnation," p. 52 (see intro., n. 20).

12. NA, Z2-3522, minutes of Saint-Germain-des-Prés.

13. Montesquieu, *Œuvres complètes*, ed. André Masson (Paris: Nagel, 1950–1955), p. 1552.

14. *Le manuel du marin chrétien* (Paris, 1851), p. 31. G. Fournier in his *Hydrographie* (see chap. 2, n. 39) does not go as far as this, since he does not consider atheism. He writes "that it is necessary for the blasphemer either to believe that God does not see him or to have lost his fear of justice" (p. 692).

15. François Berriot, *Athéismes et athéistes au XVIᵉ siècle en France* (Lille: Atelier national de reproduction des thèses, 1984), pp. 855ff. The author cites in this regard the *De tribus impostoribus*, published in Amsterdam in the early 1680s. [The *De tribus impostoribus* (Treatise of the three impostors) holds a prominent place in the clandestine culture of unbelief in European history. It was as much the popular focus of legend for its blasphemous attack on revealed religion as it was a succession of actual printed manuscripts that traded on the notorious title. The treatise's routes of circulation have been the subject of recent scholarly interest. An early instance of impious comparative religion, its interpretation of the three established faiths, or "laws," of Moses, Christ, and Mahomet as fabrications and deceptions was identified with the twelfth-century Spanish Arabian philosopher Averroës's commentary on Aristotle. It also had earlier links to Cicero's account of religion as the invention of legislators in *De natura deorum*. By the time it came to preoccupy the eighteenth-century popular imagination, an ill-

reputed ur-manuscript of this idea had, according to Renan, been variously attributed to, among others, Averroës, Boccaccio, Peter Aretino, Machiavelli, Pomponazzi, Cardano, Servetus, Campanella, Bruno, Spinoza, Hobbes, and Vanini! One early *De tribus impostoribus*, dated 1598, has been preserved, though, in a volume printed in Vienna in 1753 (reedited by "Philomeste junior" [G. Brunet] in 1860). Significant French versions entitled *Traité des trois imposteurs* appeared in 1721, 1760, and 1768 (ascribed to Emperor Frederick II of Hohenstaufen), with the second volume of a text from 1719, *La Vie et l'Esprit de Mr. Benoit de Spinosa* [sic], corresponding closely to these later versions. Derided by Voltaire and Grimm for the simplicity and demagogic coarseness of its "imposture" thesis, it nevertheless went through several editions to become one of the widest circulating tracts of radical skepticism and Spinozistic materialism during the eighteenth century. See *Traité des trois imposteurs: Manuscrit clandestin du début du VIIIᵉ siècle*, ed. Pierre Rétat (Saint-Etienne: Editions de l'Université de Saint-Etienne, 1973), pp. 7–20; and *The Treatise of the Three Impostors and the Problem of Enlightenment*, tr. and ed. Abraham Anderson (London: Rowman and Littlefield, 1997), pp. ix–xiv.—Trans.]

16. [Molière, *Don Juan*, first performed in 1665, translated by Kenneth McLeish (London: Nick Hern Books, 1997), act 3, pp. 35–36. The lines in French from the critical edition (Amsterdam, 1683) of the play can be found in Molière, *Le Festin de Pierre (Dom Juan)*, ed. Joan DeJean (Paris: Droz, 1999), pp. 121–122.—Trans.]

17. Dorimon and Villiers are the authors of two earlier versions of *Don Juan*. For the chevalier de Roquelaure material, see René Pintard, "Une histoire du libertinage au XVIIᵉ siècle," *Revue d'histoire de la philosophie* (1937): 22.

18. Prince de Conti, *Traité de la comédie* (Paris, 1666), quoted by Christin, "Sur la condamnation," p. 56 (see intro., n. 20).

19. J. Morel, "A propos de la scène du pauvre dans *Dom Juan*," *Revue d'histoire littéraire de la France*, nos. 5–6 (1972): 939–944.

20. J. Rouzeaud, ed., *Etudes sur le "Dom Juan" de Molière* (Paris, 1993); Patrick Danfrey, "*Dom Juan*" ou la critique de la raison comique (Paris: Champion, 1993), part 2, chap. 1.

21. J. Gerson, *Centilogium de implusibus*, vol. 3, p. 154.

22. Dedieu, *L'administration*, pp. 43–45 (see chap. 2, n. 4).

23. Dedieu brings up even this type of blasphemy: "I do not believe in God for three months" (ibid., p. 45).

24. J. Pouillon, "Remarques sur le verbe croire," in *La fonction symbolique: Essais d'anthropologie*, ed. Michel Izard and Pierre Smith (Paris: Gallimard, 1979), pp. 43–51.

25. Remonstrance from 1645 quoted by Taveneaux, *Le catholicisme*, p. 250 (see chap. 3, n. 10). This slippage between blasphemy and anticlericalism is further

alluded to, very clearly, in several bishop's letters from the seventeenth and eighteenth centuries. In one from May 10, 1718, written by Cardinal de Bissy, bishop of Meaux, we read: "Charges will be brought against all persons who shall swear, blapheme, say, sing, write or commit things abusive of, offending, and opposing the respect that we harbor for the holy Name of God, of the holy Virgin his Mother, of all the saints, of ecclesiastics both temporal and monastic, [or] against our holy mysteries and also against people vested with official dignity." (NA, A.D. I 23 A [item 22]).

26. The authorities of the consistory of Sainte-Marie-aux-Mines in the seventeenth century (1635–1685) made a clear distinction between the blasphemy of an insult against elders, deacons, or the pastor even if, in the majority of cases, the offenders were themselves one of these officers. I thank M. Magdeleine for having made this source available to me.

27. Departmental Archives of the Rhône, 2B 31 (March 1740), quoted by Ferrand, "Blasphémateurs," p. 129 (see chap. 7, n. 12).

28. All these examples are in Ferrand, ibid., pp. 129–130.

29. NA, Z2 3 580, quoted by Debaret, "Le blasphème," p. 78 (see chap. 5, n. 19).

30. NA, Z2 781 (August 1667), quoted by Audard, "Le blasphème," p. 78 (see chap. 4, n. 36).

31. "Proof of the paltry piety and devotion they have before God," exclaimed a priest offended by a blasphemer in a church in Beaujolais (Ferrand, "Blasphémateurs," p. 130).

32. As brought out by Henry, writing on Neuchâtel at the end of the eighteenth century and beginning of the nineteenth, *Crime*, pp. 648ff. (see chap. 1, n. 39).

33. Departmental Archives of the Rhône, 10 G 3 776 (December 1750), quoted by Ferrand, "Blasphémateurs," p. 130.

13. WHAT BLASPHEMY SAID ABOUT SOCIETY

1. [—Ainsi (dist le moyne), à ces diables, ce pendent qu'ilz durent! Vertus Dieu qu'en eust faict ce boyteux? Le cor Dieu! il prent plus de plaisir quand on luy faict present d'un bon couble de beufz!

—Comment (dist Ponocrates), vous jurez, Frere Jean?

—Ce n'est (dist le moyne) que pour orner mon langaige. Ce sont couleurs de rethorique Ciceroniane.

The French given above is taken from *Gargantua*, vol. 2 of *Oeuvres de François Rabelais*, ed. Abel Lefranc (Paris: Champion, 1913), bk. 1, chap. 39, p. 337. For the quotation from the English translation given in the text, see François Rabelais, *The Very Horrific Life of the Great Gargantua, Father of Pantagruel*, bk. 1 of *The Complete Works of François Rabelais*, tr. Donald M. Frame (Berkeley: University of

California Press, 1991), chap. 39, p. 92. The "it" discussed is a hare Frère Jean says he has stolen from a lackey who was taking it to Lord Maulévrier.—Trans.]

2. Delumeau underscores the extreme frequency of impious expressions such as "By God" [*par Dieu*], "For the love of God" [*pour Dieu*], "By God's side" [*ventre Dieu*], and "I deny God" [*je renie Dieu*] occurring in French theatrical works of the fifteenth and sixteenth centuries and speaks even of "1,366 occurrences in the entirety of the works studied" (*Un chemin d'histoire*, p. 41 [see chap. 2, n. 37]).

3. For the quotation in the text, see Departmental Archives of Lot-et-Garonne, B 1 418, quoted by Hanlon, "Les rituels," p. 267 (see chap. 7, n. 40).

4. For the description of the ritual, I refer to the pioneering article of Hanlon (ibid.), which, however, says not a word about blasphemy.

5. NA, Z2 4 034, bailiwick of Saint-Denis (1671), quoted by Véronique Bezault, "Le blasphème au XVII siècle dans le bailliage de Saint-Denis" (master's thesis, University of Paris X, 1996).

6. Robert Muchembled, *La violence*, pp. 253–254 (see chap. 6, n. 20).

7. On the debate surrounding language and its relation with politics and the absolutist construction, I refer to M. Fogel, who sets forth with clarity the problem's given in *Les cérémonies de l'information en France du XVIᵉ au XVIIIᵉ siècle* (Paris: Fayard, 1989), pp. 293–326; and to Marc Fumaroli, "La prose De l'Etat: Charles Paschal, théoricien de style royal," *La diplomatie de l'esprit: De Montaigne à La Fontaine* (Paris: Hermann, 1994), pp. 59–124, and in particular, pp. 93–111.

8. Norbert Elias, *La civilisation des mœurs*, tr. from the German (2d ed.) by Pierre Kamnitzer (Paris: Calmann-Lévy, 1973), pp. 180–185.

9. Robert Muchembled, *Culture populaire et culture des élites dans la France moderne (XVIᵉ–XVIIIᵉ siècles): Essai*, 2d. ed. (Paris: Flammarion, 1984), preface. [*Popular Culture and Elite Culture in France, 1400–1750*, tr. Lydia Cochrane (Baton Rouge: Louisiana State University Press, 1985).] On the subject of the development of civility among the nobility, one can allude to the foundation of academies at the end of the sixteenth and early seventeenth centuries. Following the initiative of Antoine Pluvinel, and installed in several cities of the kingdom of France, they were to favor the birth of a "new, more moderate and self-controlled gentleman."

10. Quoted by Châtellier, *La religion des pauvres*, p. 194 (see chap. 2, n. 46).

11. Des Essarts, *Dictionnaire* (see chap. 9, n. 18), quoted by Belmas, "La montée," p. 21 (see chap. 4, n. 8).

12. Taveneaux, *Le catholicisme*, p. 181 (see chap. 3, n. 10). Cf. also Roger Chartier, Marie-Madeleine Compère, and Dominique Julia, *L'éducation en France du XVIᵉ au XVIIIᵉ siècle* (Paris: Société d'éducation et d'enseignement supérieur, 1976).

13. NA, Z2 452 (October 28, 1664), quoted by Audard, "Le blasphème," p. 101 (chap. 4, n. 36).

14. Catherine Villiers de Billy, *Instructions historiques, dogmatiques, et morales en faveur des laboureurs* (Paris, 1746).

15. Ibid., p. 234. Cf. also the opinion of J.-B. Robinet in his *Dictionnaire universel*, s.v. "blasphemy" (see chap. 9, n. 67). In the eighteenth-century theater, the bourgeois character continuously uses improper language, punctuating his sentences with "By Jove!" [*parbleu*], "the devil!" [*morbleu*]. Cf. Nivelle de la Chaussée, *La fausse antipathie*, quoted by L. Croq, "Les bourgeois de Paris au XVIIIᵉ siècle: Identification d'une catégorie sociale polymorphe" (doctoral thesis, University of Paris I, 1998), p. 76.

16. See for example the observations of Le Brun de La Rochette, *Le procès*, pp. 4–5 (see chap. 4, n. 35); or A. de Montchrestien, *Traité de l'économie politique*, bk. 1.

17. NA, Y 9 523-A, Châtelet de Paris (June–November 1723).

18. Louis-Sébastien Mercier, *Tableau de Paris* (1782–1788), reprinted in *Le Paris de Louis-Sébastien Mercier: Cartes et index toponymique*, ed. Jean-Claude Bonnet, Anne Le Fur, and Jean Sellier (Paris: Mercure de France, 1994), vol. 1, pp. 439–441. Spirited thanks to Sabine Juratic for guiding my attention to this text.

19. Ibid., vol. 1, p. 439.

20. Michel Foucault, *Folie et déraison: Histoire de la folie à l'âge classique* (Paris: Plon, 1961), "Le nouveau partage," part 3, chap. 2, pp. 460–506.

21. J. Wright, *A sermon delivered at the long Room, Marble Street, on Tuesday evening, April 8, 1817, for which a prosecution is commenced on a charge of blasphemy* (Liverpool: F. B. Wright, 1817), quoted by Lawton, *Blasphemy*, p. 3 (see intro., n. 21).

22. Delumeau, *La peur* (see chap. 1, n. 34), pp. 400–403, and not *Le péché* (see intro., n. 4) as Favret-Saada erroneously cites it in "Rushdie," p. 253 (see intro., n. 18).

23. Favret-Saada, ibid., p. 254. I refer directly to her demonstration without really taking it up here.

24. Delumeau, *La peur*, pp. 401–403.

25. Muchembled, *L'invention*, pp. 76–81 (see chap. 12, n. 8). See there the references to J. Gerson and Jacques du Clercq.

26. Favret-Saada, "Rushdie," p. 254.

27. Delumeau, *Un chemin d'histoire*, p. 42 (see chap. 2, n. 37).

28. For example, Deschamps's *Ballades*, 145–149 ("Contre ceux qui jurent Dieu"), *Œuvres complètes*, (Paris, 1878), vol. 1, pp. 271–277. I thank J.-P. Boudet for having alerted me to these texts.

29. Christin, "Du Solt," particularly pp. 58–60 (see chap. 6, n. 19); and Christin, "Matériaux," pp. 68–77 (see intro., n. 25).

CONCLUSION: BLASPHEMY'S COMEBACK

1. *Catéchisme de l'Eglise catholique* Fr. ed. (Paris, 1992): "Blasphemy consists of uttering, in thought or out loud, words of hatred, reproach, defiance against God;

of speaking ill of God; of not showing respect towards Him in one's words; of abusing the holy Name of God" (sec. 2:148, pp. 442–443).

2. Mortal sin has "as its intention [*pour objet*] a serious matter committed in full consciousness and of set purpose" (ibid., p. 391).

3. One would need to do a thorough inventory, or bookkeeping, for each of the episcopates, of the bishop's letters that take up this subject, as Pichette has done for the church in Canada. He counted "only" thirty-nine bishop's letters between 1849 and 1951 that devote (very uneven) elaborations to the subject (*Le guide*, p. 137 [see chap. 4, n. 2]).

4. Pastoral letter of March 25, 1943, quoted by Pichette, ibid., pp. 148–149.

5. In western Europe today only Belgium, Portugal, and France (excepting Alsace and the department of the Moselle) have no antiblasphemy laws on the books (Dartevelle, *Blasphèmes* [see chap. 4, n. 26]).

6. In this sense it will come as no surprise that it was in Italy, Spain, and Quebec—lands with strong Christian traditions until a recent period—that for a long time blasphemy remained deep-rooted. It played its role as an expression of resistance to the heavy, heavy social and cultural inertia of Catholicism.

7. E. Benveniste, "La blasphémie et l'euphémie," in *L'Analyse du langage théologique: Le nom de Dieu; actes du colloque organisé par le Centre international d'études humanistes et par l'Institut d'études philosophiques de Rome, Rome, 5–11 janvier 1969*, ed. Enrico Castelli (Paris: Aubier, 1969), pp. 71–73.

8. [After the composition of the French edition of this book, the Iranian government ended its endorsement of the fatwa issued by the late Ayatollah Ruhollah Khomeini. Under Islamic law, however, only the person who issued such a decree can revoke it. Sickeningly, certain hard-line Iranian groups have renewed calls for Rushdie's assassination.—Trans.]

9. For example: two judgments in Spain in 1983, one in Austria in 1987, a trial in Germany in 1985 (Dartevelle, *Blasphèmes*, pp. 85–92, 107–110, 117).

10. Among others one can cite J.-L. Godard's film *Hail Mary* (*Je vous salue Marie*), Véronique Samson's song "Allah," and the pictorial demonstration titled *Treize à table* in Nantes in 1994. But the work by Marcel Paquet, *Merde à Jésus, Souvenirs de José de Nazareth: Roman* (Paris: Editions de la Différence, 1989) has not it seems been the object of any accusations, on the part of religious authorities, for being blasphemous.

11. *La Croix*, January 7, 1992.

12. M. Péronnet, "De la profanisation," in *Foi, fidélité, amitié en Europe à la période moderne: Mélanges offerts à Robert Sauzet*, ed. Brigitte Maillard (Tours: Publications de l'Université de Tours, 1995), pp. 421–427. Péronnet defines *profanization* as the "process that, starting with an initial situation—the analysis of the sacred—mobilizes elements which lead gradually to the erosion of universal value founded on the sacred by another universal value defined with reference to

the sacred as profane." (I would amend the last part of the passage to read: "defined *initially*.")

13. J. Cheyronnaud, "Un blasphème très contemporain: *La Marseillaise* de Gainsbourg," *Injures et blasphèmes*, thematic issue, *Mentalités*, no. 2 (1989): 151–159.

14. Humanity, as "a sacred history," joins here a fundamental anthropological dimension of Christianity (for example, I Paul, 1 Corinthians 3). See, for example, F. Bourdeau, "Fin du sacré, sainteté du profane," *Forma Gregis*, no. 1 (1974): 1–94.

| BIBLIOGRAPHY

Primary Sources

A Note on References. Citations for material from documents in the Departmental Archives (Archives départementales, B and G series) and Communal Archives (Archives communales) are given in the notes. For the National Archives, the collections classified as *Z2* (ordinary royal and segnioral jurisdictions); *A.D. III* (criminal laws); and *Y 9* and *Y 10* (Châtelet de Paris) constitute the major series that I have selectively consulted.

RELIGIOUS SOURCES

A., J.-M. *Le blasphème.* Paris, 1882.

Abelly, L. *Les principes de la morale chrétienne.* Paris, 1670.

Azpicuelta. *Abrégé du manuel et très sage doctrine.* Fr. tr. Paris, 1602.

Bauny, E. *Somme des péchez qui se commettent en tous estats.* Paris, 1633.

Benedicti, J. de. *La somme des péchez et des remèdes d'iceux.* Fr. ed. Paris, 1601.

Bergier, N.-S. *Un théologien au siècle des Lumières, N.-S. Bergier: Correspondance (1770–1790).* Edited by A. Jobert. Lyon, 1987.

Bernier, H. *Le doute légitime sur l'apparition miraculeuse de la Très Sainte Vierge Marie.* Angers, 1859.

Bertaut, B. *Le directeur des confesseurs.* Paris, 1638.

Besoigne. *Principes de la justice chrétienne.* Paris, 1764.

Binsfeld, P. *La théologie des pasteurs, et autres prestres ayans charge des ames.* Fr. tr. Rouen, 1640.

Blanchard, A. *Essay d'exhortation pour les estats différens des malades.* Paris, 1713.

Blasphème flétri, Le. [Anonymous.] Paris-Toulouse, 1861.

Bluteau, V. *Le catéchisme catholique, d'après saint Thomas d'Aquin, disposé suivant le plan du catéchisme du concile de Trente, à l'usage des catéchistes, des institutions religieuses et des fidèles avec un choix de nombreux traits historiques.* Paris, 1860.

Bressanvido, I. *Instructions morales de la doctrine chrétienne.* Fr. tr. Lyon, 1859.

Cuppé, P. *Le ciel ouvert à tous les hommes ou Traité théologique par lequel, sans rien déranger des pratiques de la religion, on prouve solidement par l'Ecriture sainte et par la raison que tous les hommes sont sauvés.* London, 1783.

Daon R. *Conduite des confesseurs dans le tribunal de la Pénitence.* Paris, 1738.

Eudes, J. *Le bon confesseur.* Paris, 1686.

Floriot, P. *Morale chrétienne rapportée aux instructions que Jésus-Christ nous a données dans l'oraison dominicale.* Rouen, 1672.

Fornari, M. *Instructions des confesseurs.* Fr. tr. Lyon, 1674.

Gaultier, J. *Table chronologique de l'estat du christianisme comprenant . . . le rapport des vieilles hérésies aux modernes et douze principales vérités catholiques établies contre la R.P.R. par l'Ecriture Sainte et preuvées de siècle en siècle par les Saints Pères de ce temps-là.* Lyon, 1673.

Genêt, F. *Théologie morale.* Paris, 1676.

Godeau, A. *La morale chrétienne.* Paris, 1709.

Grenade, L. de. *Le guide des pécheurs.* Fr. tr. Paris, 1627.

Le Semellier, J. L. *Conférences ecclésiastiques sur le Décalogue.* Brussels, 1759.

Liguori, A. de. *Le confesseur des gens de campagne.* Paris, 1830.

——. *Instructions et sermons sur les préceptes du Décalogue et sur les sacrements.* Fr. tr. Paris, 1827.

Loarte, G. *Instructions pour les confesseurs.* Fr. tr. Lyon, 1674.

Maillard, O. *Sermons et poésies.* Nantes, 1877.

Mangin, A. de. *La science des confesseurs.* Paris, 1758.

Marche, P. *Nouveau manuel de l'archiconfrérie réparatrice.* Paris, 1858.

Marguet, J. [pseud., abbé Daux]. *Essai sur le blasphème.* Besançon, 1823.

Migne, J.-P., ed. *Collection intégrale et universelle des Orateurs sacrés du premier et du second ordre . . . et collection intégrale, ou choisie, de la plupart des orateurs du troisième ordre.* 99 vols. (Petit Montrouge, 1844):

Ballet, F. *Sermon XVI.* Vol. 49.

Beurrier, V.-T. *Sermon VII.* Vol. 56.

Billot, J. *Prônes réduits en pratiques, pour les dimanches et fêtes principales de l'année.* Vol. 40.

Chevassu, J. *Conférences sur les commandements.* Vol. 94.

Encyclopédie théologique. Vol. 31 (*Dictionnaire de théologie morale*).

Fromentières, J.-L. de. *Sermon pour le jour de la circoncision.* Vol. 8.

Foucault, N. *Prône des dimanches.* Vol. 88.

Gambart, A. *Instructions sur les commandements de Dieu.* Vol. 89.

Girard, N. *Petits prônes* (11e dimanche après la Pentecôte). Vol. 92.

L'Avocat, R. *Sermon XLVI.* Vol. 18.

——. *Dictionnaire moral ou la science universelle de la chaire.* Vol. 19.

Lejeune, J. *Sermon XLVII.* Vol. 3.

Loriot, L. *Morale* (Sermon LXI). Vol. 31.

Paris, S. de. *Sermon XXXII* and *Panégyrique du Saint Nom de Jésus*. Vol. 33.

Villecourt. *Explication des commandements de Dieu*. Vol. 82.

Milhard, P. *L'inventaire des cas de conscience*. Toulouse, 1611.

———. *Le vraye guide des curez, vicaires et confesseurs*. Rouen, 1613.

Parisot, A. *La réparation du blasphème et de la profanation du dimanche*. Nancy, 1883.

Pontas, J. *Dictionnaire des cas de conscience*. Paris, 1715.

Port-Maurice, L. de. *Traité de confession générale*. Paris, 1826.

Possevin, J.-B. *Pratique dorée de la charge et office des curés*. Fr. tr. Paris, 1619.

Régnault, V. *De la prudence des confesseurs*. Paris, 1616.

Richelieu, A. du Plessis de. *Instruction du chrestien*. Poitiers, 1621.

Les sept trompettes pour réveiller les pécheurs. Translated by C. Jouye. Rouen, 1645.

Servais, P. *La sœur Marie de Saint-Pierre de la Sainte-Famille*. Saint-Dizier, n.d. [ca. 1880].

Stern, J., ed. *La Salette: Documents authentiques, 1847–1849*. Paris, 1980–1984.

Thomassin. *Le blasphème foudroyé par les carreaux du ciel et de la terre*. Paris, 1666.

Tolet, F. *L'instruction des prêtres qui contient sommairement tous les cas de conscience*. Lyon, 1628.

Turlot, N. *Thrésor de la doctrine chrétienne*. Lyon, 1651.

Valentin, J. *Examen raisonné ou décisions théologiques sur les commandements de Dieu et de l'Eglise*. Paris, 1839.

Villalobos, H. de. *Somme de théologie morale*. Fr. ed. Rouen, 1635.

Villars, P. de. *Traité sommaire et invectif contre les vains sermens, fréquens juremens et exécrables blasphèmes dont ce siècle est tout infect*. Lyon, 1596.

Villiers de Billy, C. *Instructions historiques, dogmatiques et morales en faveur des laboureurs*. Paris, 1746.

Vincent de Paul. *Sermons pour les missions des campagnes*. Edited by Jeanmaire. Paris, 1859.

JURIDICAL SOURCES

Beccaria, C. B. *Des délits et des peines*. Paris, 1773.

Blackstone, W. *Commentaries on the Laws of England*. Oxford, 1768.

Brillon, P.-J. *Dictionnaire des arrêts ou jurisprudence universelle*. Paris, 1717.

Brissot de Warville, J.-P. *Les moyens d'adoucir la rigueur des lois pénales en France*. Châlons-sur-Marne, 1781.

Dareau, F. *Traité des injures dans l'ordre judiciaire*. Paris, 1775.

Delamare, N. *Traité de la police*. Paris, 1727.

Denissart, J.-B. *Collection de décisions nouvelles et de notions relatives à la jurisprudence.* Paris, 1754.

Durand de Maillane, P.-T. *Dictionnaire de droit canonique et de pratique bénéficiale.* 2d ed. Lyon, 1770.

Guyot, ed. *Répertoire universel et raisonné de jurisprudence civile, criminelle, canonique et bénéficiale.* Paris, 1776.

Jousse, D. *Traité de justice criminelle en France.* Paris, 1771.

La Poix de Fréminville, de. *Dictionnaire ou traité de police générale.* Paris, 1758.

La Roche-Flavin, B. de. *Recueil des déclarations du roy et arrêts de la Cour de Parlement.* Paris, n. d. [ca. 1686].

L'Averdy, C. C. F. de. *Code pénal ou recueil des principales ordonnances.* 4th ed. Paris, 1777.

Le Brun de La Rochette, C. *Le procès civil et criminel.* Rouen, 1609.

Muyart de Vouglans, P. F. *Les lois criminelles de France dans leur ordre naturel.* Paris, 1780.

Papon, J. *Recueil d'arrêts notables des cours souveraines en France.* 4th ed. Lyon, 1569.

Priori, L. *Pratica criminale secondo il ritto delle leggi della Serenissima Repubblica di Venezia.* Venice, 1644.

Rousseaud de La Combe, G. du. *Traité des matières criminelles.* Paris, 1741.

Vermeil, F. M. *Essai sur les réformes à faire dans notre législation criminelle.* Paris, 1781.

MISCELLANEOUS SOURCES

Aulard, F.-A., ed. *La Société des Jacobins.* Vol. 6. Paris, 1897.

Barbeyrac, J. *Traité du jeu.* 3d ed. Amsterdam, 1737.

Bayle, P. *De la tolérance: Commentaire philosophique sur ces paroles de Jésus-Christ "Contrains-les d'entrer."* Edited by J.-M. Gros. Paris, 1992.

Durand, Y., ed. *Les cahiers de doléances des paroisses du bailliage de Troyes pour les Etats généraux de 1614.* Paris, 1966.

Dussaulx, J. *De la passion du jeu.* Paris, 1779.

Frain du Tremblay, J. *Conversations morales sur les jeux et les divertissements.* Paris, 1685.

Lachèvre, F., ed. *Le procès du poète Théophile de Viau.* Paris, 1909.

La Placette, J. *Traité des jeux-de-hazard défendu contre les objections de M. de Joncourt, et de quelques autres.* La Haye, 1714.

L'Estoile, P. de. *Journal.* Edited by L. R. Lefebvre. Paris, 1886.

Mercier, L.-S. *Tableau de Paris.* 1782–1788. In *Le Paris de Louis-Sébastien Mercier: Cartes et index toponymique,* edited by J.-C. Bonnet, A. Le Fur, and J. Sellier. Paris, 1994.

Minière, O. de. *Discours véritable sur ce qui est advenu à trois blasphémateurs ordinaires.* Angoulême, 1600.

Pepys, S. *Journal.* Fr. tr. Paris, 1994. [*The Diary of Samuel Pepys.* 1825. Edited by Henry B. Wheatley, 2 vols. New York: Random House, 1946.]

Sorbin, A. *Exhortation à la noblesse pour la dissuader et détourner des duels.* Paris, 1578.

Thiers, J.-B. *Traité des jeux et des divertissements qui peuvent être permis ou qui doivent être défendus aux chrétiens selon les règles de l'Eglise et le sentiment des Pères.* Paris, 1686.

Underhille, E. B., ed. *Tracts of Liberty of Conscience (1614–1661).* New York, 1846.

Viette, B. de. *Punition divine et exemplaire d'un blasphémateur.* Lyon, 1612.

Secondary Sources

Adam, A. *Théophile de Viau et la libre-pensée française en 1620.* 2d ed. Geneva, 1966.

Alibert, J. *Joseph de Maistre, Etat et Religion.* Paris, 1990.

Allier, R. *La cabale des dévôts: 1627–1666.* Geneva, 1972.

Artonne, A., L. Guizard, and O. Pontel. *Répertoire des statuts synodaux.* Paris, 1963.

Audard, H. "Le blasphème au village: Les pratiques blasphématoires dans les campagnes parisiennes (1660–1710)." Master's thesis, University of Paris I, 1995.

Aulard, F.-A. *Le culte de la Raison et le culte de l'Etre Suprême (1793–1794).* Paris, 1892.

Aymles, G. E. "Unbelief in Seventeenth-Century England." In *Puritans and Revolutionaries: Essays in Seventeenth-Century History,* edited by D. Pennington and K. Thomas. Oxford, 1978.

Beaulande, V. "Le blasphème et les blasphémateurs à la fin du Moyen Age dans la France du nord." D.E.A. thesis, University of Reims, 1994.

Beck, R. *Jour du Seigneur, jour de fête, jour de repos: Les mutations du dimanche en France (1700–1900).* Paris, 1997.

Belmas, E. "La police des cultes et des mœrs en France sous l'Ancien Régime." Graduate thesis, University of Paris I, 1980.

Bénichi, R. *Le duel et le blasphème à Paris au temps de Louis XIII.* D.E.A. thesis, University of Paris, 1956.

Bennassar, B., et al., eds. *L'Inquisition espagnole (XVIe–XIXe siècles).* Paris, 1979

Berriot, F. *Athéismes et athéistes au XVIe siècle en France.* Lille, 1984.

Bertoni, M. *La ligue réparatrice des blasphèmes contre la Très Sainte Vierge Marie: Une démarche de la pensée religieuse, mariale, et franciscaine de la Corse et plus particulièrement de l'Ile Rousse au début du XXe siècle.* Sisco, 1982.

Bezault, V. "Le blasphème au XVIIe siècle dans le bailliage de Saint-Denis." Master's thesis, University of Paris X, 1996.

Bianchi, S. "Recherches sur la déchristianisation dans le district de Corbeil (1793–1797)." Graduate thesis, University of Paris I, 1976.

Billacois, F. *Le duel dans la société française aux XVIe et XVIIe siècles: Essai de psychologie historique.* Paris, 1986.

Boureau, A. *Le simple corps du roi: L'impossible sacralité des souverains français (XVe–XVIIIe siècles).* Paris, 1988.

Boureau, A., and C. S. Ingerlrom, eds. *La royauté sacrée dans le monde chrétien: Actes du colloque de Royaumont, 1989.* Paris, 1992.

Cabantous, A. "Du blasphème au blasphémateur: Jalons pour une histoire (XVIe–XIXe siècle)." In *Blasphèmes et libertés, Colloque de Bruxelles, 10 février 1990, organisé par la Ligue pour l'abolition des lois réprimant le blasphème et le droit de s'exprimer librement,* edited by P. Dartevelle, P. Denis, and J. Robyn, pp. 11–32. Paris, 1993.

——. "Le blasphème de l'abbé Bergier." *Homo Religiosus, Autour de Jean Delumeau,* pp. 468–476. Paris, 1997.

Cariou, P. *Les idéalités casuistiques: Un directeur de conscience au XVIIe siècle, Jacques de Sainte-Beuve (1613–1677).* Paris, 1979.

Casagrande, C., and S. Vecchio. *Les péchés de la langue: Discipline et éthique de la parole dans la culture médiévale.* Fr. tr. Paris, 1991.

Castelli, E., ed. *L'analyse du langage théologique: Le nom de Dieu; Actes du colloque organisé par le Centre international d'études humanistes et par l'Institut d'études philosophiques de Rome, Rome, 5–11 janvier 1969.* Paris, 1969.

Chartier, R. *Les origines culturelles de la Révolution française.* Paris, 1990. [*The Cultural Origins of the French Revolution.* Translated by L. G. Cochrane. Durham, 1991.]

Châtellier, L. *La religion des pauvres: Les missions rurales en Europe et la formation du catholicisme moderne, XVIe–XIXe siècles.* Paris, 1993.

Cheyronnaud, J., E. Claverie, and J. Favret-Saada, eds. *Paroles d'outrages.* Thematic issue, *Ethnologie française* 22, no. 3 (1992).

Christin, O. "Du Solt nit schweren bey Sein Namen: Matériaux pour servir à l'histoire du blasphème (1450–1550)" and "Matériaux pour servir à l'histoire du blasphème." Parts 1 and 2, respectively. *Bulletin de la Mission historique française en Allemagne,* no. 29 (1994): 56–67; and no. 3 (1996): 67–85.

——. "Sur la condamnation du blasphème (XVIe–XVIIe siècles)." *Revue d'histoire de l'Eglise de France* 80, no. 204 (janvier–juin 1994): 43–64.

Clark, P. *The English Alehouse: A Social History (1200–1830).* London, 1983.

Cottret, B. "Ecce homo: La crise de l'incarnation royale en Angleterre (1649–1688–1701)." In *Le Christ entre orthodoxie et lumières: Actes du colloque tenu à Genève en août 1993,* edited by M. C. Pitassi. Geneva, 1994.

Cozzi, G. "Note su tribunali e procedure penali a Venezia nel '700," *Revista Storica Italiana*, no. 4 (1965): 931–952.

Davis, J. C. *Fear, Myth, and History: The Ranters and the Historians*. Cambridge, 1986.

Davis, N. Z. *Pour sauver sa vie: Les récits de pardon au XVIe siècle*. Fr. tr. Paris, 1988. [*Fiction in the Archives: Pardon Tales and Their Tellers in Sixteenth-Century France*. Stanford, 1987.]

Debaret, S. "Le blasphème parisien au XVIIe siècle (1610–1671)." Master's thesis, University of Paris I, 1994.

Deconninck-Brossard, F. *Vie politique, sociale et religieuse en Grande-Bretagne d'après les sermons préchés ou publiés dans le nord de l'Angleterre (1738–1760)*. Lille, 1984.

Dedieu, J.-P. *L'administration de la foi: L'Inquisition de Tolède (XVIe–XVIIIe siècles)*. Madrid, 1989.

Delahaye, H. "Note sur la légende de la lettre du Christ tombée du ciel." *Bulletin de l'Académie royale de Belgique* (1899): 171–213.

Delumeau, J. *L'aveu et le pardon: Les difficultés de la confession, XIIIe–XVIIIe siècles*. Paris, 1991.

——. *Un chemin d'histoire: Chrétienté et christianisation*. Paris, 1981.

——. *La péché et la peur*. Paris, 1981. [*Sin and Fear: The Emergence of a Western Guilt Culture, 13th–18th Centuries*. Translated by E. Nicholson. New York, 1991.]

——. *La peur en Occident (XIVe–XVIIIe siècles): Une cité assiégée*. Paris, 1978.

Derosas, R. "Moralità e giustizia a Venezia nel '500–600. Gli escuttori contro la bestemmia." In *Stato, società e giustizia nella Repubblica veneta (sec. XV–XVIII)*, edited by G. Cozzi, pp. 433–528. Rome, 1981.

Dyonnet, N. "Impiétés provinciales au XVIIIe siècle." *Histoire, Economie, Société*, no. 3 (1990): 391–421.

Escamilla-Colin, M. *Crimes et châtiments dans l'Espagne inquisitoriale (1659–1734)*. Paris, 1992.

Ferrand, R. "Blasphémateurs et sacrilèges en Lyonnais et Beaujolais (1679–1789)." Master's thesis, Lumière University (Lyon II), 1989.

Florida, R. E. "British Law and Socinianism in the 17th and 18th Centuries." In *Socinianism and its Role in the Culture of the 16th to 18th Centuries*, edited by L. Szczucki. Warsaw, 1983.

Flynn, M. "Blasphemy and the Play of Anger in Sixteenth-Century Spain." *Past and Present* 149 (Nov. 1995): 29–56.

Gauvard, C. *De grace especial: Crime, Etat, et société en France à la fin du Moyen Age*. Paris, 1991.

Genêt, J. *L'énigme des sermons du curé d'Ars: Etudes sur la prédication de Saint Jean-Marie Vianney suivie de l'analyse critique et du texte de six sermons*. Paris, 1961.

Ginzburg, C. *Le fromage et les vers: L'univers d'un meunier au XVIe siècle*. Fr. tr. Paris, 1980. [*The Cheese and the Worms: The Cosmos of a Sixteenth-Century Miller*. Translated by John Tedeschi and Anne Tedeschi. Baltimore, 1980.]

Grussi, O. *La vie quotidienne des joueurs sous l'Ancien Régime à Paris et à la Cour*. Paris, 1985.

Guillemaut, C. *Pierre-Louis Parisis*. Arras, 1916–1917.

Guilleminot, S. "La justice d'Ancien Régime au XVIIe siècle: Onze mille cas dans le présidial de Caen." *Histoire, Economie, Société*, no. 2 (1988): 187–208.

Guillet, C. *La rumeur de Dieu: Apparitions, prophéties, et miracles sous la Restauration*. Paris, 1994.

Hanlon, G. "Les rituels de l'agression en Aquitaine au XVIIe siècle." *Annales E.S.C.*, no. 2 (1985): 244–268.

Henry, P. *Crime, justice et société dans la principauté de Neuchâtel au XVIIIe siècle (1707–1806)*. Neuchâtel, 1984.

Hernandez-Bermejo, M. A. "La moralizacion en el siglo XVIII: Analisis de une Fuente; Los libros de visita." *Norba* 4 (1983).

Hildesheimer, F. "Parler dangereusement en *1793*." In *1793, La patrie en danger: Actes du 2ème colloque international organisé par les Archives départementales de l'Oise, samedi 23 et dimanche 24 octobre 1993*," pp. 157–171. Beauvais, 1996.

Hill, C. *Le monde à l'envers: Les idées radicales au cours de la Révolution anglaise*. Fr. tr. Paris, 1977. [*The World Turned Upside Down: Radical Ideas During the English Revolution*. London, 1972.]

Hofmann, C. "Justice et société dans le bailliage seigneurial de Saint-Denis en France dans la seconde moitié du XVIIe siècle." Thesis, Ecole Nationale des Chartes, 1992.

Hughes, G. *Swearing: A Social History of Foul Language, Oaths, and Profanity in English*. Cambridge, Mass., and Oxford, U.K., 1991.

Huston, N. *Dire et interdire: Eléments de jurologie*. Paris, 1980.

Injures et blasphèmes. Thematic issue, *Mentalités*, no. 2 (1989). (See especially the articles by E. Belmas, A. Cabantous, J. Cheyronnaud, R. Hardy, O. Christin, and F. Hildesheimer.)

Jansénisme et révolution: Actes du colloque de Versailles tenu au Palais des Congrès les 13 et 14 octobre 1984, vol. 39, *Chroniques de Port-Royal*, Paris, 1990.

Jones, J. R., ed. *Liberty Secured?* Stanford, 1992.

Jonsen, A., and S. Toulmin. *The Abuse of Casuistry: A History of Moral Reasoning*. Berkeley, 1988.

Lamour, E. "Le débat sur le sacrilège (loi du 4 janvier 1825)." Master's thesis, University of Paris I, 1988.

Langlois, C. "La conjoncture miraculaire à la fin de la Restauration." *Revue d'histoire de la spiritualité* (1973): 227–241.

Lapasset, M. "La morale en action d'une petite société rurale au XVIIIe siècle: Justice seigneuriale de l'abbaye d'Hautvilliers, bailliage de Reims." *Etudes champenoises*, no. 4 (1979): 11–24.

Lauret, B. "Tu ne prononceras pas à tort le nom de Dieu." In *Blasphèmes et libertés, Colloque de Bruxelles, 10 février 1990, organisé par la Ligue pour l'abolition des lois réprimant le blasphème et le droit de s'exprimer librement*, edited P. Dartevelle, P. Denis, and J. Robyn, pp. 33–48. Paris, 1993.

Lawton, D. *Blasphemy*. Philadelphia and London, 1993.

Lebigre, A. *Les Grands Jours d'Auvergne: Désordre et répression au XVIIe siècle*. Paris, 1976.

Le Bras, G. *Etudes de sociologie religieuse*. Paris, 1955.

Lecharny, H. "L'injure à Paris au XVIIIe siècle: Un aspect de la violence au quotidien." *Revue d'histoire moderne et contemporaine* 36 (October–December 1989): 559–585.

Lefebvre-Teillard, A. *Les officialités à la veille du Concile de Trente*. Paris, 1973.

Lefranc, M.-G. "Blasphèmes et blasphémateurs dans le royaume de Valence (XVIe–XVIIIe siècles)." Master's thesis, University of Toulouse-Le-Mirail, 1976.

Lemercier, P. *Les justices seigneuriales de la région parisienne de 1580 à 1789*. Paris, 1933.

Lespagnon, J.-H. *La loi du sacrilège*. Paris, 1935.

Leutenbauer, S. *Das Delikt der Gotteslästerung in des bayerischen Gesetzgebung*. Cologne-Vienna, 1984.

Levy, L. *Treason Against God: A History of the Offense of Blasphemy*. New York, 1981.

Lewis, G., and J. Mitchell. *Blasphemer and Reformer: A Study of James Leslie*. Aberdeen, 1984.

Lottin, A. *Lille, citadelle de la Contre-Réforme? (1598–1668)*. Dunkirk, 1984.

Lourmière, N. "Le blasphème à Paris dans la première moitié du XVIIIe siècle." Master's thesis, University of Paris I, 1994.

Lutaud, O. *Winstanley: Socialisme et christianisme sous Cromwell*. Paris, 1976.

Mandon, G. *La société périgourdine au siècle des Lumières: Le clergé paroissial*. Périgueux, 1982.

Mandrou, R. *Magistrats et sorciers au XVIIe siècle: Une analyse de psychologie historique*. Paris, 1968.

Meisma, K. O. *Spinoza et son cercle*. Fr. tr. Paris, 1983.

Merrick, J. W. *The Desacralization of the French Monarchy in the Eighteenth Century*. Baton Rouge, 1990.

Merricksay, A. *Le Châtelet et la répression de la criminalité à Paris en 1770*. Graduate thesis, University of Paris IV, 1984.

Muchembled, R. *L'invention de l'homme moderne*. Paris, 1988.

——. *Le temps des supplices: De l'obéissance sous les rois absolus (XVe–XVIIIe siècles)*. Paris, 1992.

———. *La violence au village: Sociabilité et comportements populaires en Artois du XVᵉ au XVIIᵉ siècles*. Paris, 1989.

Nooker, G. D. *A History of the Crime of Blasphemy*. London, 1922.

Perez-Munoz, I. *Pecar, delinquir y castigar: El tribunal eclesiastico de Soria en el siglo XVI y XXII*. Caceres, 1992.

Pernot, M. *Etude sur la vie religieuse de la campagne lorraines à la fin du XVIIᵉ siècle: Le visage du Xaintois d'après la visite canonique de 1687*. Nancy, 1971.

Pichette, J.-P. *Le guide raisonné des jurons*. Montréal, 1980.

Piozza-Donati, M.-J. "Le procès contre Matteo Gazzotto, modénais soupçonné d'hérésie à la fin du XVIᵉ siècle," *Mélanges de l'Ecole française de Rome* 89 (1977): 945–982.

Pitt-Rivers, J. *Anthropologie de l'honneur: La mésaventure de Sichem*. Fr. tr. Paris, 1983. [*The Fate of Shechem or the Politics of Sex: Essays in the Anthropology of the Mediterranean*. London, 1980.]

Plessix-Buisset, C. *Le criminel devant ses juges en Bretagne aux XVIᵉ–XVIIᵉ siècles*. Paris, 1988.

Porret, M. "Rêver de s'enrichir ou s'enrichir en rêvant." *Revue d'histoire moderne et contemporaine* 38 (1991): 17–36.

Porter plainte, stratégie villageoise et justice en Ile-de-France (XVIIᵉ–XVIIIᵉ siècles). Thematic issue, *Droit et culture*, no. 19 (1990).

Rey-Mermet, T. *La morale selon saint Alphonse de Liguori*. Paris, 1987.

Robbe, D. *Crime et religion au XVIIIᵉ siècle: Blasphémateurs et sacrilèges jugés en appel au Parlement de Paris*. Master's thesis, University of Paris X, 1969.

Sabean, D. *Power in the Blood: Popular Culture and Village Discourse in Early Modern Germany*. Cambridge, 1984.

Seguin, J.-P. *L'information en France avant le périodique: 517 canards imprimés entre 1529 et 1631*. Paris, 1964.

Sevrin, E. *Les missions religieuses en France sous la Restauration (1815–1830)*. 2 vols. Paris, 1948, 1959.

Soman, A. *Sorcellerie et justice criminelle, le Parlement de Paris, XVIᵉ–XVIIIᵉ siècles*. Brookfield, Vt., 1992.

Tallon, A. *La Compagnie du Saint-Sacrement, 1629–1667: Spiritualité et société*. Paris, 1990.

Tessier, R. *Le sacré*. Paris, 1991.

Thomas, K. *Religion and the Decline of Magic*. New York, 1971.

Tuttle, E. *Religion et idéologie dans la Révolution anglaise (1647–1649)*. Paris, 1989.

Van Damme, S. "Théophile de Viau et les Jésuites: Procès et polémique littéraires au XVIIᵉ siècle." D.E.A. thesis, Ecole des Hautes Etudes en Sciences Sociales, 1994.

EUROPEAN PERSPECTIVES
A Series in Social Thought and Cultural Criticism
Lawrence D. Kritzman, Editor